RIN-NE

りんね

Story and Art by
Rumiko Takahashi

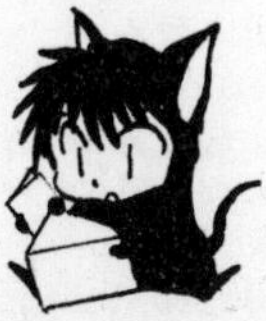

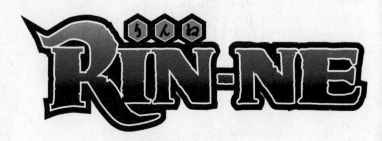

RIN-NE

りんね

Characters

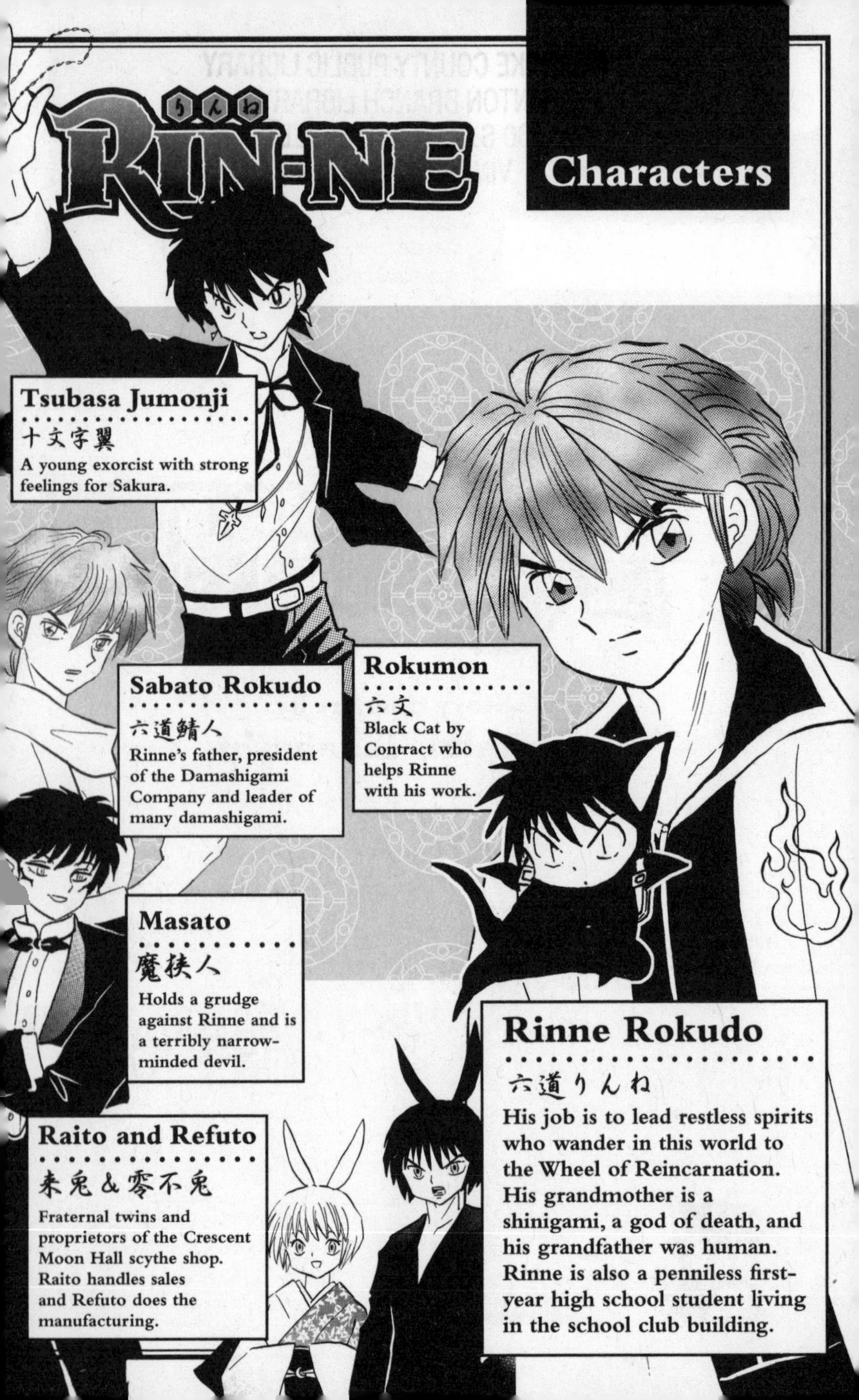

Tsubasa Jumonji

十文字翼

A young exorcist with strong feelings for Sakura.

Rokumon

六文

Black Cat by Contract who helps Rinne with his work.

Sabato Rokudo

六道鯖人

Rinne's father, president of the Damashigami Company and leader of many damashigami.

Masato

魔狭人

Holds a grudge against Rinne and is a terribly narrow-minded devil.

Rinne Rokudo

六道りんね

His job is to lead restless spirits who wander in this world to the Wheel of Reincarnation. His grandmother is a shinigami, a god of death, and his grandfather was human. Rinne is also a penniless first-year high school student living in the school club building.

Raito and Refuto

来兎&零不兎

Fraternal twins and proprietors of the Crescent Moon Hall scythe shop. Raito handles sales and Refuto does the manufacturing.

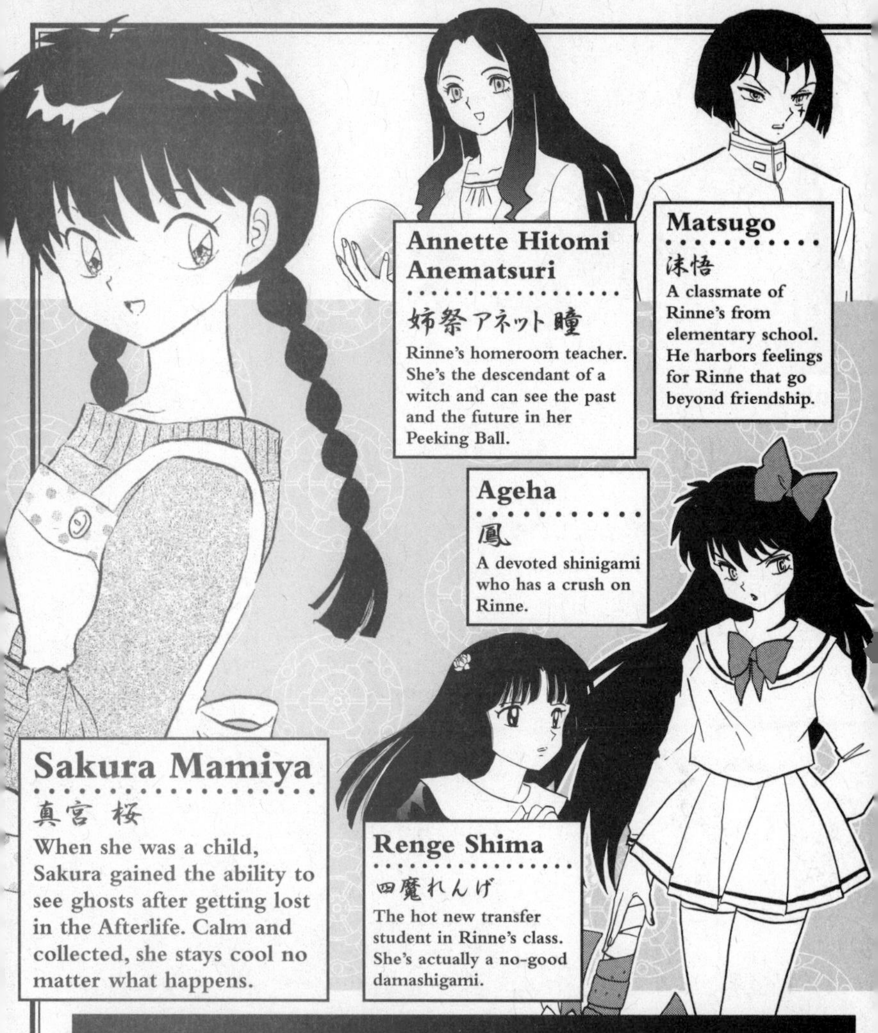

Sakura Mamiya

真宮 桜

When she was a child, Sakura gained the ability to see ghosts after getting lost in the Afterlife. Calm and collected, she stays cool no matter what happens.

Annette Hitomi Anematsuri

姉祭アネット瞳

Rinne's homeroom teacher. She's the descendant of a witch and can see the past and the future in her Peeking Ball.

Matsugo

沫悟

A classmate of Rinne's from elementary school. He harbors feelings for Rinne that go beyond friendship.

Ageha

鳳

A devoted shinigami who has a crush on Rinne.

Renge Shima

四魔れんげ

The hot new transfer student in Rinne's class. She's actually a no-good damashigami.

The Story So Far

Sakura, the girl who can see ghosts, and Rinne the shinigami (sort of) spend their days together, helping spirits that can't pass on reach the Afterlife, and dealing with all kinds of strange phenomena at their school.

Rinne is invited by Matsugo to attend the Elite Shinigami High's cultural festival, where he must conquer a haunted house with a history of destroying relationships. He then confronts an evil nutcracker in a tussle over some delicious crab. As usual, poor Rinne's got no time for leisure. Rinne dreams of the day he can escape his poverty, but in the meantime, he's got work to do!

RIN-NE

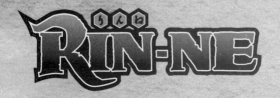

Contents

CHAPTER 269: MAKEUP LESSONS ON WAYWARD DOG CATCHING

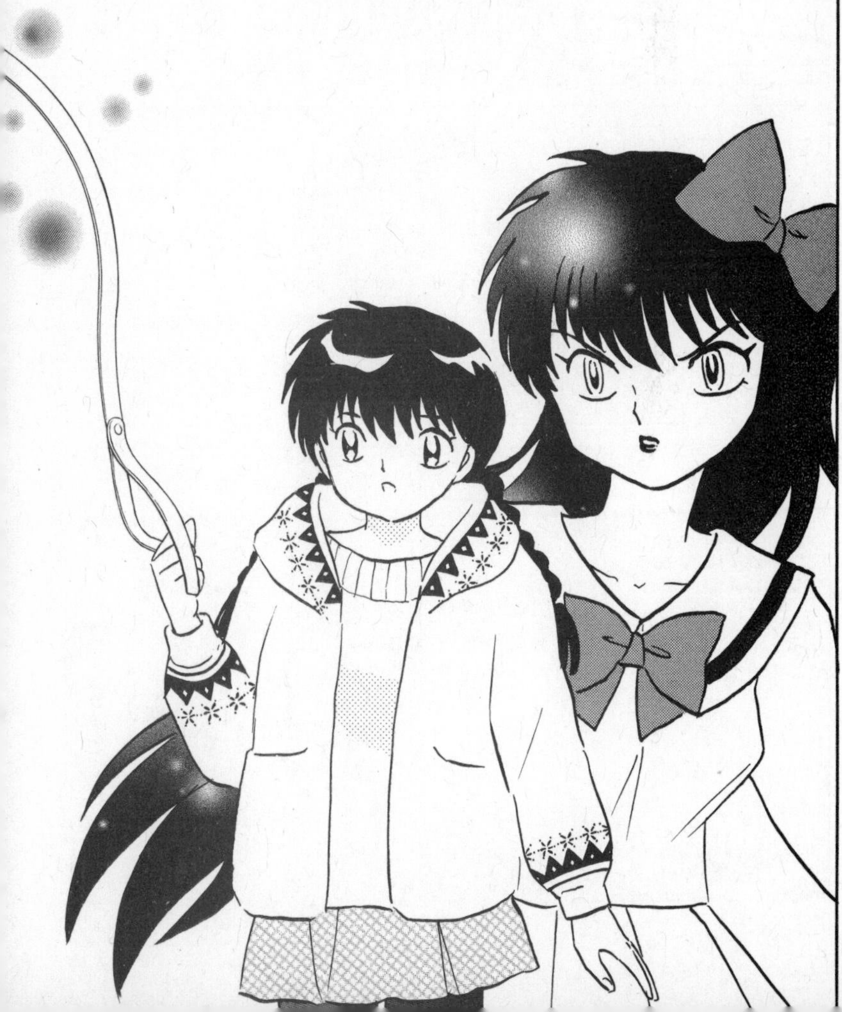

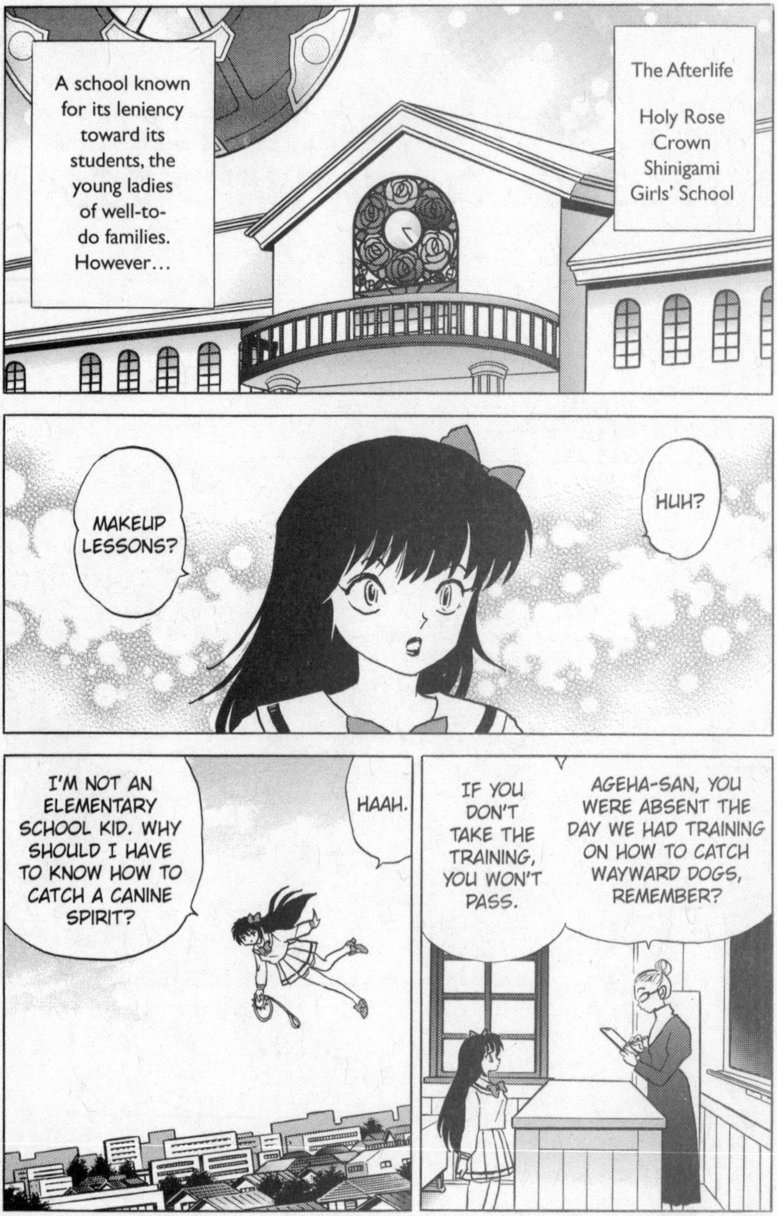
The Afterlife
Holy Rose Crown Shinigami Girls' School
A school known for its leniency toward its students, the young ladies of well-to-do families. However…
HUH?
MAKEUP LESSONS?
AGEHA-SAN, YOU WERE ABSENT THE DAY WE HAD TRAINING ON HOW TO CATCH WAYWARD DOGS, REMEMBER?
IF YOU DON'T TAKE THE TRAINING, YOU WON'T PASS.
HAAH.
I'M NOT AN ELEMENTARY SCHOOL KID. WHY SHOULD I HAVE TO KNOW HOW TO CATCH A CANINE SPIRIT?

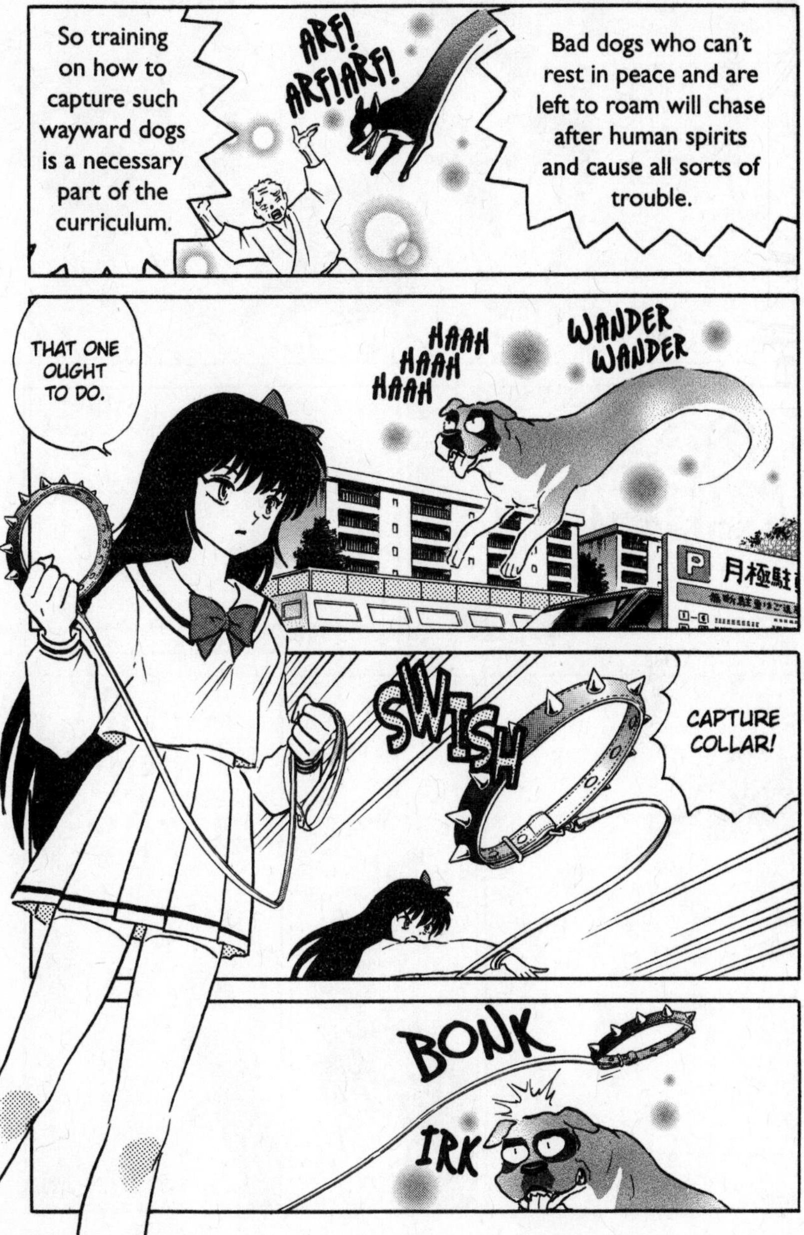
Bad dogs who can't rest in peace and are left to roam will chase after human spirits and cause all sorts of trouble.
ARF! ARF!ARF!
So training on how to capture such wayward dogs is a necessary part of the curriculum.
WANDER WANDER
HAAH HAAH HAAH
THAT ONE OUGHT TO DO.
P 月極駐
CAPTURE COLLAR!
SWISH
BONK
IRK

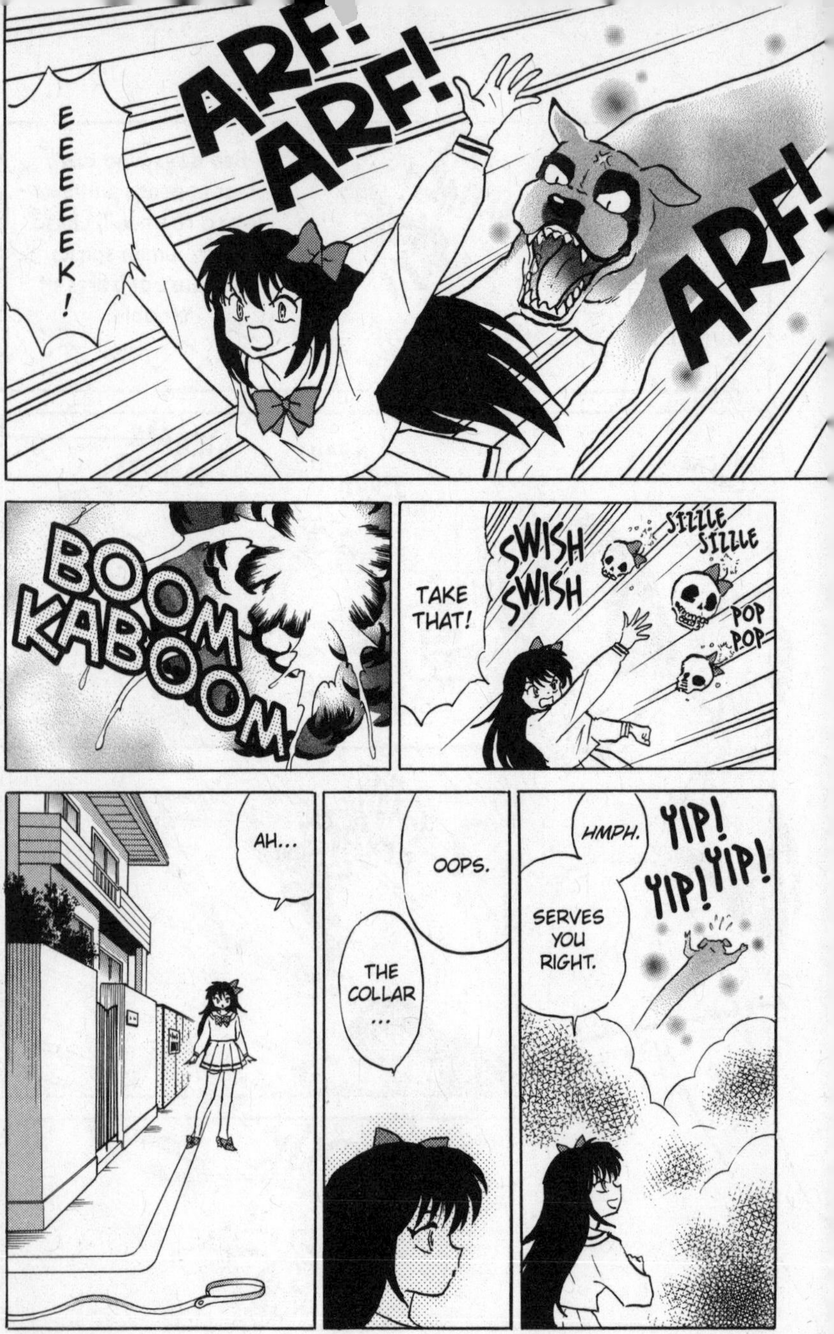
ARF!
ARF. ARF!
EEEEEEK!
SIZZLE SIZZLE
POP POP
SWISH SWISH
TAKE THAT!
BOOM KABOOM
YIP! YIP! YIP!
HMPH.
SERVES YOU RIGHT.
OOPS.
THE COLLAR...
AH...

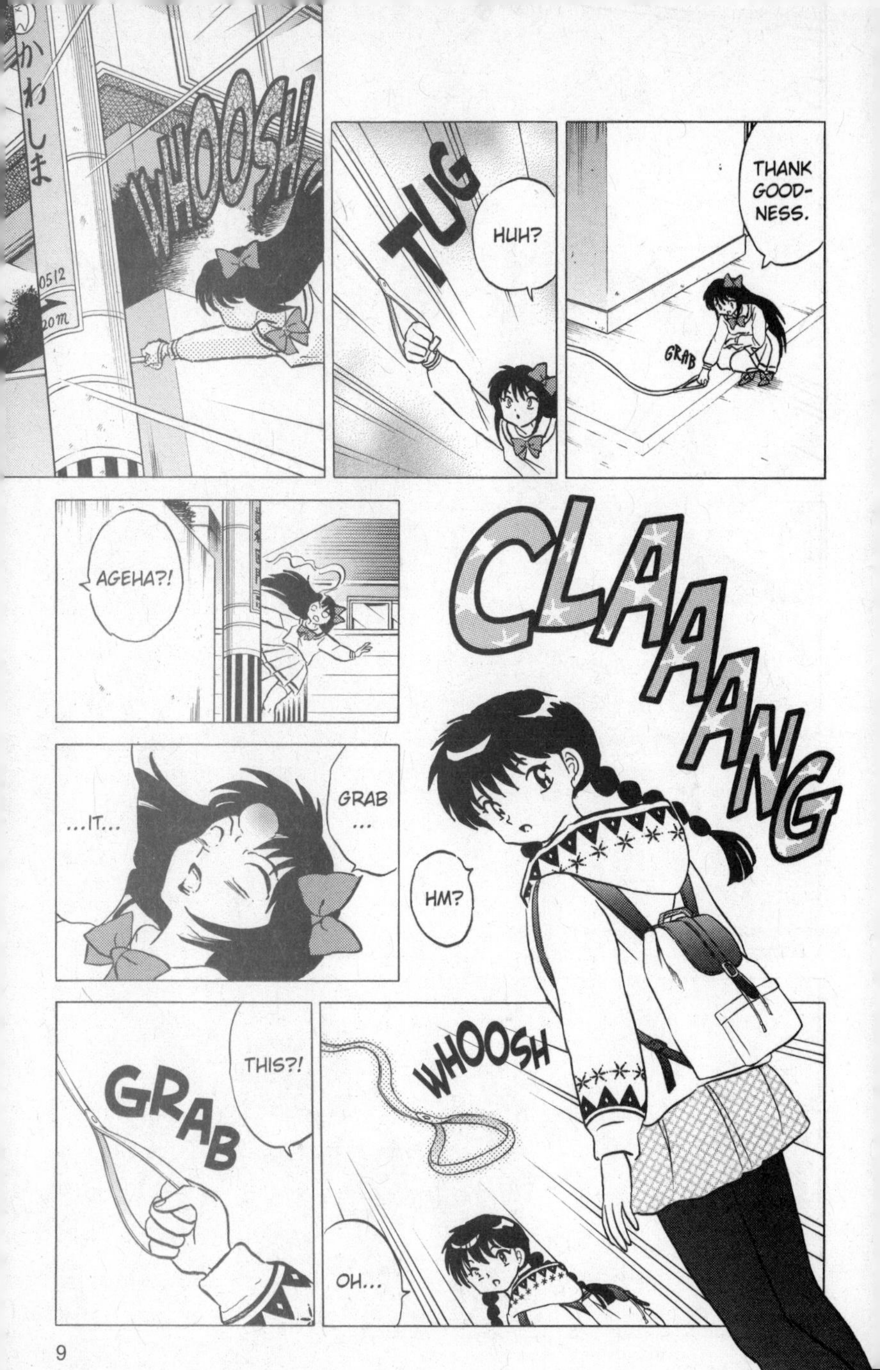
かわしま
0512
WHOOSH
TUG
HUH?
THANK GOOD-NESS.
GRAB
AGEHA?!
...IT...
GRAB ...
CLAAANG
HM?
GRAB
THIS?!
WHOOSH
OH...

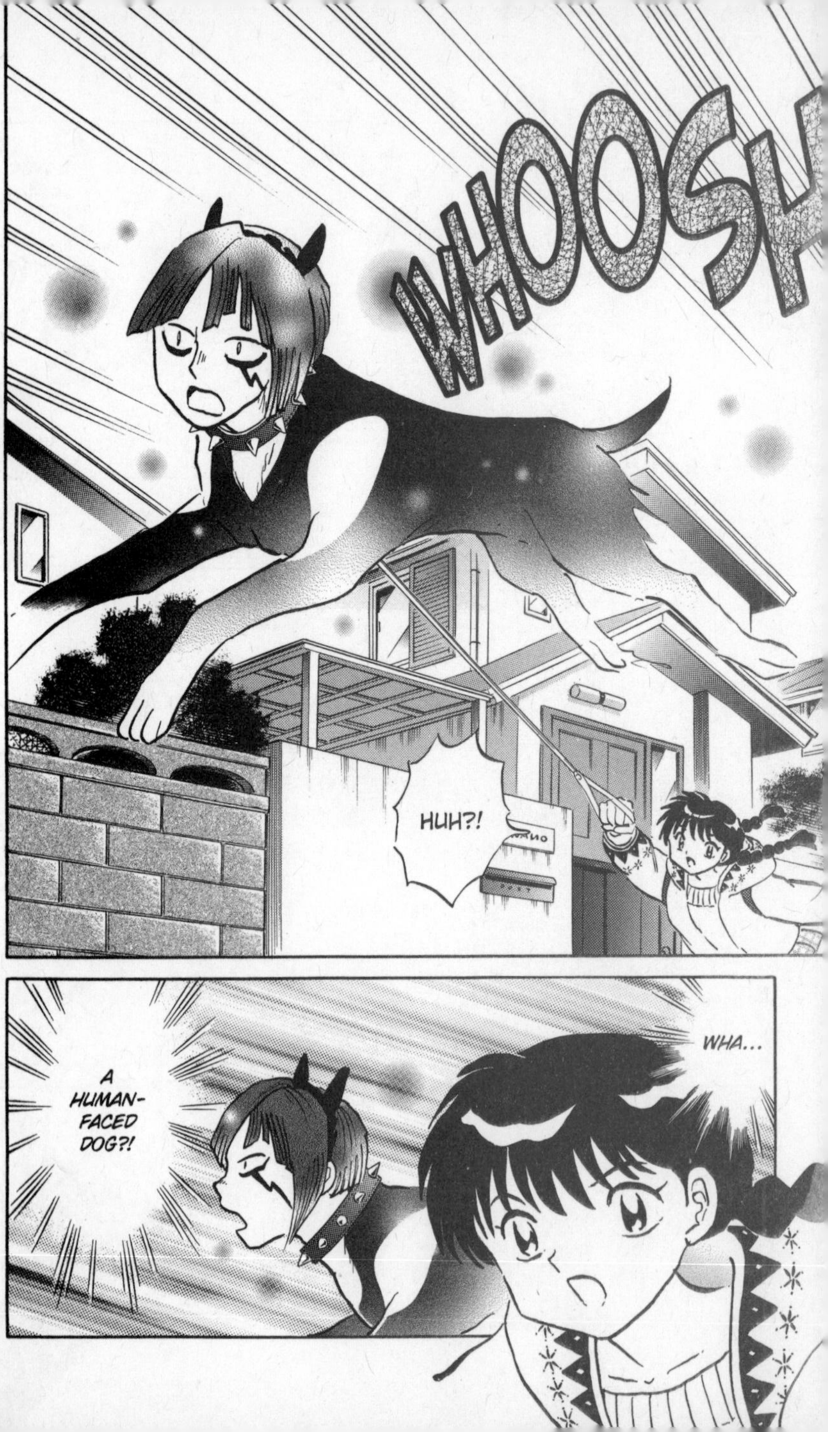
WHOOSH
HUH?!
WHA...
A HUMAN-FACED DOG?!

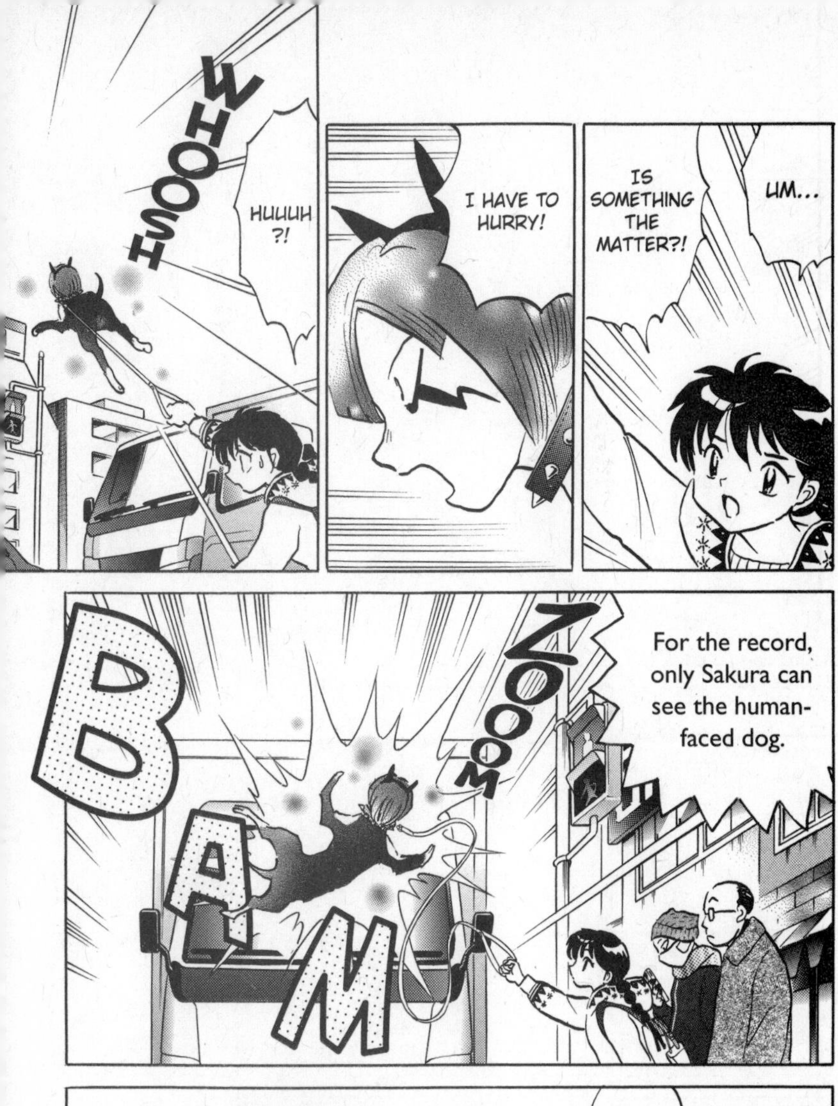
UM...
IS SOMETHING THE MATTER?!
I HAVE TO HURRY!
HUUUH ?!
WHOOOSH
For the record, only Sakura can see the human-faced dog.
ZOOOOM
BAM
Mean-while ...
AGEHA.
AGEHA-SAMA.
AH...

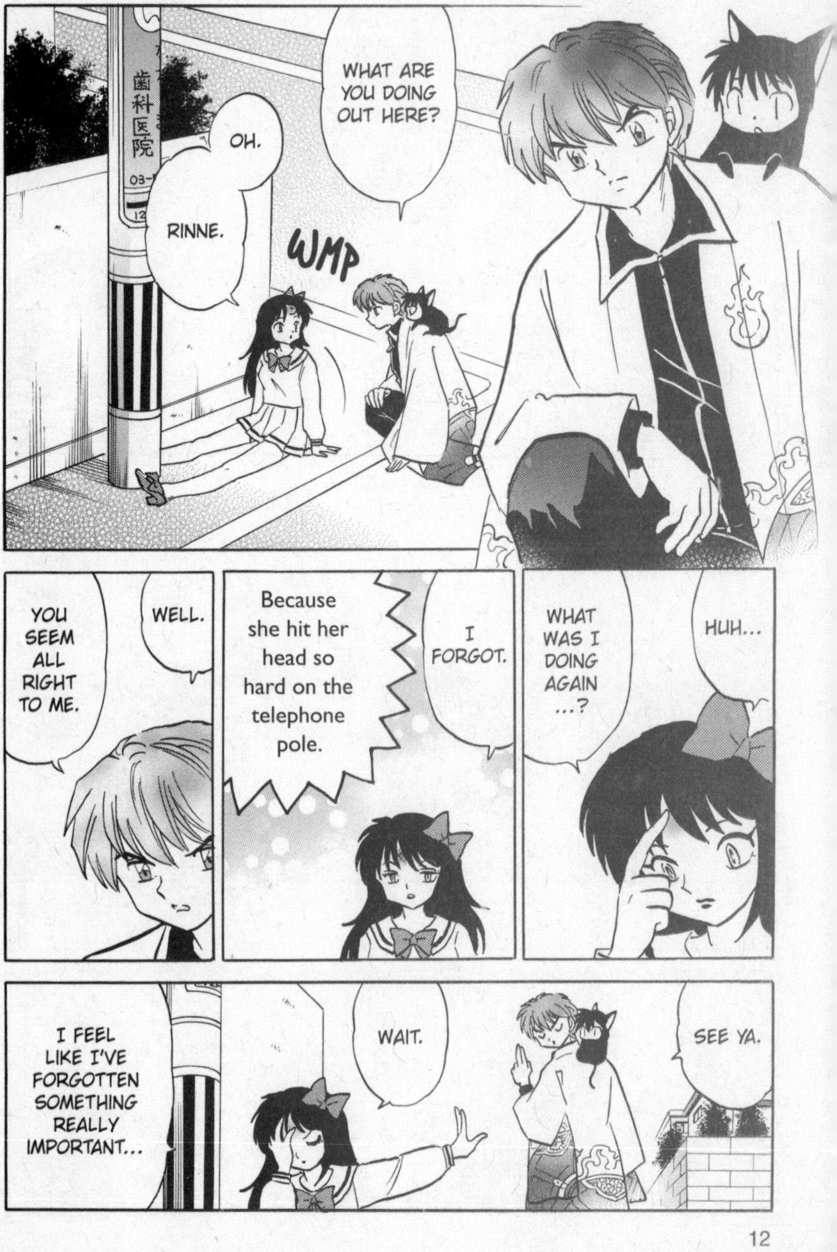
WHAT ARE YOU DOING OUT HERE?
歯科医院
OH.
RINNE.
WMP
HUH...
WHAT WAS I DOING AGAIN ...?
I FORGOT.
Because she hit her head so hard on the telephone pole.
WELL.
YOU SEEM ALL RIGHT TO ME.
SEE YA.
WAIT.
I FEEL LIKE I'VE FORGOTTEN SOMETHING REALLY IMPORTANT...

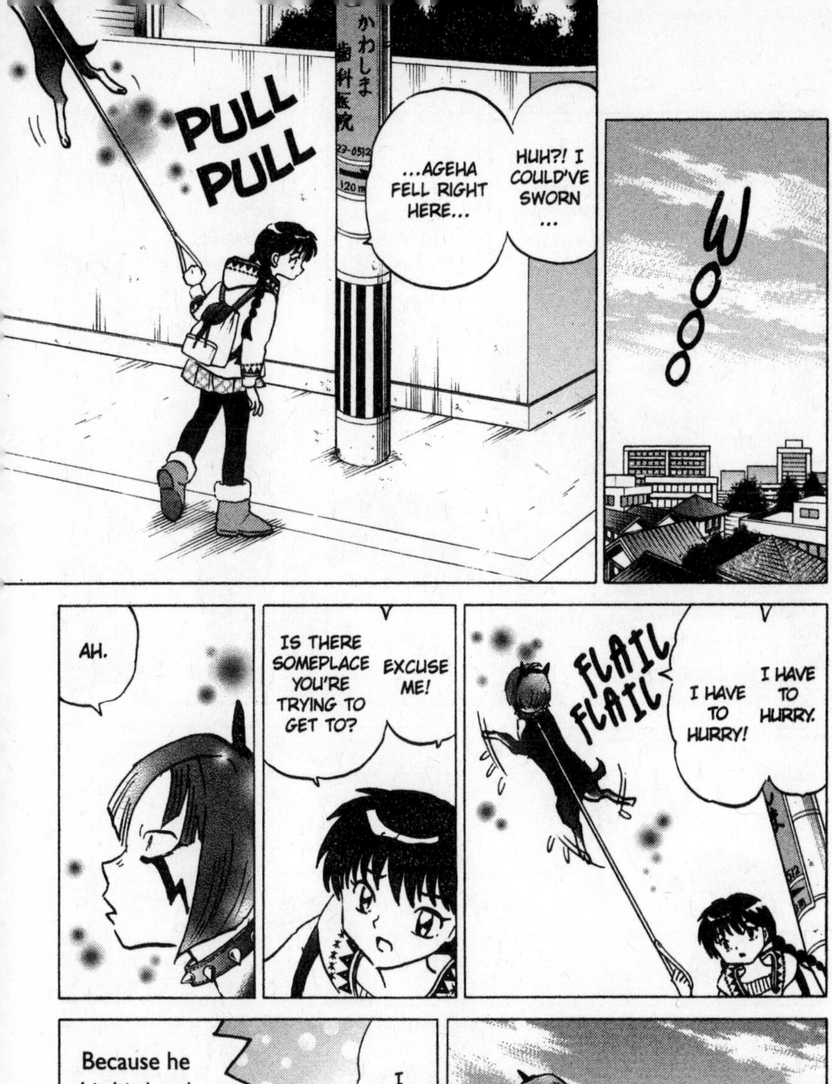
WOOOO
HUH?! I COULD'VE SWORN ...
...AGEHA FELL RIGHT HERE...
かわしま
歯科医院
PULL PULL
I HAVE TO HURRY.
I HAVE TO HURRY!
FLAIL FLAIL
EXCUSE ME!
IS THERE SOMEPLACE YOU'RE TRYING TO GET TO?
AH.
I FORGET.
Because he hit his head so hard on the truck.

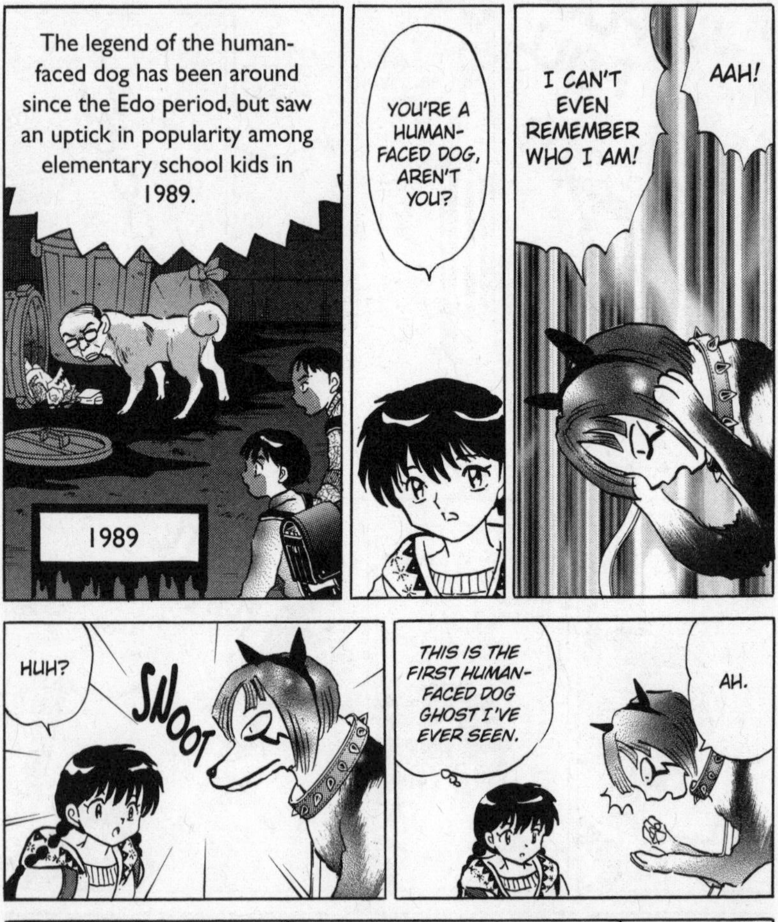
AAH!
I CAN'T EVEN REMEMBER WHO I AM!
YOU'RE A HUMAN-FACED DOG, AREN'T YOU?
The legend of the human-faced dog has been around since the Edo period, but saw an uptick in popularity among elementary school kids in 1989.
1989
AH.
THIS IS THE FIRST HUMAN-FACED DOG GHOST I'VE EVER SEEN.
SNOOT
HUH?
ARF! ARF! ARF!
HUH?! YOUR MOUTH BECAME A DOG'S MUZZLE!
WHAT'S GOING ON HERE?!

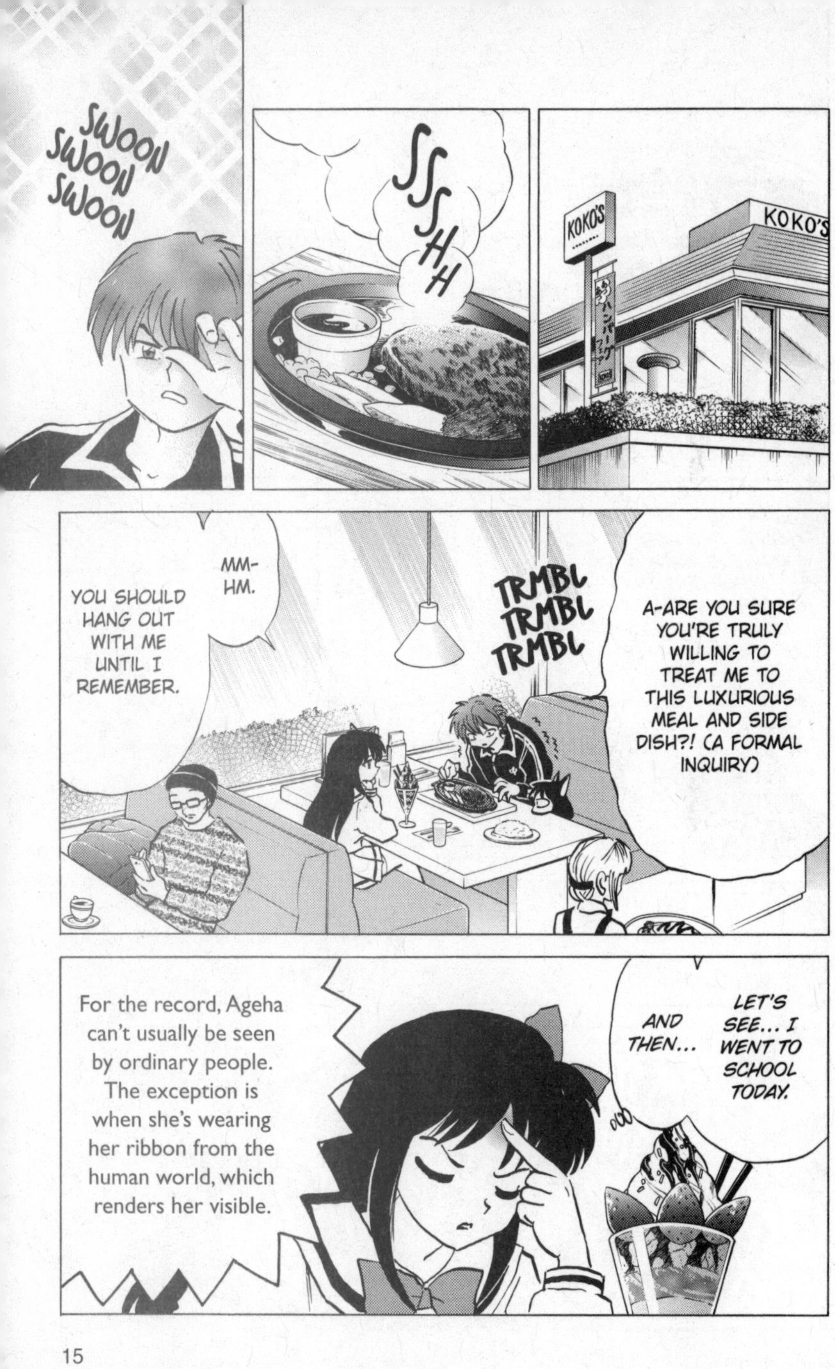
KOKO'S
KOKO'S
SSSHH
SWOON SWOON SWOON
TRMBL TRMBL TRMBL
A-ARE YOU SURE YOU'RE TRULY WILLING TO TREAT ME TO THIS LUXURIOUS MEAL AND SIDE DISH?! (A FORMAL INQUIRY)
MM-HM.
YOU SHOULD HANG OUT WITH ME UNTIL I REMEMBER.
LET'S SEE... I WENT TO SCHOOL TODAY.
AND THEN...
For the record, Ageha can't usually be seen by ordinary people. The exception is when she's wearing her ribbon from the human world, which renders her visible.

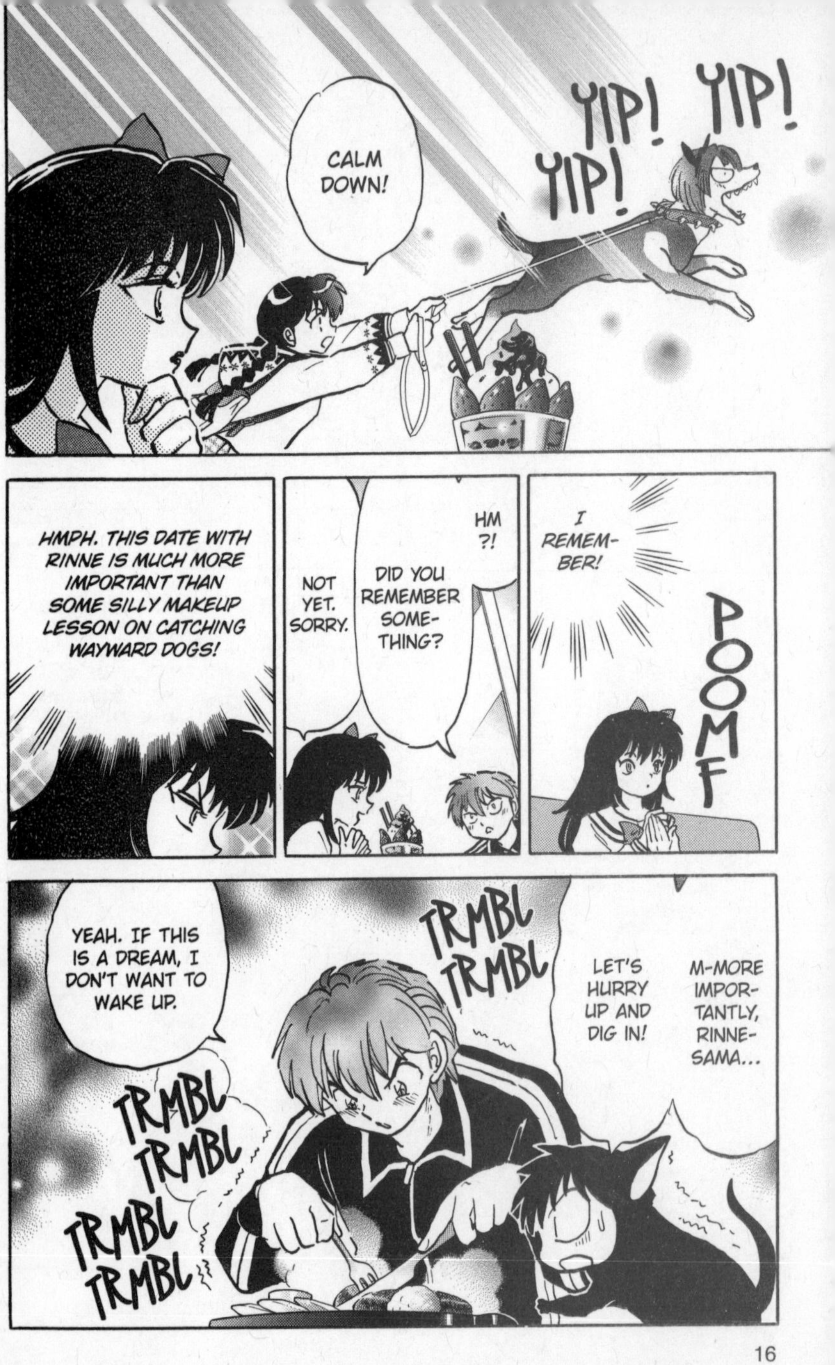
YIP! YIP!
YIP!
CALM DOWN!
I REMEMBER!
POOMF
HM?!
DID YOU REMEMBER SOMETHING?
NOT YET. SORRY.
HMPH. THIS DATE WITH RINNE IS MUCH MORE IMPORTANT THAN SOME SILLY MAKEUP LESSON ON CATCHING WAYWARD DOGS!
M-MORE IMPORTANTLY, RINNE-SAMA...
LET'S HURRY UP AND DIG IN!
TRMBL TRMBL
YEAH. IF THIS IS A DREAM, I DON'T WANT TO WAKE UP.
TRMBL TRMBL TRMBL TRMBL

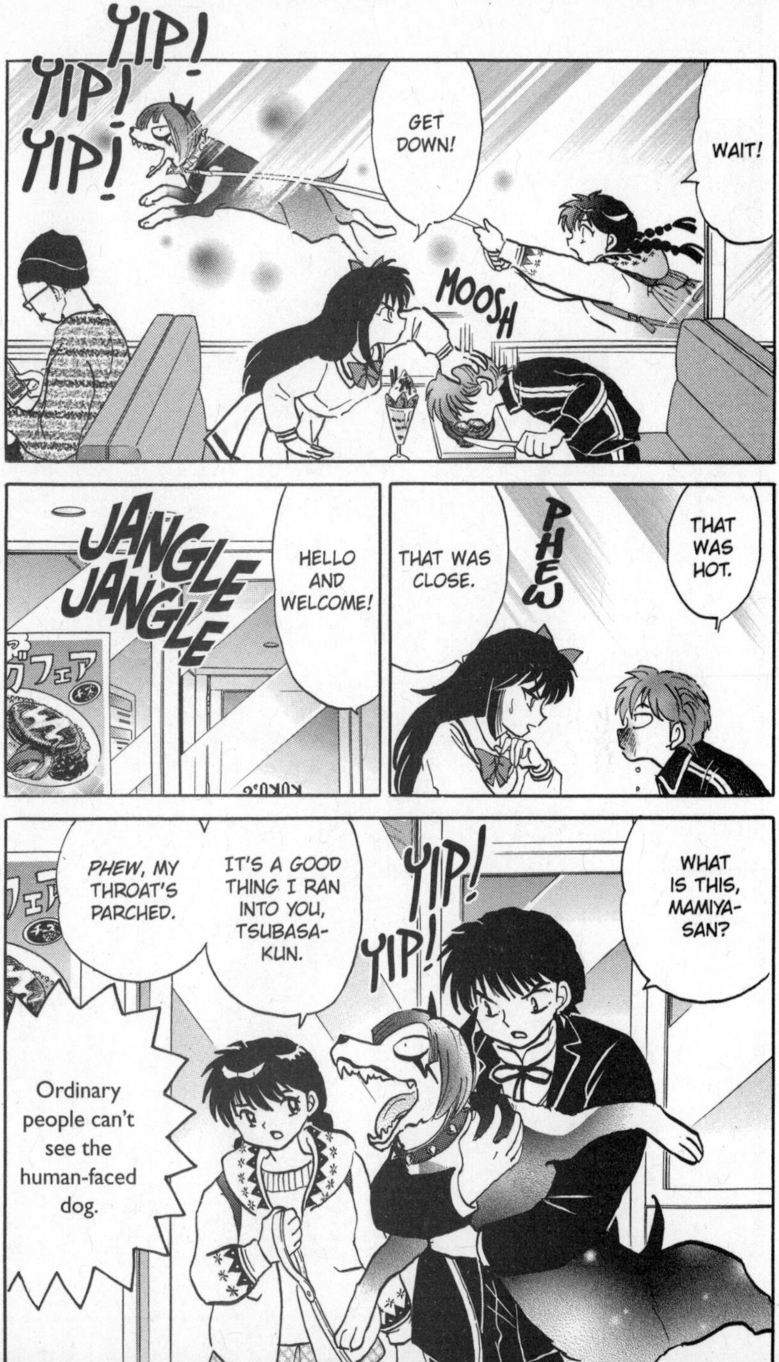
WAIT!
GET DOWN!
MOOSH
YIP! YIP! YIP!
THAT WAS HOT.
PHEW
THAT WAS CLOSE.
HELLO AND WELCOME!
JANGLE JANGLE
WHAT IS THIS, MAMIYA-SAN?
YIP! YIP!
IT'S A GOOD THING I RAN INTO YOU, TSUBASA-KUN.
PHEW, MY THROAT'S PARCHED.
Ordinary people can't see the human-faced dog.

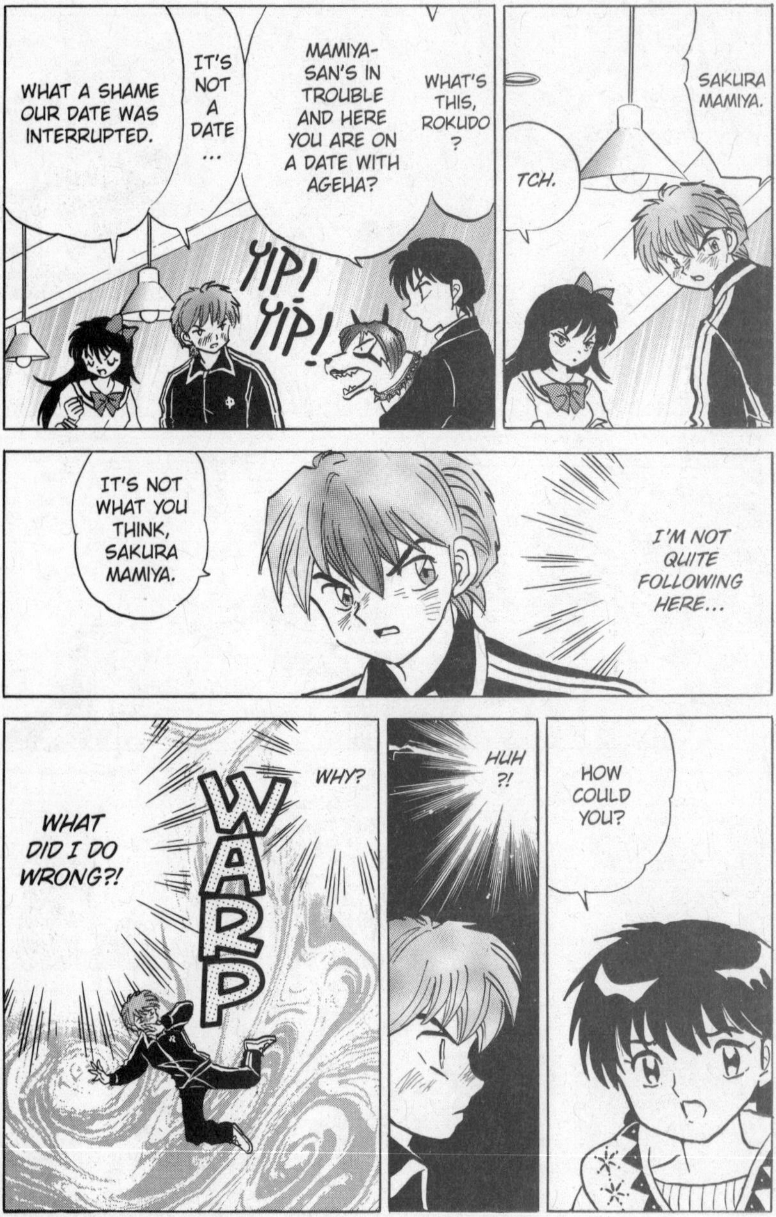
SAKURA MAMIYA.
TCH.
WHAT'S THIS, ROKUDO?
MAMIYA-SAN'S IN TROUBLE AND HERE YOU ARE ON A DATE WITH AGEHA?
IT'S NOT A DATE...
WHAT A SHAME OUR DATE WAS INTERRUPTED.
YIP! YIP!
I'M NOT QUITE FOLLOWING HERE...
IT'S NOT WHAT YOU THINK, SAKURA MAMIYA.
HOW COULD YOU?
HUH?!
WHY?
WARP
WHAT DID I DO WRONG?!

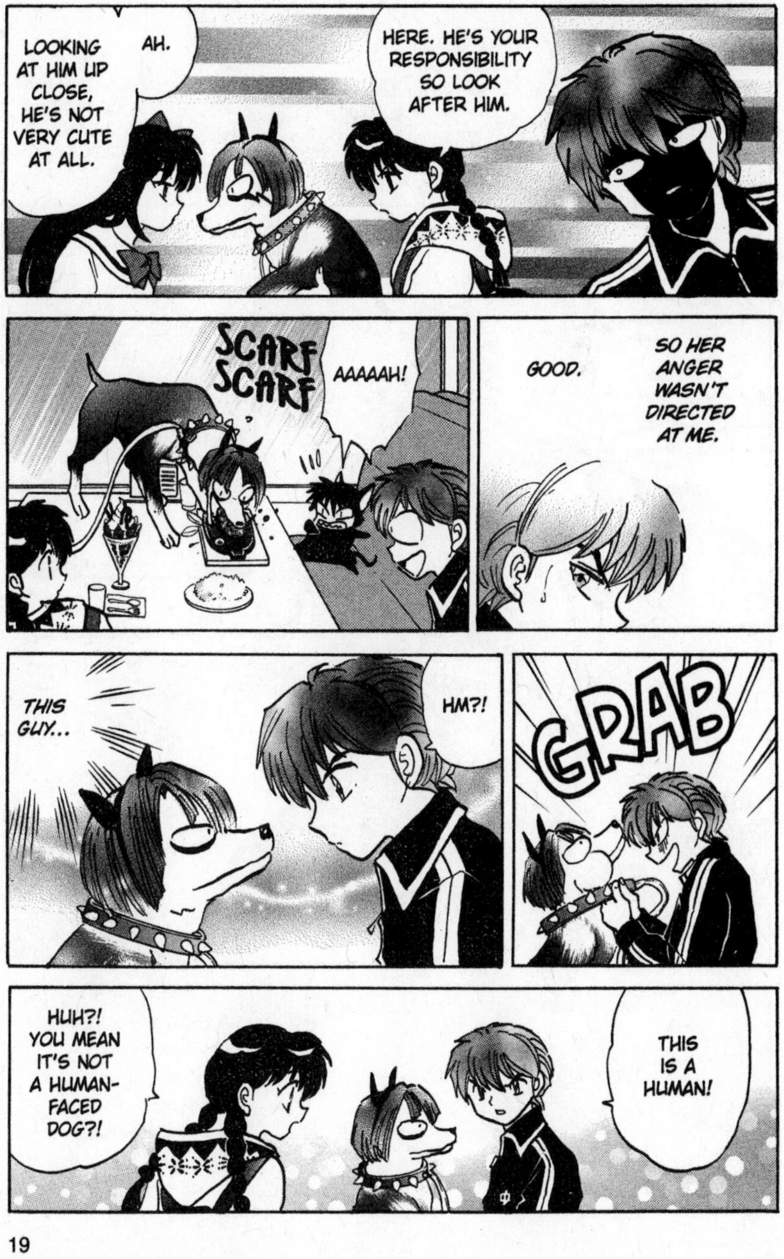
HERE. HE'S YOUR RESPONSIBILITY SO LOOK AFTER HIM.
AH.
LOOKING AT HIM UP CLOSE, HE'S NOT VERY CUTE AT ALL.
SO HER ANGER WASN'T DIRECTED AT ME.
GOOD.
AAAAAH!
SCARF SCARF
GRAB
HM?!
THIS GUY...
THIS IS A HUMAN!
HUH?! YOU MEAN IT'S NOT A HUMAN-FACED DOG?!

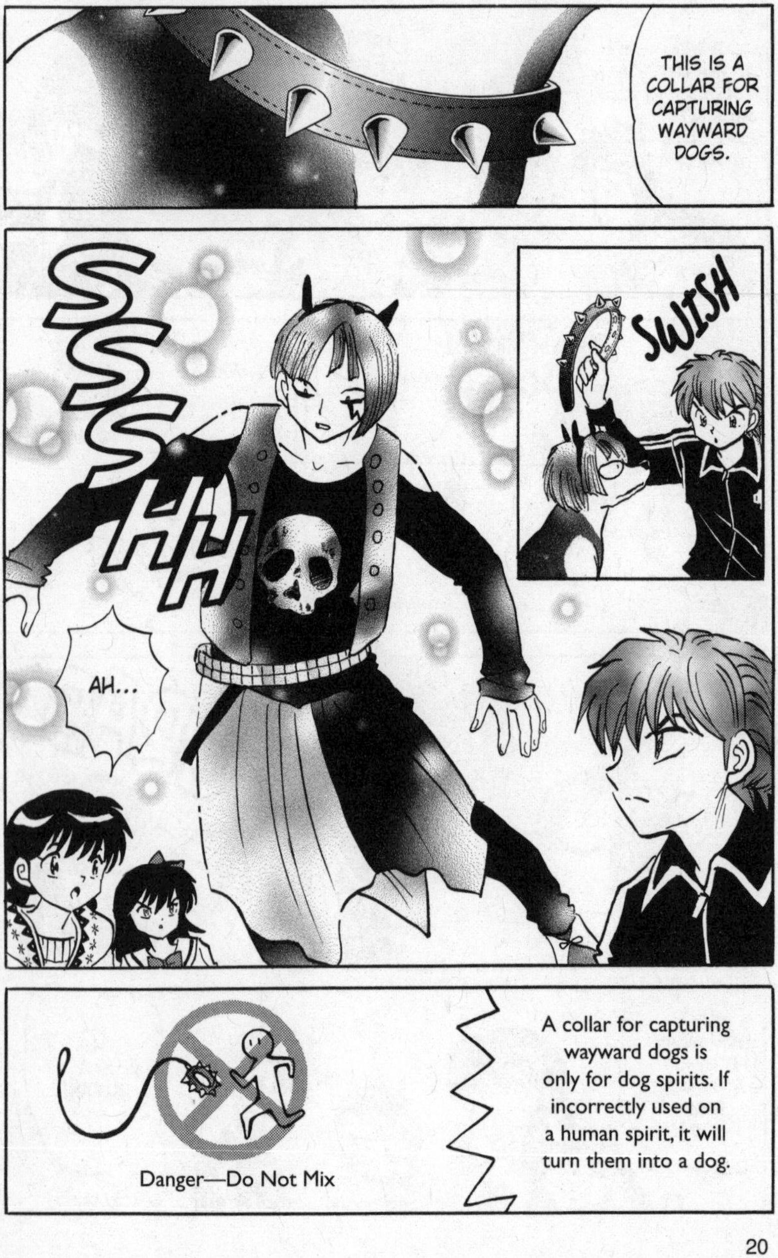
THIS IS A COLLAR FOR CAPTURING WAYWARD DOGS.
SWISH
SSSHH
AH...
A collar for capturing wayward dogs is only for dog spirits. If incorrectly used on a human spirit, it will turn them into a dog.
Danger—Do Not Mix

YOU WERE THIS CLOSE TO BECOMING A FULL-FLEDGED DOG.
AH!
AAAAH! I'VE GOT TO HURRY!
TUG
SWATCH
BOOMF
HEY! HE TURNED INTO A HUMAN-FACED DOG AGAIN.
WHY'S HE PUTTING IT ON HIMSELF?!
HE SEEMED TO BE IN A HURRY TO GET SOME-WHERE...
I REMEMBER NOW!
THE AUDITION!
POOMF
I WAS A PUNK ROCKER ON MY WAY TO AN AUDITION ONE DAY...
OH NO! I FORGOT MY CHOKER!

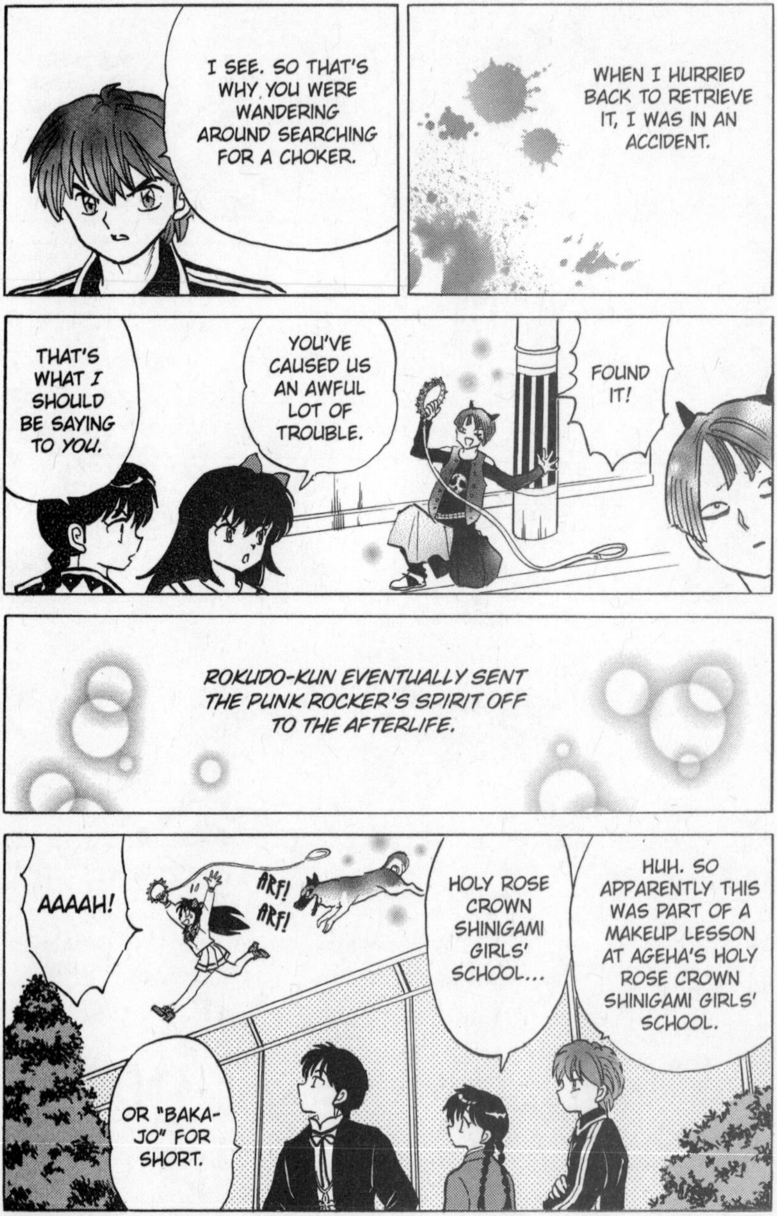
WHEN I HURRIED BACK TO RETRIEVE IT, I WAS IN AN ACCIDENT.
I SEE. SO THAT'S WHY YOU WERE WANDERING AROUND SEARCHING FOR A CHOKER.
FOUND IT!
YOU'VE CAUSED US AN AWFUL LOT OF TROUBLE.
THAT'S WHAT *I* SHOULD BE SAYING TO *YOU*.
ROKUDO-KUN EVENTUALLY SENT THE PUNK ROCKER'S SPIRIT OFF TO THE AFTERLIFE.
HUH. SO APPARENTLY THIS WAS PART OF A MAKEUP LESSON AT AGEHA'S HOLY ROSE CROWN SHINIGAMI GIRLS' SCHOOL.
HOLY ROSE CROWN SHINIGAMI GIRLS' SCHOOL...
ARF! ARF!
AAAAH!
OR "BAKA-JO" FOR SHORT.

In Japanese, "ba-ka-jo" are the three first syllables of "Rose Crown Girls." Phonetically, "baka-jo" sounds like "stupid girl."

CHAPTER 270: THE SNOWY STAIRCASE

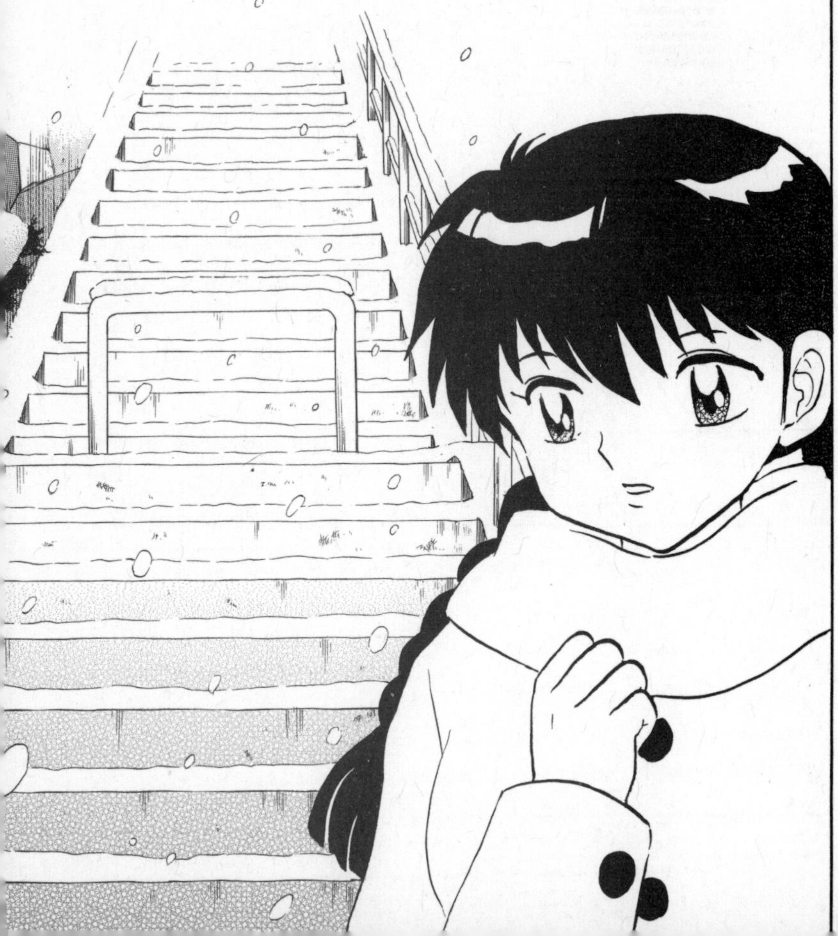

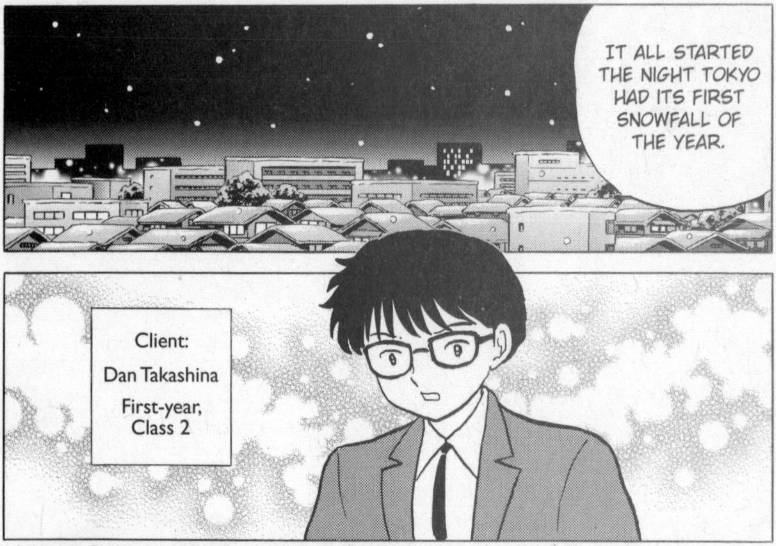
IT ALL STARTED THE NIGHT TOKYO HAD ITS FIRST SNOWFALL OF THE YEAR.
Client:
Dan Takashina
First-year, Class 2

In Japanese, Dan's last name literally means "tall stairs," and his first name can mean "step," as in a staircase.

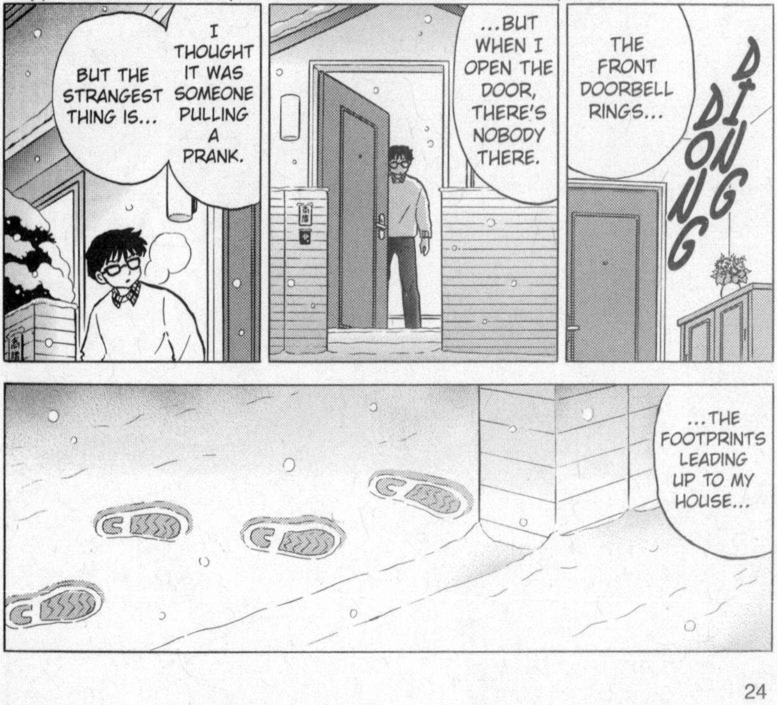
THE FRONT DOORBELL RINGS...
DING DONG
...BUT WHEN I OPEN THE DOOR, THERE'S NOBODY THERE.
I THOUGHT IT WAS SOMEONE PULLING A PRANK.
BUT THE STRANGEST THING IS...
...THE FOOTPRINTS LEADING UP TO MY HOUSE...

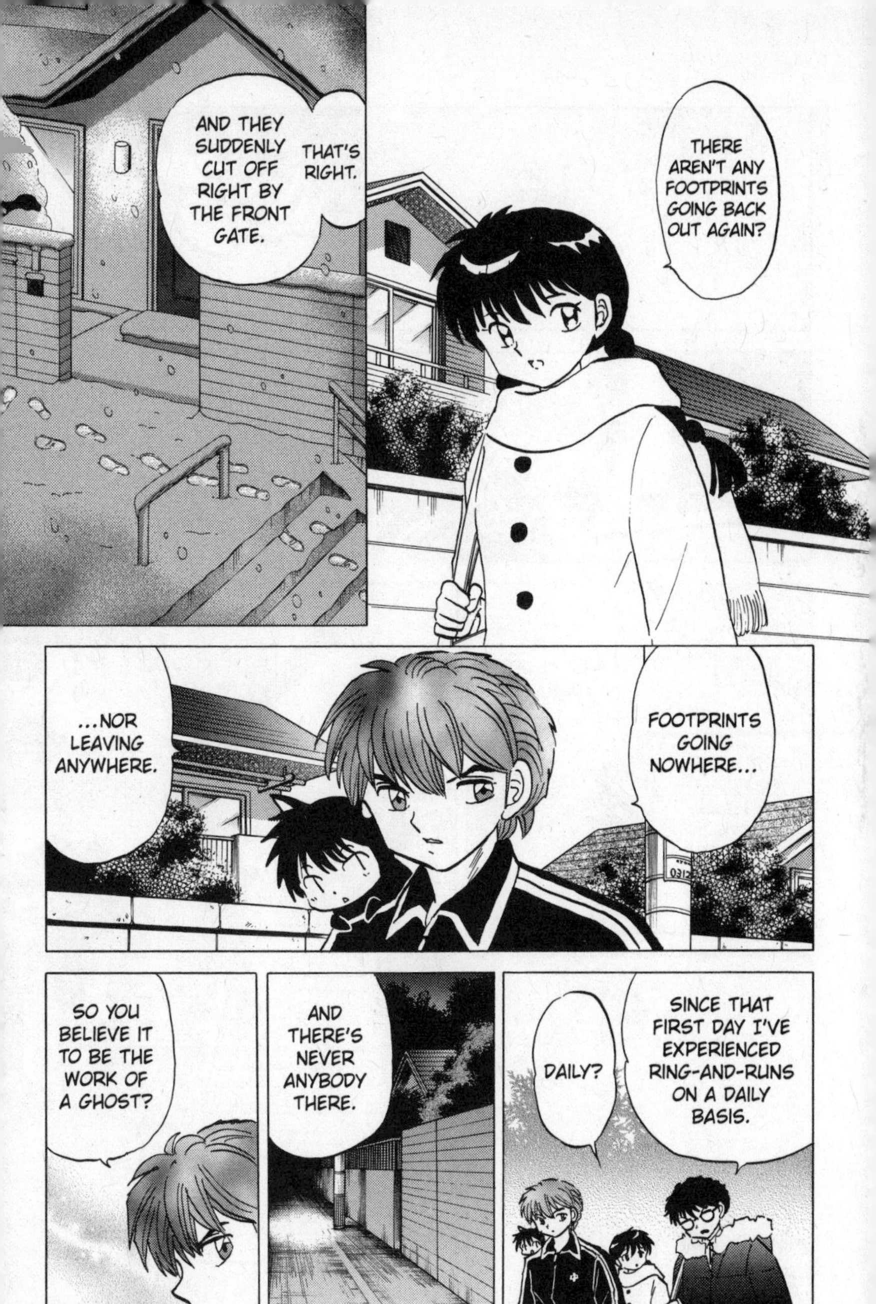
THERE AREN'T ANY FOOTPRINTS GOING BACK OUT AGAIN?
THAT'S RIGHT.
AND THEY SUDDENLY CUT OFF RIGHT BY THE FRONT GATE.
FOOTPRINTS GOING NOWHERE...
...NOR LEAVING ANYWHERE.
SINCE THAT FIRST DAY I'VE EXPERIENCED RING-AND-RUNS ON A DAILY BASIS.
DAILY?
AND THERE'S NEVER ANYBODY THERE.
SO YOU BELIEVE IT TO BE THE WORK OF A GHOST?

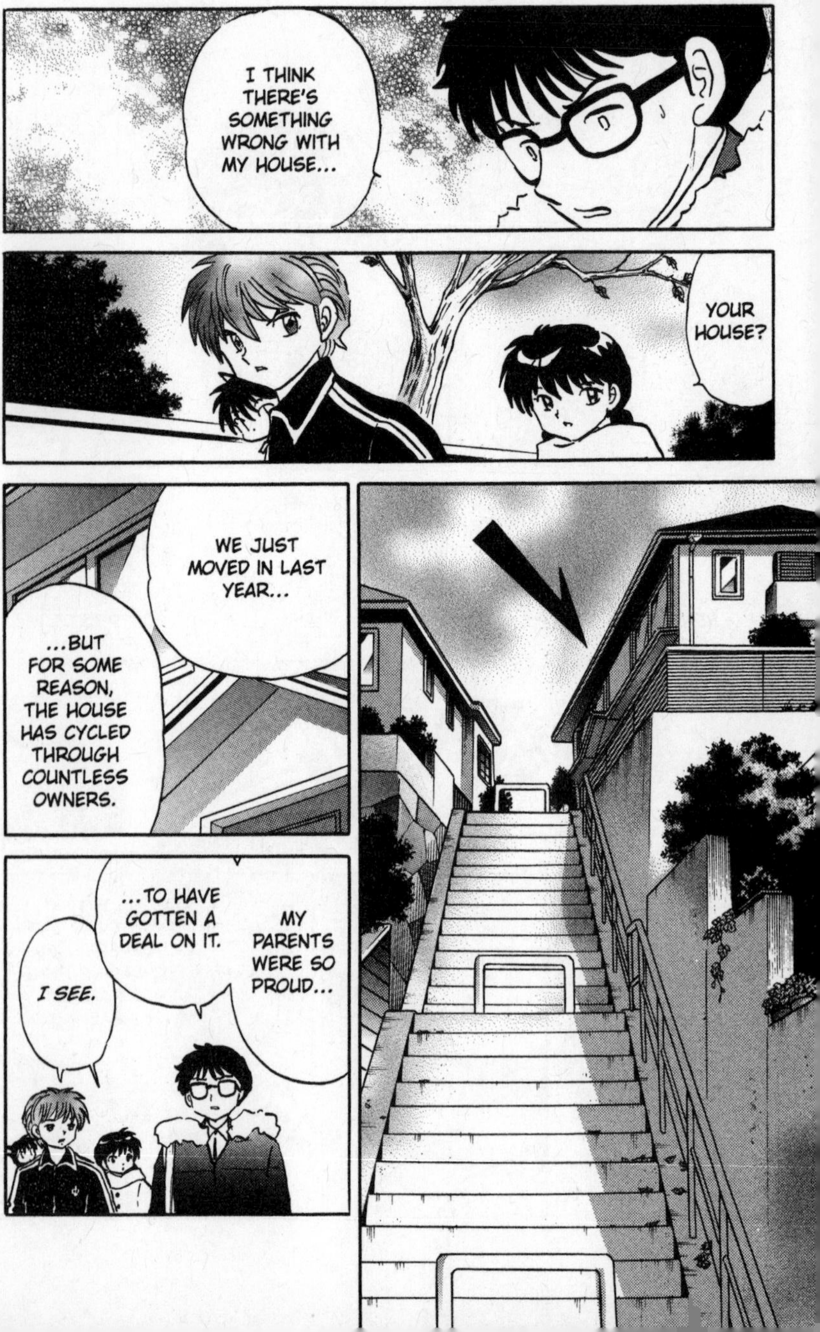
I THINK THERE'S SOMETHING WRONG WITH MY HOUSE...
YOUR HOUSE?
WE JUST MOVED IN LAST YEAR...
...BUT FOR SOME REASON, THE HOUSE HAS CYCLED THROUGH COUNTLESS OWNERS.
MY PARENTS WERE SO PROUD...
...TO HAVE GOTTEN A DEAL ON IT.
I SEE.

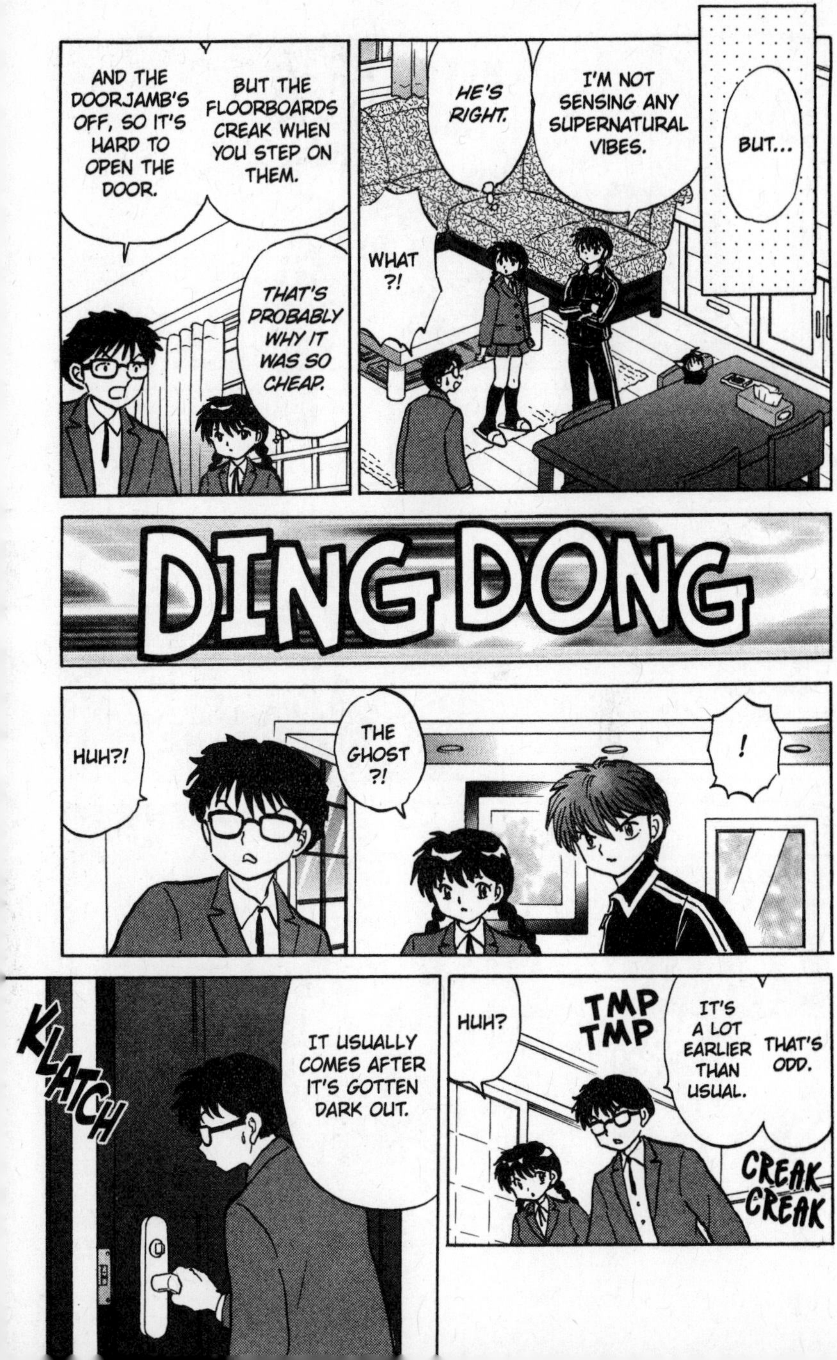
BUT...
I'M NOT SENSING ANY SUPERNATURAL VIBES.
HE'S RIGHT.
WHAT?!
BUT THE FLOORBOARDS CREAK WHEN YOU STEP ON THEM.
AND THE DOORJAMB'S OFF, SO IT'S HARD TO OPEN THE DOOR.
THAT'S PROBABLY WHY IT WAS SO CHEAP.
DING DONG
!
THE GHOST?!
HUH?!
THAT'S ODD.
IT'S A LOT EARLIER THAN USUAL.
TMP TMP
HUH?
CREAK CREAK
IT USUALLY COMES AFTER IT'S GOTTEN DARK OUT.
KLATCH

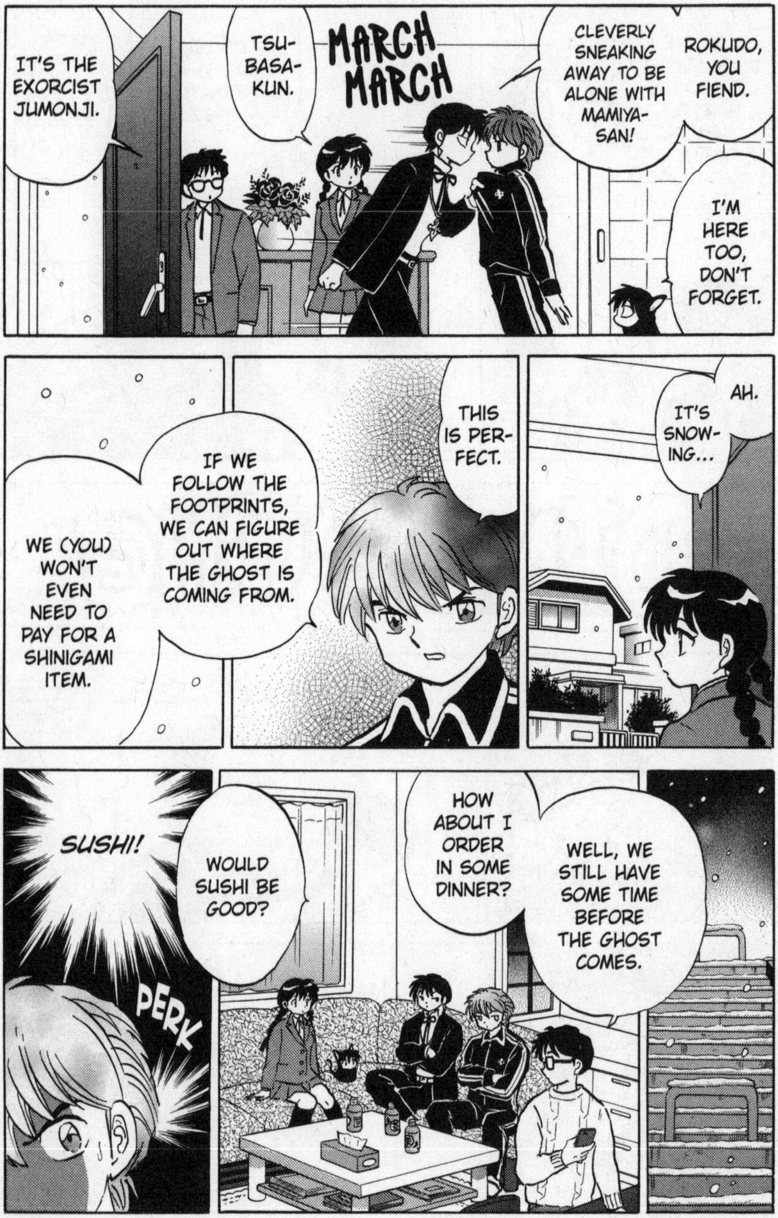
ROKUDO, YOU FIEND.
CLEVERLY SNEAKING AWAY TO BE ALONE WITH MAMIYA-SAN!
I'M HERE TOO, DON'T FORGET.
MARCH MARCH
TSU-BASA-KUN.
IT'S THE EXORCIST JUMONJI.
AH.
IT'S SNOW-ING...
THIS IS PER-FECT.
IF WE FOLLOW THE FOOTPRINTS, WE CAN FIGURE OUT WHERE THE GHOST IS COMING FROM.
WE (YOU) WON'T EVEN NEED TO PAY FOR A SHINIGAMI ITEM.
WELL, WE STILL HAVE SOME TIME BEFORE THE GHOST COMES.
HOW ABOUT I ORDER IN SOME DINNER?
WOULD SUSHI BE GOOD?
SUSHI!
PERK

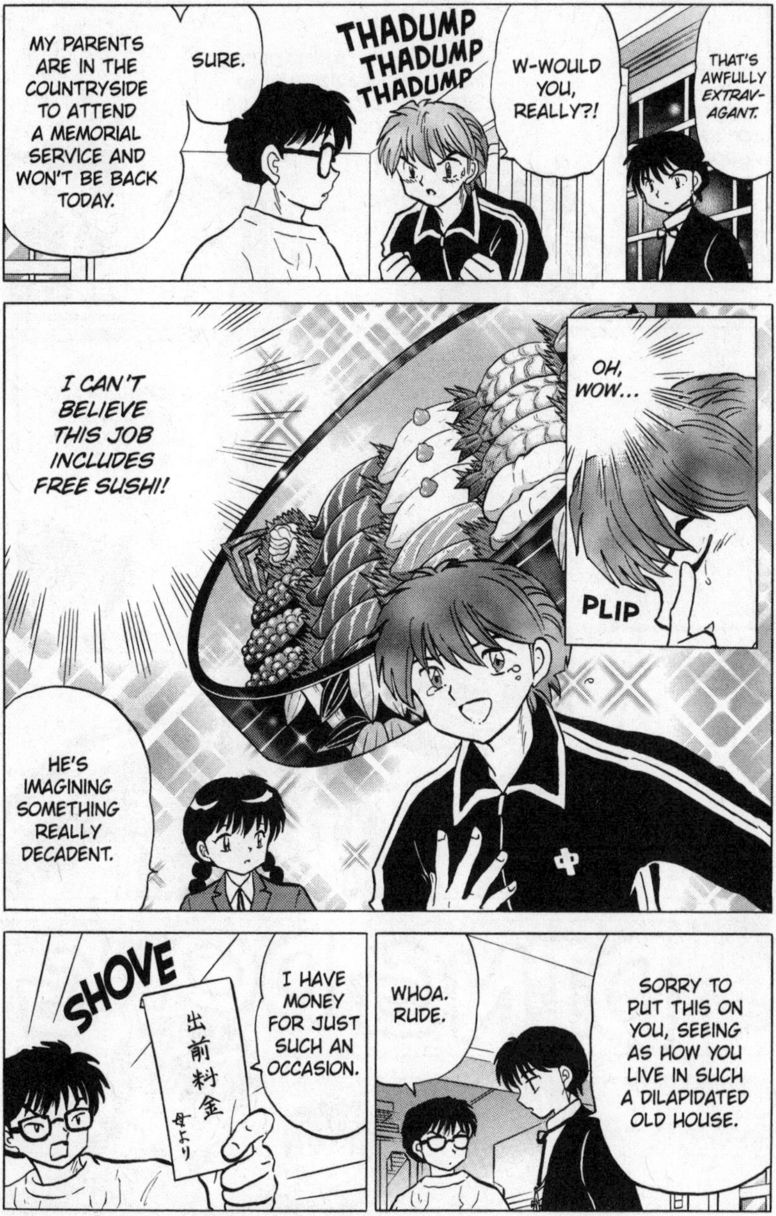
THAT'S AWFULLY EXTRAVAGANT.
W-WOULD YOU, REALLY?!
THADUMP THADUMP THADUMP
SURE.
MY PARENTS ARE IN THE COUNTRYSIDE TO ATTEND A MEMORIAL SERVICE AND WON'T BE BACK TODAY.
OH, WOW...
PLIP
I CAN'T BELIEVE THIS JOB INCLUDES FREE SUSHI!
HE'S IMAGINING SOMETHING REALLY DECADENT.
SORRY TO PUT THIS ON YOU, SEEING AS HOW YOU LIVE IN SUCH A DILAPIDATED OLD HOUSE.
WHOA. RUDE.
I HAVE MONEY FOR JUST SUCH AN OCCASION.
SHOVE
出前料金
母より
Envelope: Meal delivery money From Mom

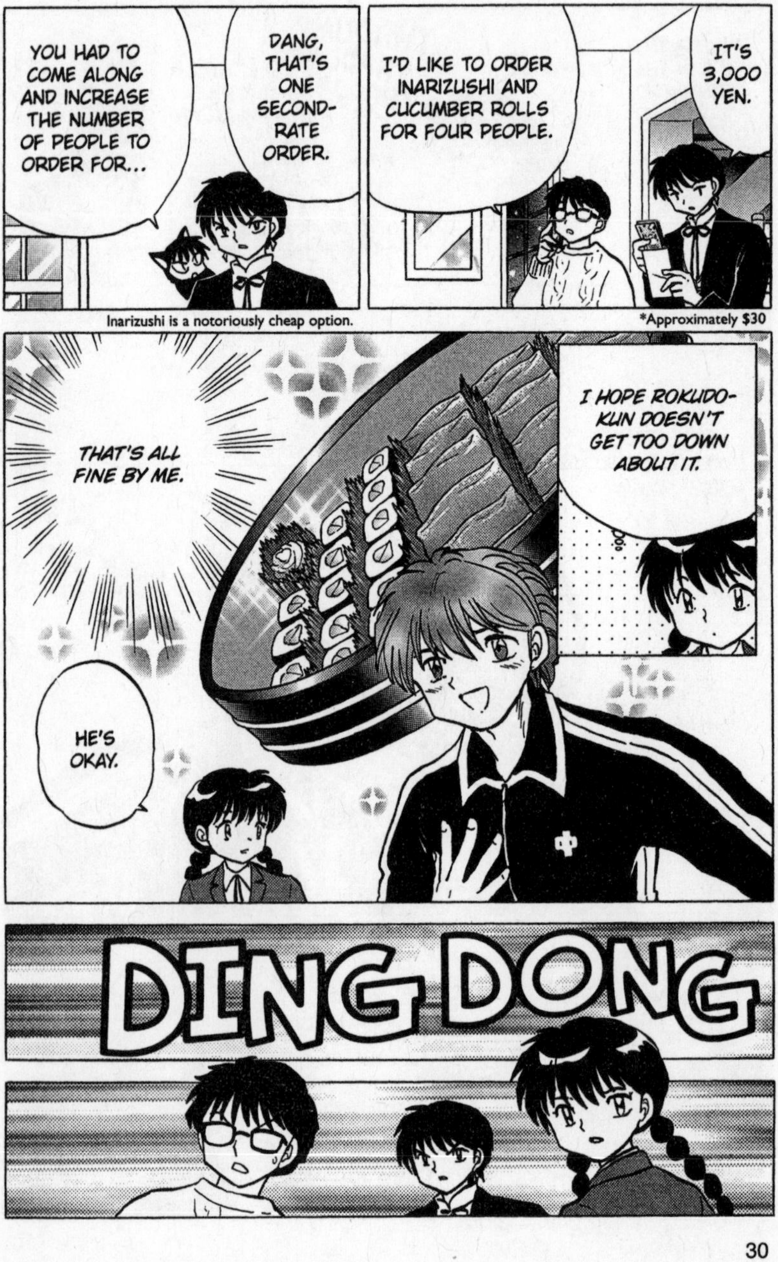
IT'S 3,000 YEN.
I'D LIKE TO ORDER INARIZUSHI AND CUCUMBER ROLLS FOR FOUR PEOPLE.
DANG, THAT'S ONE SECOND-RATE ORDER.
YOU HAD TO COME ALONG AND INCREASE THE NUMBER OF PEOPLE TO ORDER FOR...
I HOPE ROKUDO-KUN DOESN'T GET TOO DOWN ABOUT IT.
THAT'S ALL FINE BY ME.
HE'S OKAY.
DING DONG
*Approximately $30
Inarizushi is a notoriously cheap option.

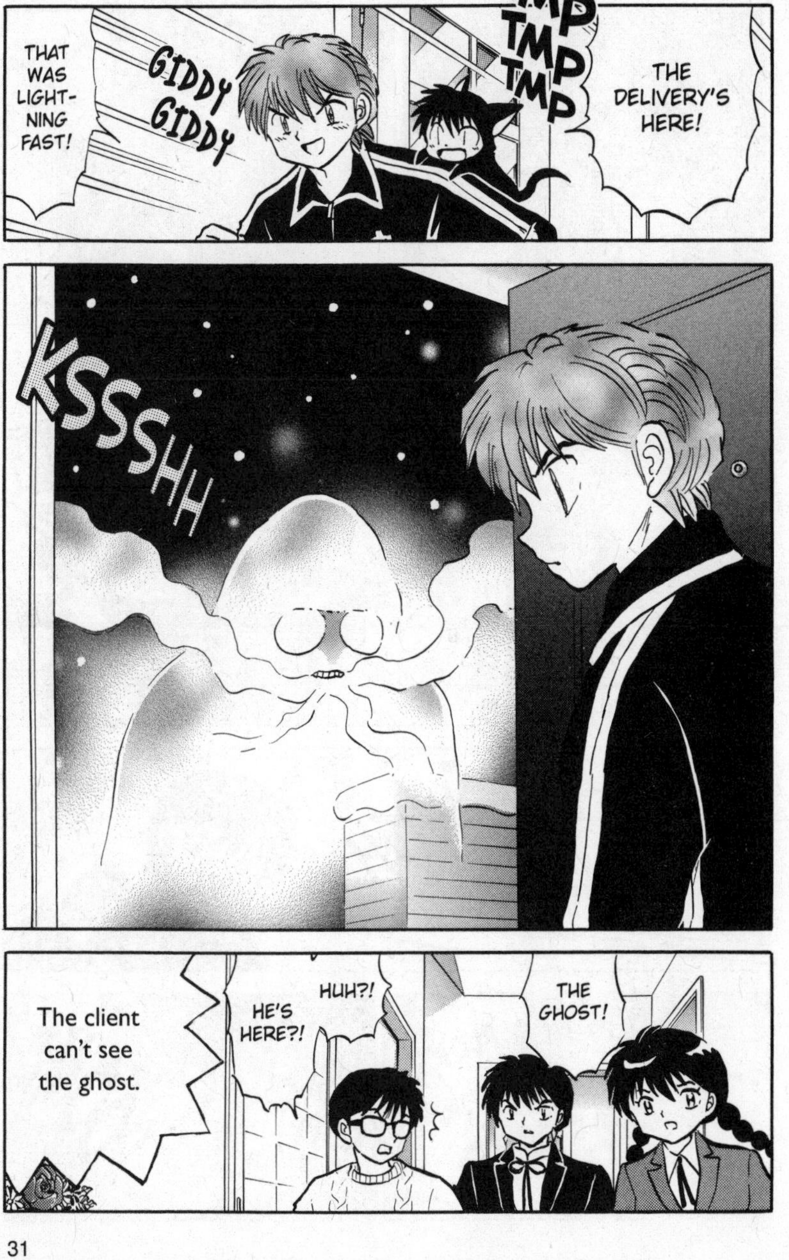
THE DELIVERY'S HERE!
TMP TMP TMP
GIDDY GIDDY
THAT WAS LIGHT-NING FAST!
KSSSHH
THE GHOST!
HUH?!
HE'S HERE?!
The client can't see the ghost.

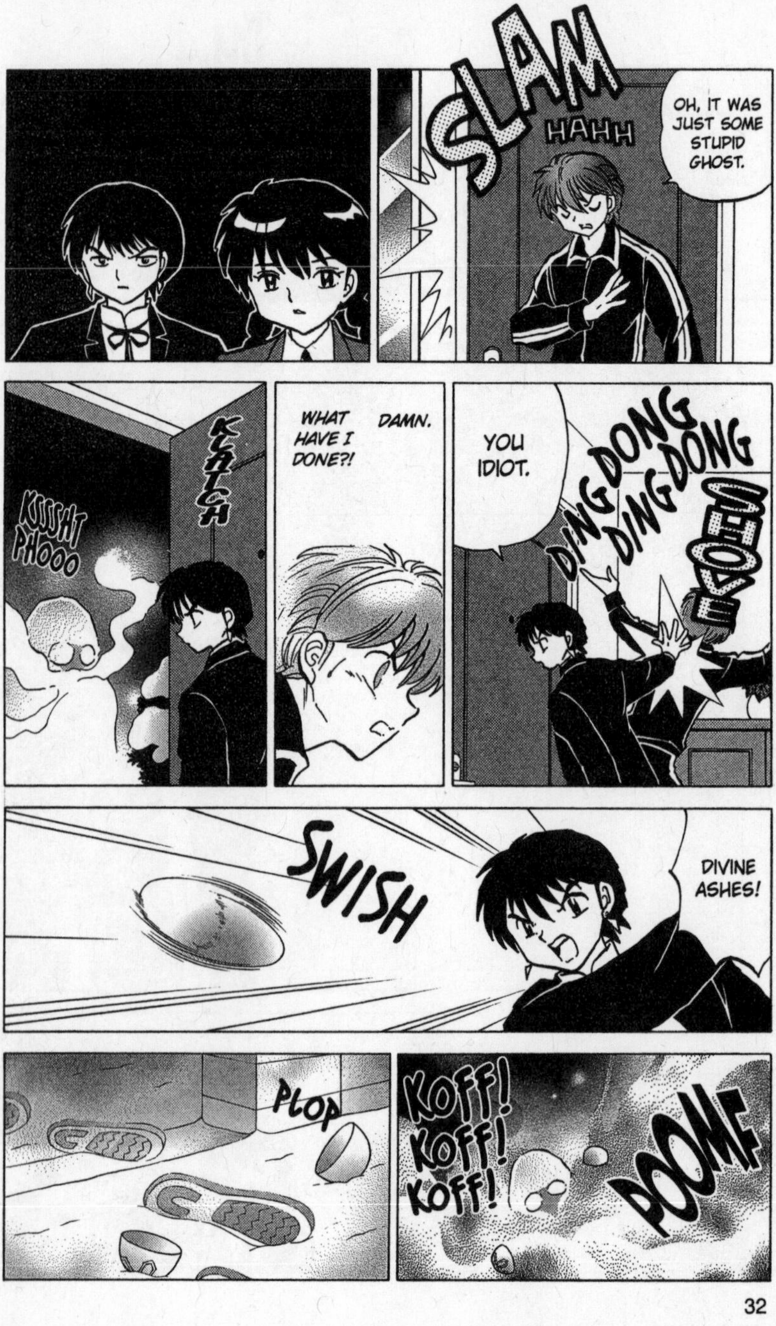
SLAM
HAHH
OH, IT WAS JUST SOME STUPID GHOST.
YOU IDIOT.
DING DONG DING DONG
SHOVE
DAMN.
WHAT HAVE I DONE?!
KLATCH
KSSSHT PHOOO
DIVINE ASHES!
SWISH
POOMF
KOFF! KOFF! KOFF!
PLOP

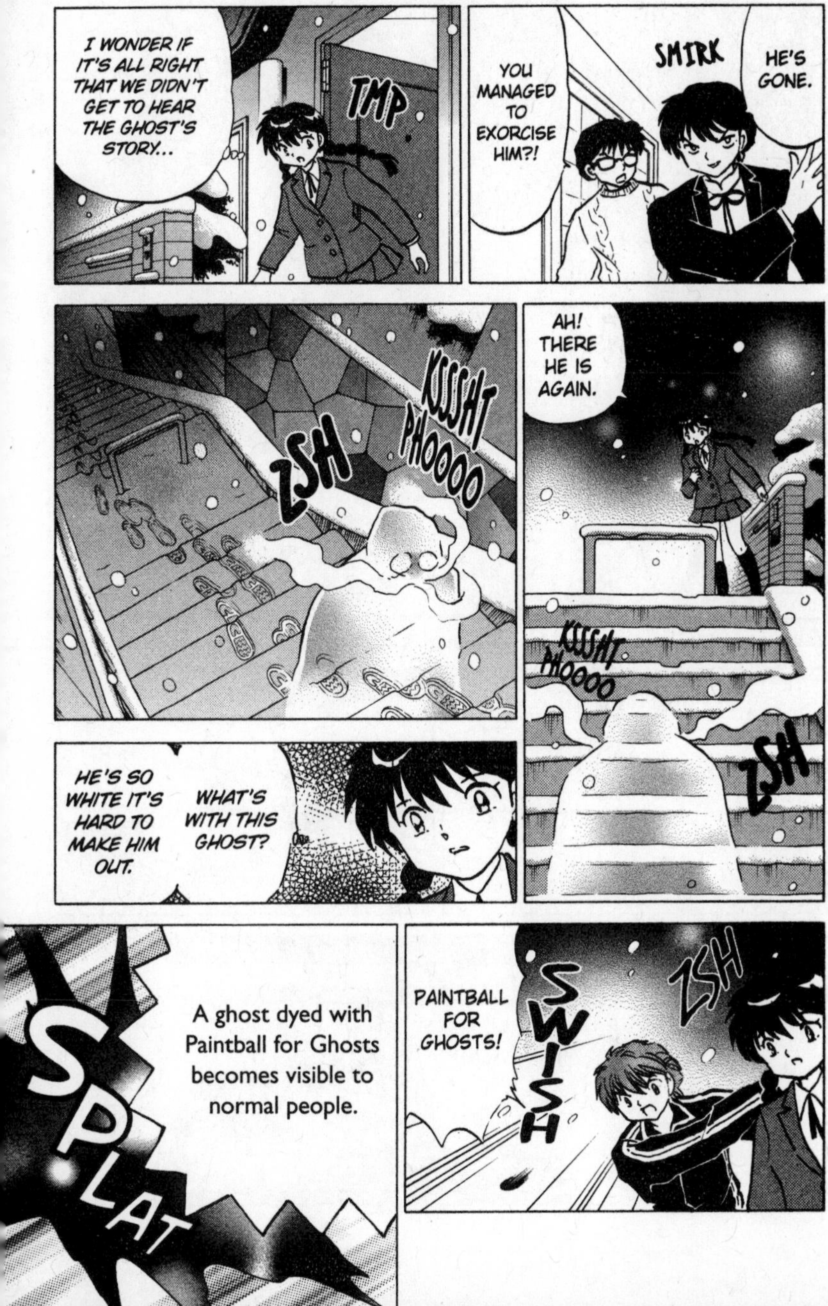
HE'S GONE.
SMIRK
YOU MANAGED TO EXORCISE HIM?!
TMP
I WONDER IF IT'S ALL RIGHT THAT WE DIDN'T GET TO HEAR THE GHOST'S STORY...
AH! THERE HE IS AGAIN.
KSSSHT PHOOOO
ZSH
KSSSHT PHOOOO
ZSH
WHAT'S WITH THIS GHOST?
HE'S SO WHITE IT'S HARD TO MAKE HIM OUT.
ZSH
SWISH
PAINTBALL FOR GHOSTS!
A ghost dyed with Paintball for Ghosts becomes visible to normal people.
SPLAT

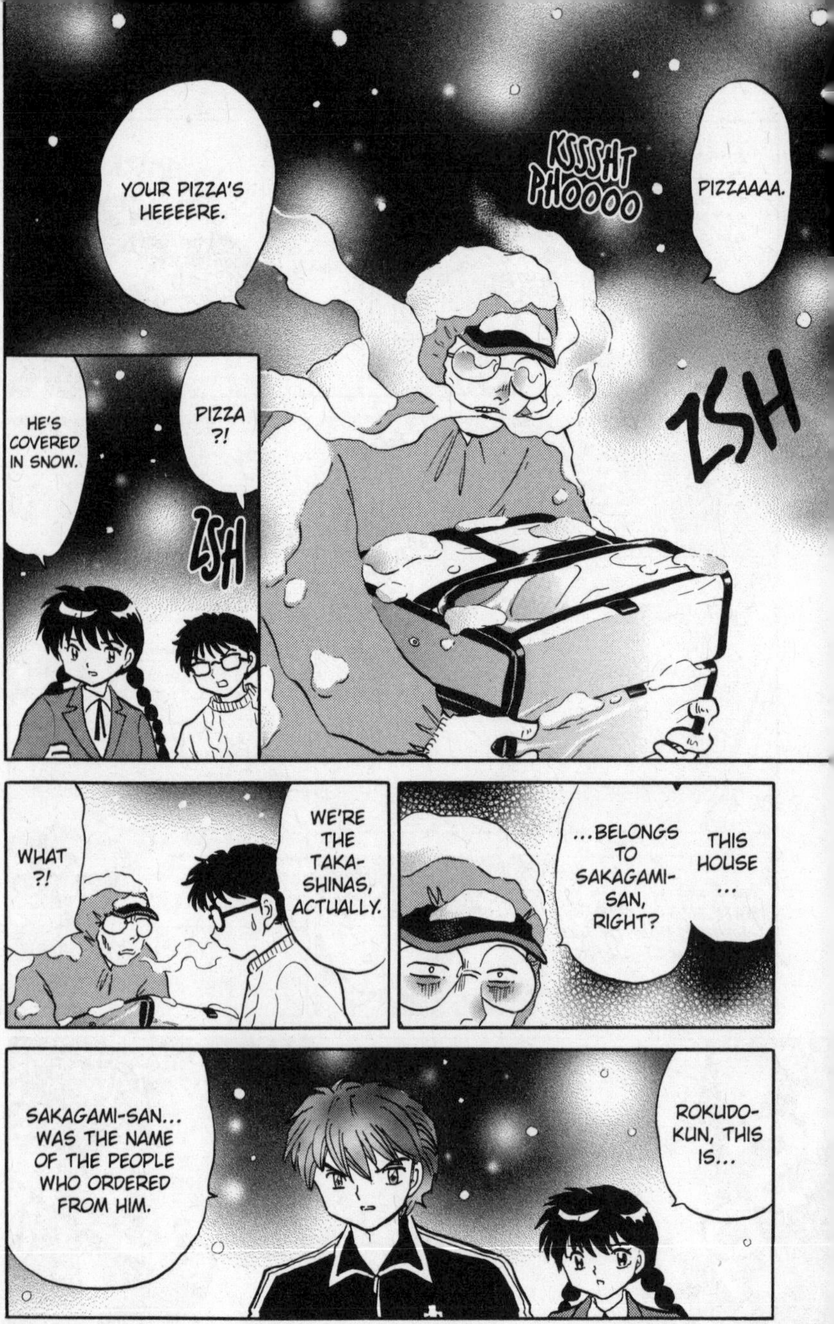
PIZZAAAA.
KSSSHT PHOOOO
YOUR PIZZA'S HEEEERE.
ZSH
PIZZA ?!
HE'S COVERED IN SNOW.
ZSH
THIS HOUSE ...
...BELONGS TO SAKAGAMI-SAN, RIGHT?
WE'RE THE TAKA-SHINAS, ACTUALLY.
WHAT ?!
ROKUDO-KUN, THIS IS...
SAKAGAMI-SAN... WAS THE NAME OF THE PEOPLE WHO ORDERED FROM HIM.

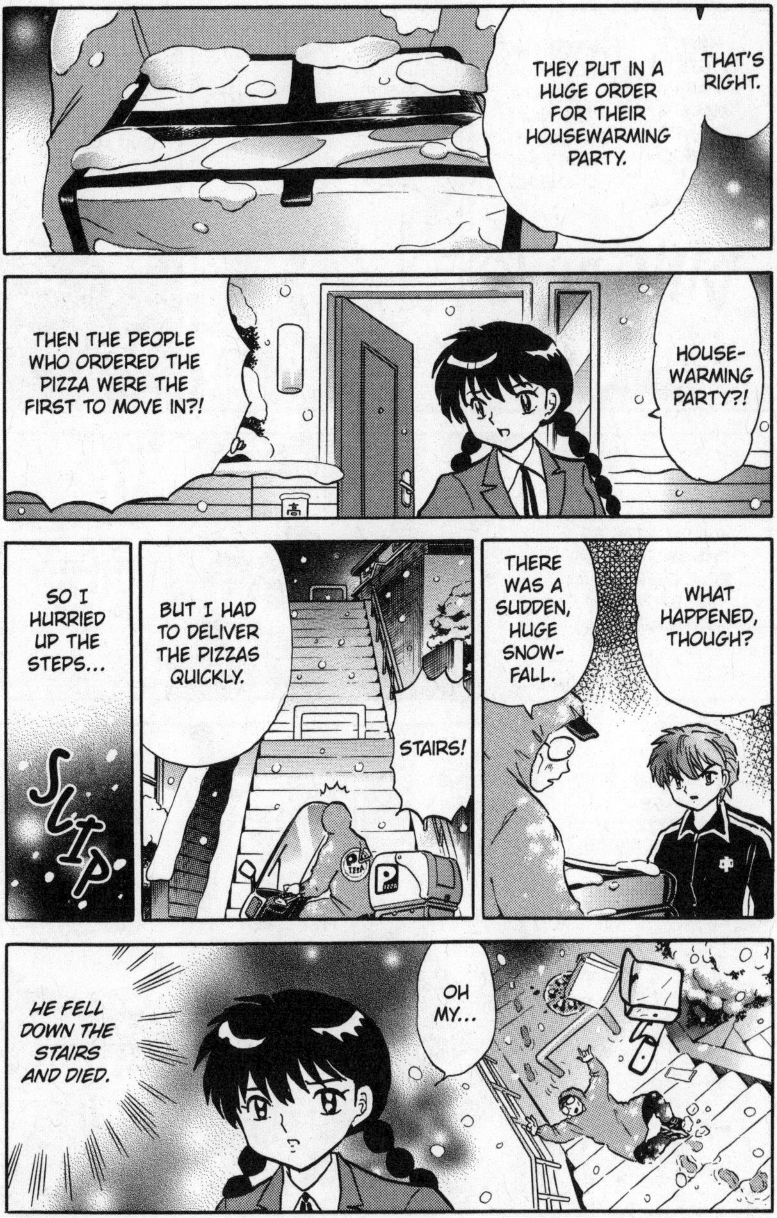
THAT'S RIGHT.
THEY PUT IN A HUGE ORDER FOR THEIR HOUSEWARMING PARTY.
HOUSE-WARMING PARTY?!
THEN THE PEOPLE WHO ORDERED THE PIZZA WERE THE FIRST TO MOVE IN?!
WHAT HAPPENED, THOUGH?
THERE WAS A SUDDEN, HUGE SNOW-FALL.
BUT I HAD TO DELIVER THE PIZZAS QUICKLY.
STAIRS!
SO I HURRIED UP THE STEPS...
SLIP
OH MY...
HE FELL DOWN THE STAIRS AND DIED.

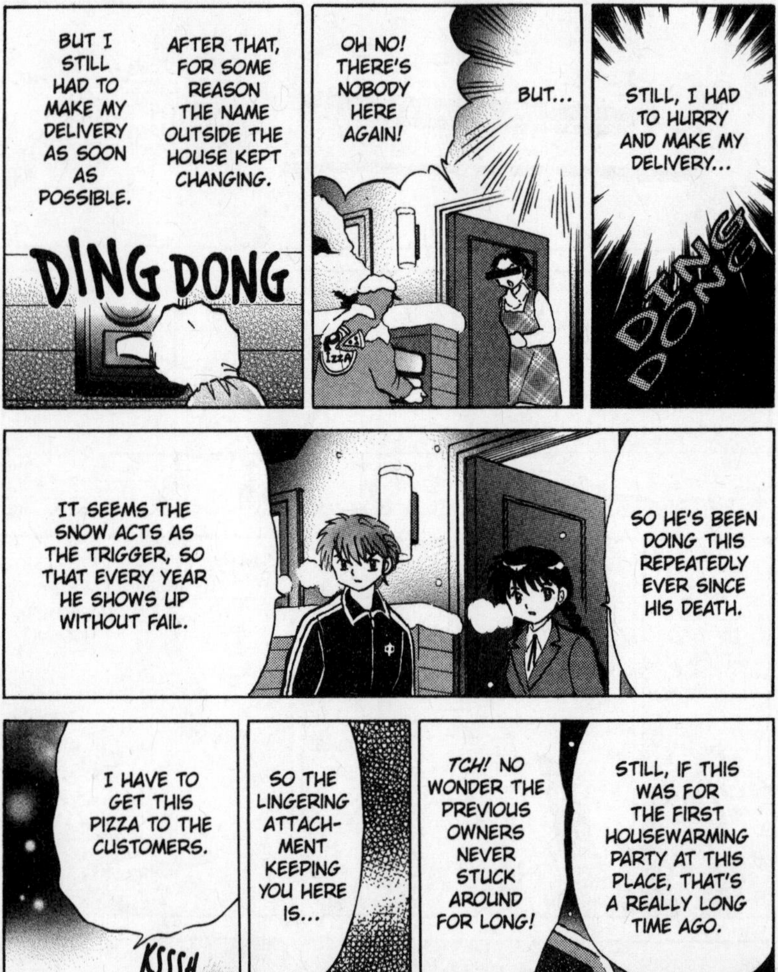
STILL, I HAD TO HURRY AND MAKE MY DELIVERY...
DING DONG
BUT...
OH NO! THERE'S NOBODY HERE AGAIN!
AFTER THAT, FOR SOME REASON THE NAME OUTSIDE THE HOUSE KEPT CHANGING.
BUT I STILL HAD TO MAKE MY DELIVERY AS SOON AS POSSIBLE.
DING DONG
SO HE'S BEEN DOING THIS REPEATEDLY EVER SINCE HIS DEATH.
IT SEEMS THE SNOW ACTS AS THE TRIGGER, SO THAT EVERY YEAR HE SHOWS UP WITHOUT FAIL.
STILL, IF THIS WAS FOR THE FIRST HOUSEWARMING PARTY AT THIS PLACE, THAT'S A REALLY LONG TIME AGO.
TCH! NO WONDER THE PREVIOUS OWNERS NEVER STUCK AROUND FOR LONG!
SO THE LINGERING ATTACH-MENT KEEPING YOU HERE IS...
I HAVE TO GET THIS PIZZA TO THE CUSTOMERS.
KSSSH PHOOO

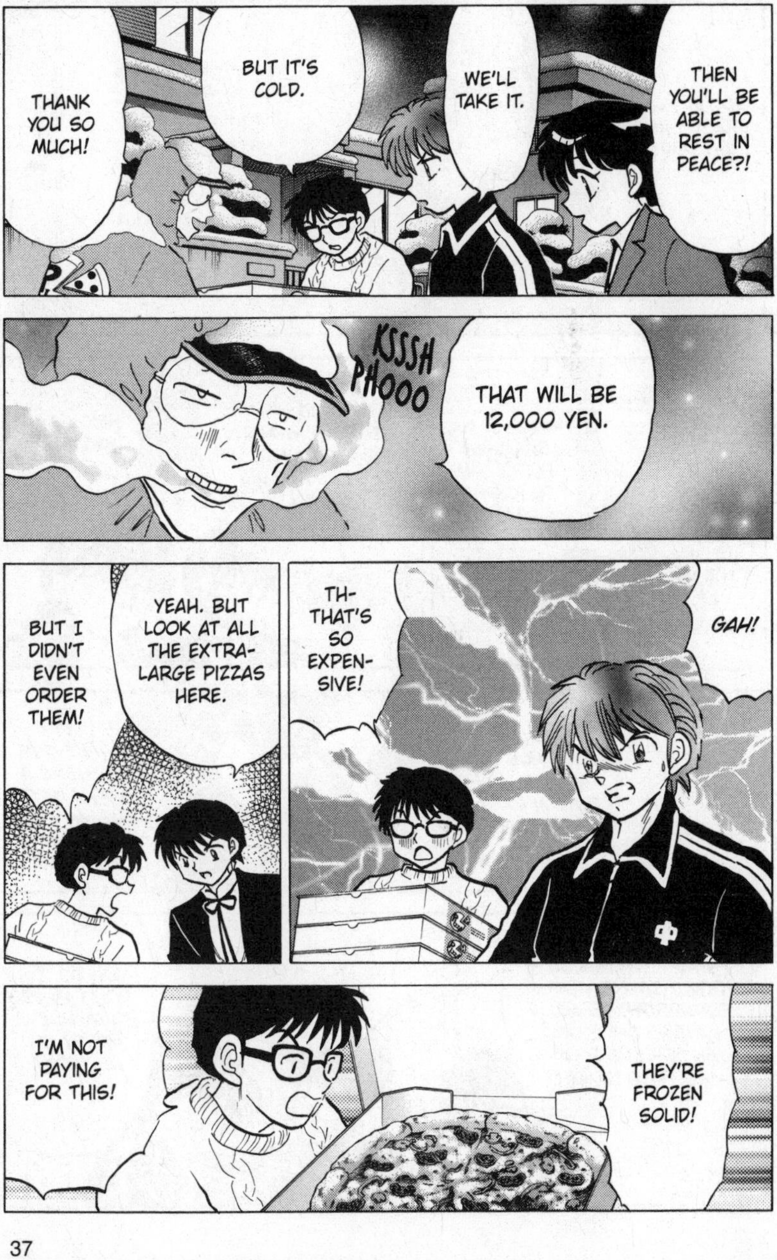
THEN YOU'LL BE ABLE TO REST IN PEACE?!
WE'LL TAKE IT.
BUT IT'S COLD.
THANK YOU SO MUCH!
THAT WILL BE 12,000 YEN.
KSSSH PHOOO
GAH!
TH-THAT'S SO EXPEN-SIVE!
YEAH. BUT LOOK AT ALL THE EXTRA-LARGE PIZZAS HERE.
BUT I DIDN'T EVEN ORDER THEM!
THEY'RE FROZEN SOLID!
I'M NOT PAYING FOR THIS!

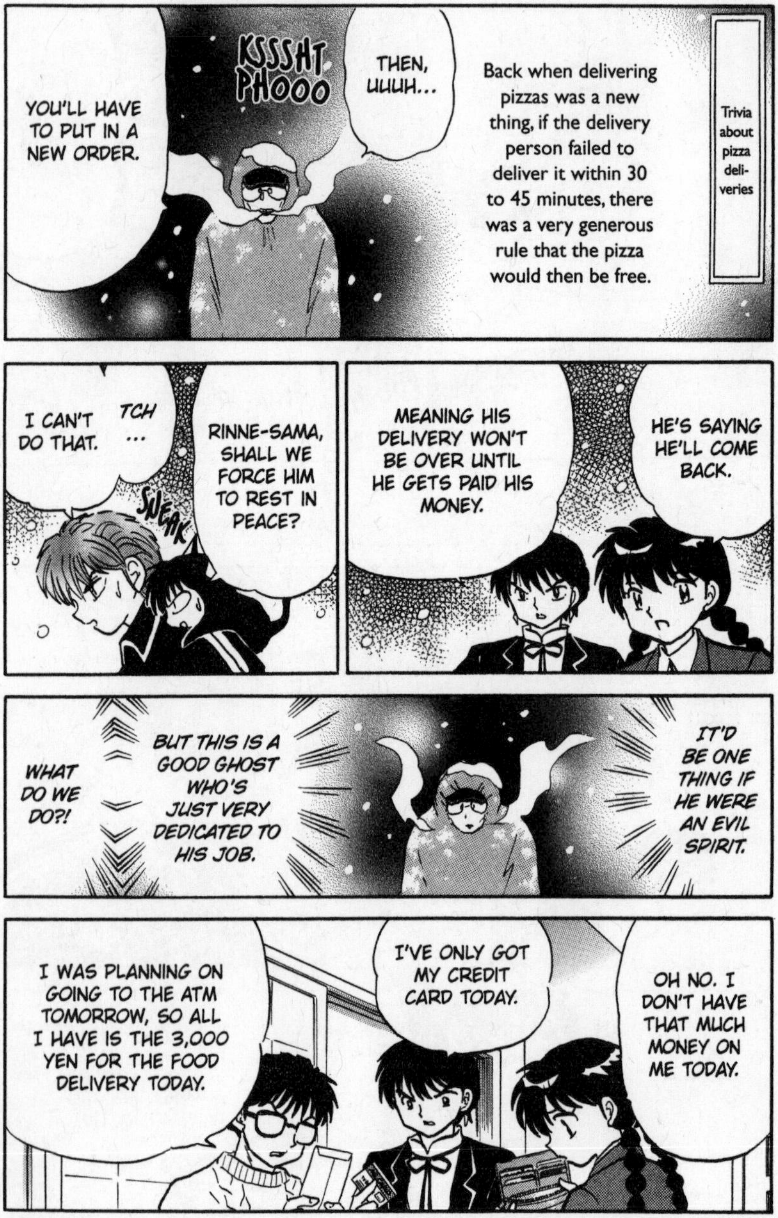
Trivia about pizza deli-veries
Back when delivering pizzas was a new thing, if the delivery person failed to deliver it within 30 to 45 minutes, there was a very generous rule that the pizza would then be free.
THEN, UUUH...
KSSSHT PHOOO
YOU'LL HAVE TO PUT IN A NEW ORDER.
HE'S SAYING HE'LL COME BACK.
MEANING HIS DELIVERY WON'T BE OVER UNTIL HE GETS PAID HIS MONEY.
RINNE-SAMA, SHALL WE FORCE HIM TO REST IN PEACE?
TCH ...
I CAN'T DO THAT.
SNEAK
IT'D BE ONE THING IF HE WERE AN EVIL SPIRIT.
BUT THIS IS A GOOD GHOST WHO'S JUST VERY DEDICATED TO HIS JOB.
WHAT DO WE DO?!
OH NO. I DON'T HAVE THAT MUCH MONEY ON ME TODAY.
I'VE ONLY GOT MY CREDIT CARD TODAY.
I WAS PLANNING ON GOING TO THE ATM TOMORROW, SO ALL I HAVE IS THE 3,000 YEN FOR THE FOOD DELIVERY TODAY.

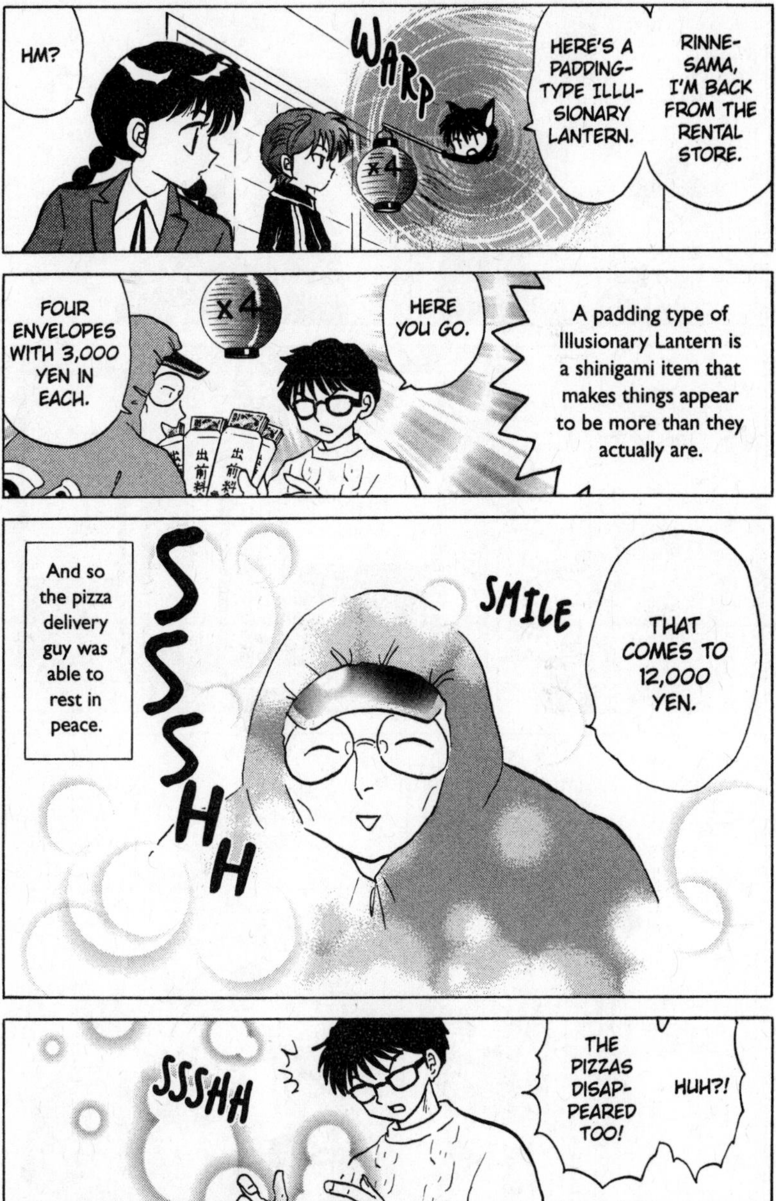
RINNE-SAMA, I'M BACK FROM THE RENTAL STORE.
HERE'S A PADDING-TYPE ILLUSIONARY LANTERN.
WARP
x4
HM?
A padding type of Illusionary Lantern is a shinigami item that makes things appear to be more than they actually are.
HERE YOU GO.
x4
FOUR ENVELOPES WITH 3,000 YEN IN EACH.
THAT COMES TO 12,000 YEN.
SMILE
SSSHH
And so the pizza delivery guy was able to rest in peace.
HUH?!
THE PIZZAS DISAPPEARED TOO!
SSSHH

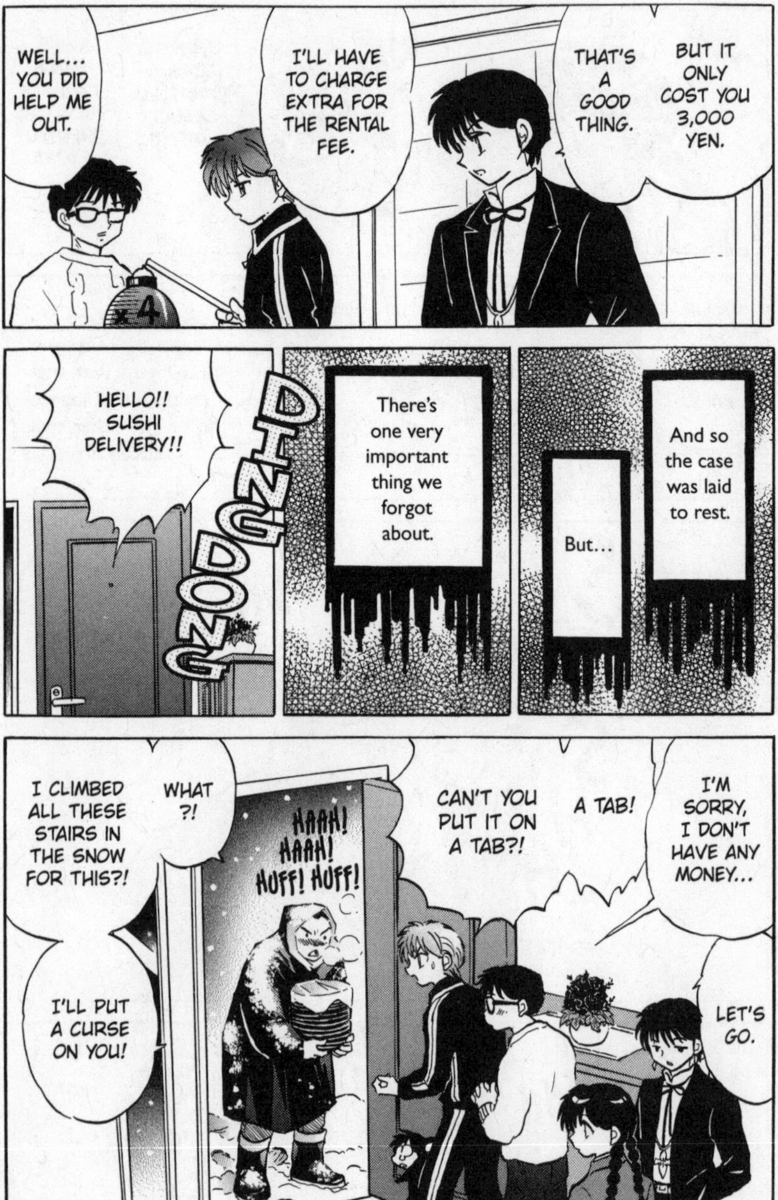
BUT IT ONLY COST YOU 3,000 YEN.
THAT'S A GOOD THING.
I'LL HAVE TO CHARGE EXTRA FOR THE RENTAL FEE.
WELL... YOU DID HELP ME OUT.
And so the case was laid to rest.
But...
There's one very important thing we forgot about.
DING DONG
HELLO!! SUSHI DELIVERY!!
I'M SORRY, I DON'T HAVE ANY MONEY...
LET'S GO.
A TAB!
CAN'T YOU PUT IT ON A TAB?!
HAAH! HAAH! HUFF! HUFF!
WHAT?!
I CLIMBED ALL THESE STAIRS IN THE SNOW FOR THIS?!
I'LL PUT A CURSE ON YOU!

CHAPTER 271: NAGARA

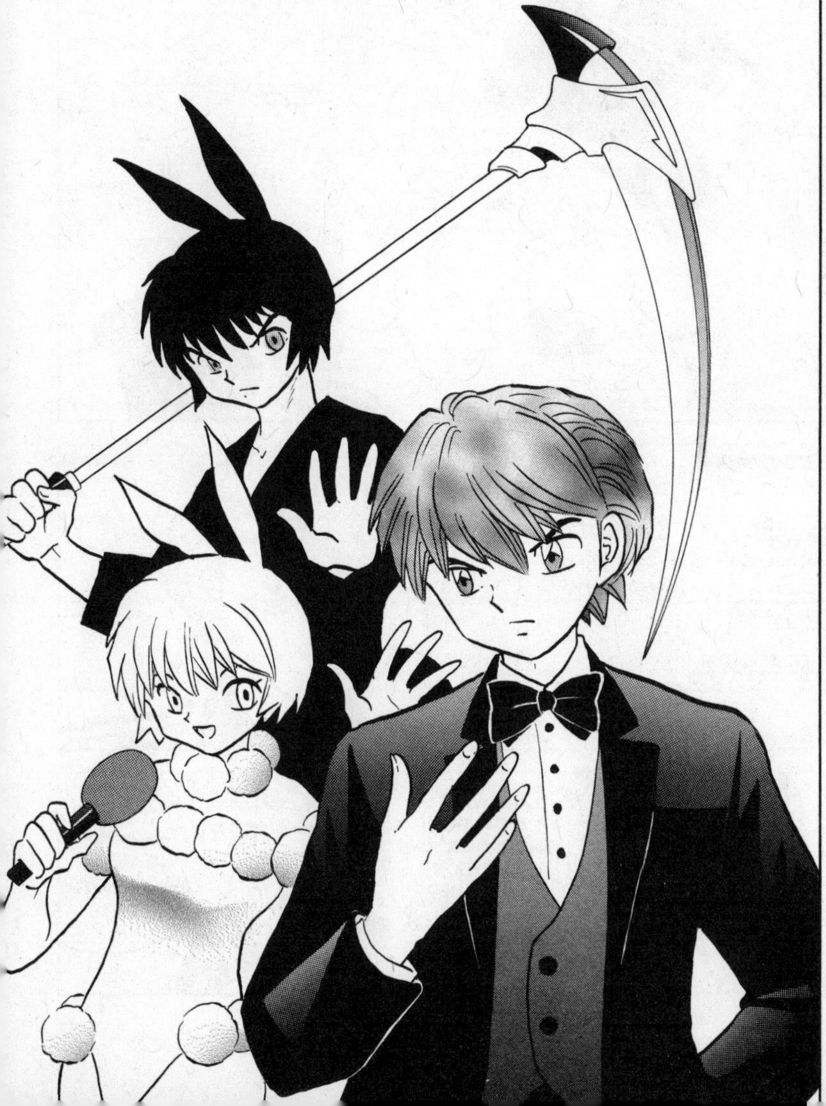

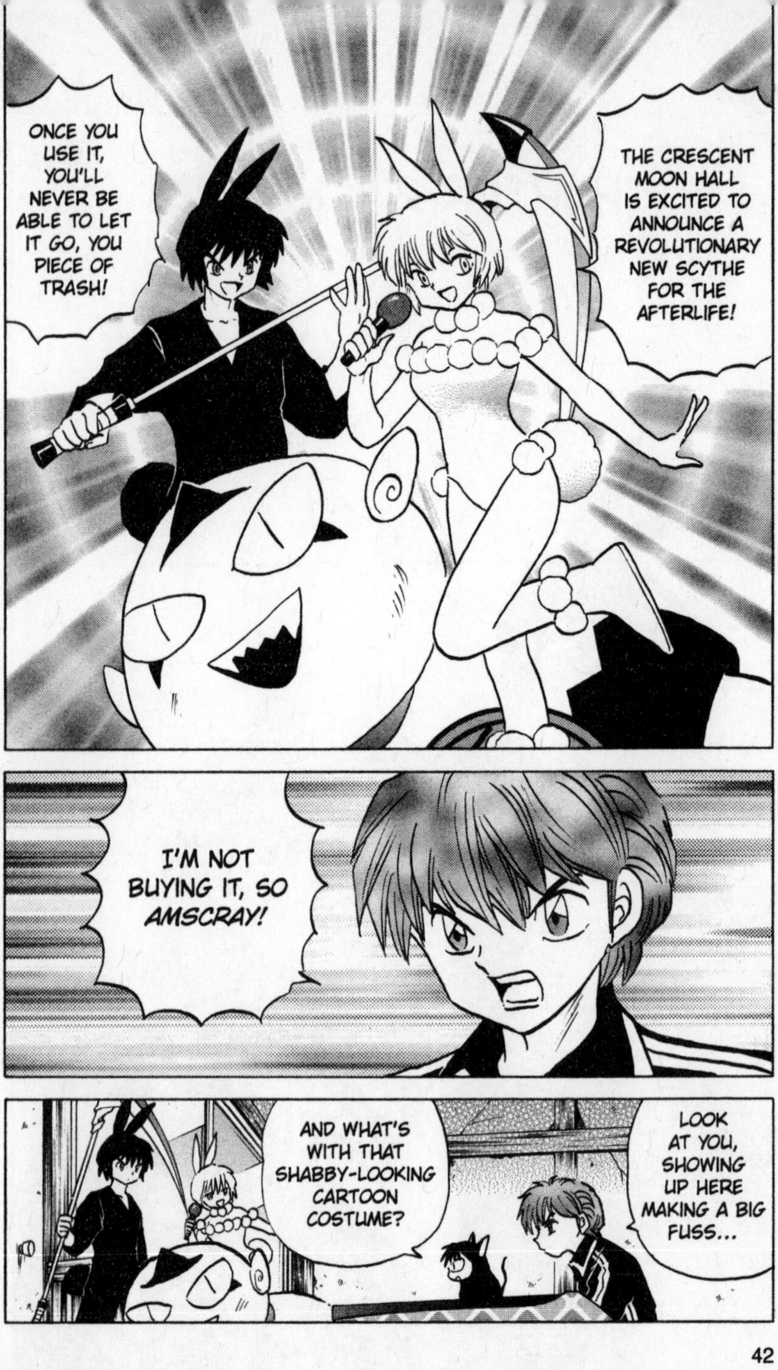
THE CRESCENT MOON HALL IS EXCITED TO ANNOUNCE A REVOLUTIONARY NEW SCYTHE FOR THE AFTERLIFE!
ONCE YOU USE IT, YOU'LL NEVER BE ABLE TO LET IT GO, YOU PIECE OF TRASH!
I'M NOT BUYING IT, SO *AMSCRAY!*
LOOK AT YOU, SHOWING UP HERE MAKING A BIG FUSS...
AND WHAT'S WITH THAT SHABBY-LOOKING CARTOON COSTUME?

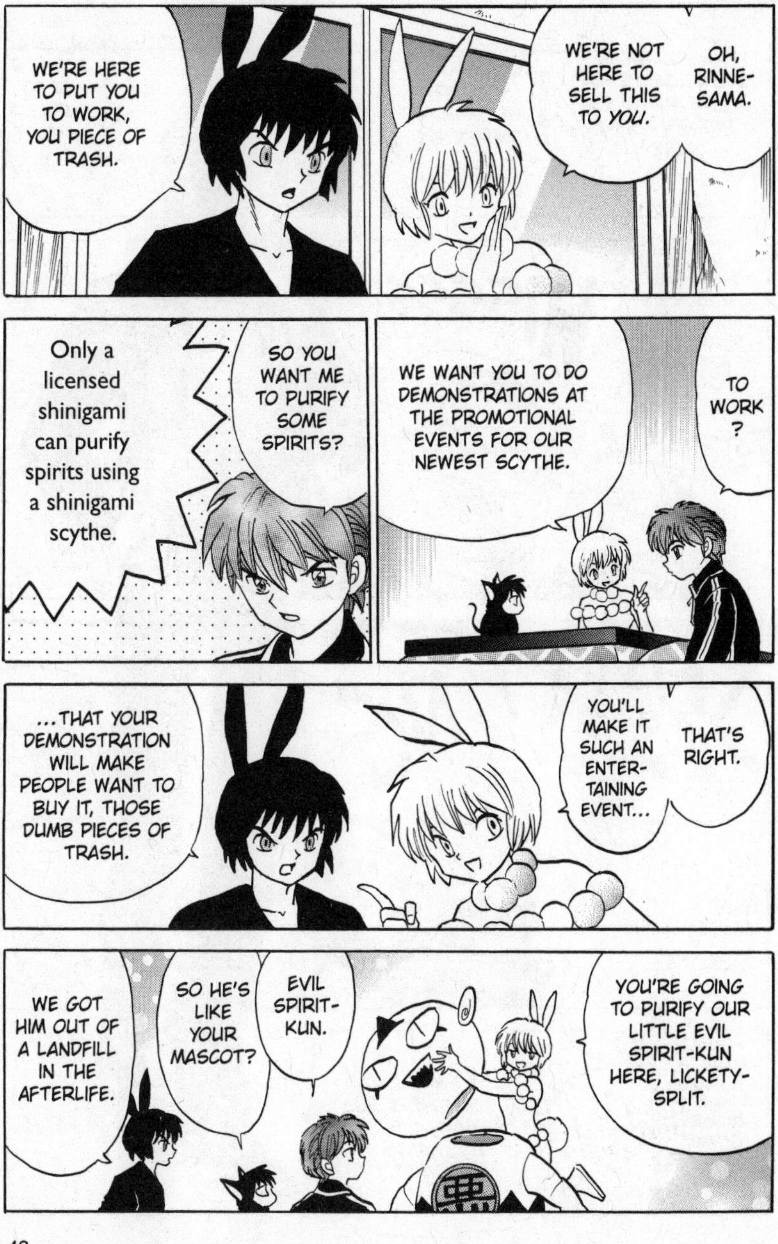
OH, RINNE-SAMA.
WE'RE NOT HERE TO SELL THIS TO *YOU*.
WE'RE HERE TO PUT YOU TO WORK, YOU PIECE OF TRASH.
TO WORK?
WE WANT YOU TO DO DEMONSTRATIONS AT THE PROMOTIONAL EVENTS FOR OUR NEWEST SCYTHE.
SO YOU WANT ME TO PURIFY SOME SPIRITS?
Only a licensed shinigami can purify spirits using a shinigami scythe.
THAT'S RIGHT.
YOU'LL MAKE IT SUCH AN ENTERTAINING EVENT...
...THAT YOUR DEMONSTRATION WILL MAKE PEOPLE WANT TO BUY IT, THOSE DUMB PIECES OF TRASH.
YOU'RE GOING TO PURIFY OUR LITTLE EVIL SPIRIT-KUN HERE, LICKETY-SPLIT.
EVIL SPIRIT-KUN.
SO HE'S LIKE YOUR MASCOT?
WE GOT HIM OUT OF A LANDFILL IN THE AFTERLIFE.

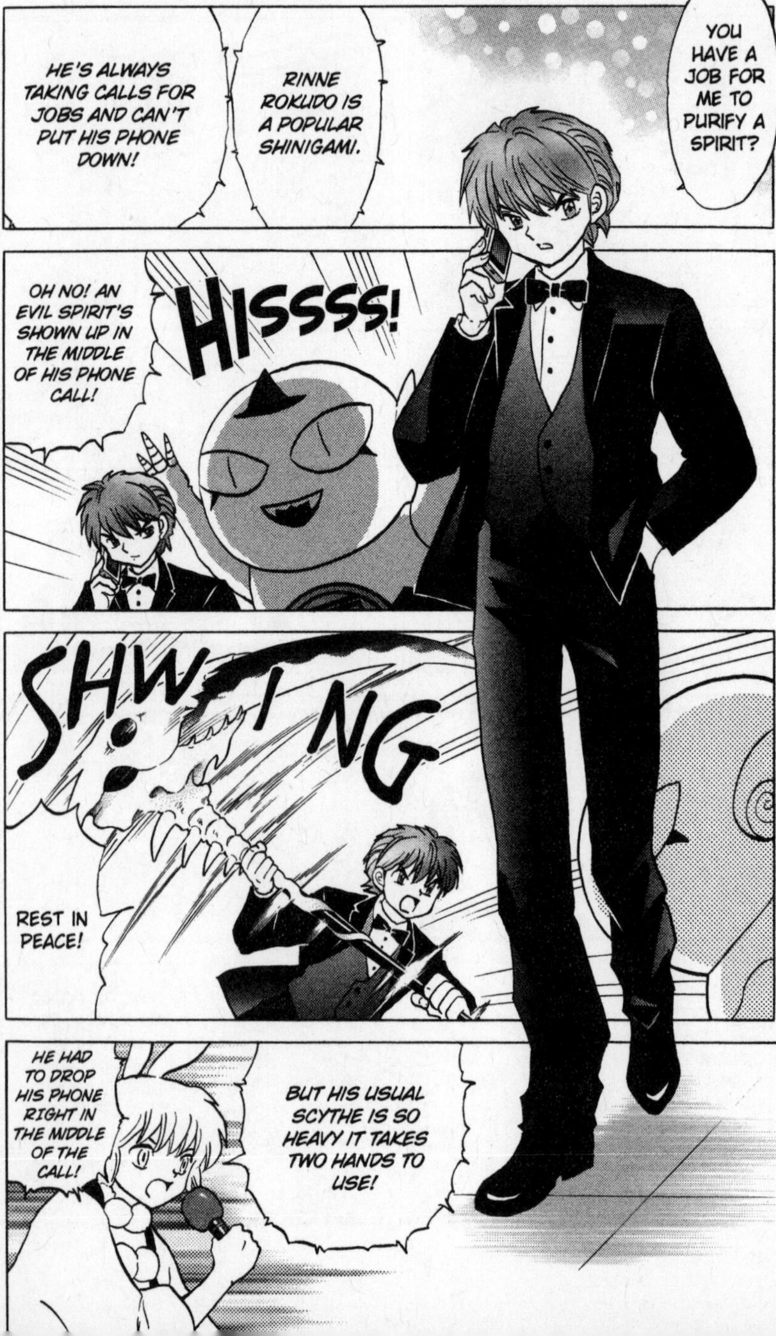
YOU HAVE A JOB FOR ME TO PURIFY A SPIRIT?
RINNE ROKUDO IS A POPULAR SHINIGAMI.
HE'S ALWAYS TAKING CALLS FOR JOBS AND CAN'T PUT HIS PHONE DOWN!
HISSSS!
OH NO! AN EVIL SPIRIT'S SHOWN UP IN THE MIDDLE OF HIS PHONE CALL!
SHWING
REST IN PEACE!
BUT HIS USUAL SCYTHE IS SO HEAVY IT TAKES TWO HANDS TO USE!
HE HAD TO DROP HIS PHONE RIGHT IN THE MIDDLE OF THE CALL!

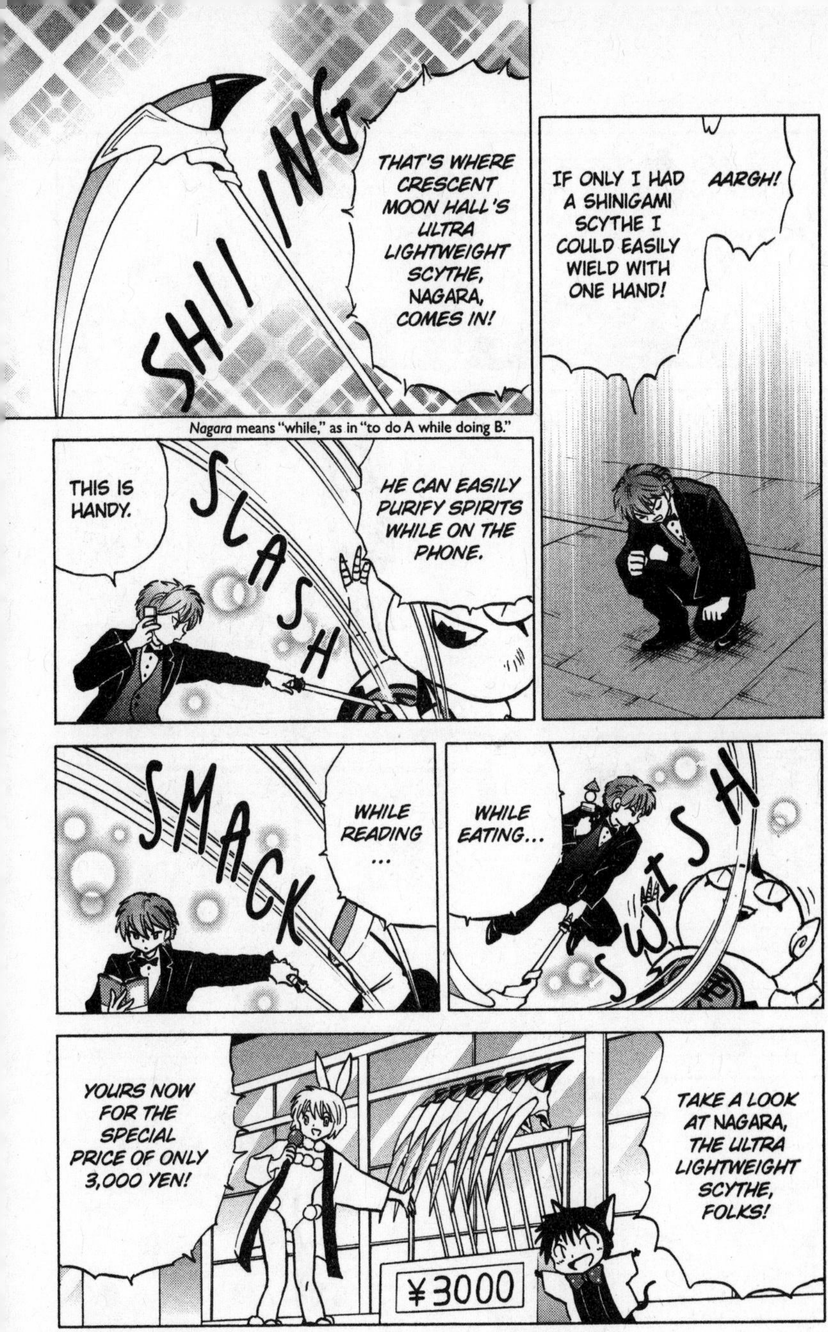
AARGH!
IF ONLY I HAD A SHINIGAMI SCYTHE I COULD EASILY WIELD WITH ONE HAND!
SHIIING
THAT'S WHERE CRESCENT MOON HALL'S ULTRA LIGHTWEIGHT SCYTHE, NAGARA, COMES IN!
HE CAN EASILY PURIFY SPIRITS WHILE ON THE PHONE.
SLASH
THIS IS HANDY.
SWISH
WHILE EATING...
WHILE READING...
SMACK
TAKE A LOOK AT NAGARA, THE ULTRA LIGHTWEIGHT SCYTHE, FOLKS!
¥3000
YOURS NOW FOR THE SPECIAL PRICE OF ONLY 3,000 YEN!

Nagara means "while," as in "to do A while doing B."

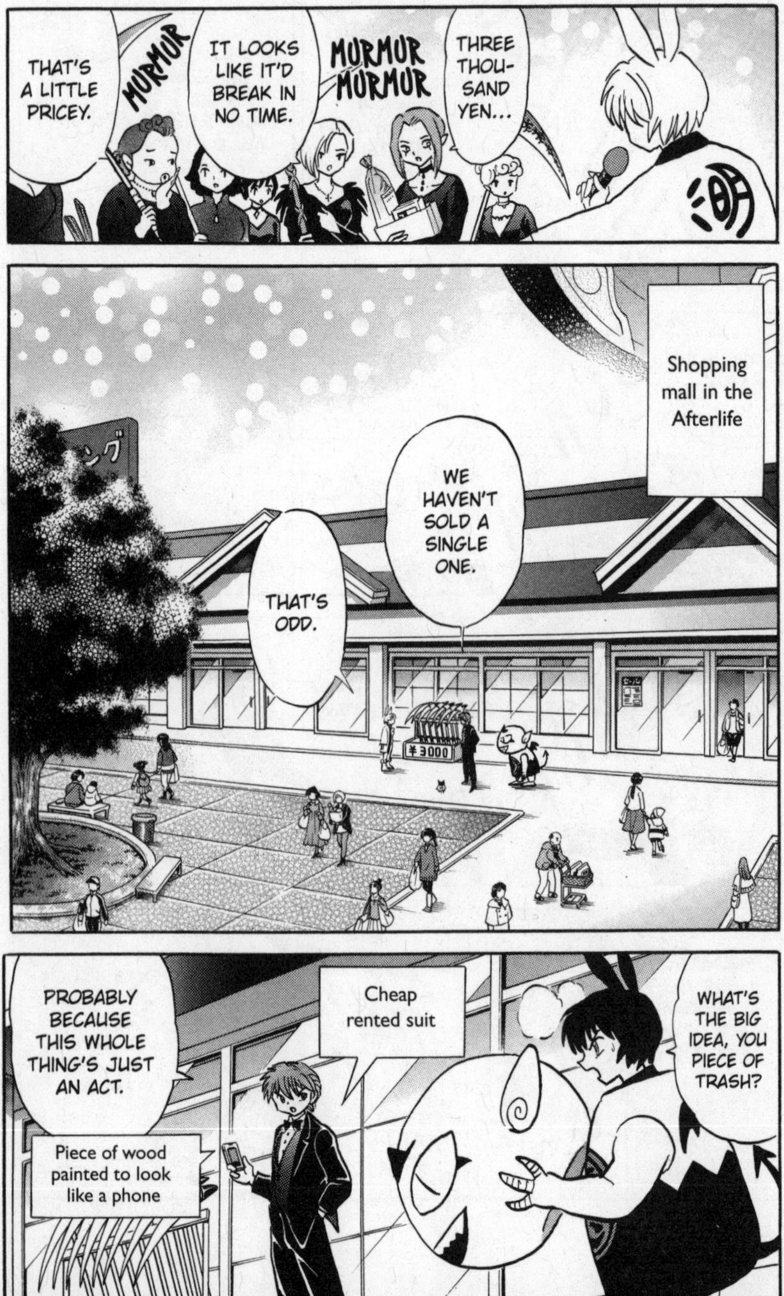
THREE THOU-SAND YEN...
MURMUR MURMUR
IT LOOKS LIKE IT'D BREAK IN NO TIME.
MURMUR
THAT'S A LITTLE PRICEY.
Shopping mall in the Afterlife
WE HAVEN'T SOLD A SINGLE ONE.
THAT'S ODD.
¥3000
WHAT'S THE BIG IDEA, YOU PIECE OF TRASH?
Cheap rented suit
PROBABLY BECAUSE THIS WHOLE THING'S JUST AN ACT.
Piece of wood painted to look like a phone

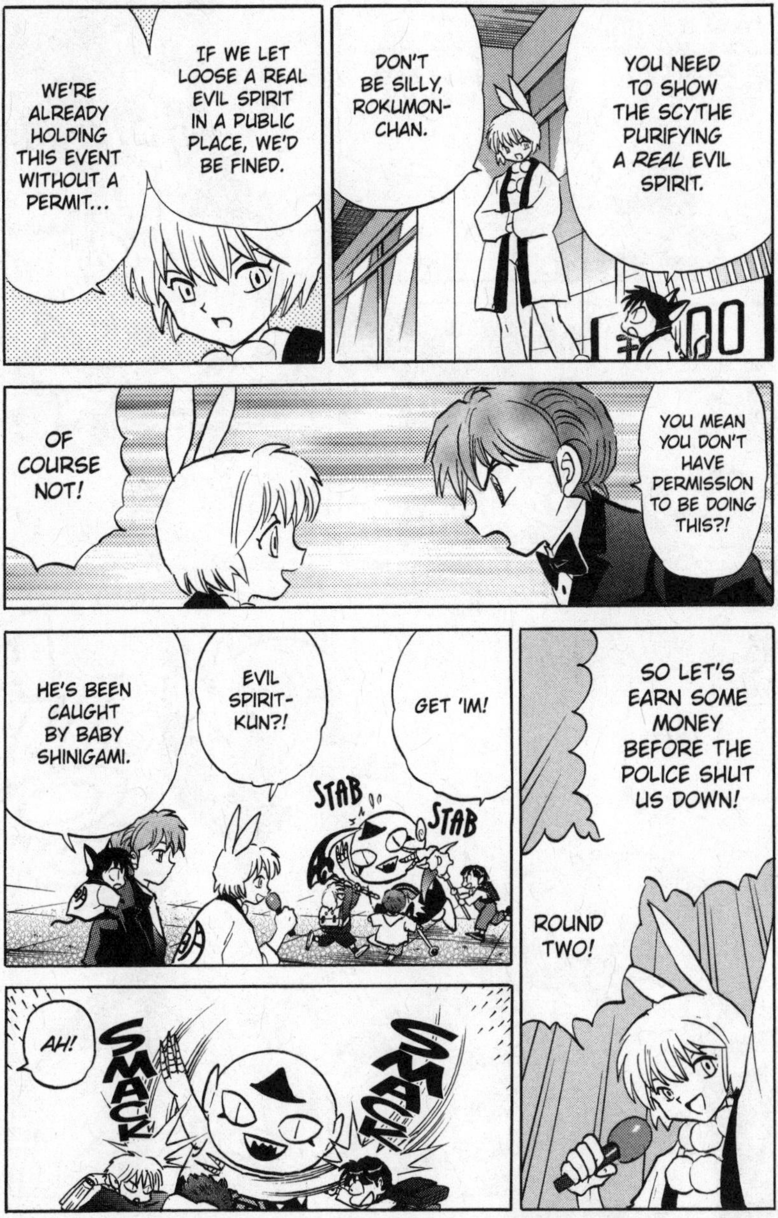
YOU NEED TO SHOW THE SCYTHE PURIFYING A *REAL* EVIL SPIRIT.
DON'T BE SILLY, ROKUMON-CHAN.
IF WE LET LOOSE A REAL EVIL SPIRIT IN A PUBLIC PLACE, WE'D BE FINED.
WE'RE ALREADY HOLDING THIS EVENT WITHOUT A PERMIT...
YOU MEAN YOU DON'T HAVE PERMISSION TO BE DOING THIS?!
OF COURSE NOT!
SO LET'S EARN SOME MONEY BEFORE THE POLICE SHUT US DOWN!
ROUND TWO!
GET 'IM!
STAB
STAB
EVIL SPIRIT-KUN?!
HE'S BEEN CAUGHT BY BABY SHINIGAMI.
SMACK
SMACK
AH!

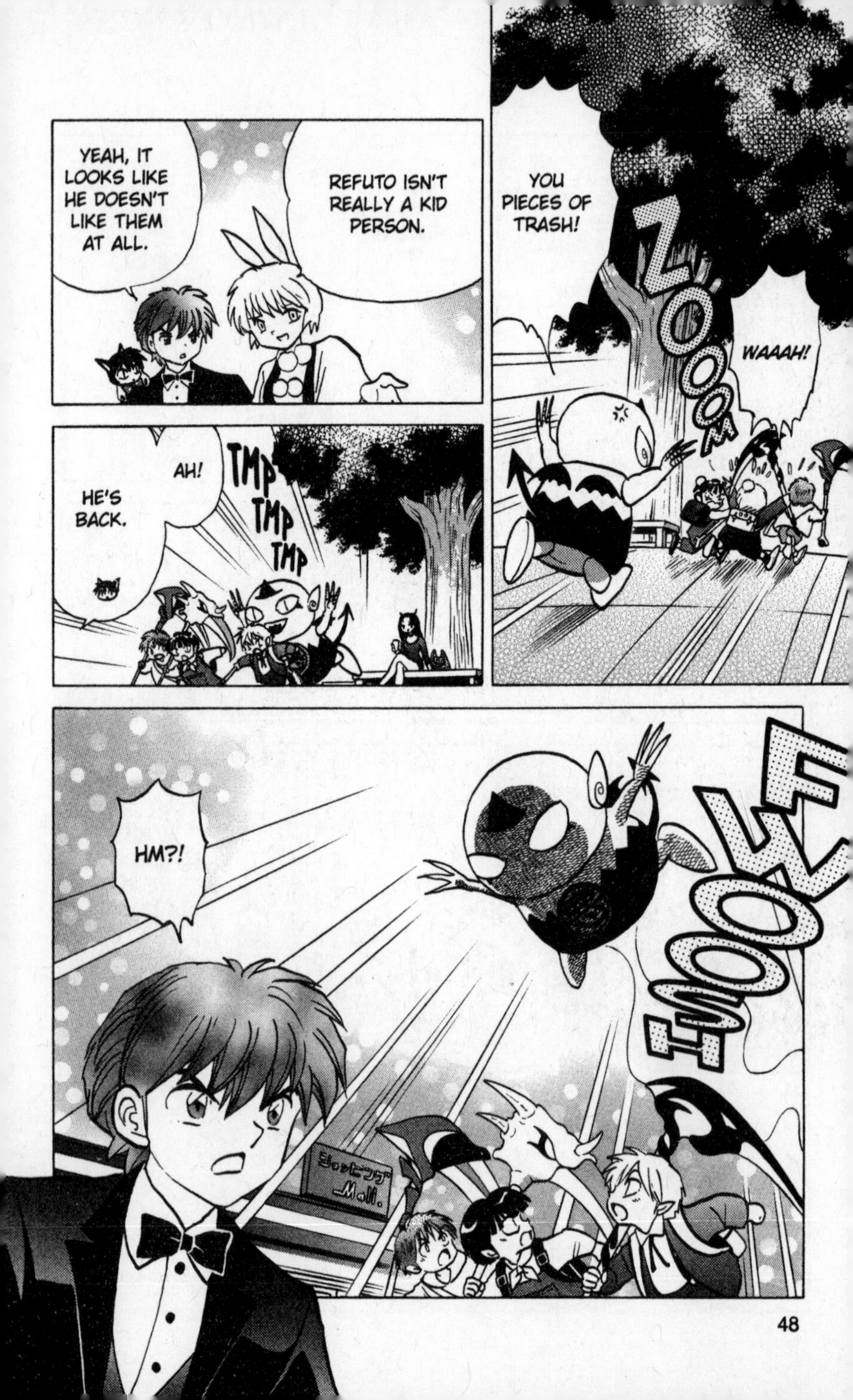
YOU PIECES OF TRASH!
ZOOOOM
WAAAH!
REFUTO ISN'T REALLY A KID PERSON.
YEAH, IT LOOKS LIKE HE DOESN'T LIKE THEM AT ALL.
TMP TMP TMP
AH!
HE'S BACK.
WHOOSH
HM?!
ショッピング Mall.

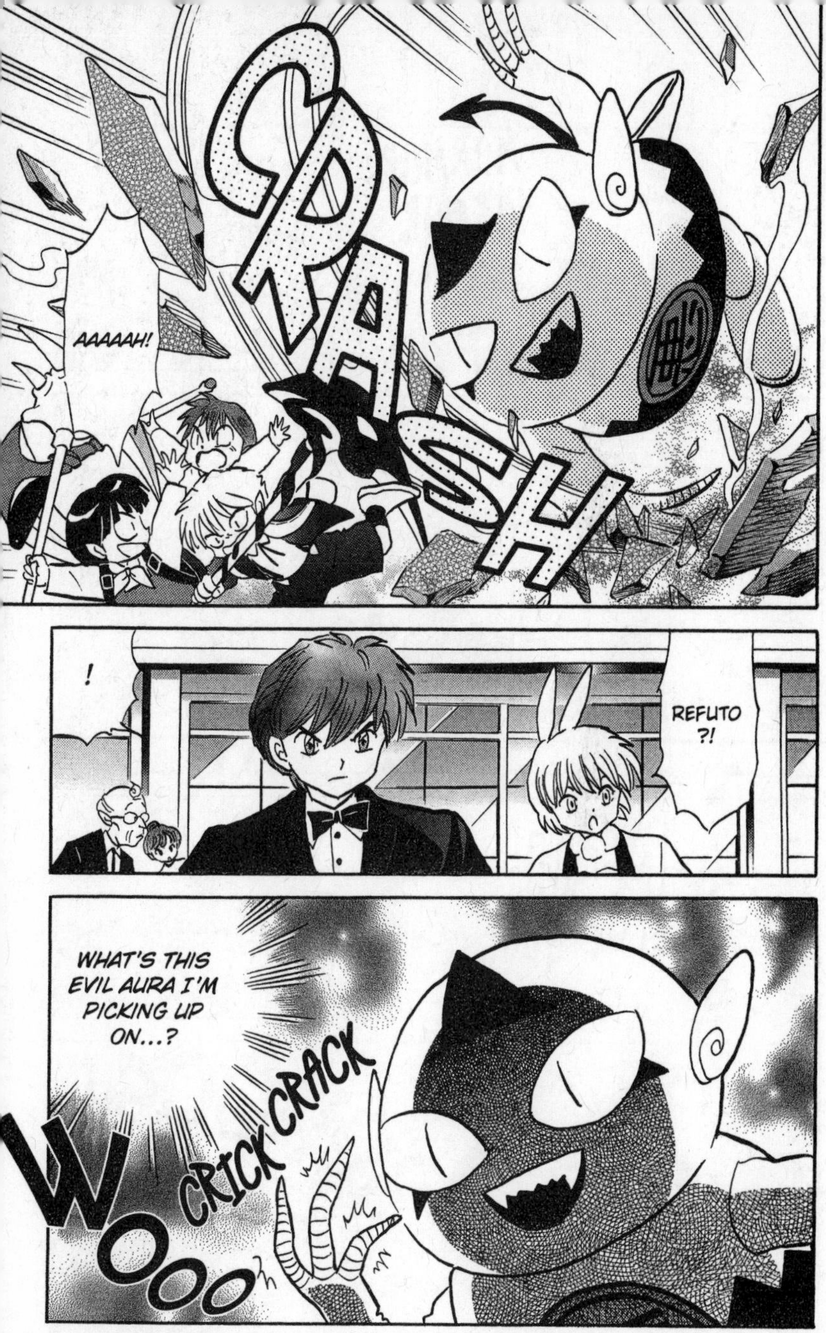
CRASH
AAAAAH!
REFUTO ?!
!
WHAT'S THIS EVIL AURA I'M PICKING UP ON...?
CRICK CRACK
WOOOO

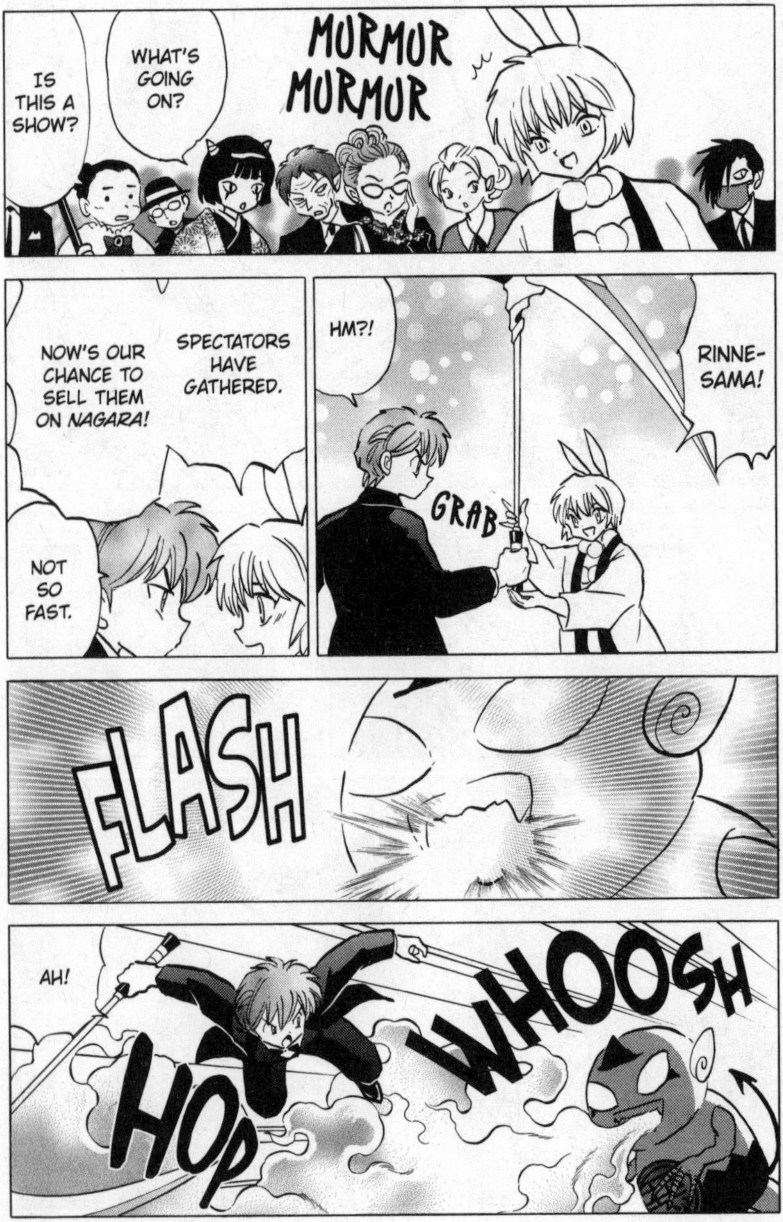
MURMUR MURMUR
WHAT'S GOING ON?
IS THIS A SHOW?
RINNE-SAMA!
HM?!
GRAB
SPECTATORS HAVE GATHERED.
NOW'S OUR CHANCE TO SELL THEM ON *NAGARA*!
NOT SO FAST.
FLASH
WHOOSH
HOP
AH!

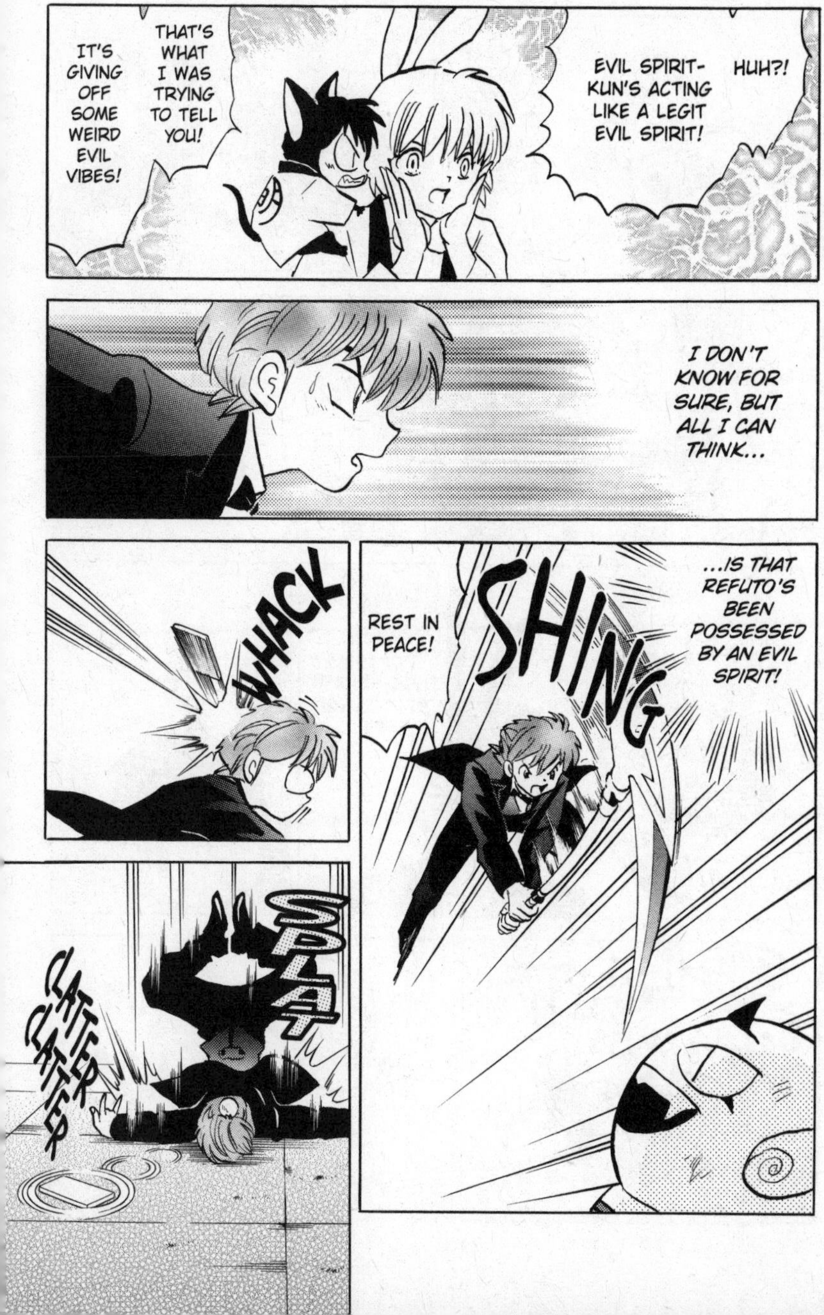
HUH?!
EVIL SPIRIT-KUN'S ACTING LIKE A LEGIT EVIL SPIRIT!
THAT'S WHAT I WAS TRYING TO TELL YOU!
IT'S GIVING OFF SOME WEIRD EVIL VIBES!
I DON'T KNOW FOR SURE, BUT ALL I CAN THINK...
...IS THAT REFUTO'S BEEN POSSESSED BY AN EVIL SPIRIT!
SHING
REST IN PEACE!
WHACK
SPLAT
CLATTER CLATTER

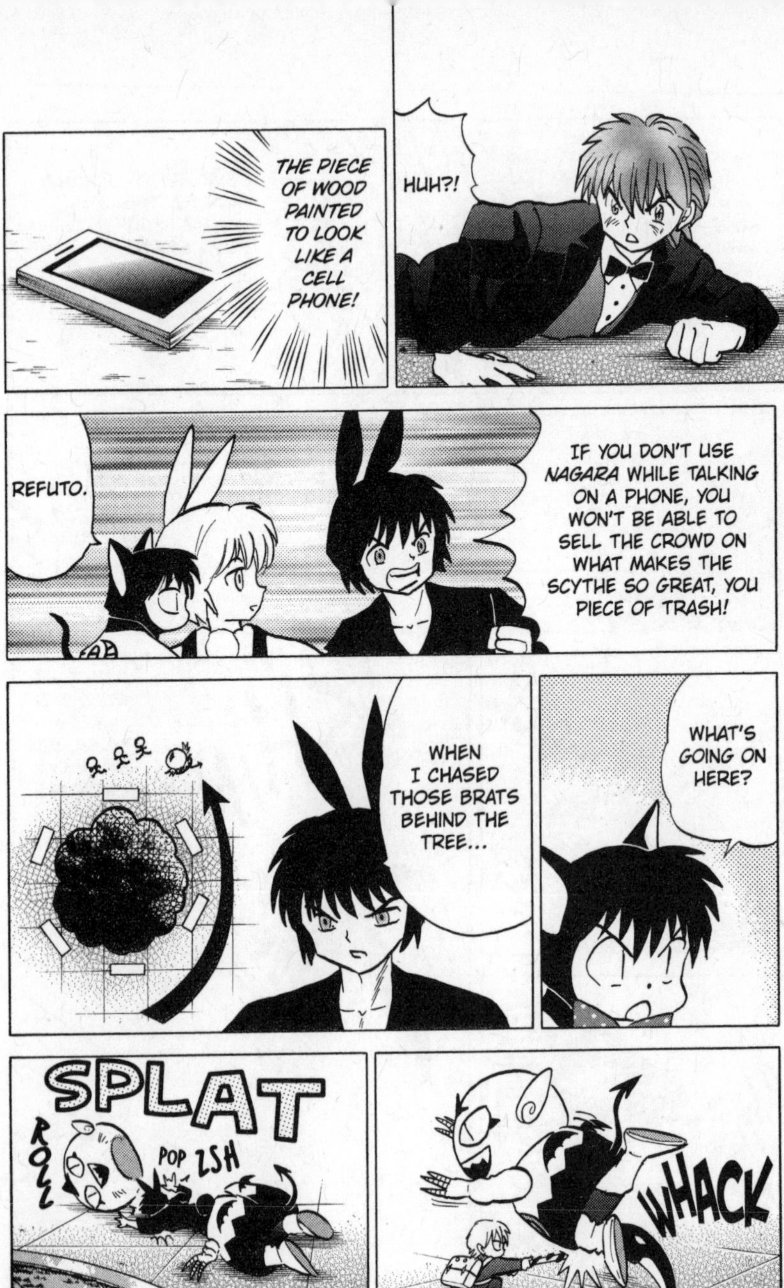
HUH?!
THE PIECE OF WOOD PAINTED TO LOOK LIKE A CELL PHONE!
IF YOU DON'T USE *NAGARA* WHILE TALKING ON A PHONE, YOU WON'T BE ABLE TO SELL THE CROWD ON WHAT MAKES THE SCYTHE SO GREAT, YOU PIECE OF TRASH!
REFUTO.
WHAT'S GOING ON HERE?
WHEN I CHASED THOSE BRATS BEHIND THE TREE...
WHACK
SPLAT
ZSH
POP
ROLL

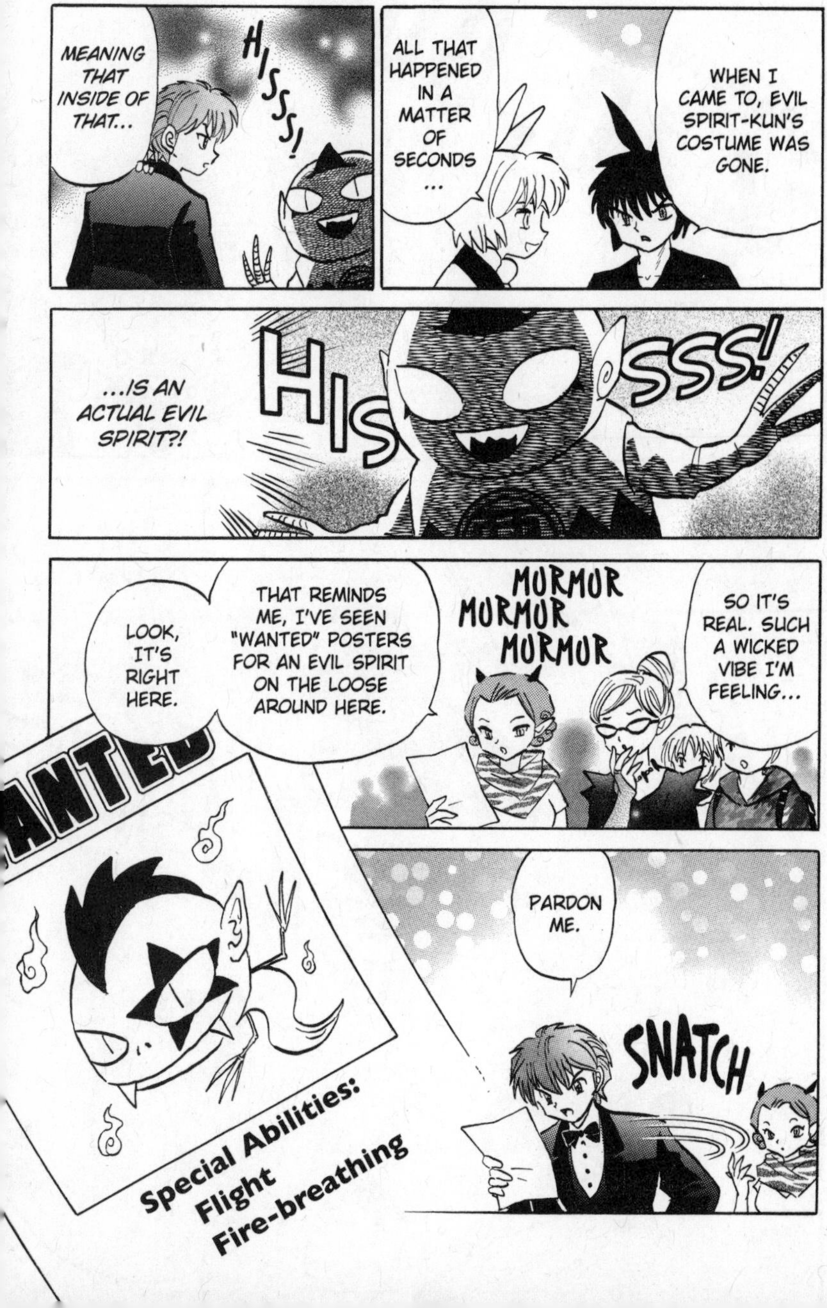
WHEN I CAME TO, EVIL SPIRIT-KUN'S COSTUME WAS GONE.
ALL THAT HAPPENED IN A MATTER OF SECONDS ...
HISSS!
MEANING THAT INSIDE OF THAT...
HISSSSS!
...IS AN ACTUAL EVIL SPIRIT?!
SO IT'S REAL. SUCH A WICKED VIBE I'M FEELING...
MURMUR MURMUR MURMUR
THAT REMINDS ME, I'VE SEEN "WANTED" POSTERS FOR AN EVIL SPIRIT ON THE LOOSE AROUND HERE.
LOOK, IT'S RIGHT HERE.
PARDON ME.
SNATCH
ANTED
Special Abilities:
Flight
Fire-breathing

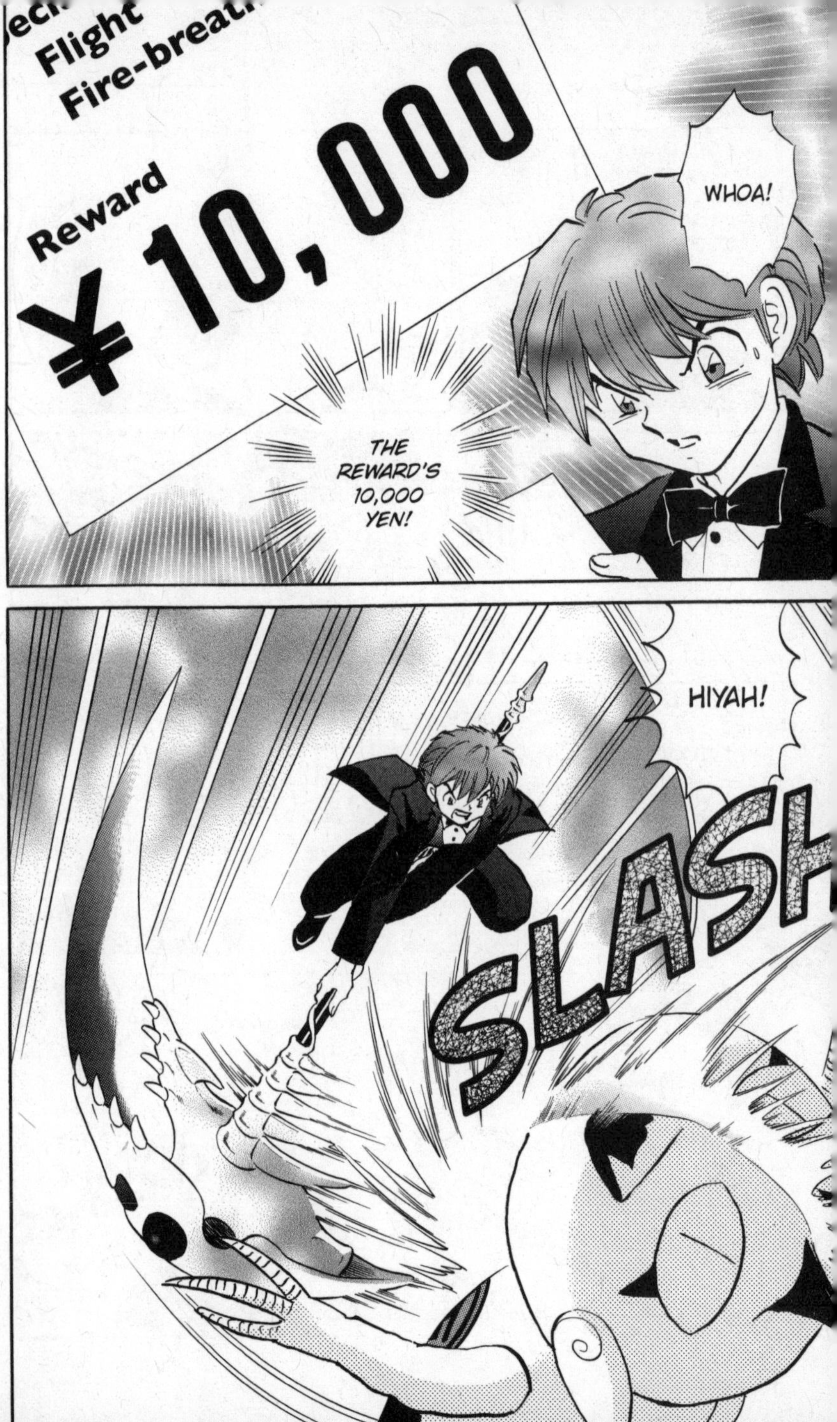
WHOA!
Flight
Fire-breat
Reward
¥10,000
THE REWARD'S 10,000 YEN!
HIYAH!
SLASH

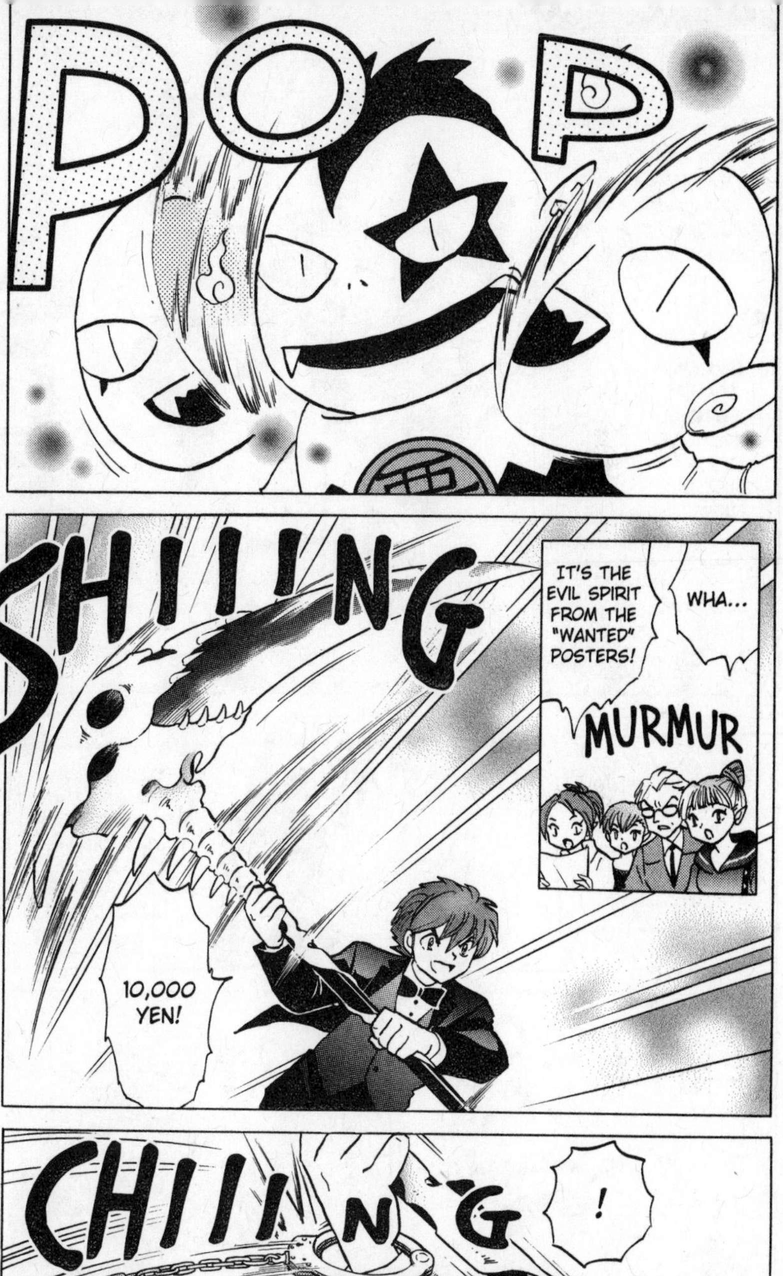
POP
WHA...
IT'S THE EVIL SPIRIT FROM THE "WANTED" POSTERS!
MURMUR
SHIIING
10,000 YEN!
!
CHIIING

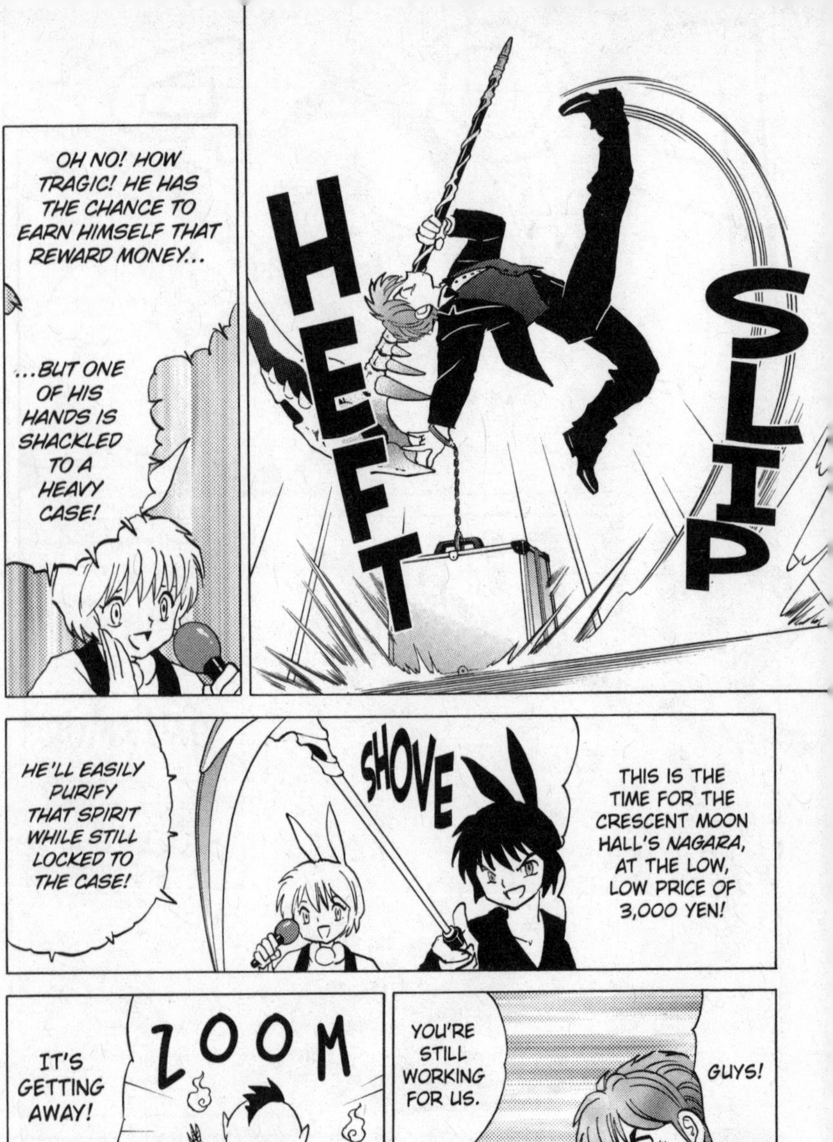
SLIP
HEFT
OH NO! HOW TRAGIC! HE HAS THE CHANCE TO EARN HIMSELF THAT REWARD MONEY...
...BUT ONE OF HIS HANDS IS SHACKLED TO A HEAVY CASE!
THIS IS THE TIME FOR THE CRESCENT MOON HALL'S NAGARA, AT THE LOW, LOW PRICE OF 3,000 YEN!
SHOVE
HE'LL EASILY PURIFY THAT SPIRIT WHILE STILL LOCKED TO THE CASE!
GUYS!
YOU'RE STILL WORKING FOR US.
JANGLE
ZOOM
IT'S GETTING AWAY!

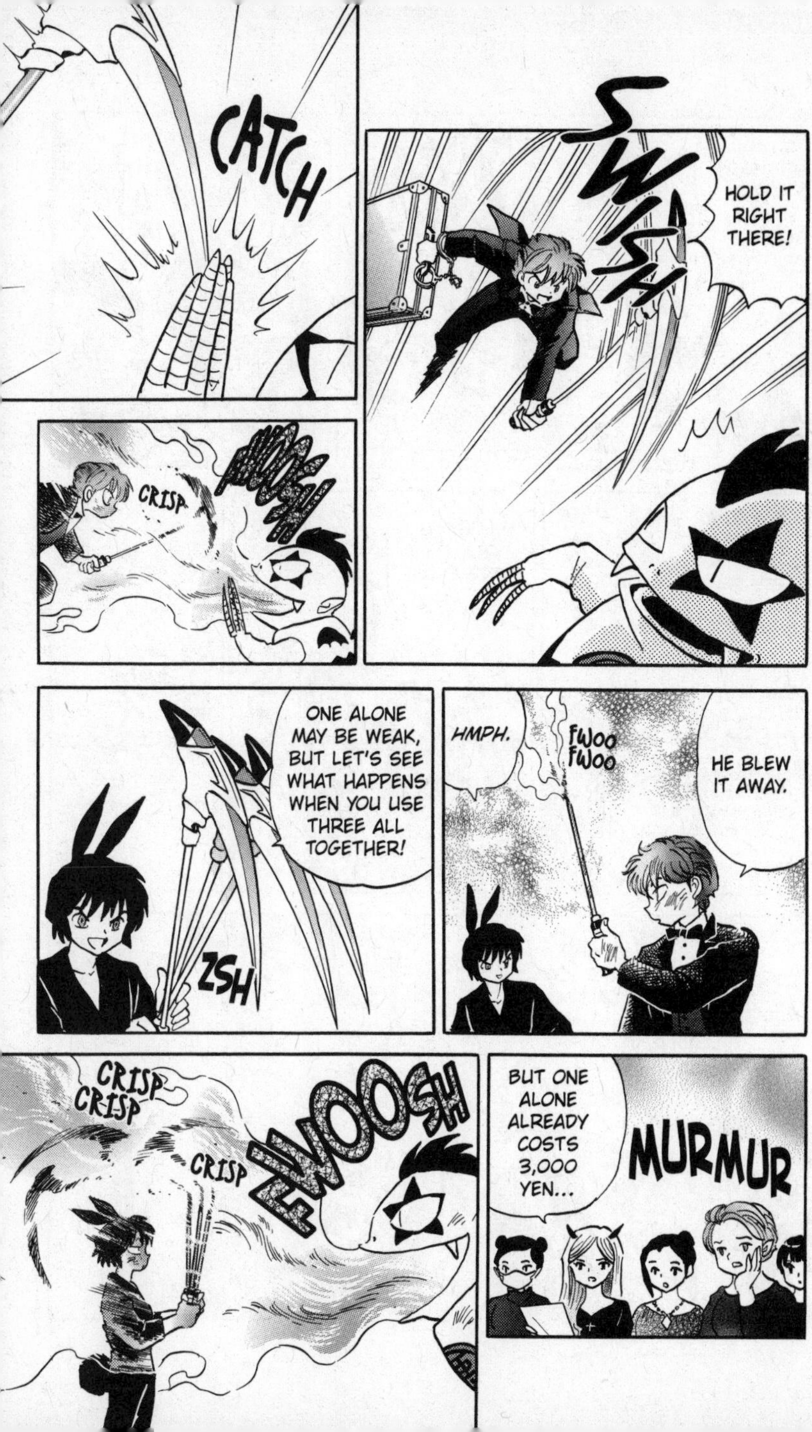
SWISH
HOLD IT RIGHT THERE!
CATCH
CRISP
PWOOSH
HE BLEW IT AWAY.
FWOO FWOO
HMPH.
ONE ALONE MAY BE WEAK, BUT LET'S SEE WHAT HAPPENS WHEN YOU USE THREE ALL TOGETHER!
ZSH
BUT ONE ALONE ALREADY COSTS 3,000 YEN...
MURMUR
CRISP CRISP
ZWOOSH
CRISP

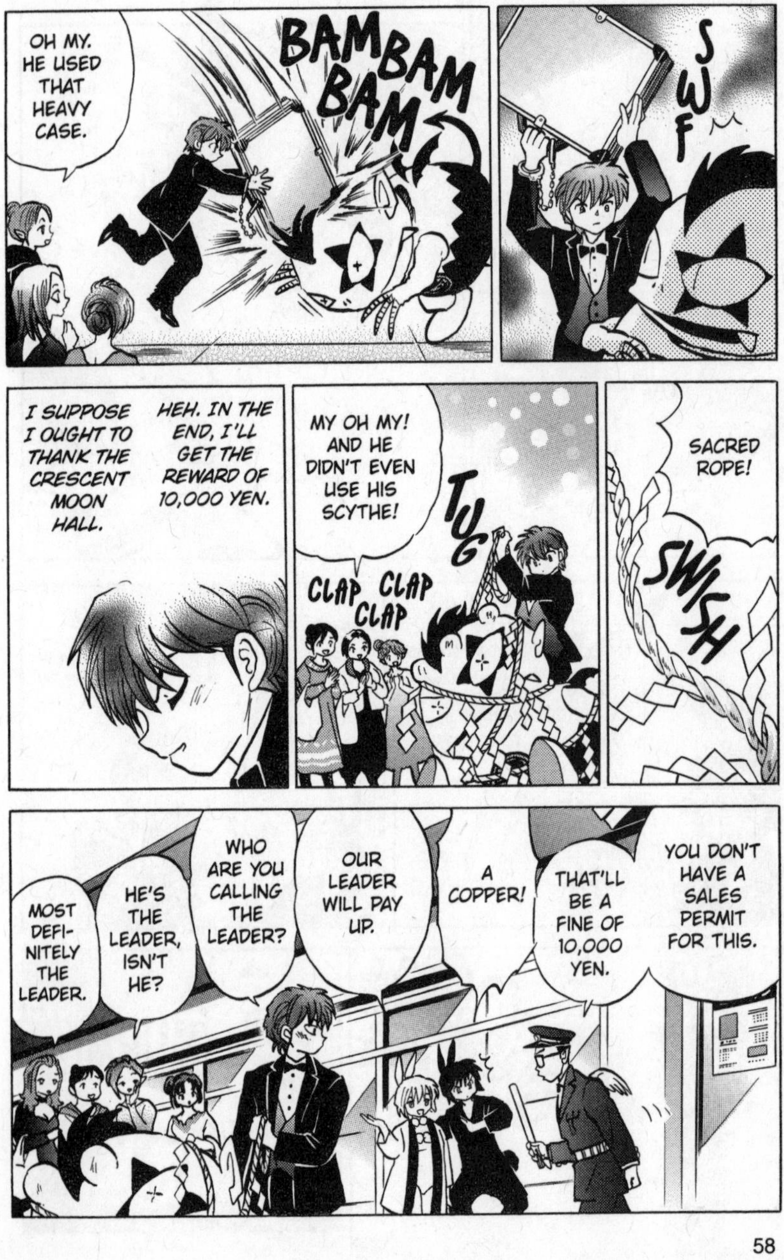
SWF
BAM BAM BAM
OH MY. HE USED THAT HEAVY CASE.
SACRED ROPE!
SWISH
MY OH MY! AND HE DIDN'T EVEN USE HIS SCYTHE!
TUG
CLAP CLAP CLAP
HEH. IN THE END, I'LL GET THE REWARD OF 10,000 YEN.
I SUPPOSE I OUGHT TO THANK THE CRESCENT MOON HALL.
YOU DON'T HAVE A SALES PERMIT FOR THIS.
THAT'LL BE A FINE OF 10,000 YEN.
A COPPER!
OUR LEADER WILL PAY UP.
WHO ARE YOU CALLING THE LEADER?
HE'S THE LEADER, ISN'T HE?
MOST DEFI-NITELY THE LEADER.

CHAPTER 272: APOLOGIZE AT THE FAMILY ALTAR

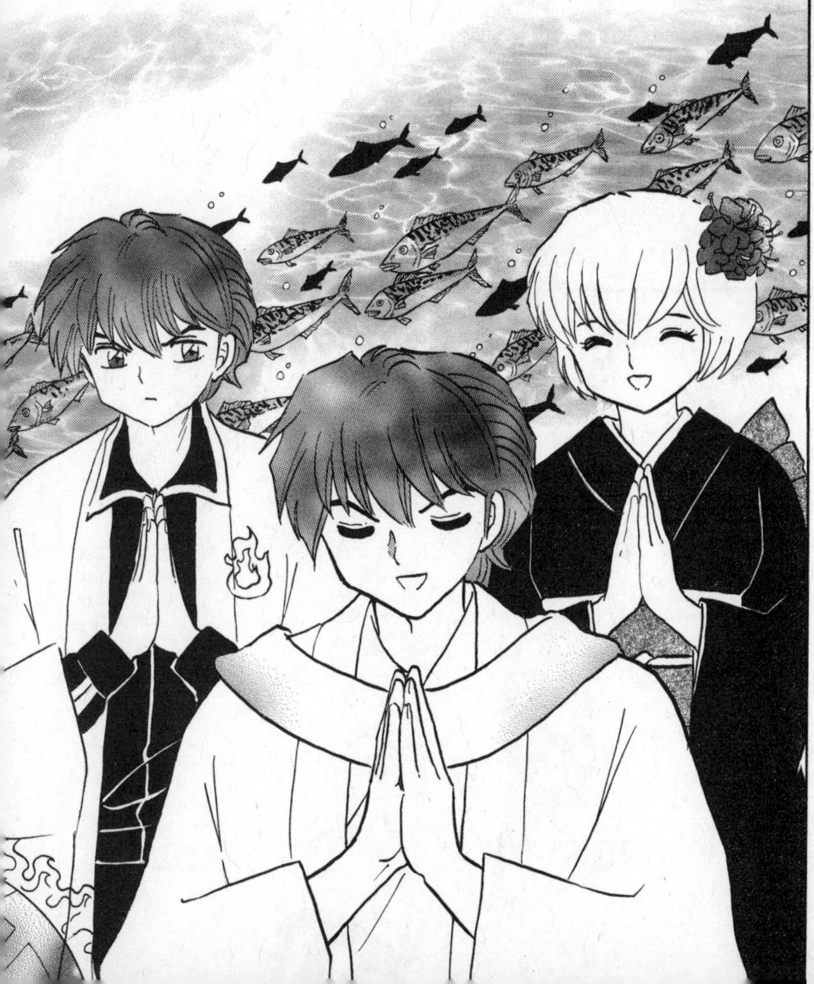

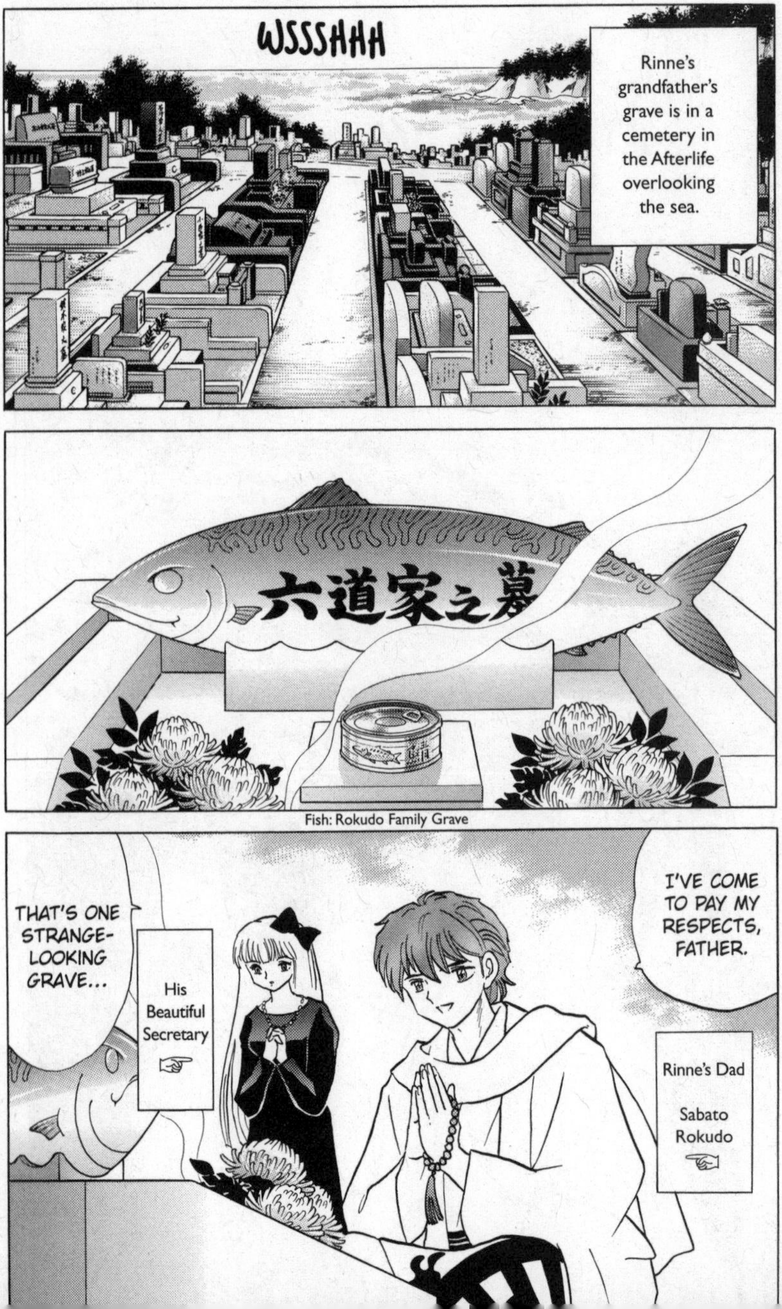
WSSSHHH
Rinne's grandfather's grave is in a cemetery in the Afterlife overlooking the sea.
六道家之墓
Fish: Rokudo Family Grave
I'VE COME TO PAY MY RESPECTS, FATHER.
Rinne's Dad Sabato Rokudo
His Beautiful Secretary
THAT'S ONE STRANGE-LOOKING GRAVE...

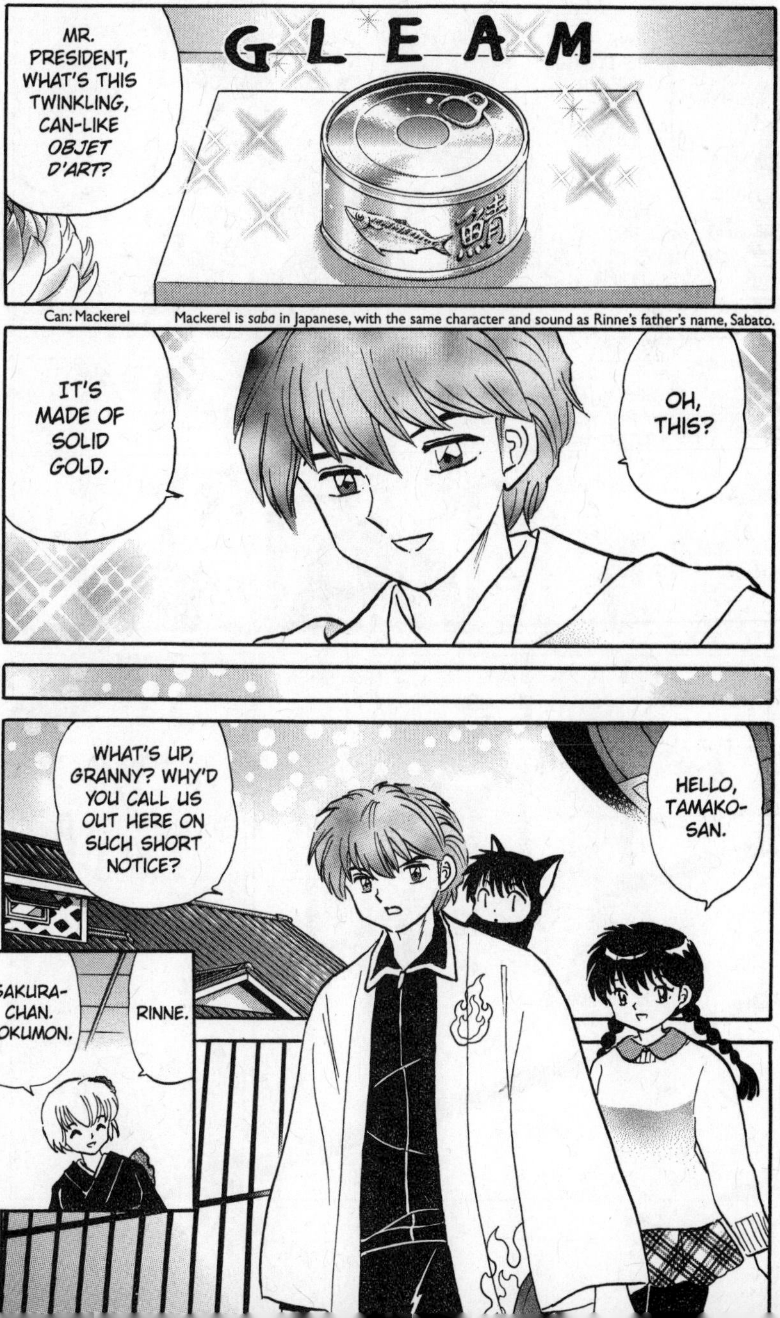
GLEAM
MR. PRESIDENT, WHAT'S THIS TWINKLING, CAN-LIKE OBJET D'ART?
OH, THIS?
IT'S MADE OF SOLID GOLD.
HELLO, TAMAKO-SAN.
WHAT'S UP, GRANNY? WHY'D YOU CALL US OUT HERE ON SUCH SHORT NOTICE?
RINNE.
SAKURA-CHAN. ROKUMON.
Can: Mackerel

Mackerel is *saba* in Japanese, with the same character and sound as Rinne's father's name, Sabato.

DON'T CALL ME G-R-A-N-N-Y!
NOOGIE NOOGIE NOOGIE
OW OW OW OW OW OW.
WE HAVE TO DO THIS EVERY SINGLE TIME.
SHE WOULDN'T HAVE IT ANY OTHER WAY.
A THIEF?
IT SEEMS HE'S BEEN PROWLING AROUND MY HOME SINCE YESTERDAY.
I'M AT MY WIT'S END.
BA BA
I SEE.
PLEASE CATCH HIM FOR ME, RINNE.

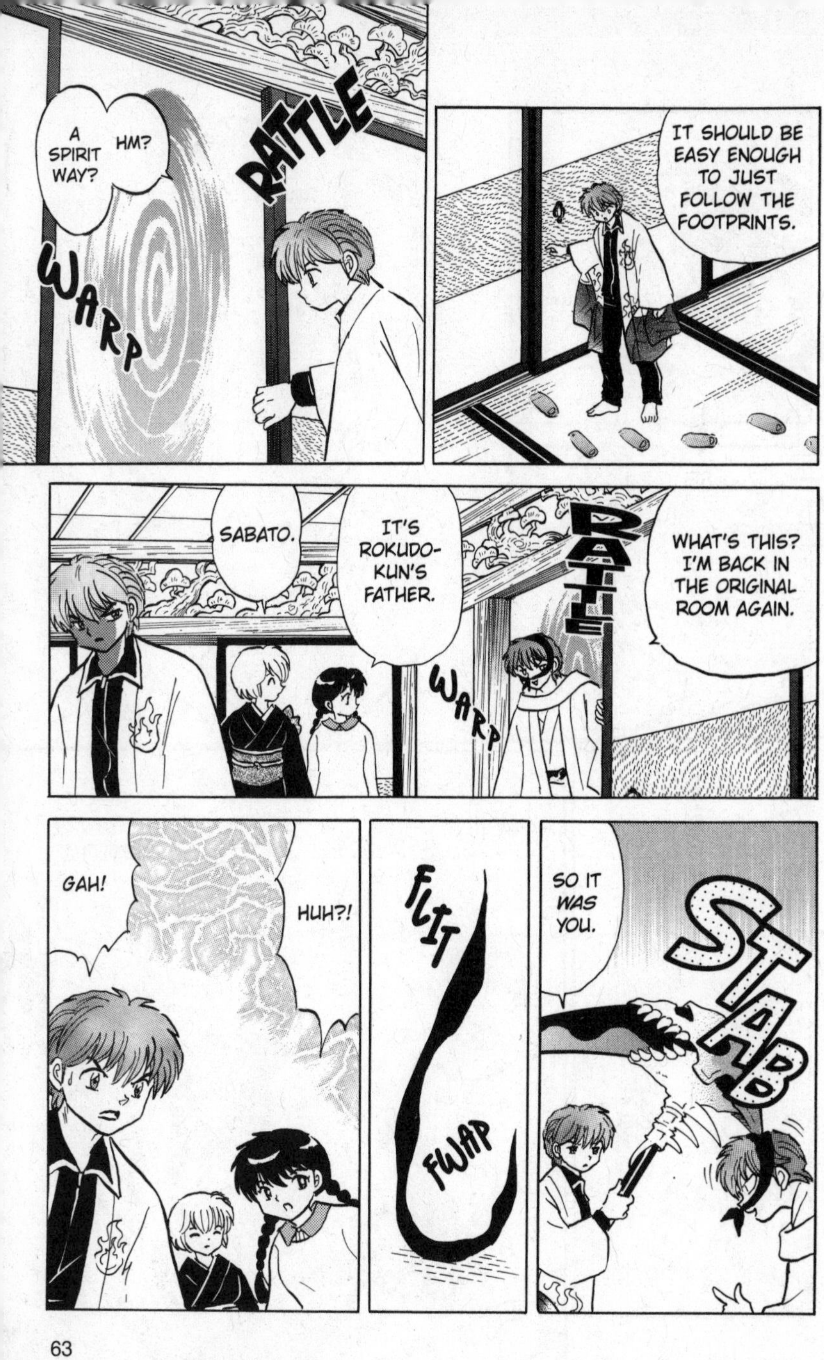
IT SHOULD BE EASY ENOUGH TO JUST FOLLOW THE FOOTPRINTS.
RATTLE
HM?
A SPIRIT WAY?
WARP
WHAT'S THIS? I'M BACK IN THE ORIGINAL ROOM AGAIN.
RATTLE
WARP
IT'S ROKUDO-KUN'S FATHER.
SABATO.
SO IT WAS YOU.
STAB
FLIT
FWAP
HUH?!
GAH!

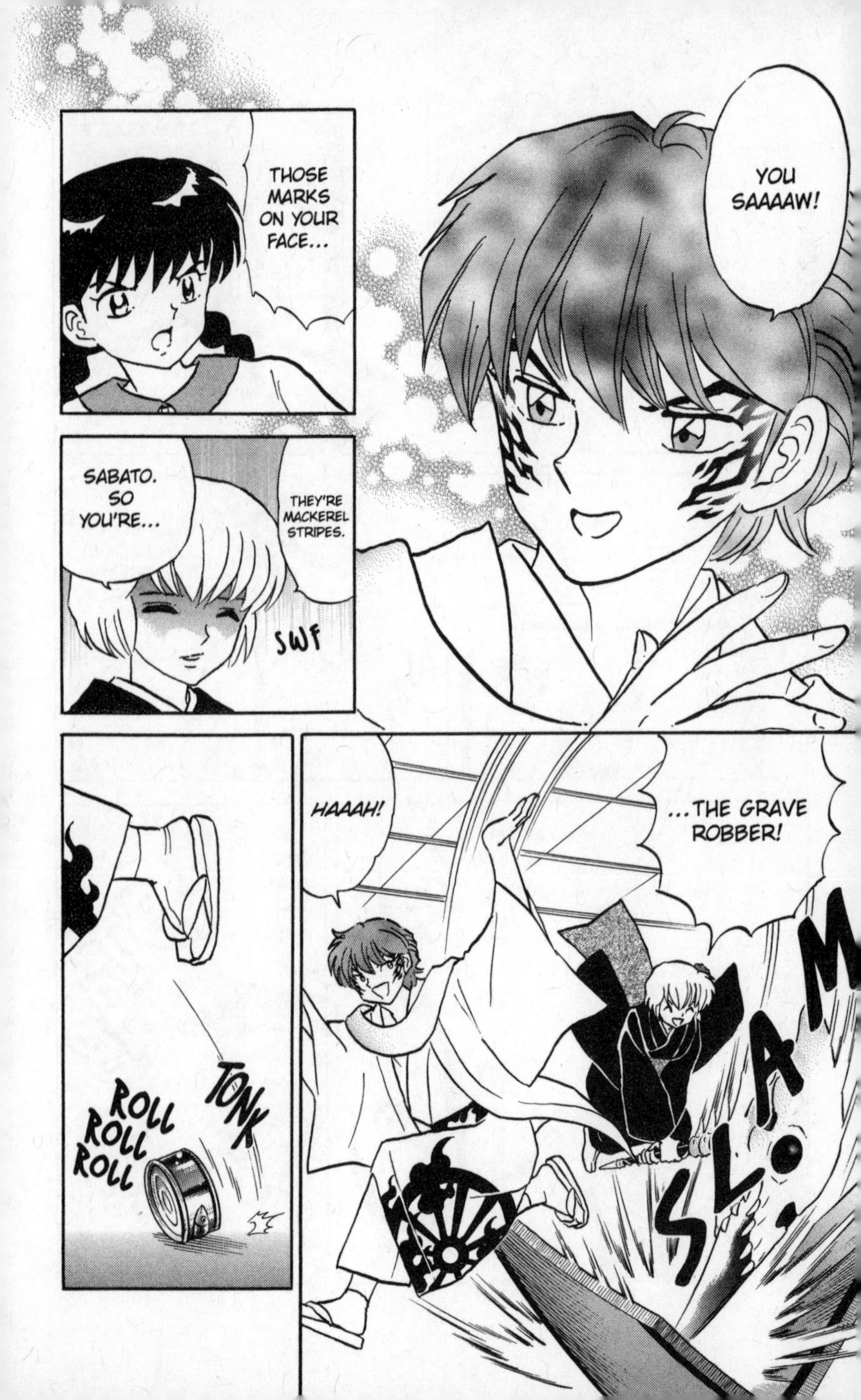
YOU SAAAAW!
THOSE MARKS ON YOUR FACE...
THEY'RE MACKEREL STRIPES.
SABATO. SO YOU'RE...
SWF
...THE GRAVE ROBBER!
HAAAH!
SLAM
TONK
ROLL ROLL ROLL

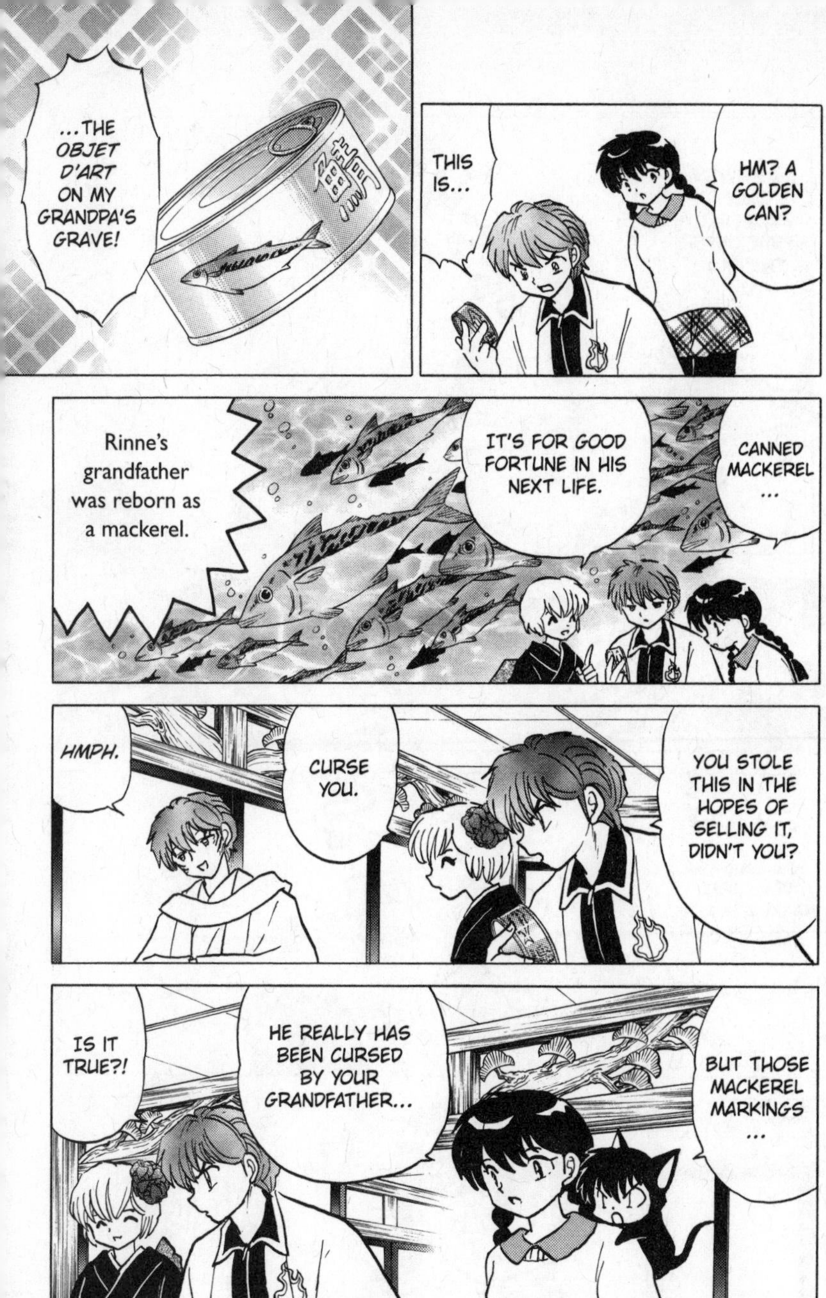
HM? A GOLDEN CAN?
THIS IS...
...THE OBJET D'ART ON MY GRANDPA'S GRAVE!
CANNED MACKEREL ...
IT'S FOR GOOD FORTUNE IN HIS NEXT LIFE.
Rinne's grandfather was reborn as a mackerel.
YOU STOLE THIS IN THE HOPES OF SELLING IT, DIDN'T YOU?
CURSE YOU.
HMPH.
BUT THOSE MACKEREL MARKINGS ...
HE REALLY HAS BEEN CURSED BY YOUR GRANDFATHER...
IS IT TRUE?!

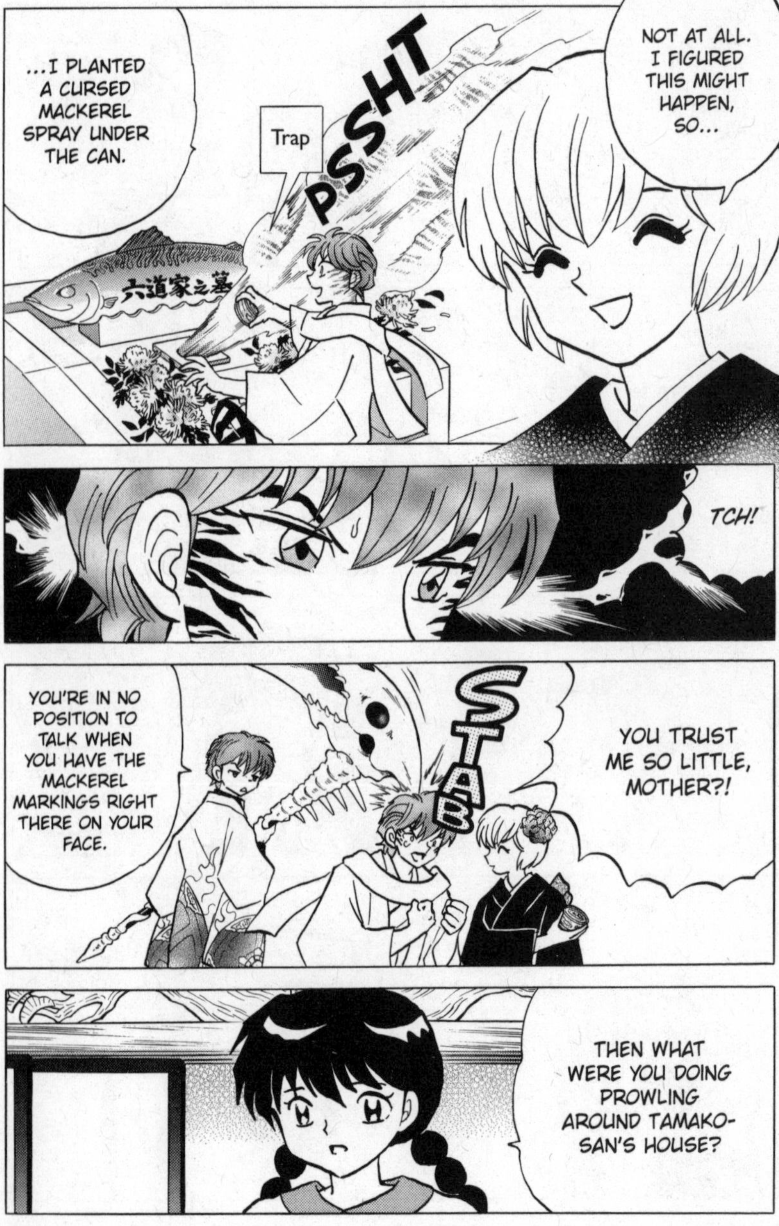
NOT AT ALL. I FIGURED THIS MIGHT HAPPEN, SO...
PSSHT
Trap
...I PLANTED A CURSED MACKEREL SPRAY UNDER THE CAN.
六道家之墓
TCH!
YOU TRUST ME SO LITTLE, MOTHER?!
STAB
YOU'RE IN NO POSITION TO TALK WHEN YOU HAVE THE MACKEREL MARKINGS RIGHT THERE ON YOUR FACE.
THEN WHAT WERE YOU DOING PROWLING AROUND TAMAKO-SAN'S HOUSE?

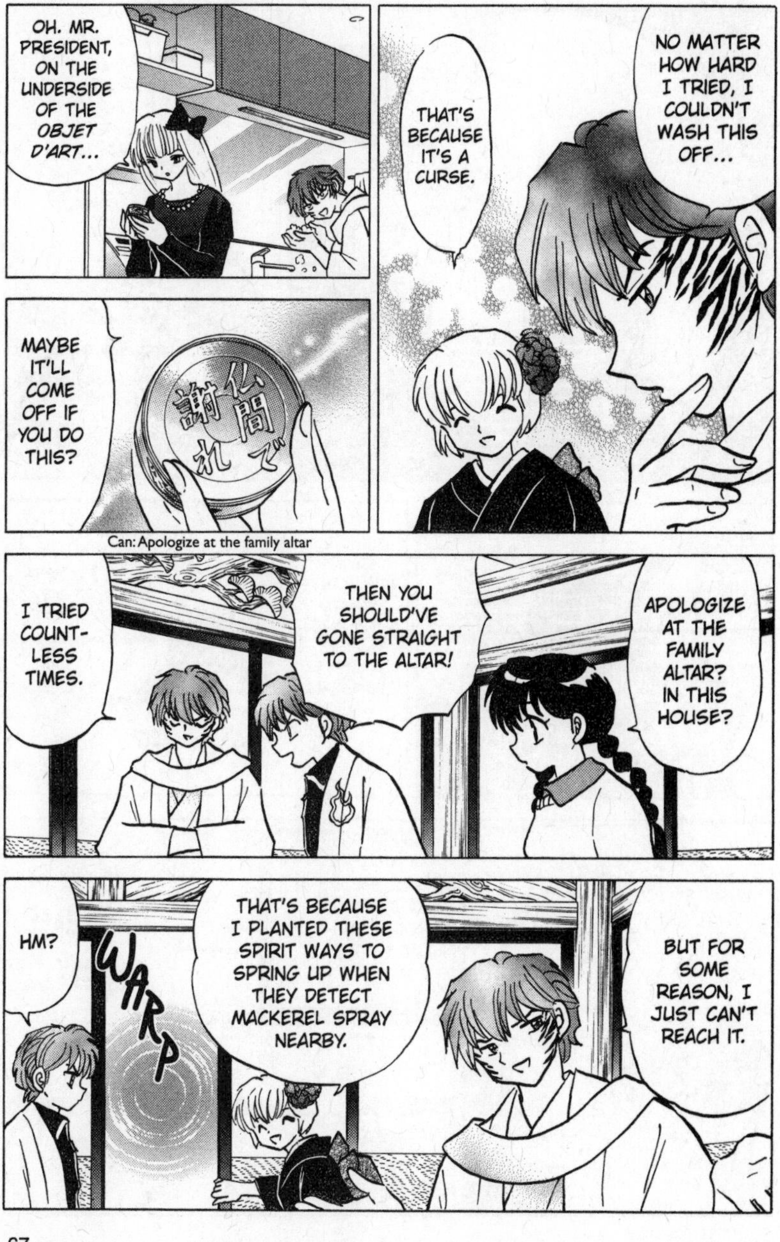
NO MATTER HOW HARD I TRIED, I COULDN'T WASH THIS OFF...
THAT'S BECAUSE IT'S A CURSE.
OH. MR. PRESIDENT, ON THE UNDERSIDE OF THE *OBJET D'ART*...
MAYBE IT'LL COME OFF IF YOU DO THIS?
仏間で謝れ
Can: Apologize at the family altar
APOLOGIZE AT THE FAMILY ALTAR? IN THIS HOUSE?
THEN YOU SHOULD'VE GONE STRAIGHT TO THE ALTAR!
I TRIED COUNTLESS TIMES.
BUT FOR SOME REASON, I JUST CAN'T REACH IT.
THAT'S BECAUSE I PLANTED THESE SPIRIT WAYS TO SPRING UP WHEN THEY DETECT MACKEREL SPRAY NEARBY.
WARP
HM?

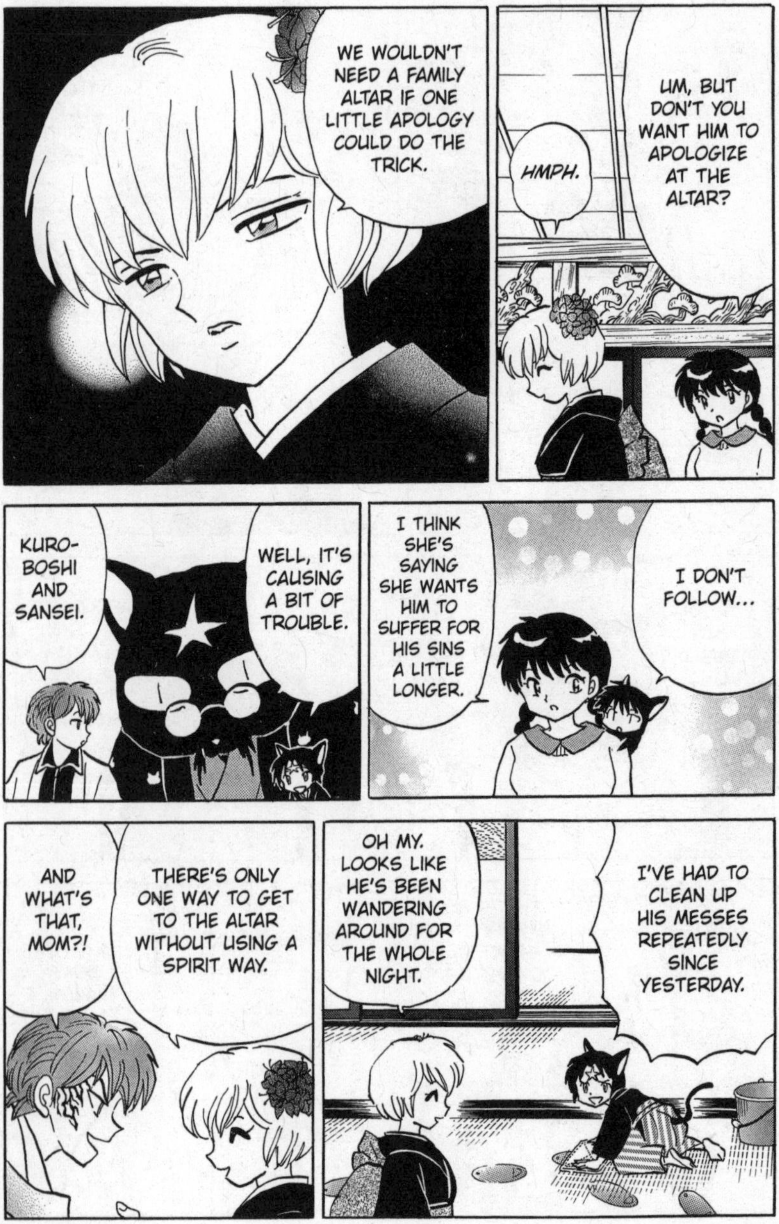
UM, BUT DON'T YOU WANT HIM TO APOLOGIZE AT THE ALTAR?
HMPH.
WE WOULDN'T NEED A FAMILY ALTAR IF ONE LITTLE APOLOGY COULD DO THE TRICK.
I DON'T FOLLOW...
I THINK SHE'S SAYING SHE WANTS HIM TO SUFFER FOR HIS SINS A LITTLE LONGER.
WELL, IT'S CAUSING A BIT OF TROUBLE.
KURO-BOSHI AND SANSEI.
I'VE HAD TO CLEAN UP HIS MESSES REPEATEDLY SINCE YESTERDAY.
OH MY. LOOKS LIKE HE'S BEEN WANDERING AROUND FOR THE WHOLE NIGHT.
THERE'S ONLY ONE WAY TO GET TO THE ALTAR WITHOUT USING A SPIRIT WAY.
AND WHAT'S THAT, MOM?!

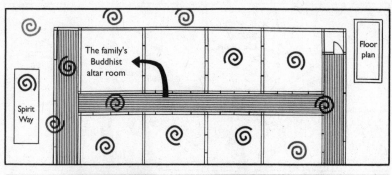

Floor plan

The family's Buddhist altar room

Spirit Way

RATTLE

YOU HAVE TO GET THROUGH THIS ROOM.

MESS

Family altar room

I ALMOST FORGOT THIS IS A WOMAN WHO DOESN'T LIKE TO TIDY UP.

OH...

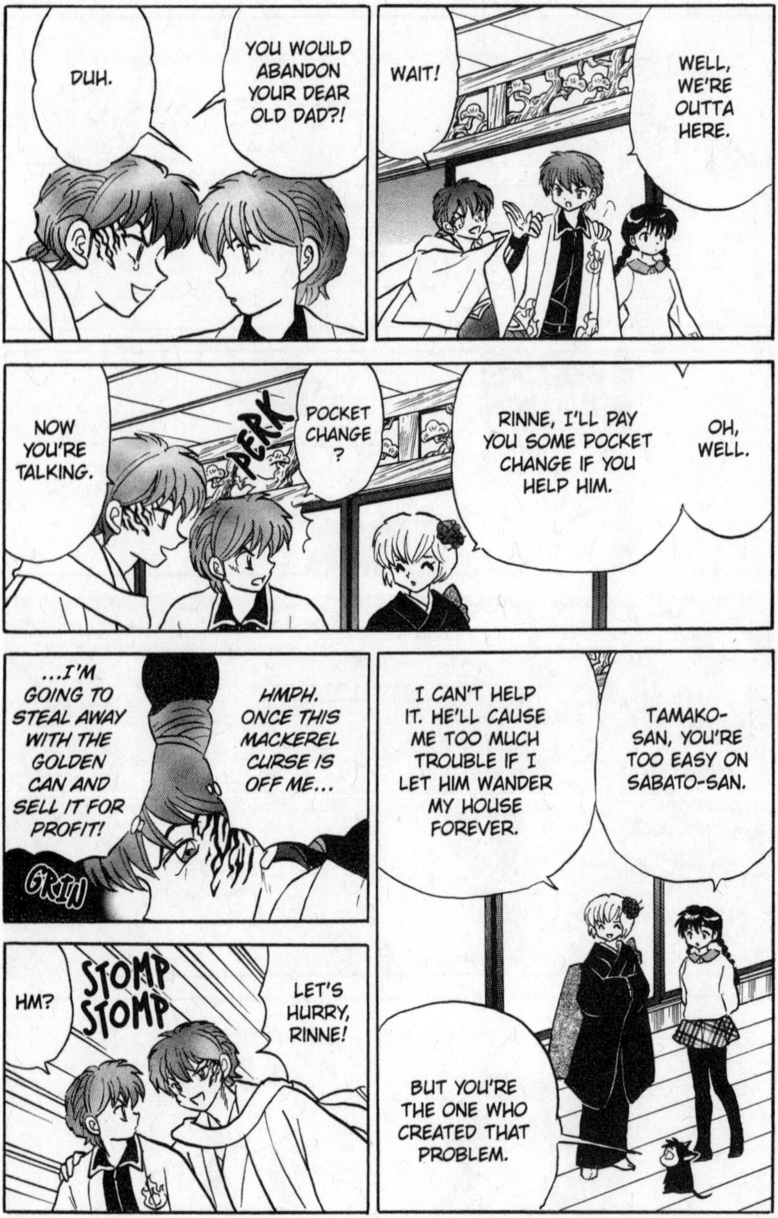
WELL, WE'RE OUTTA HERE.
WAIT!
YOU WOULD ABANDON YOUR DEAR OLD DAD?!
DUH.
OH, WELL.
RINNE, I'LL PAY YOU SOME POCKET CHANGE IF YOU HELP HIM.
POCKET CHANGE?
PERK
NOW YOU'RE TALKING.
TAMAKO-SAN, YOU'RE TOO EASY ON SABATO-SAN.
I CAN'T HELP IT. HE'LL CAUSE ME TOO MUCH TROUBLE IF I LET HIM WANDER MY HOUSE FOREVER.
BUT YOU'RE THE ONE WHO CREATED THAT PROBLEM.
HMPH. ONCE THIS MACKEREL CURSE IS OFF ME...
...I'M GOING TO STEAL AWAY WITH THE GOLDEN CAN AND SELL IT FOR PROFIT!
GRIN
LET'S HURRY, RINNE!
STOMP STOMP
HM?

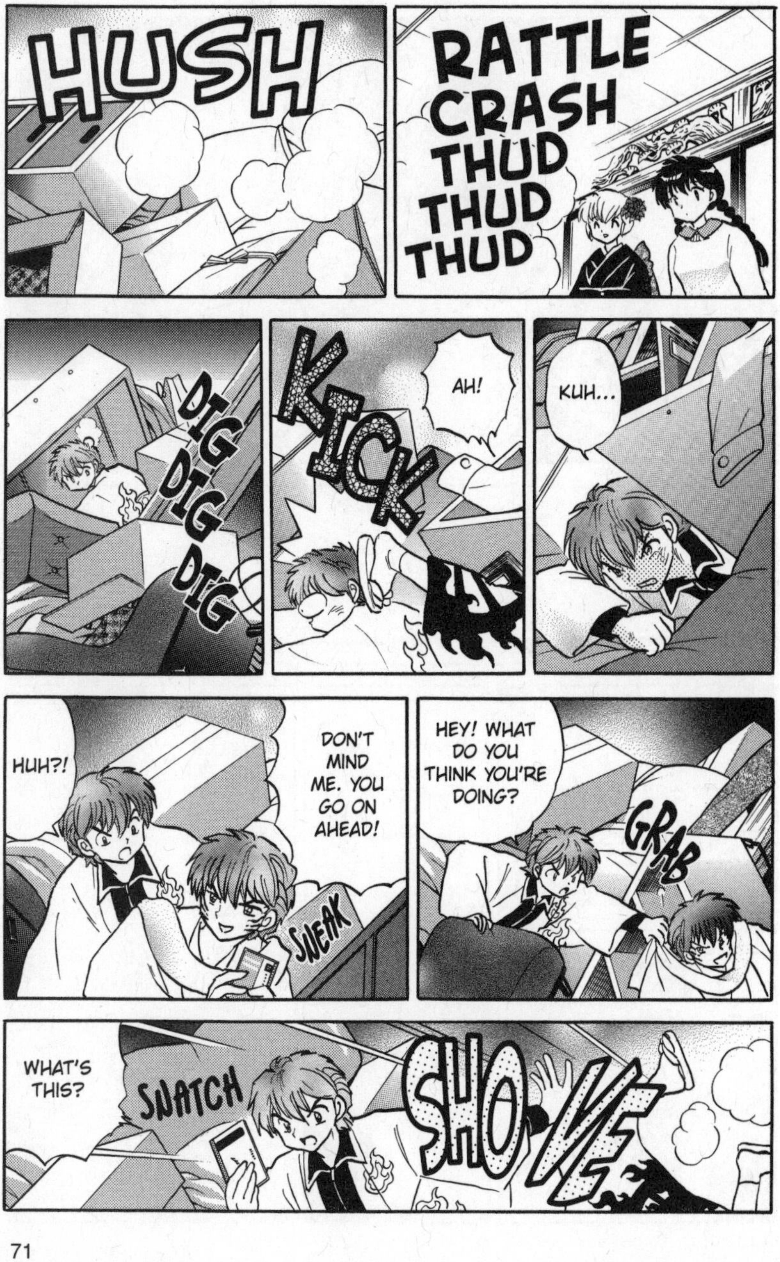
RATTLE
CRASH
THUD
THUD
THUD
HUSH
KUH...
AH!
KICK
DIG
DIG
DIG
DIG
HEY! WHAT DO YOU THINK YOU'RE DOING?
GRAB
DON'T MIND ME. YOU GO ON AHEAD!
HUH?!
SNEAK
SHOVE
SNATCH
WHAT'S THIS?

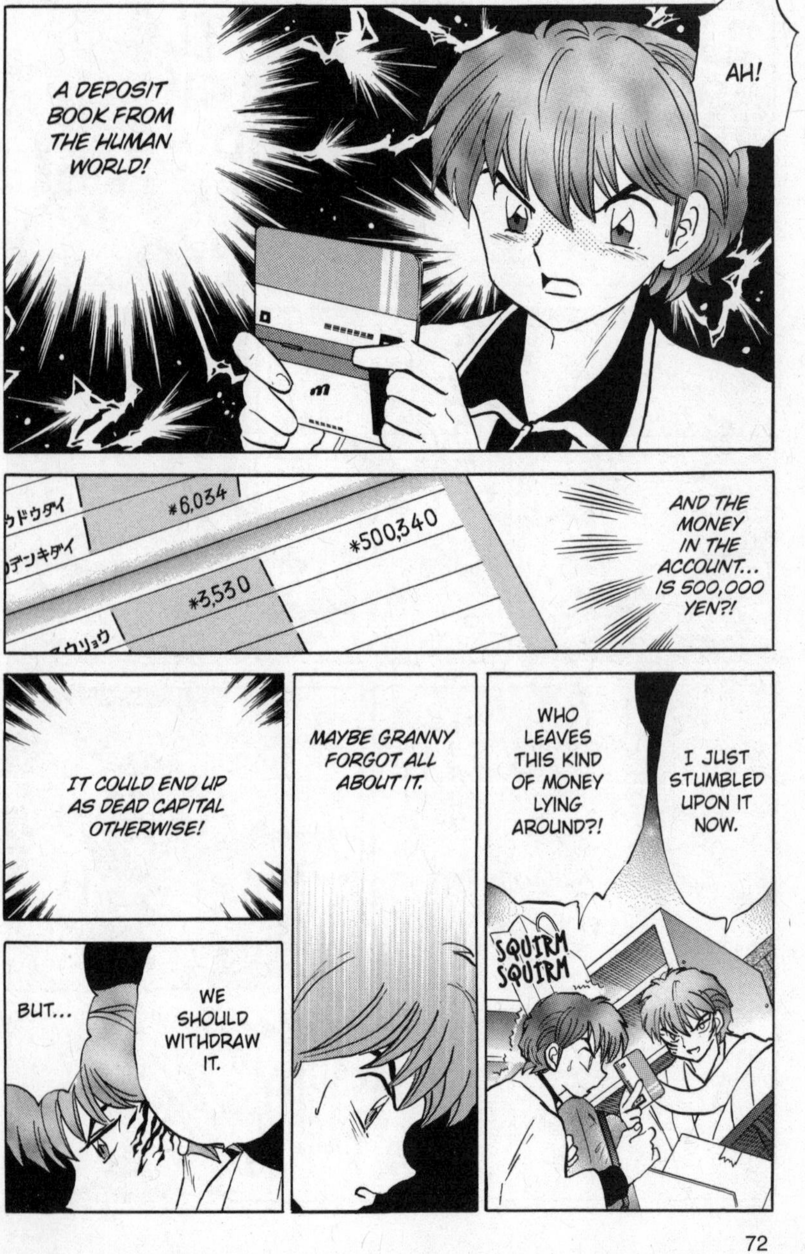
AH!
A DEPOSIT BOOK FROM THE HUMAN WORLD!
AND THE MONEY IN THE ACCOUNT... IS 500,000 YEN?!
*6,034
*500,340
*3,530
I JUST STUMBLED UPON IT NOW.
WHO LEAVES THIS KIND OF MONEY LYING AROUND?!
SQUIRM SQUIRM
MAYBE GRANNY FORGOT ALL ABOUT IT.
IT COULD END UP AS DEAD CAPITAL OTHERWISE!
WE SHOULD WITHDRAW IT.
BUT...

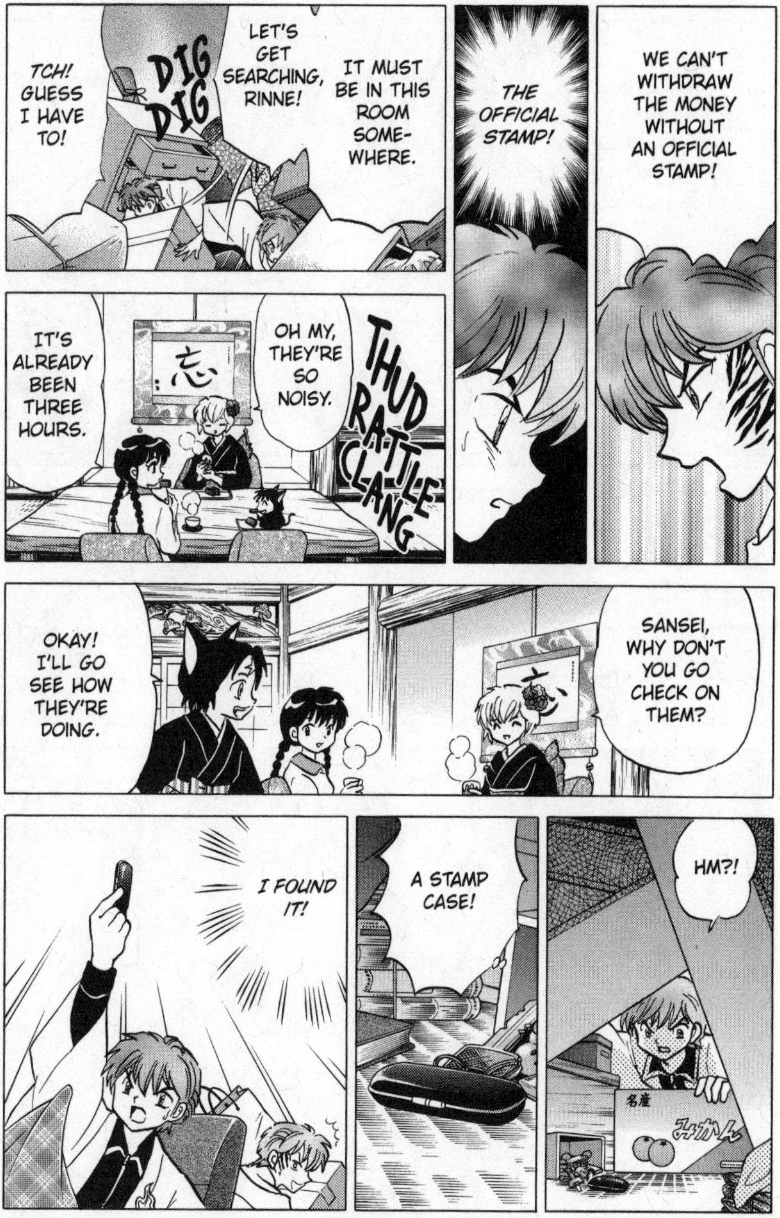
WE CAN'T WITHDRAW THE MONEY WITHOUT AN OFFICIAL STAMP!
THE OFFICIAL STAMP!
IT MUST BE IN THIS ROOM SOME-WHERE.
LET'S GET SEARCHING, RINNE!
DIG DIG
TCH! GUESS I HAVE TO!
THUD RATTLE CLANG
OH MY, THEY'RE SO NOISY.
IT'S ALREADY BEEN THREE HOURS.
SANSEI, WHY DON'T YOU GO CHECK ON THEM?
OKAY! I'LL GO SEE HOW THEY'RE DOING.
HM?!
名産
みかん
A STAMP CASE!
I FOUND IT!

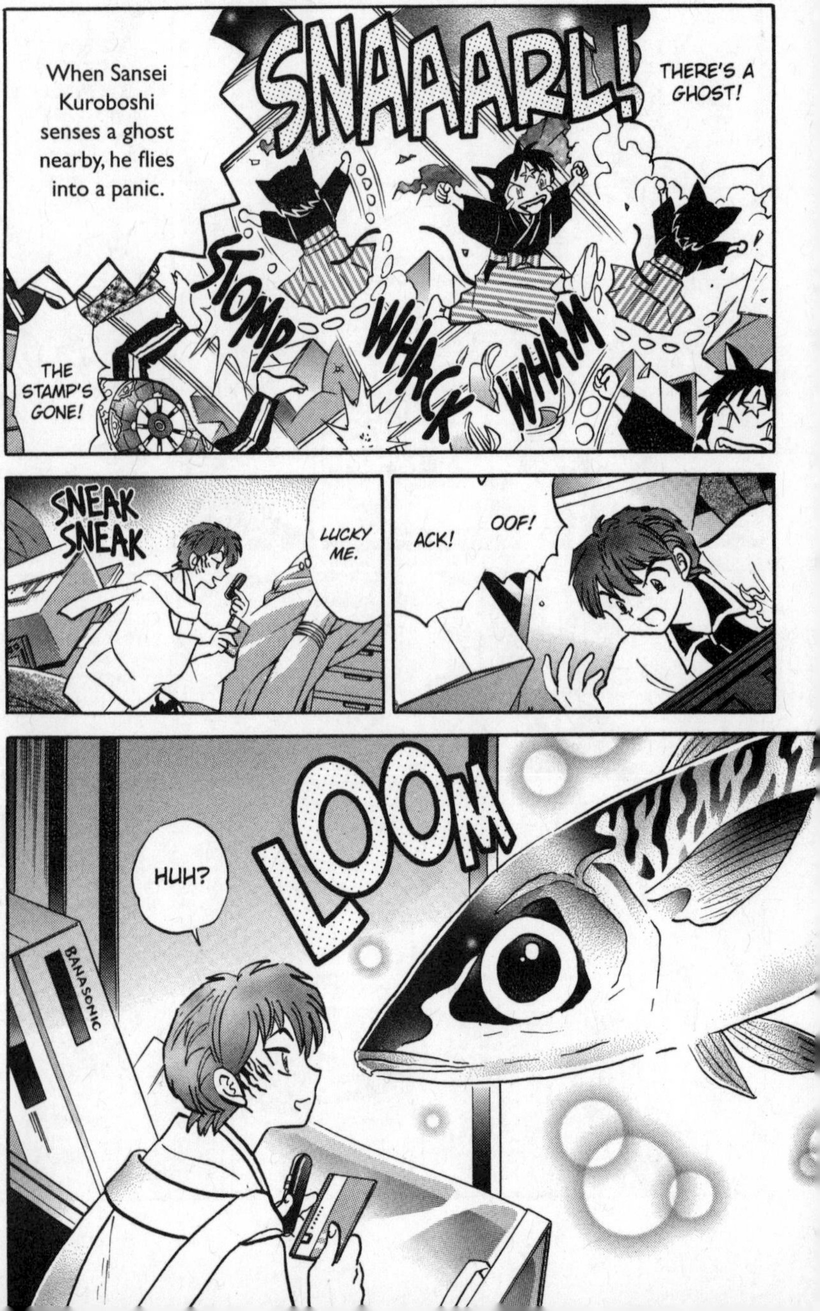
THERE'S A GHOST!
SNAAARL!
When Sansei Kuroboshi senses a ghost nearby, he flies into a panic.
WHAM
WHACK
STOMP
THE STAMP'S GONE!
OOF!
ACK!
LUCKY ME.
SNEAK SNEAK
LOOM
HUH?
BANASONIC

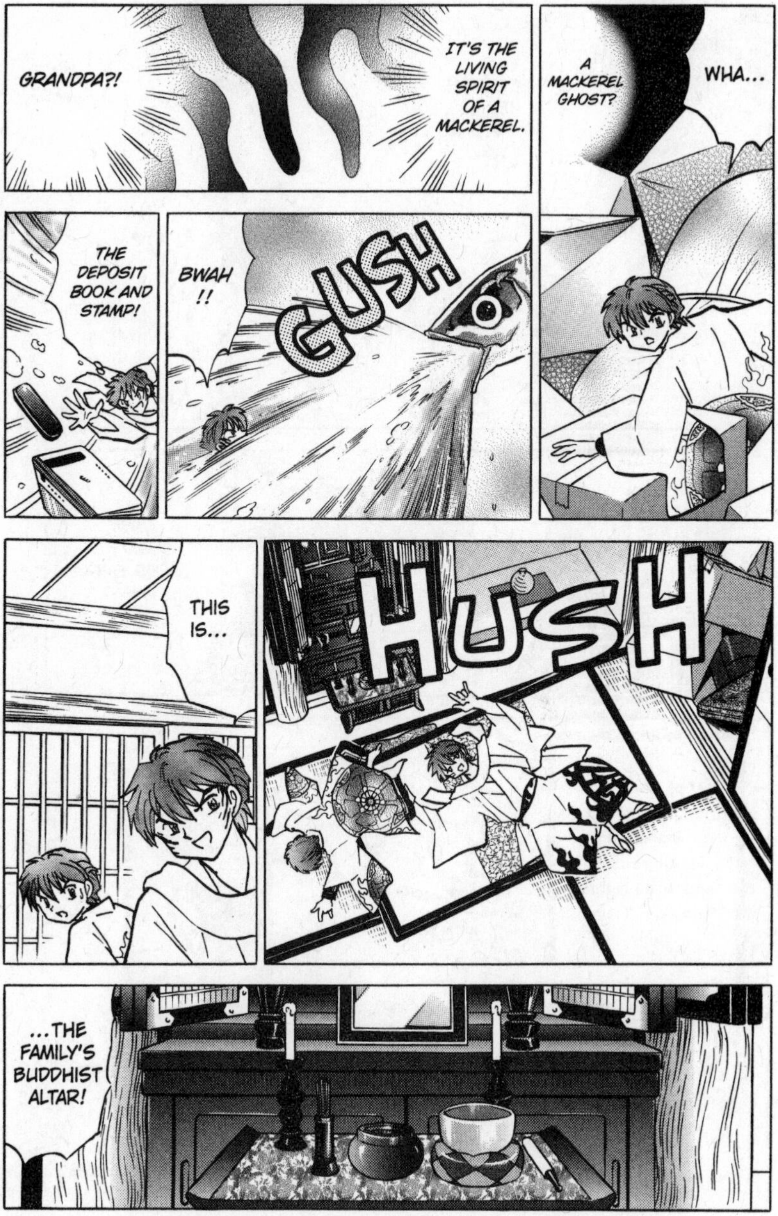
WHA...
A MACKEREL GHOST?
IT'S THE LIVING SPIRIT OF A MACKEREL.
GRANDPA?!
GUSH
BWAH !!
THE DEPOSIT BOOK AND STAMP!
HUSH
THIS IS...
...THE FAMILY'S BUDDHIST ALTAR!

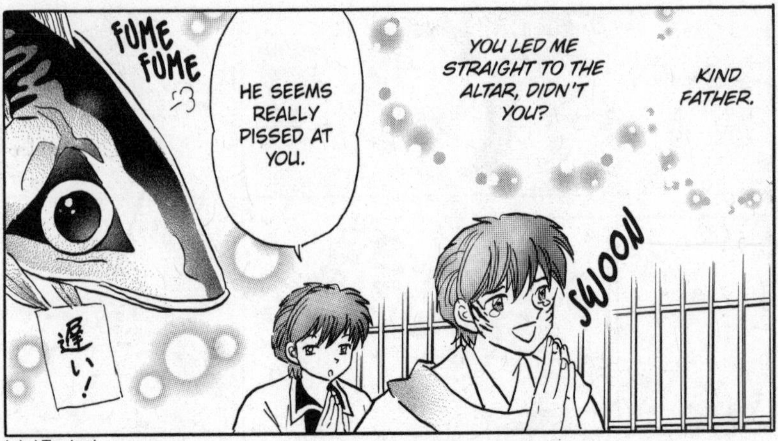
KIND FATHER.
YOU LED ME STRAIGHT TO THE ALTAR, DIDN'T YOU?
SWOON
HE SEEMS REALLY PISSED AT YOU.
FUME FUME
遅い!

Label: Too late!

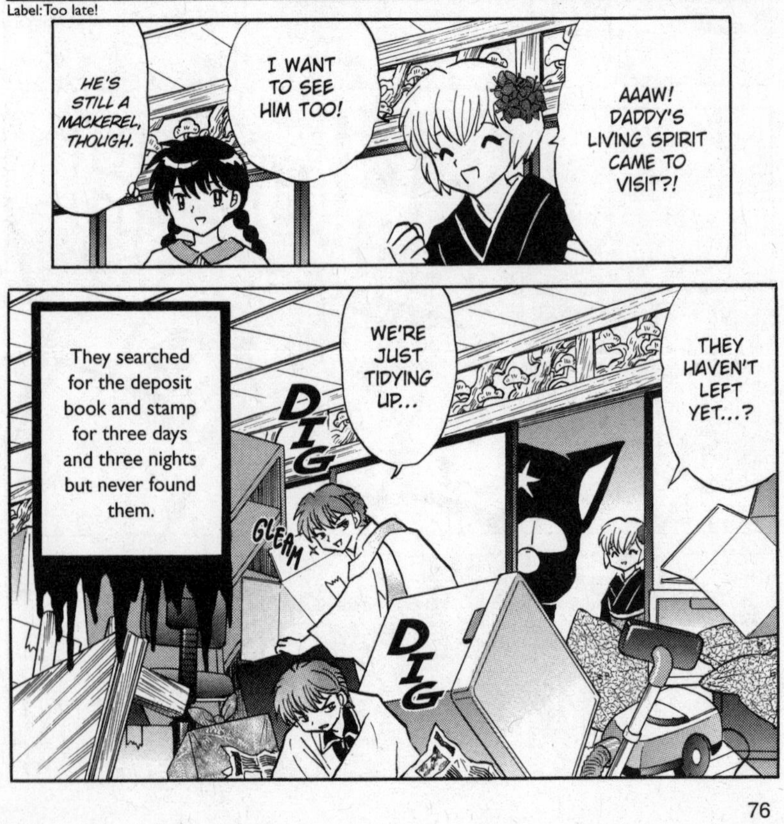
AAAW! DADDY'S LIVING SPIRIT CAME TO VISIT?!
I WANT TO SEE HIM TOO!
HE'S STILL A MACKEREL, THOUGH.
THEY HAVEN'T LEFT YET...?
WE'RE JUST TIDYING UP...
DIG
GLEAM
DIG
They searched for the deposit book and stamp for three days and three nights but never found them.

CHAPTER 273: THE CURSE OF OVERSPENDING

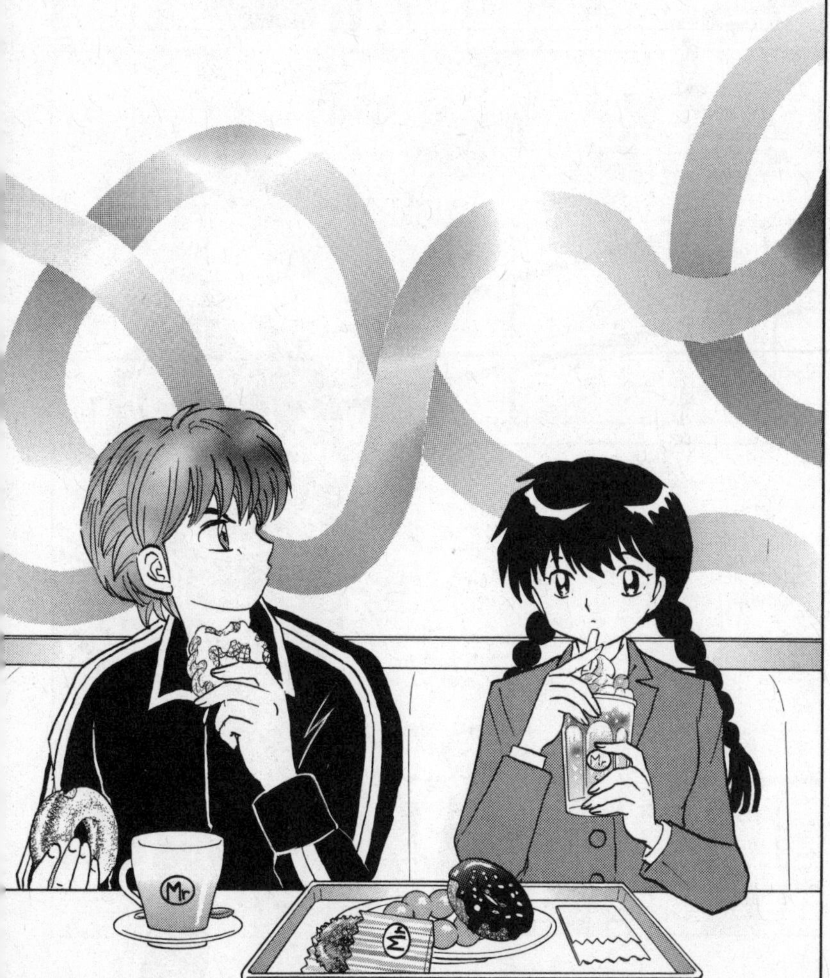

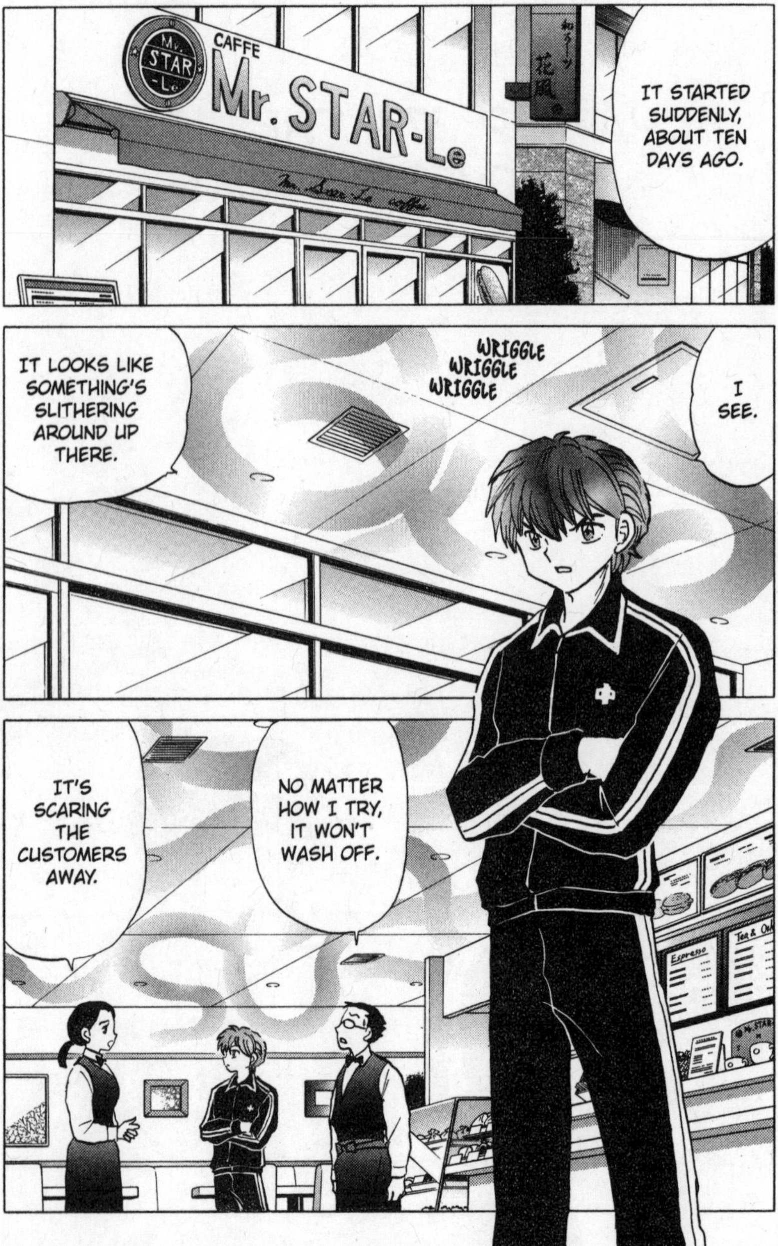
CAFFE
Mr. STAR-Le
IT STARTED SUDDENLY, ABOUT TEN DAYS AGO.
I SEE.
WRIGGLE WRIGGLE WRIGGLE
IT LOOKS LIKE SOMETHING'S SLITHERING AROUND UP THERE.
NO MATTER HOW I TRY, IT WON'T WASH OFF.
IT'S SCARING THE CUSTOMERS AWAY.

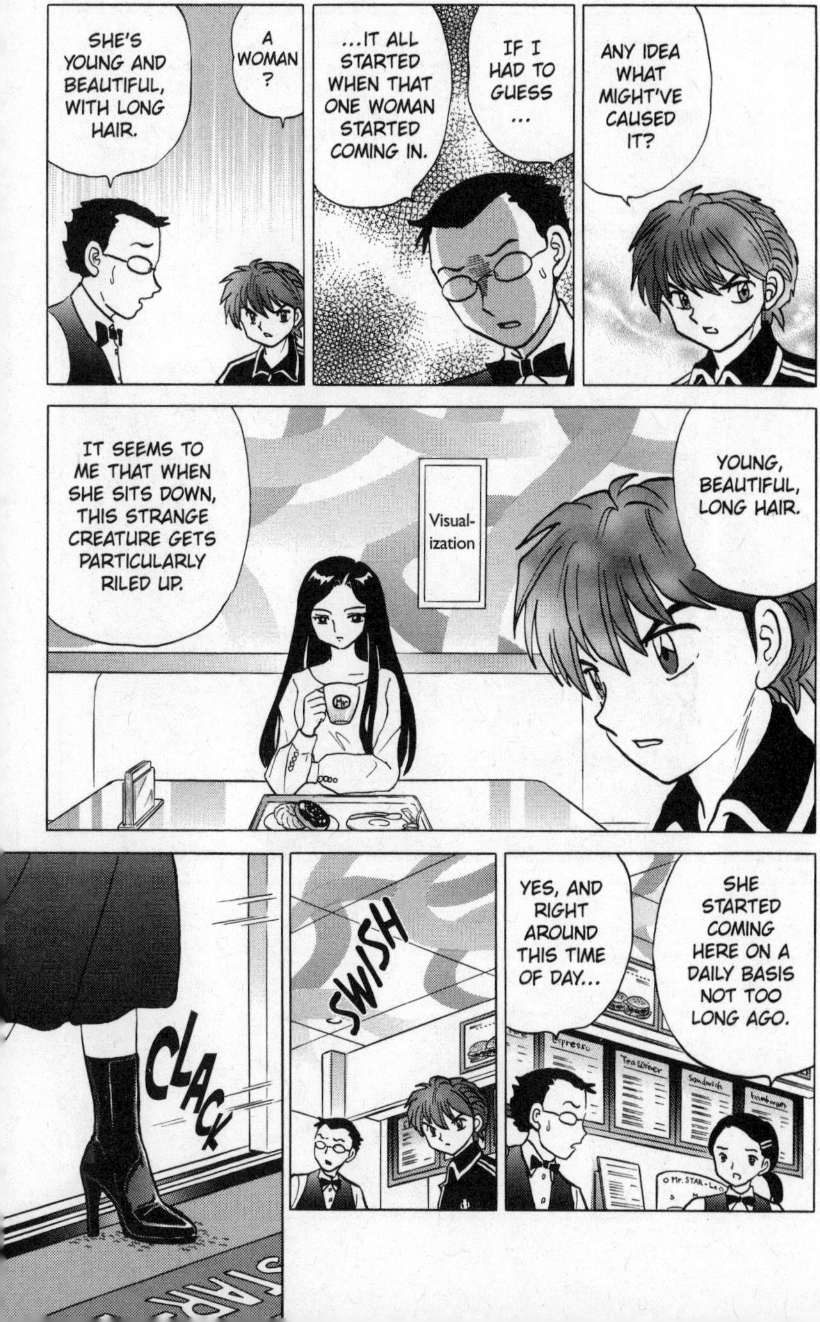
ANY IDEA WHAT MIGHT'VE CAUSED IT?
IF I HAD TO GUESS...
...IT ALL STARTED WHEN THAT ONE WOMAN STARTED COMING IN.
A WOMAN?
SHE'S YOUNG AND BEAUTIFUL, WITH LONG HAIR.
YOUNG, BEAUTIFUL, LONG HAIR.
Visual-ization
IT SEEMS TO ME THAT WHEN SHE SITS DOWN, THIS STRANGE CREATURE GETS PARTICULARLY RILED UP.
SHE STARTED COMING HERE ON A DAILY BASIS NOT TOO LONG AGO.
YES, AND RIGHT AROUND THIS TIME OF DAY...
SWISH
CLACK

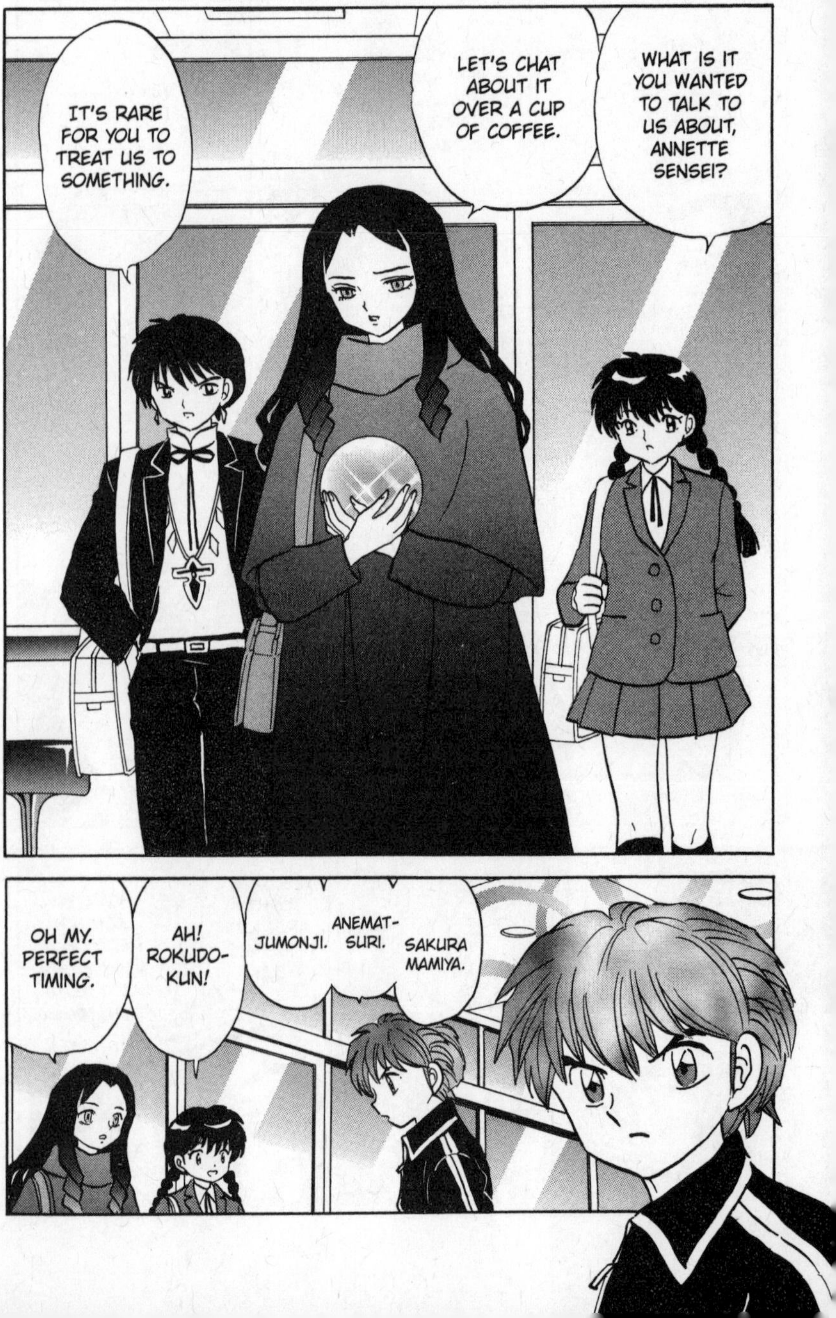
WHAT IS IT YOU WANTED TO TALK TO US ABOUT, ANNETTE SENSEI?
LET'S CHAT ABOUT IT OVER A CUP OF COFFEE.
IT'S RARE FOR YOU TO TREAT US TO SOMETHING.
SAKURA MAMIYA.
ANEMAT-SURI.
JUMONJI.
AH! ROKUDO-KUN!
OH MY. PERFECT TIMING.

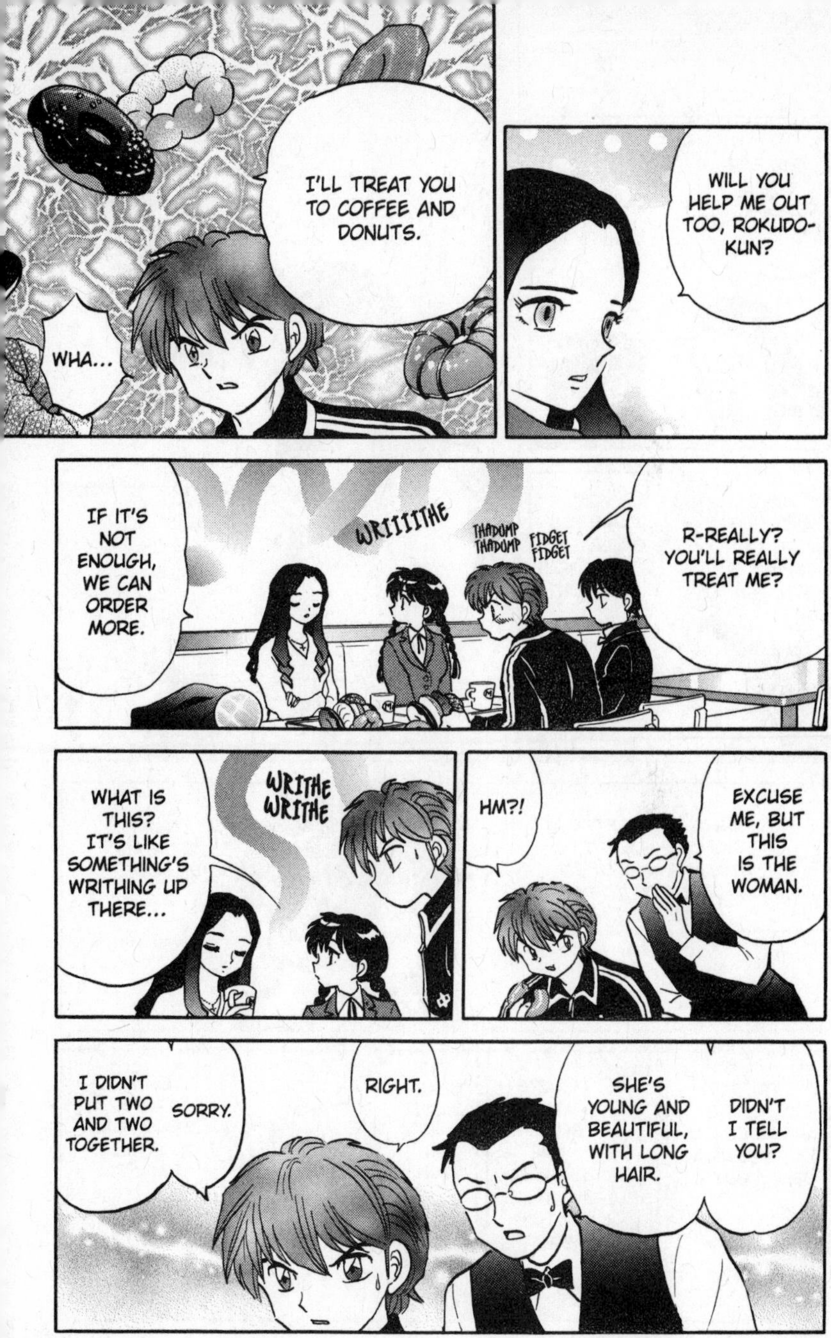
WILL YOU HELP ME OUT TOO, ROKUDO-KUN?
I'LL TREAT YOU TO COFFEE AND DONUTS.
WHA...
R-REALLY? YOU'LL REALLY TREAT ME?
FIDGET FIDGET
THADUMP THADUMP
WRIIIITHE
IF IT'S NOT ENOUGH, WE CAN ORDER MORE.
EXCUSE ME, BUT THIS IS THE WOMAN.
HM?!
WRITHE WRITHE
WHAT IS THIS? IT'S LIKE SOMETHING'S WRITHING UP THERE...
DIDN'T I TELL YOU?
SHE'S YOUNG AND BEAUTIFUL, WITH LONG HAIR.
RIGHT.
SORRY.
I DIDN'T PUT TWO AND TWO TOGETHER.

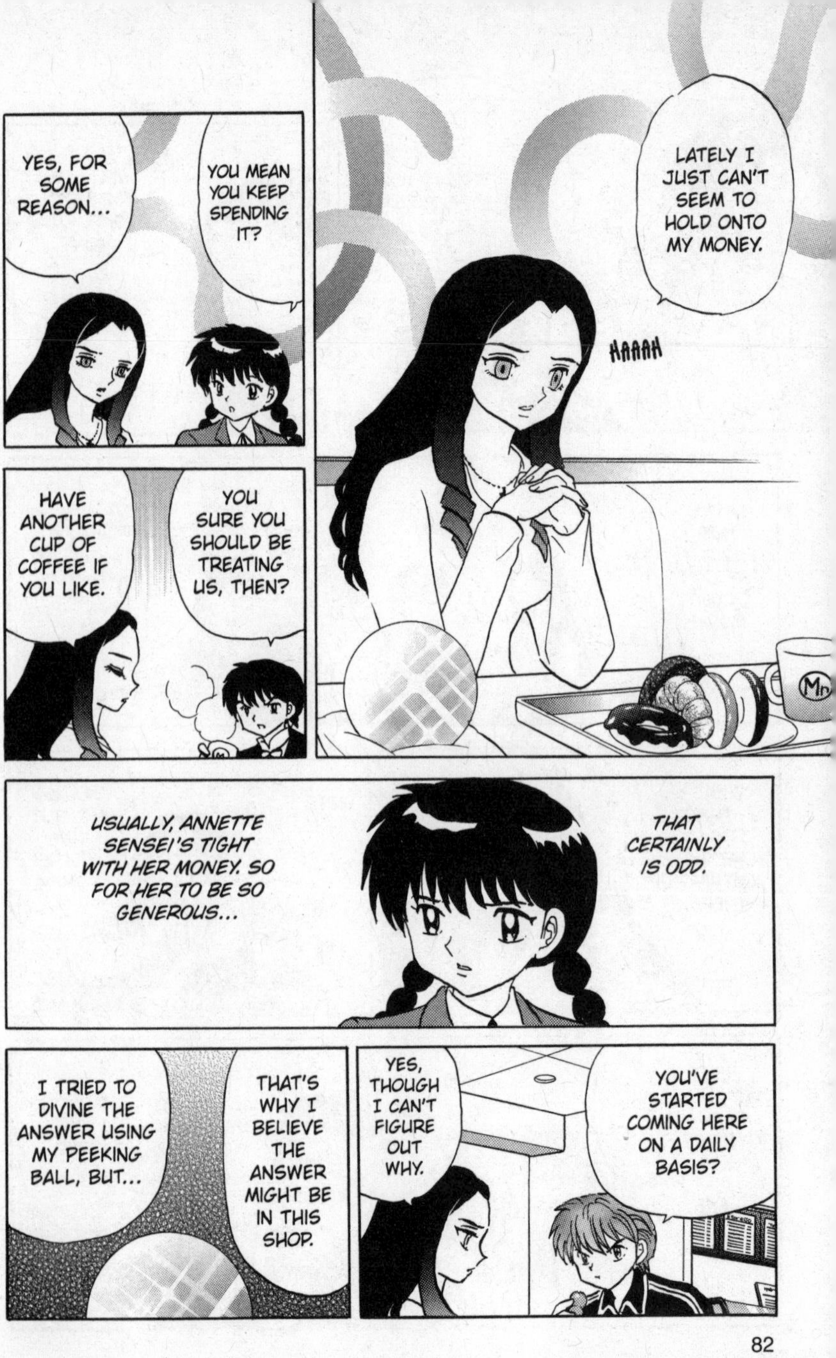
LATELY I JUST CAN'T SEEM TO HOLD ONTO MY MONEY.
HAAAH
YOU MEAN YOU KEEP SPENDING IT?
YES, FOR SOME REASON...
YOU SURE YOU SHOULD BE TREATING US, THEN?
HAVE ANOTHER CUP OF COFFEE IF YOU LIKE.
THAT CERTAINLY IS ODD.
USUALLY, ANNETTE SENSEI'S TIGHT WITH HER MONEY. SO FOR HER TO BE SO GENEROUS...
YOU'VE STARTED COMING HERE ON A DAILY BASIS?
YES, THOUGH I CAN'T FIGURE OUT WHY.
THAT'S WHY I BELIEVE THE ANSWER MIGHT BE IN THIS SHOP.
I TRIED TO DIVINE THE ANSWER USING MY PEEKING BALL, BUT...

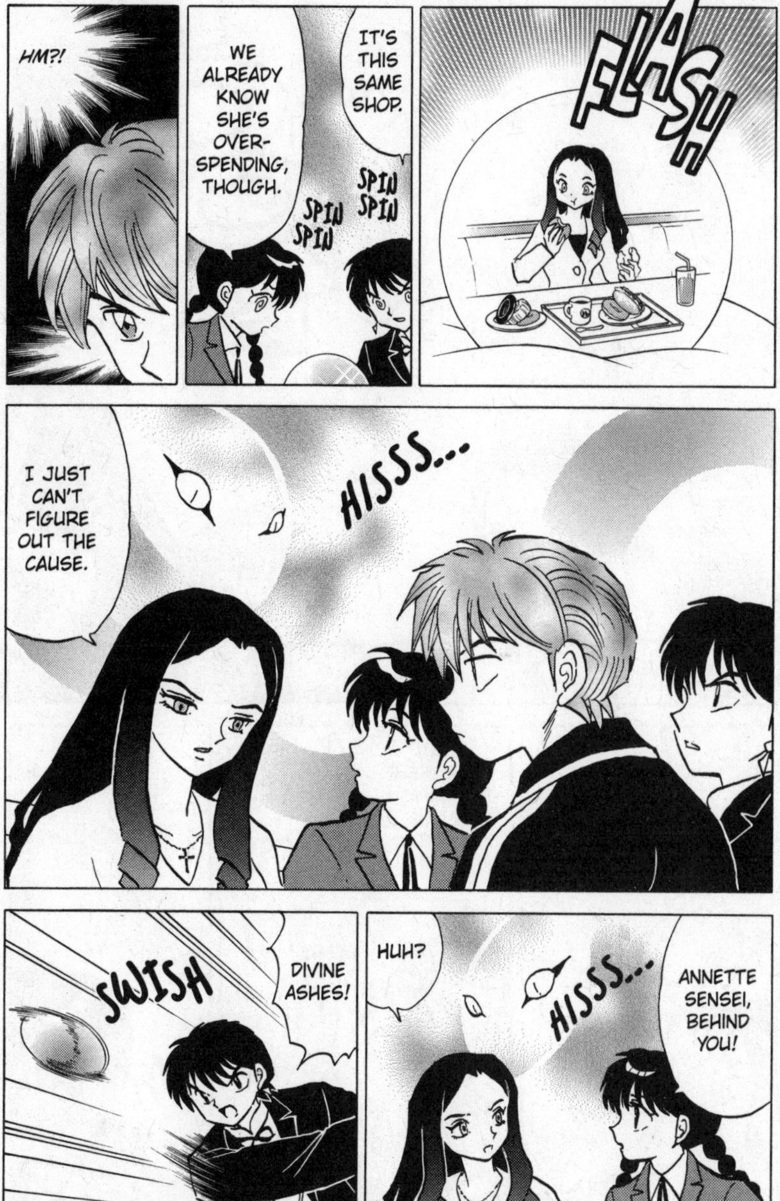
FLASH
IT'S THIS SAME SHOP.
WE ALREADY KNOW SHE'S OVER-SPENDING, THOUGH.
SPIN SPIN
SPIN SPIN
HM?!
I JUST CAN'T FIGURE OUT THE CAUSE.
HISSS...
ANNETTE SENSEI, BEHIND YOU!
HISSS...
HUH?
DIVINE ASHES!
SWISH

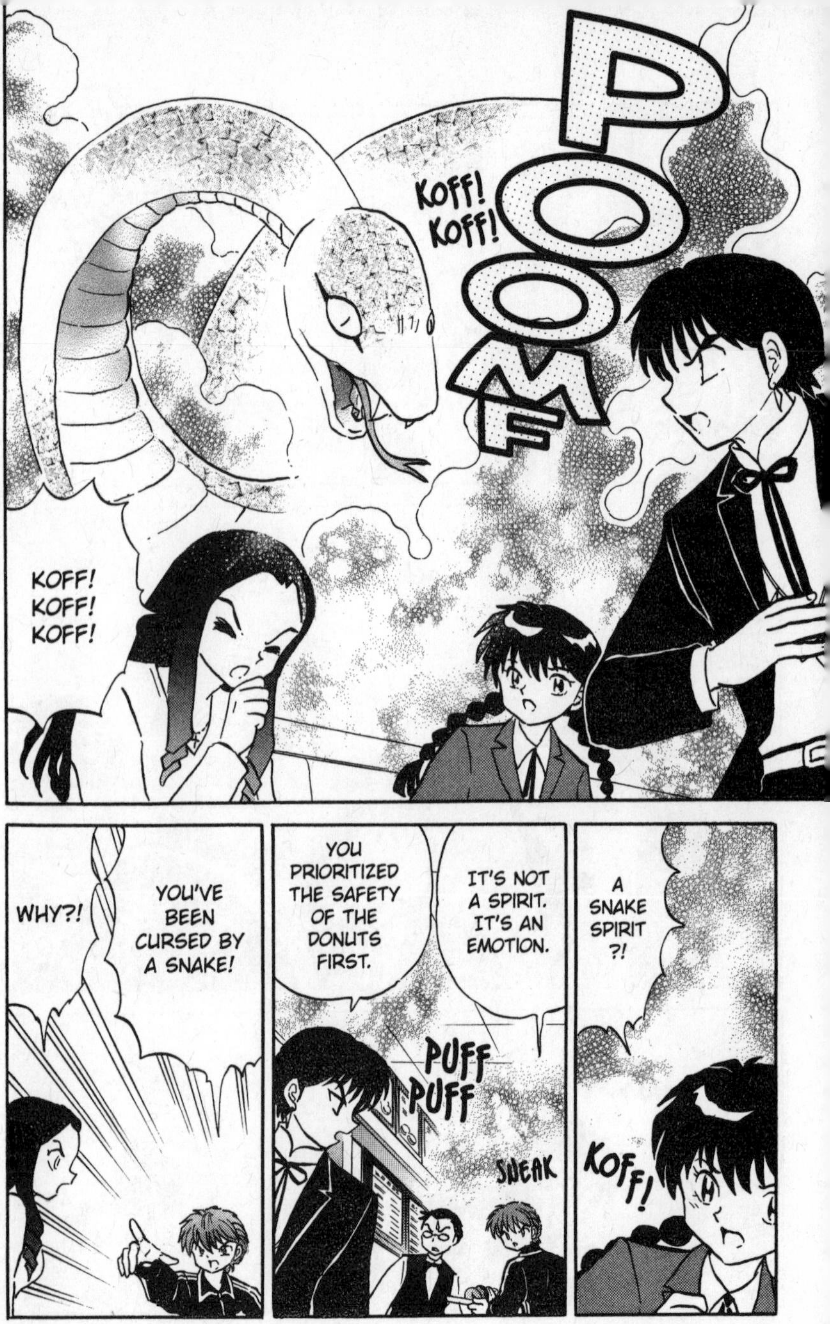
POOMF
KOFF! KOFF!
KOFF! KOFF! KOFF!
A SNAKE SPIRIT ?!
KOFF!
IT'S NOT A SPIRIT. IT'S AN EMOTION.
YOU PRIORITIZED THE SAFETY OF THE DONUTS FIRST.
PUFF PUFF
SNEAK
YOU'VE BEEN CURSED BY A SNAKE!
WHY?!

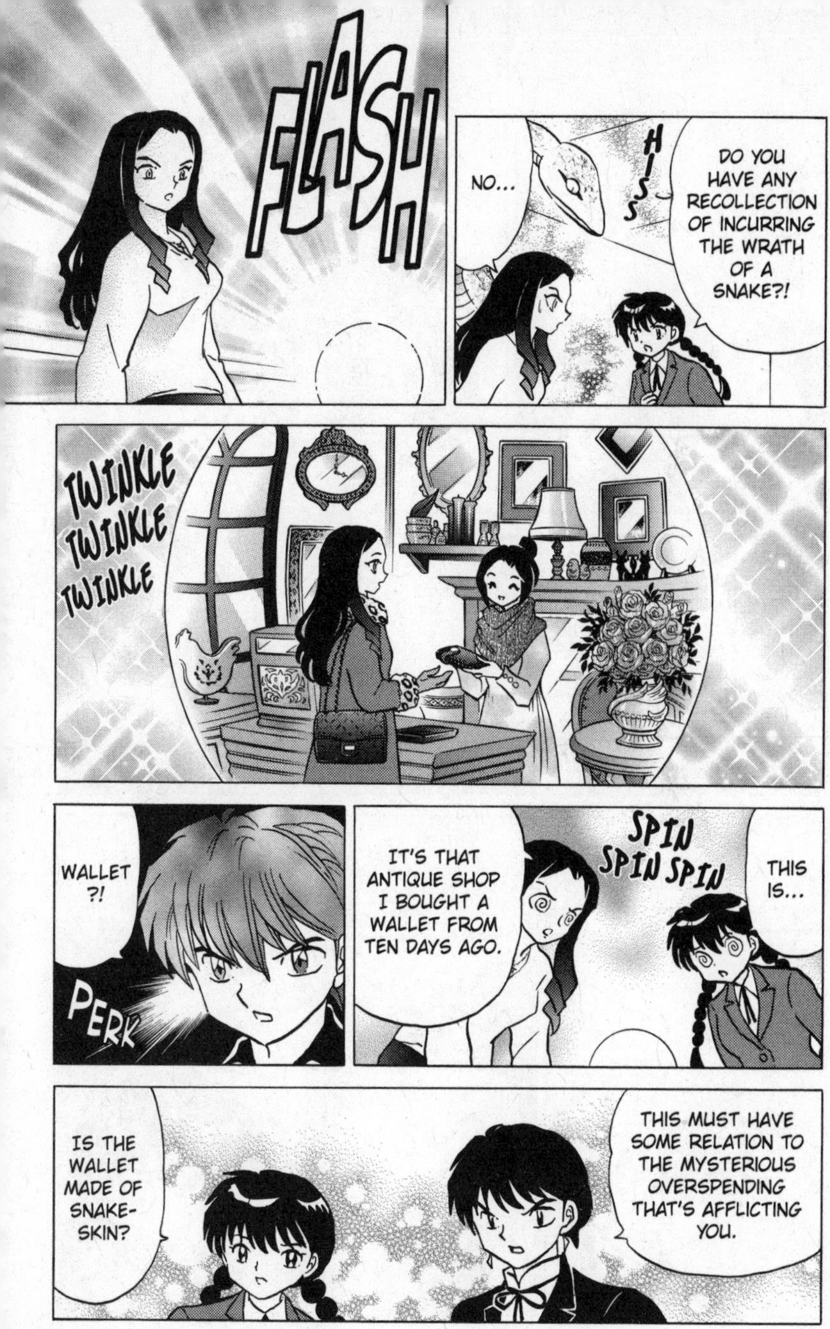
DO YOU HAVE ANY RECOLLECTION OF INCURRING THE WRATH OF A SNAKE?!
HISS
NO...
FLASH
TWINKLE TWINKLE TWINKLE
THIS IS...
SPIN SPIN SPIN
IT'S THAT ANTIQUE SHOP I BOUGHT A WALLET FROM TEN DAYS AGO.
WALLET ?!
PERK
THIS MUST HAVE SOME RELATION TO THE MYSTERIOUS OVERSPENDING THAT'S AFFLICTING YOU.
IS THE WALLET MADE OF SNAKE-SKIN?

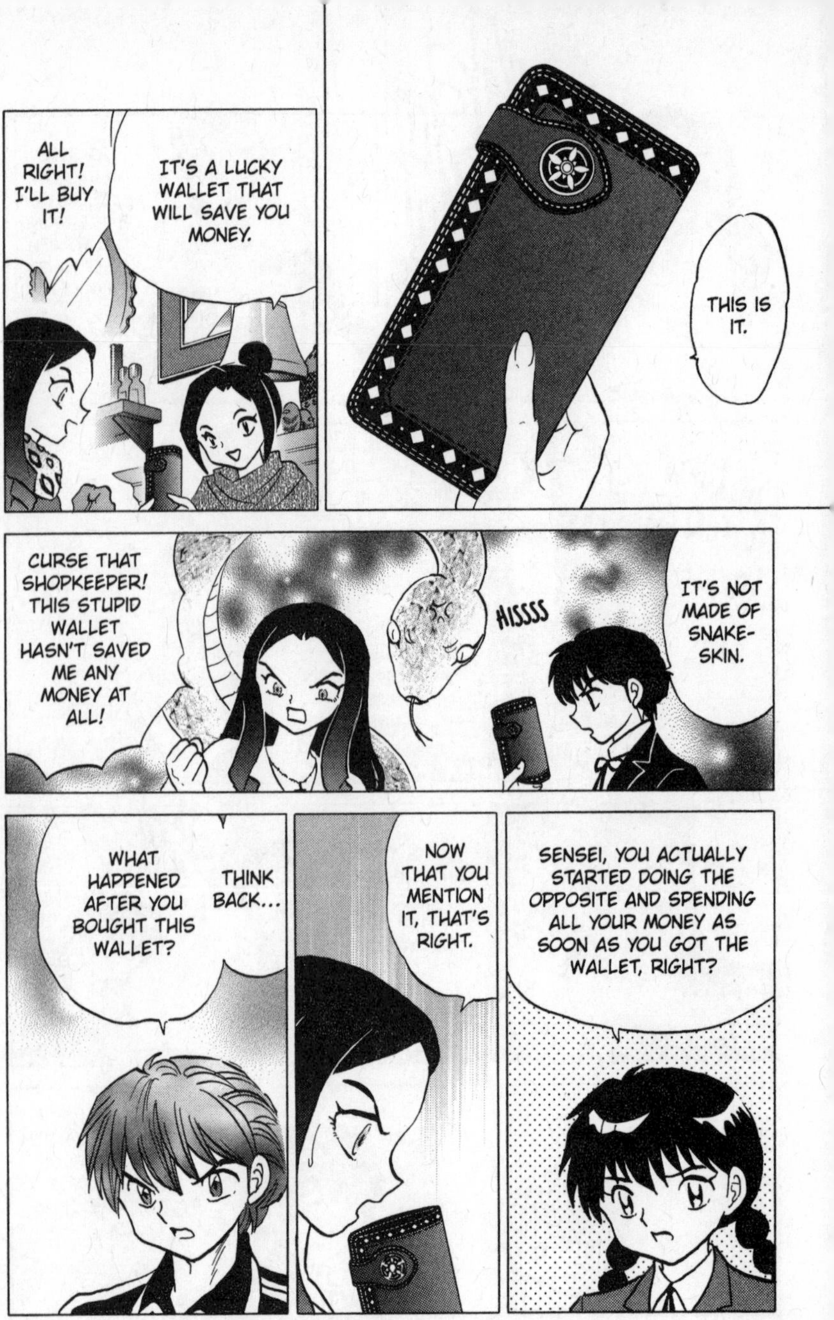
THIS IS IT.
IT'S A LUCKY WALLET THAT WILL SAVE YOU MONEY.
ALL RIGHT! I'LL BUY IT!
IT'S NOT MADE OF SNAKE-SKIN.
HISSSS
CURSE THAT SHOPKEEPER! THIS STUPID WALLET HASN'T SAVED ME ANY MONEY AT ALL!
SENSEI, YOU ACTUALLY STARTED DOING THE OPPOSITE AND SPENDING ALL YOUR MONEY AS SOON AS YOU GOT THE WALLET, RIGHT?
NOW THAT YOU MENTION IT, THAT'S RIGHT.
THINK BACK...
WHAT HAPPENED AFTER YOU BOUGHT THIS WALLET?

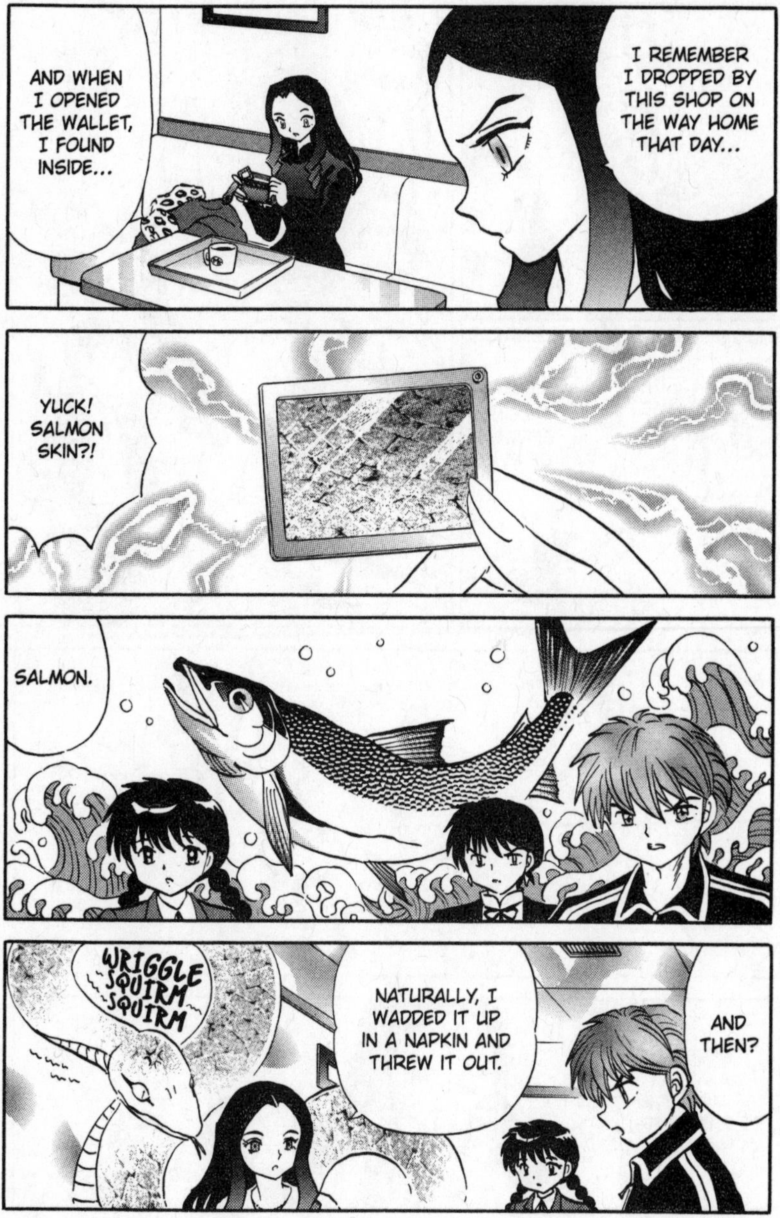
I REMEMBER I DROPPED BY THIS SHOP ON THE WAY HOME THAT DAY...
AND WHEN I OPENED THE WALLET, I FOUND INSIDE...
YUCK! SALMON SKIN?!
SALMON.
AND THEN?
NATURALLY, I WADDED IT UP IN A NAPKIN AND THREW IT OUT.
WRIGGLE SQUIRM SQUIRM

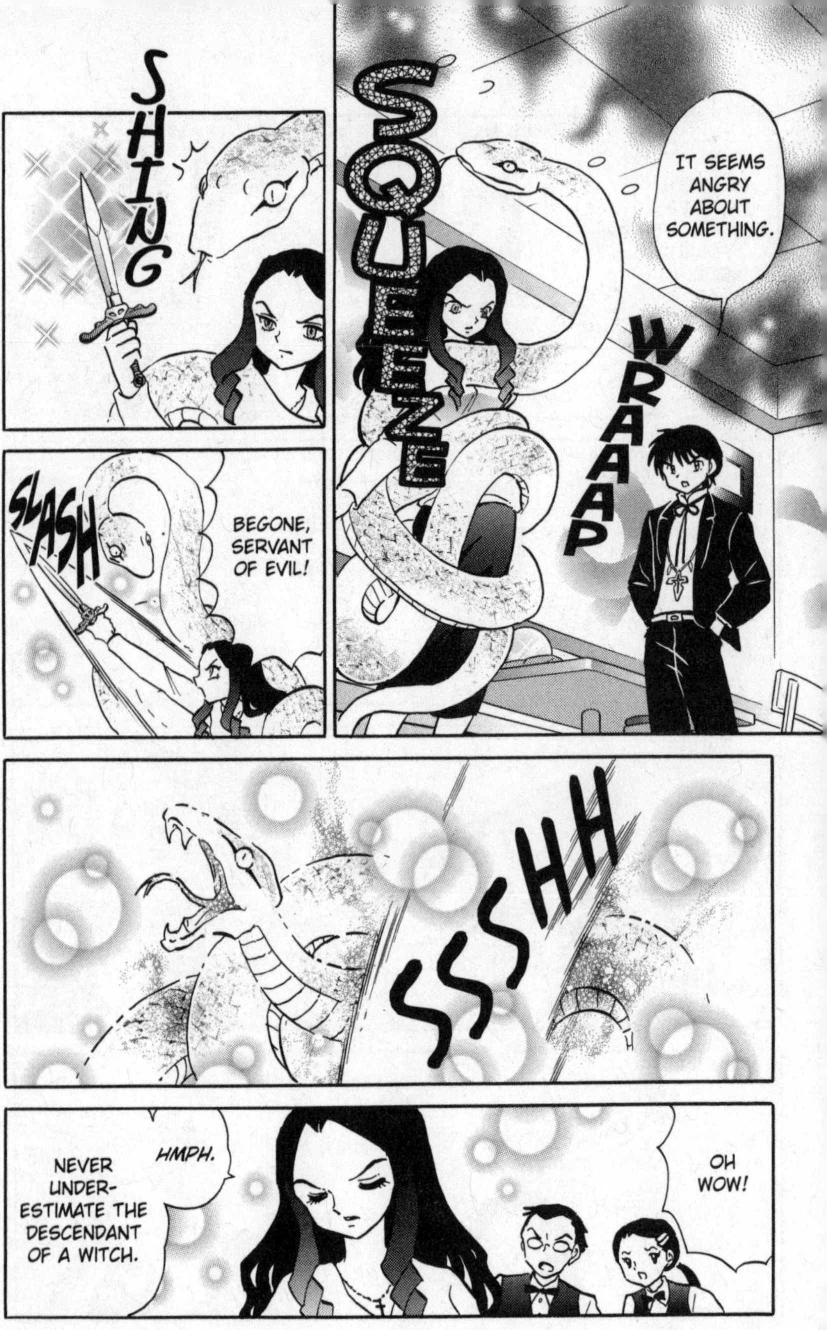
IT SEEMS ANGRY ABOUT SOMETHING.
SQUEEZE
WRAAAP
SHING
SLASH
BEGONE, SERVANT OF EVIL!
SSSHH
OH WOW!
HMPH.
NEVER UNDER-ESTIMATE THE DESCENDANT OF A WITCH.

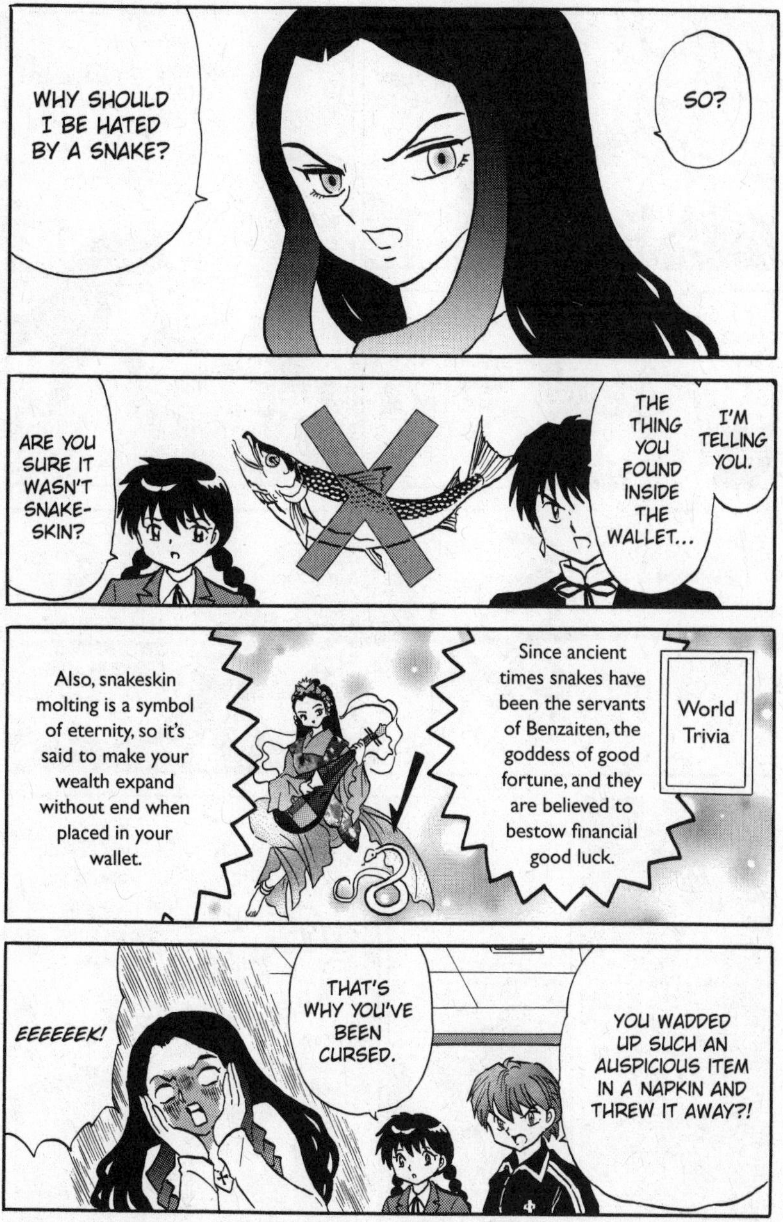
SO?
WHY SHOULD I BE HATED BY A SNAKE?
I'M TELLING YOU.
THE THING YOU FOUND INSIDE THE WALLET...
ARE YOU SURE IT WASN'T SNAKE-SKIN?
World Trivia
Since ancient times snakes have been the servants of Benzaiten, the goddess of good fortune, and they are believed to bestow financial good luck.
Also, snakeskin molting is a symbol of eternity, so it's said to make your wealth expand without end when placed in your wallet.
YOU WADDED UP SUCH AN AUSPICIOUS ITEM IN A NAPKIN AND THREW IT AWAY?!
THAT'S WHY YOU'VE BEEN CURSED.
EEEEEEK!

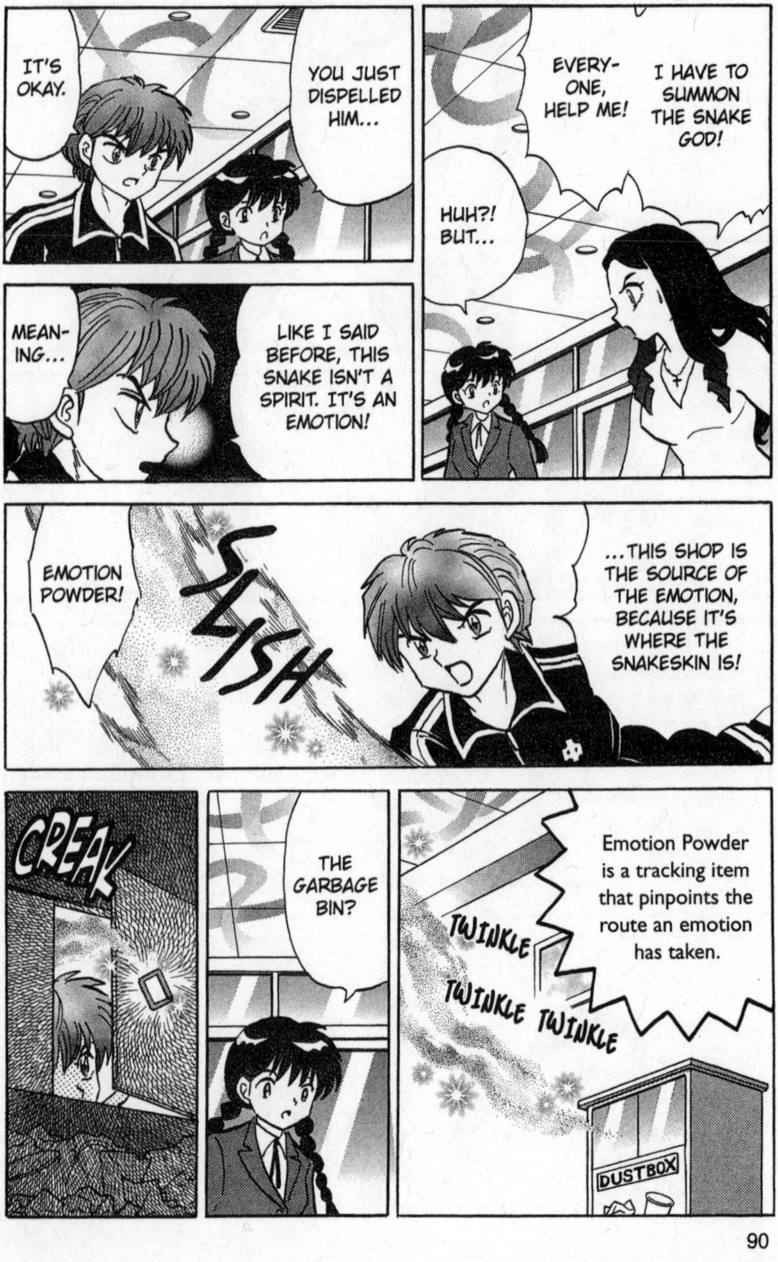
I HAVE TO SUMMON THE SNAKE GOD!
EVERY-ONE, HELP ME!
HUH?! BUT...
YOU JUST DISPELLED HIM...
IT'S OKAY.
LIKE I SAID BEFORE, THIS SNAKE ISN'T A SPIRIT. IT'S AN EMOTION!
MEAN-ING...
...THIS SHOP IS THE SOURCE OF THE EMOTION, BECAUSE IT'S WHERE THE SNAKESKIN IS!
SLISH
EMOTION POWDER!
Emotion Powder is a tracking item that pinpoints the route an emotion has taken.
TWINKLE
TWINKLE TWINKLE
DUSTBOX
THE GARBAGE BIN?
CREAK

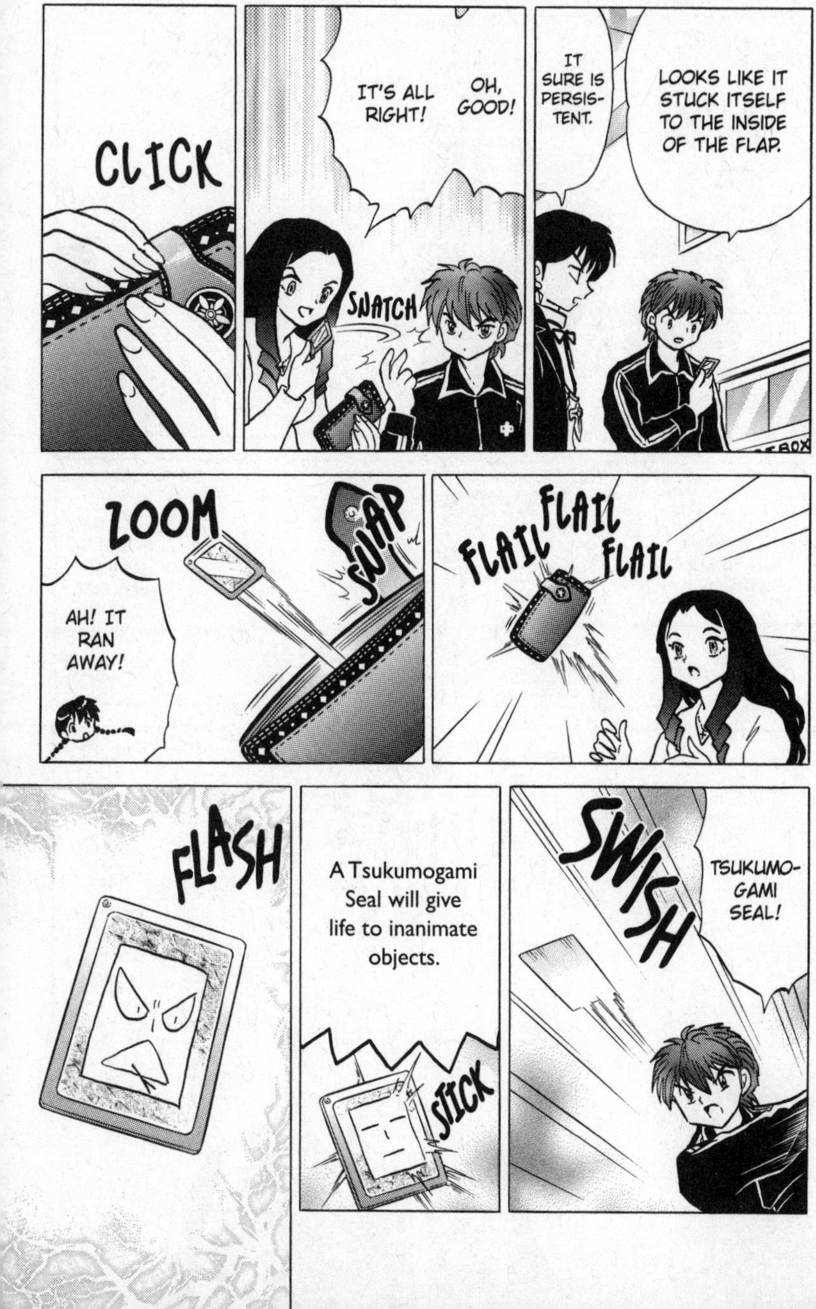
LOOKS LIKE IT STUCK ITSELF TO THE INSIDE OF THE FLAP.
IT SURE IS PERSIS-TENT.
OH, GOOD!
IT'S ALL RIGHT!
SNATCH
CLICK
FLAIL FLAIL FLAIL
SNAP
ZOOM
AH! IT RAN AWAY!
SWISH
TSUKUMO-GAMI SEAL!
A Tsukumogami Seal will give life to inanimate objects.
STICK
FLASH

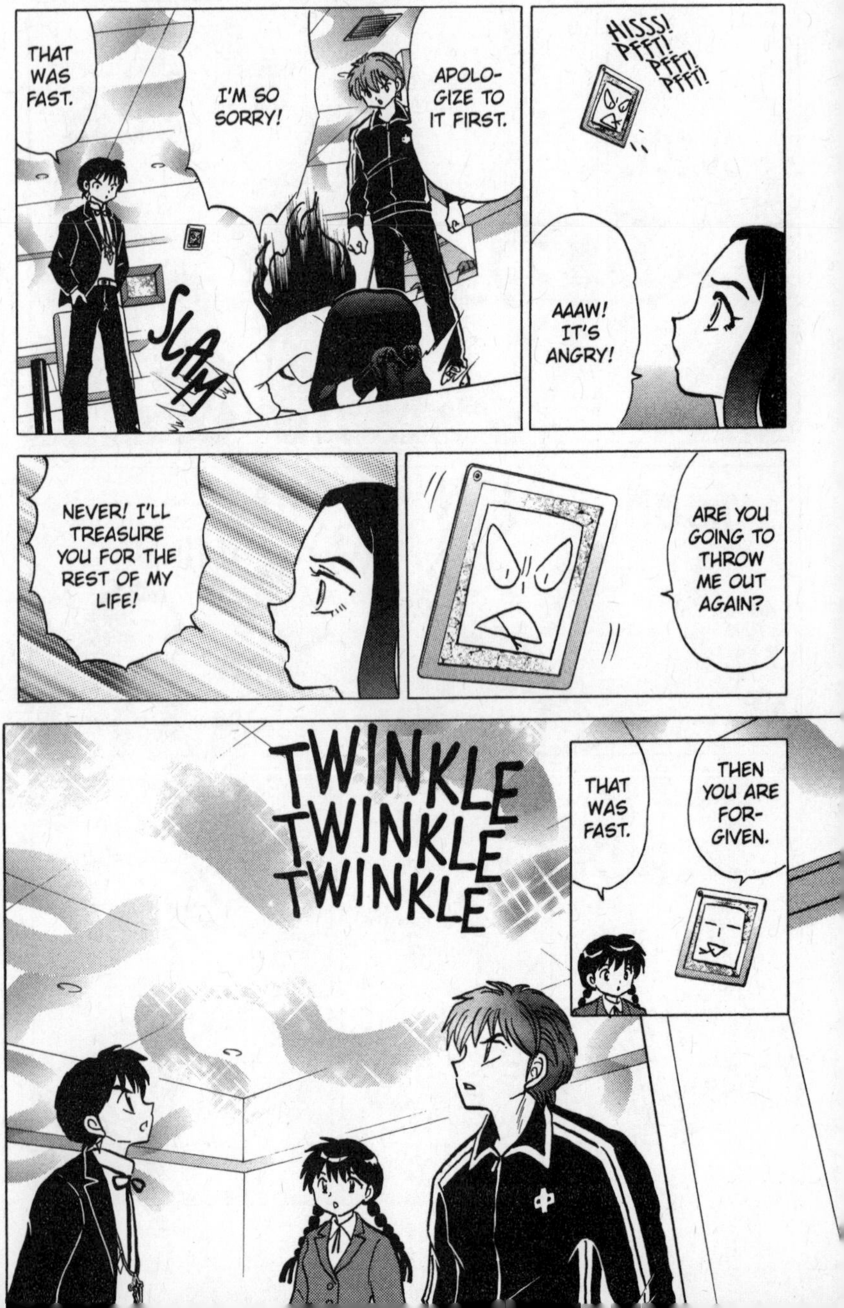
HISSS! PFFT! PFFT! PFFT!
AAAW! IT'S ANGRY!
APOLO-GIZE TO IT FIRST.
I'M SO SORRY!
THAT WAS FAST.
SLAM
ARE YOU GOING TO THROW ME OUT AGAIN?
NEVER! I'LL TREASURE YOU FOR THE REST OF MY LIFE!
THEN YOU ARE FOR-GIVEN.
THAT WAS FAST.
TWINKLE TWINKLE TWINKLE

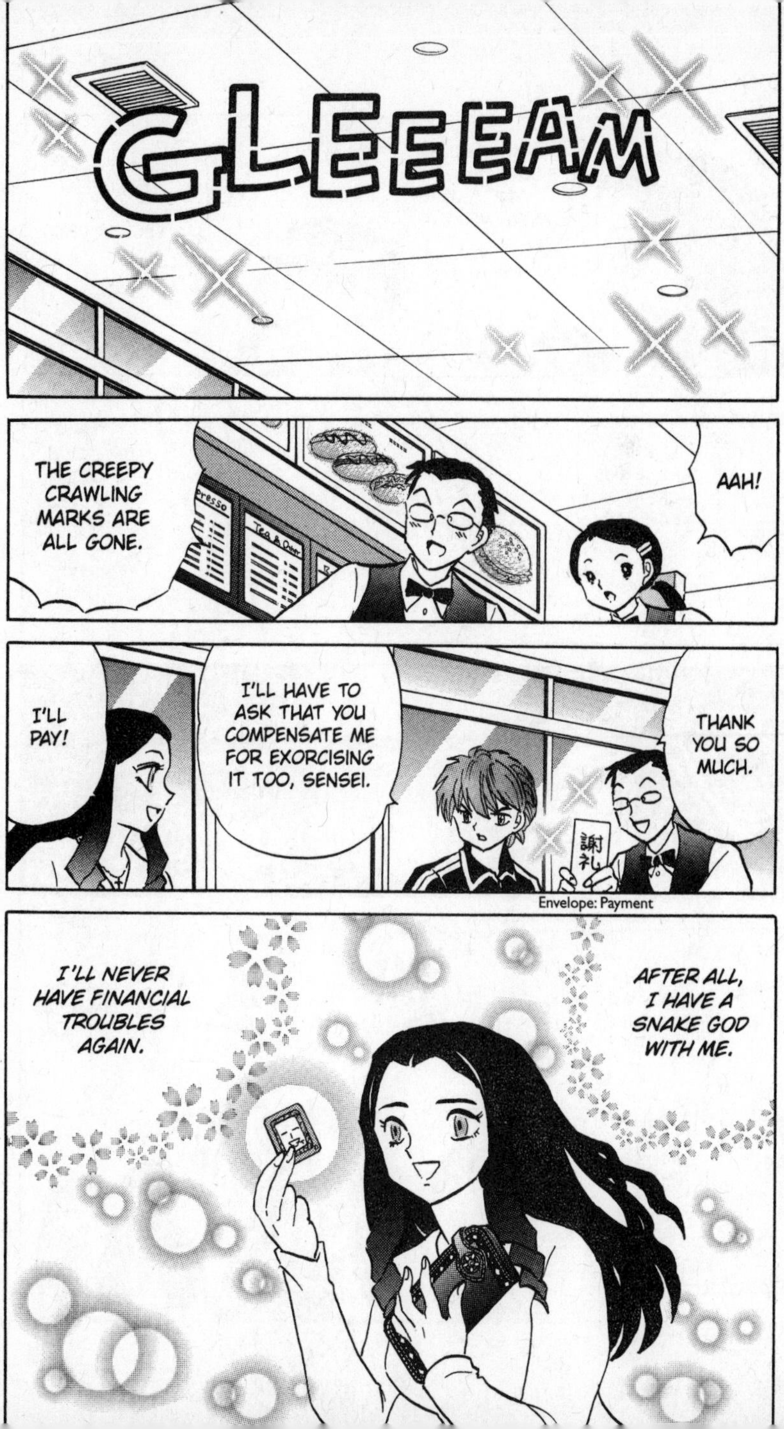
GLEEEAM
AAH!
THE CREEPY CRAWLING MARKS ARE ALL GONE.
THANK YOU SO MUCH.
謝礼
I'LL HAVE TO ASK THAT YOU COMPENSATE ME FOR EXORCISING IT TOO, SENSEI.
I'LL PAY!
Envelope: Payment
AFTER ALL, I HAVE A SNAKE GOD WITH ME.
I'LL NEVER HAVE FINANCIAL TROUBLES AGAIN.

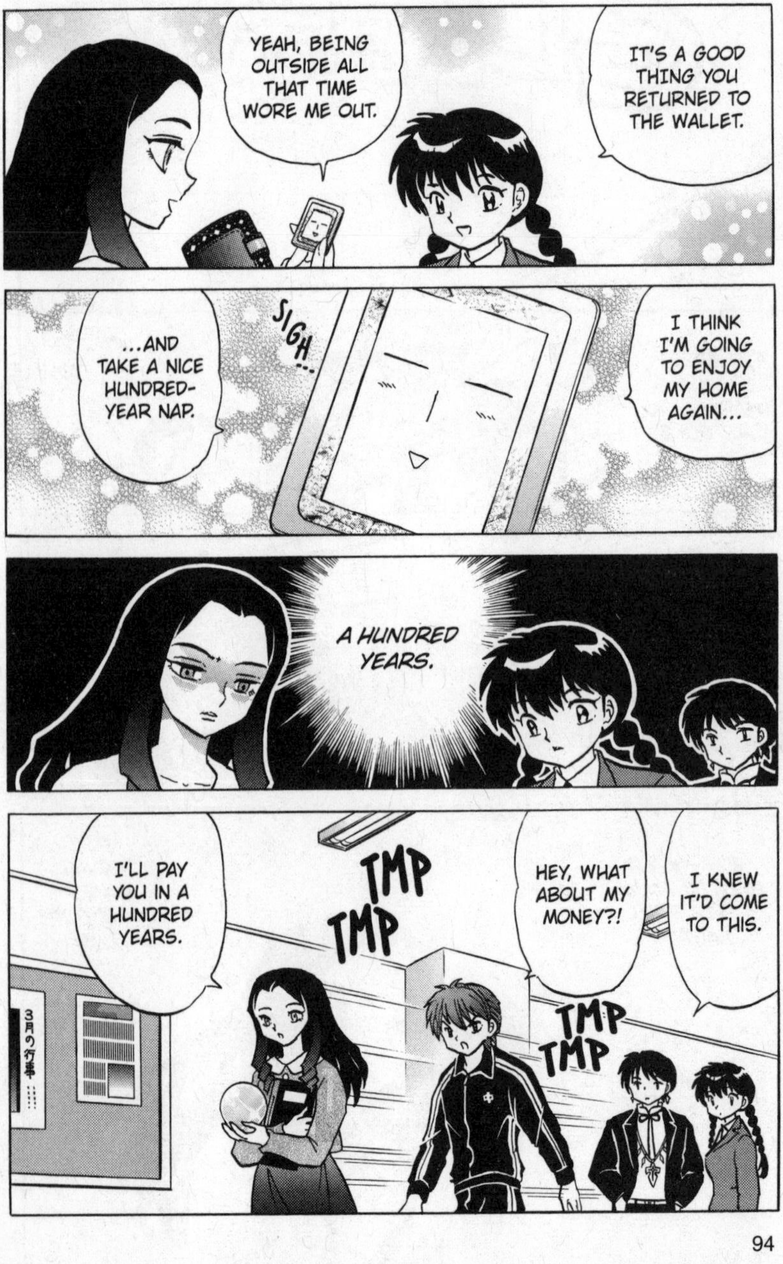
IT'S A GOOD THING YOU RETURNED TO THE WALLET.
YEAH, BEING OUTSIDE ALL THAT TIME WORE ME OUT.
I THINK I'M GOING TO ENJOY MY HOME AGAIN...
SIGH...
...AND TAKE A NICE HUNDRED-YEAR NAP.
A HUNDRED YEARS.
I KNEW IT'D COME TO THIS.
TMP TMP
HEY, WHAT ABOUT MY MONEY?!
TMP TMP
I'LL PAY YOU IN A HUNDRED YEARS.
3月の行事

CHAPTER 274: ASHES AND YEARNING

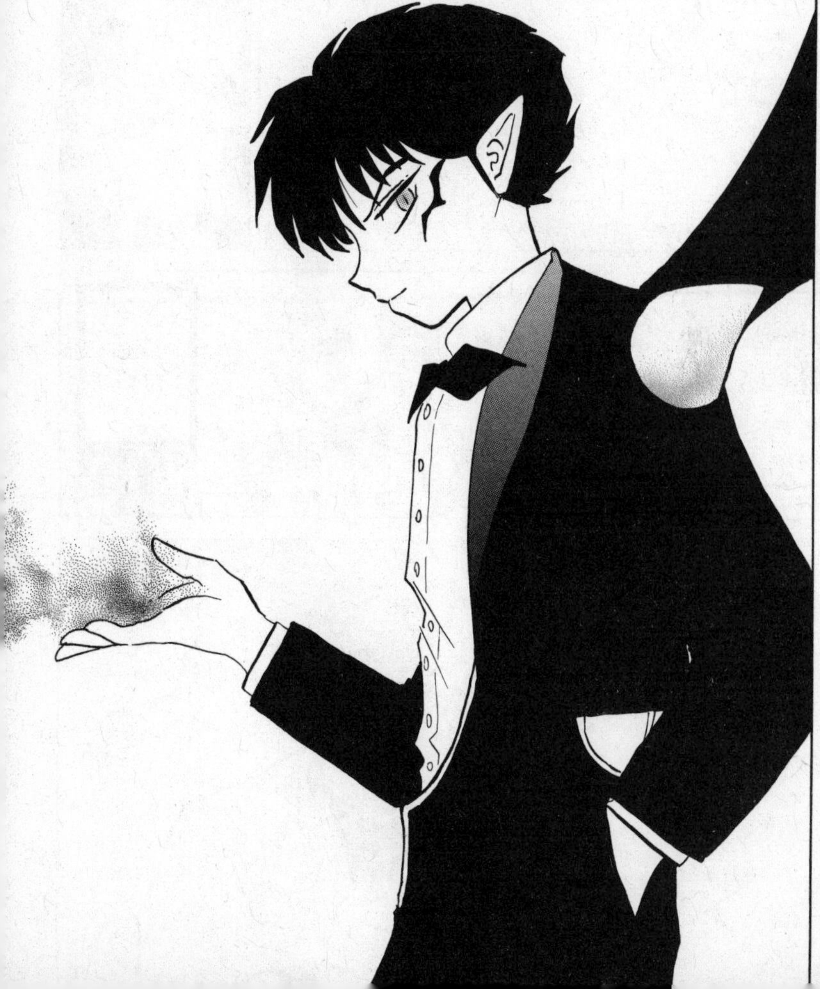

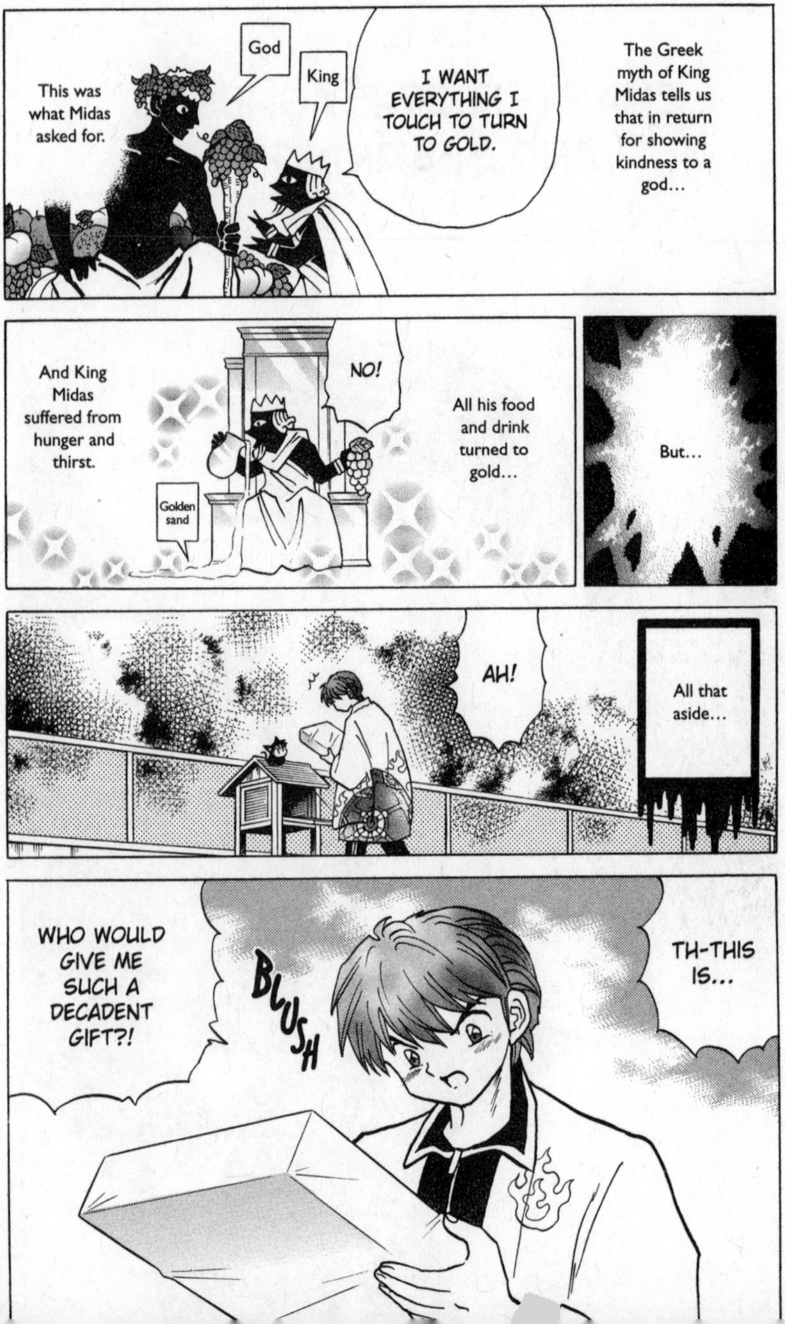
The Greek myth of King Midas tells us that in return for showing kindness to a god...
I WANT EVERYTHING I TOUCH TO TURN TO GOLD.
King
God
This was what Midas asked for.
But...
All his food and drink turned to gold...
NO!
Golden sand
And King Midas suffered from hunger and thirst.
All that aside...
AH!
TH-THIS IS...
BLUSH
WHO WOULD GIVE ME SUCH A DECADENT GIFT?!

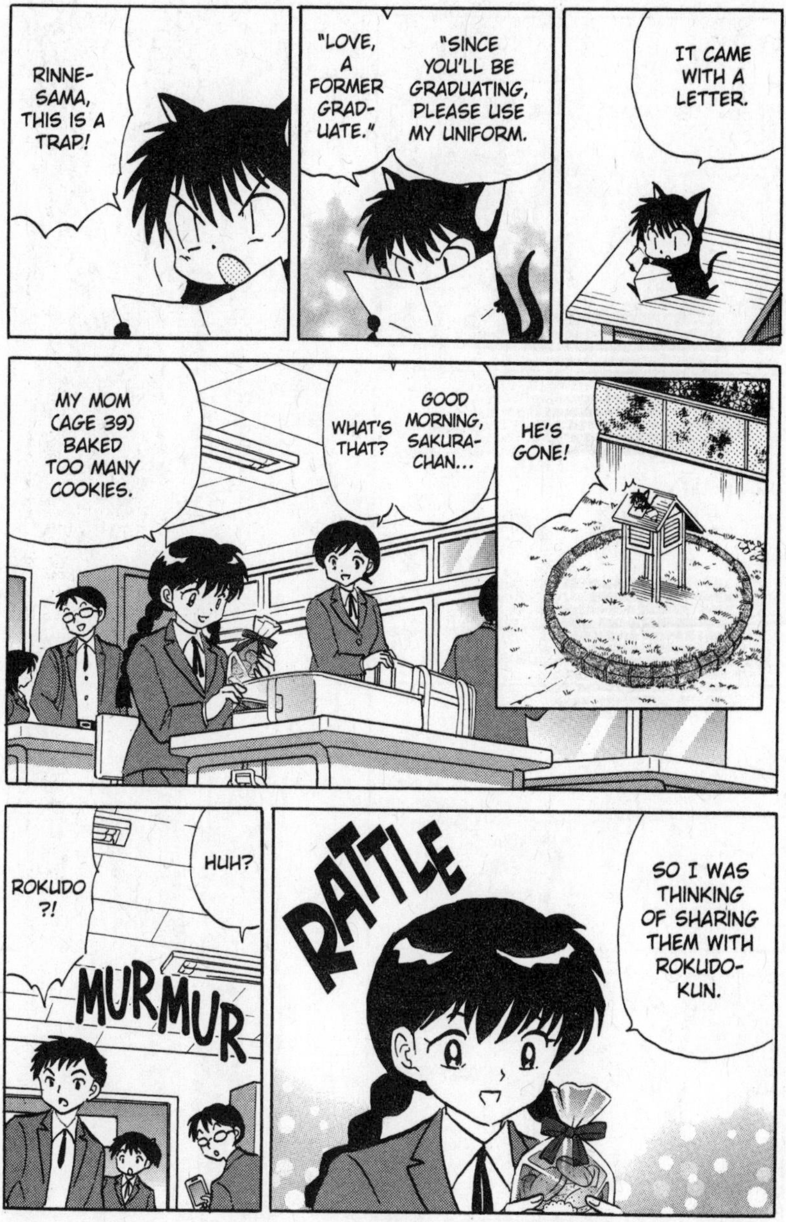
IT CAME WITH A LETTER.
"SINCE YOU'LL BE GRADUATING, PLEASE USE MY UNIFORM.
"LOVE, A FORMER GRADUATE."
RINNE-SAMA, THIS IS A TRAP!
HE'S GONE!
GOOD MORNING, SAKURA-CHAN...
WHAT'S THAT?
MY MOM (AGE 39) BAKED TOO MANY COOKIES.
SO I WAS THINKING OF SHARING THEM WITH ROKUDO-KUN.
RATTLE
HUH?
ROKUDO?!
MURMUR

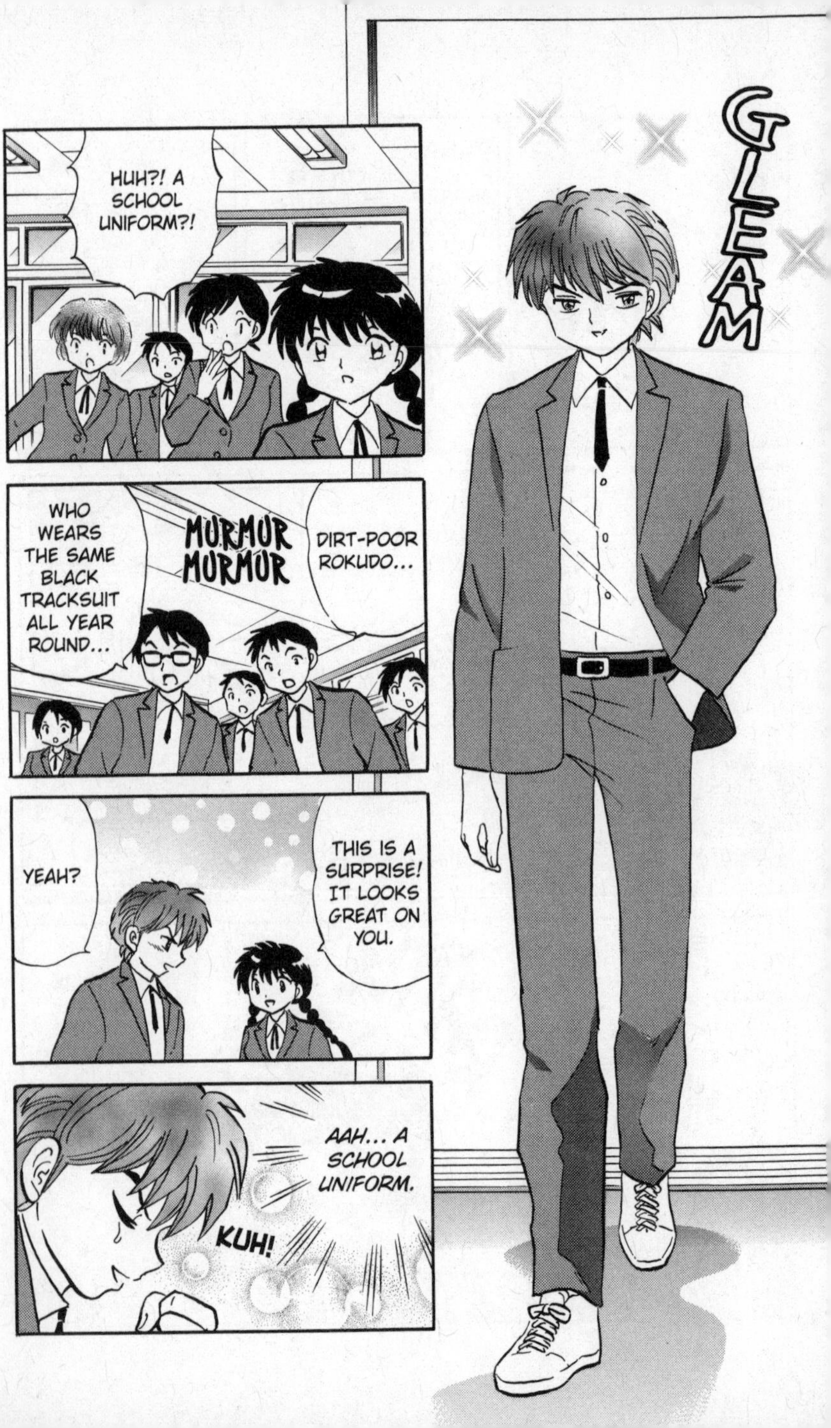
GLEAM
HUH?! A SCHOOL UNIFORM?!
DIRT-POOR ROKUDO...
MURMUR MURMUR
WHO WEARS THE SAME BLACK TRACKSUIT ALL YEAR ROUND...
THIS IS A SURPRISE! IT LOOKS GREAT ON YOU.
YEAH?
AAH... A SCHOOL UNIFORM.
KUH!

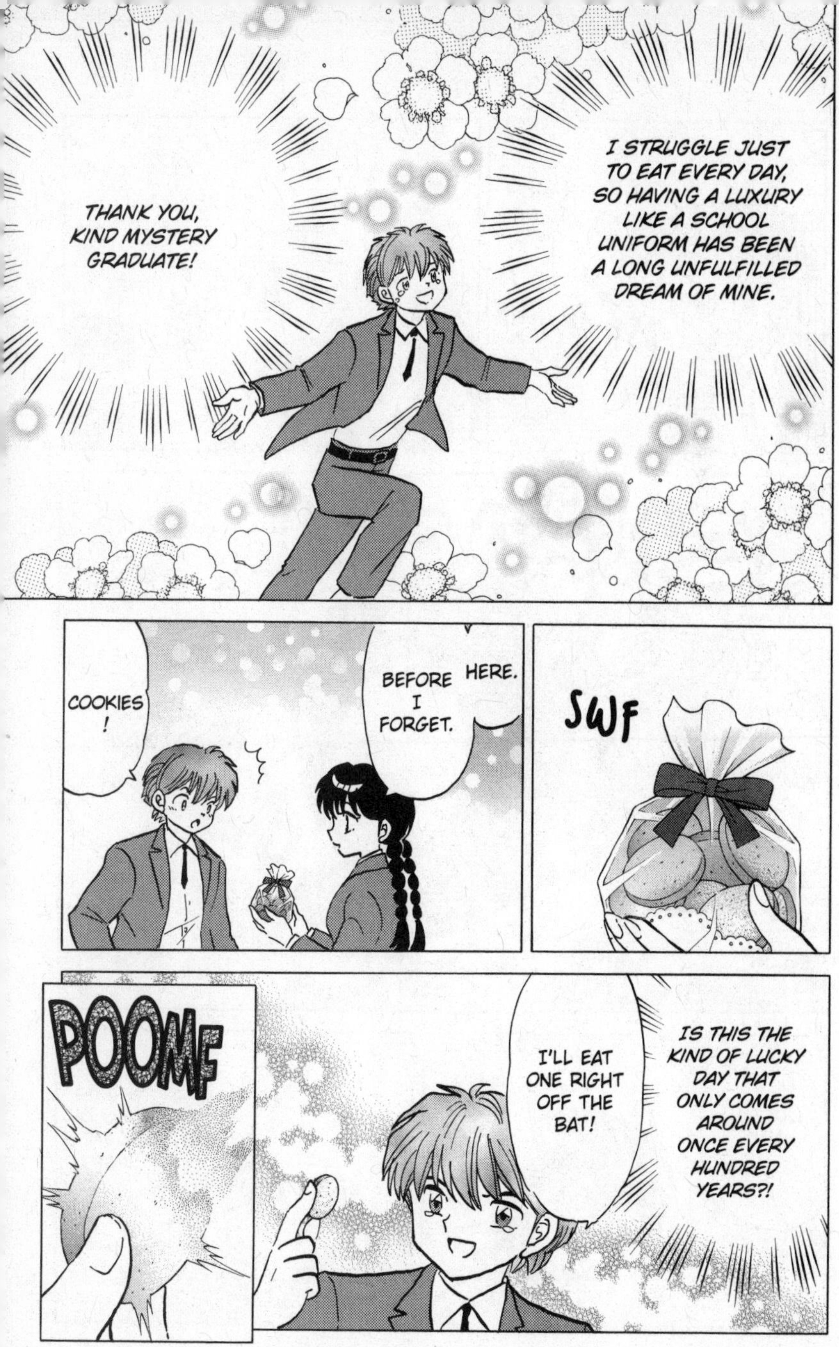
I STRUGGLE JUST TO EAT EVERY DAY, SO HAVING A LUXURY LIKE A SCHOOL UNIFORM HAS BEEN A LONG UNFULFILLED DREAM OF MINE.
THANK YOU, KIND MYSTERY GRADUATE!
SWF
HERE.
BEFORE I FORGET.
COOKIES!
IS THIS THE KIND OF LUCKY DAY THAT ONLY COMES AROUND ONCE EVERY HUNDRED YEARS?!
I'LL EAT ONE RIGHT OFF THE BAT!
POOMF

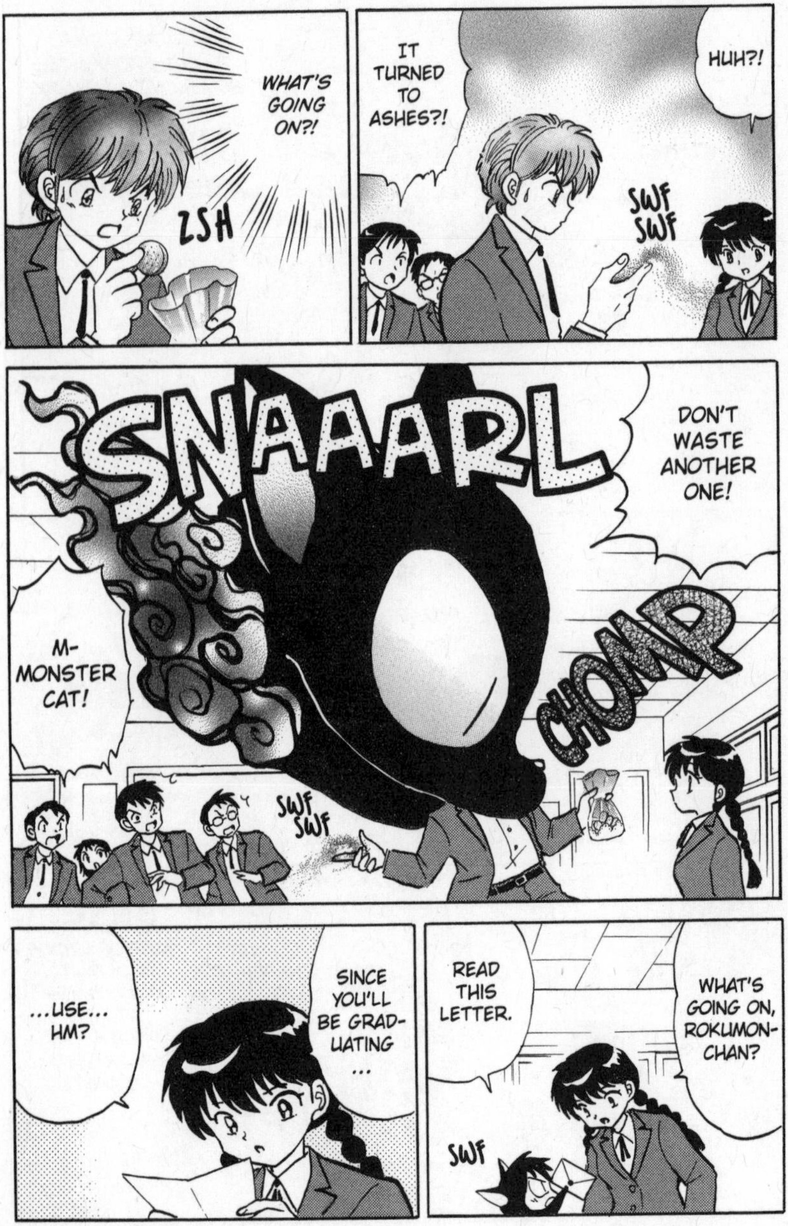
HUH?!
IT TURNED TO ASHES?!
SWF SWF
WHAT'S GOING ON?!
ZSH
SNAAARL
DON'T WASTE ANOTHER ONE!
CHOMP
M-MONSTER CAT!
SWF SWF
WHAT'S GOING ON, ROKUMON-CHAN?
READ THIS LETTER.
SWF
SINCE YOU'LL BE GRAD-UATING ...
...USE... HM?

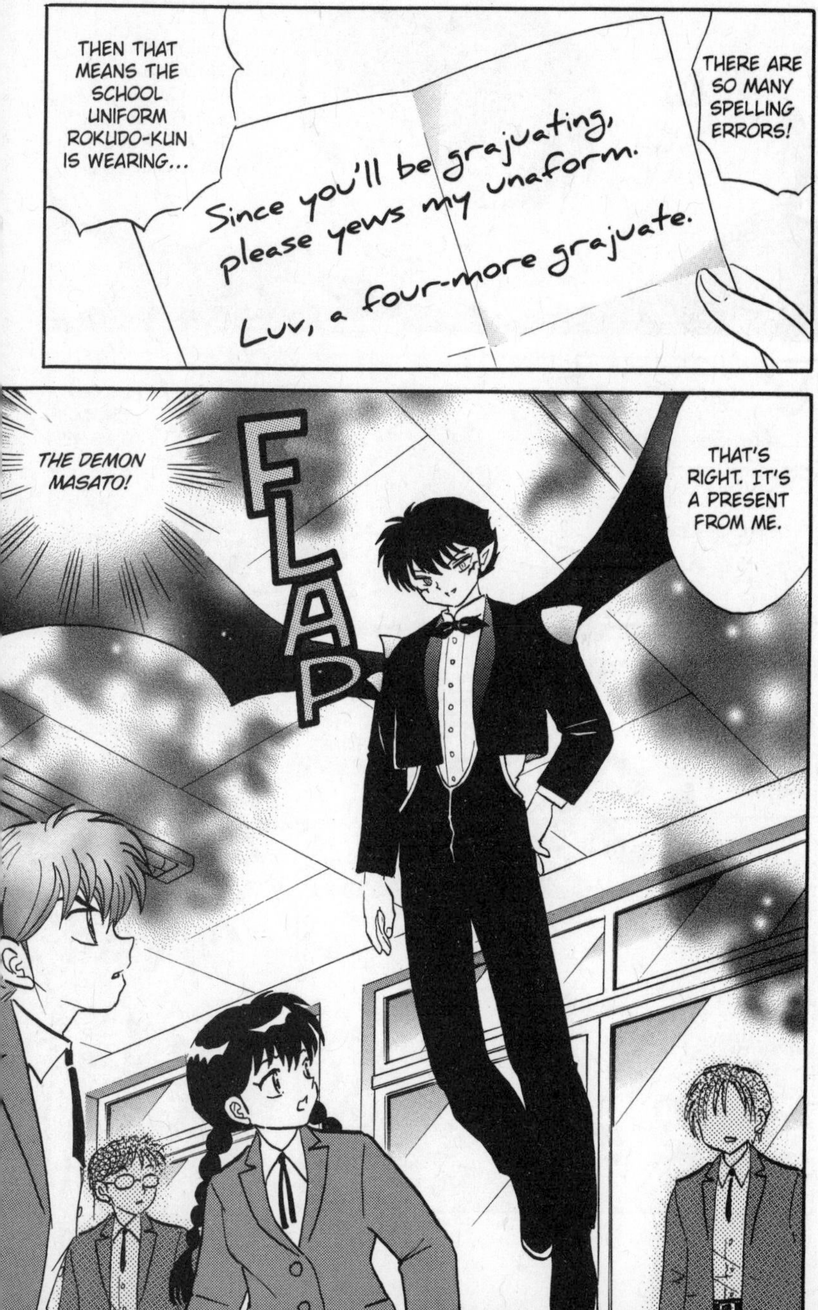
Since you'll be grajuating, please yews my unaform.
Luv, a four-more grajuate.
THERE ARE SO MANY SPELLING ERRORS!
THEN THAT MEANS THE SCHOOL UNIFORM ROKUDO-KUN IS WEARING...
THAT'S RIGHT. IT'S A PRESENT FROM ME.
FLAP
THE DEMON MASATO!

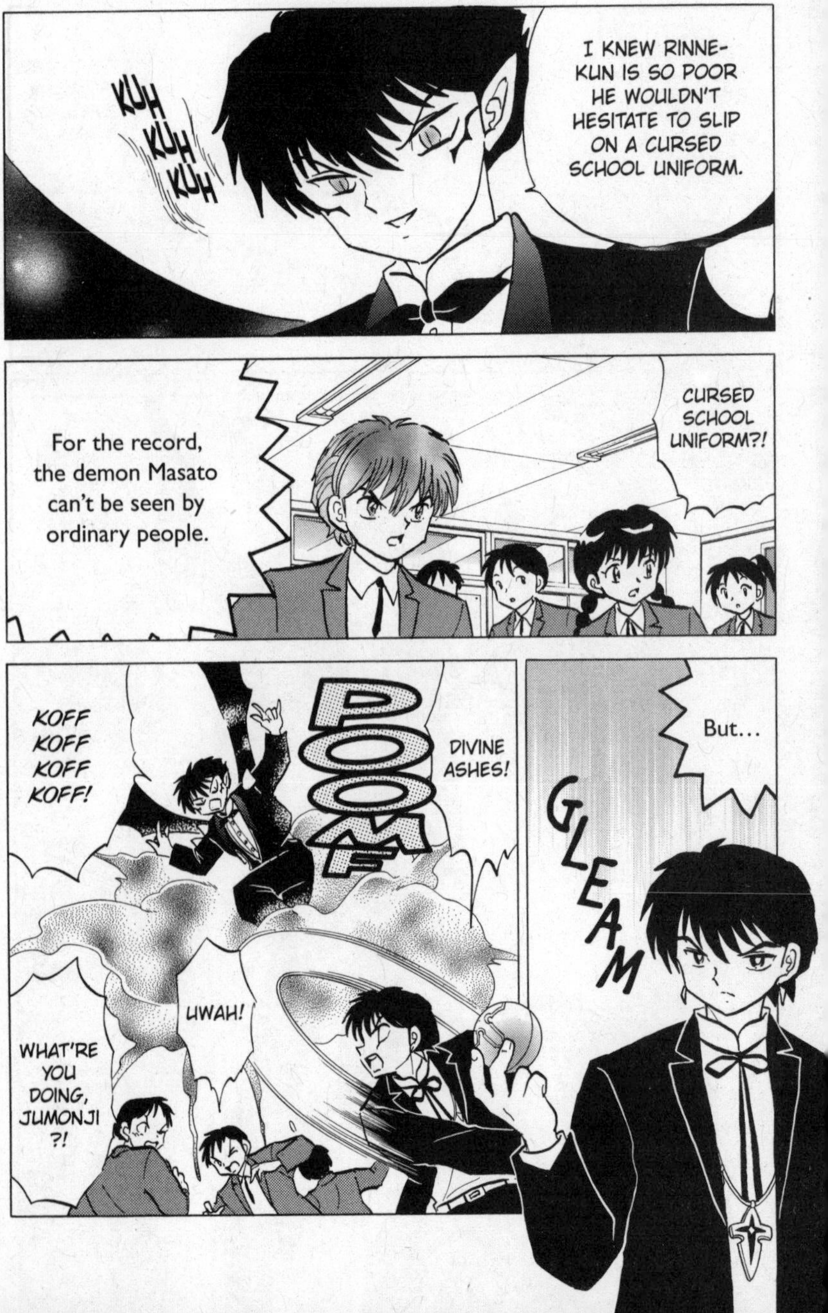
I KNEW RINNE-KUN IS SO POOR HE WOULDN'T HESITATE TO SLIP ON A CURSED SCHOOL UNIFORM.
KUH KUH KUH
CURSED SCHOOL UNIFORM?!
For the record, the demon Masato can't be seen by ordinary people.
But…
GLEAM
DIVINE ASHES!
POOF
KOFF KOFF KOFF KOFF!
UWAH!
WHAT'RE YOU DOING, JUMONJI?!

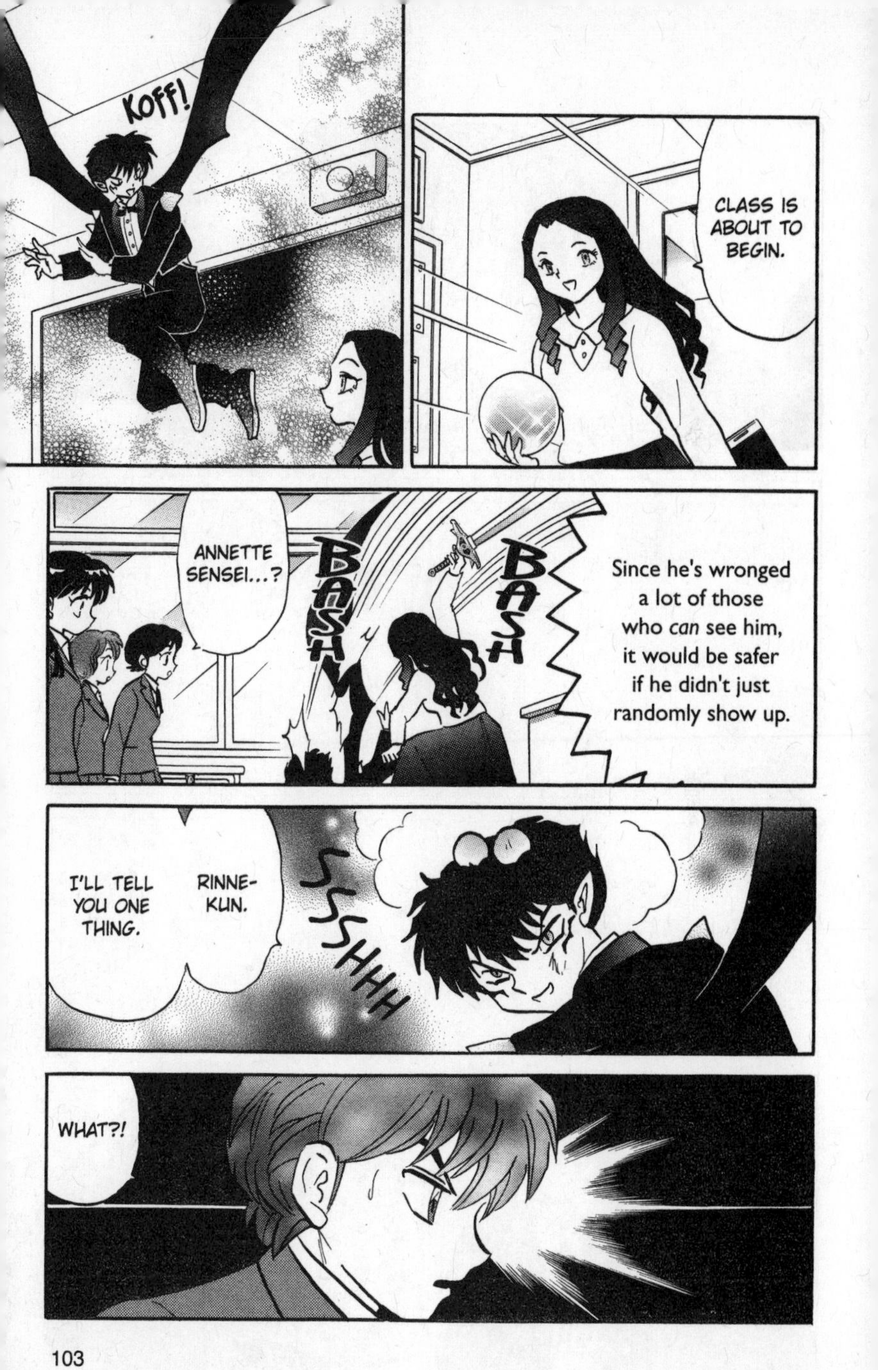
CLASS IS ABOUT TO BEGIN.
KOFF!
Since he's wronged a lot of those who *can* see him, it would be safer if he didn't just randomly show up.
BASH
BASH
ANNETTE SENSEI...?
RINNE-KUN.
I'LL TELL YOU ONE THING.
SSSHHHH
WHAT?!

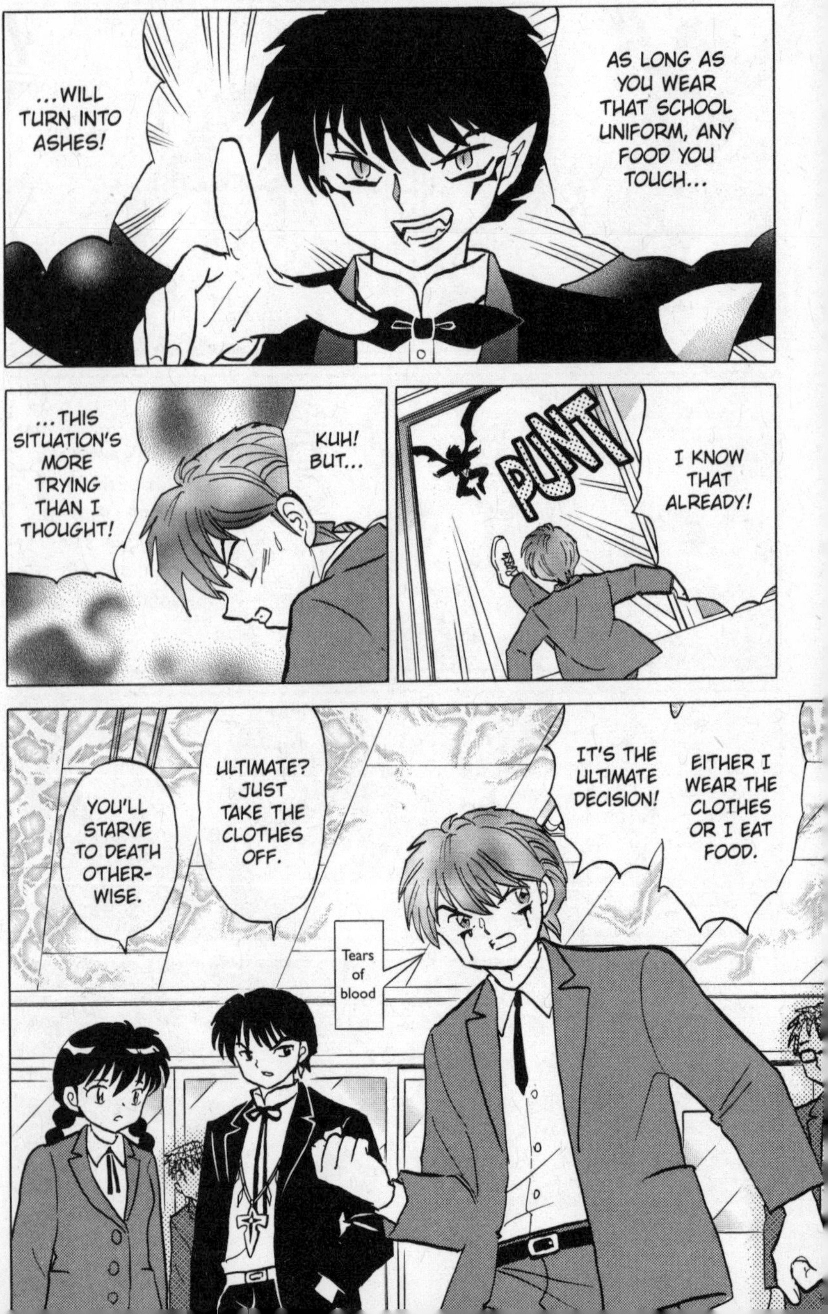
AS LONG AS YOU WEAR THAT SCHOOL UNIFORM, ANY FOOD YOU TOUCH...
...WILL TURN INTO ASHES!
PUNT
I KNOW THAT ALREADY!
KUH! BUT...
...THIS SITUATION'S MORE TRYING THAN I THOUGHT!
EITHER I WEAR THE CLOTHES OR I EAT FOOD.
IT'S THE ULTIMATE DECISION!
ULTIMATE? JUST TAKE THE CLOTHES OFF.
YOU'LL STARVE TO DEATH OTHERWISE.
Tears of blood

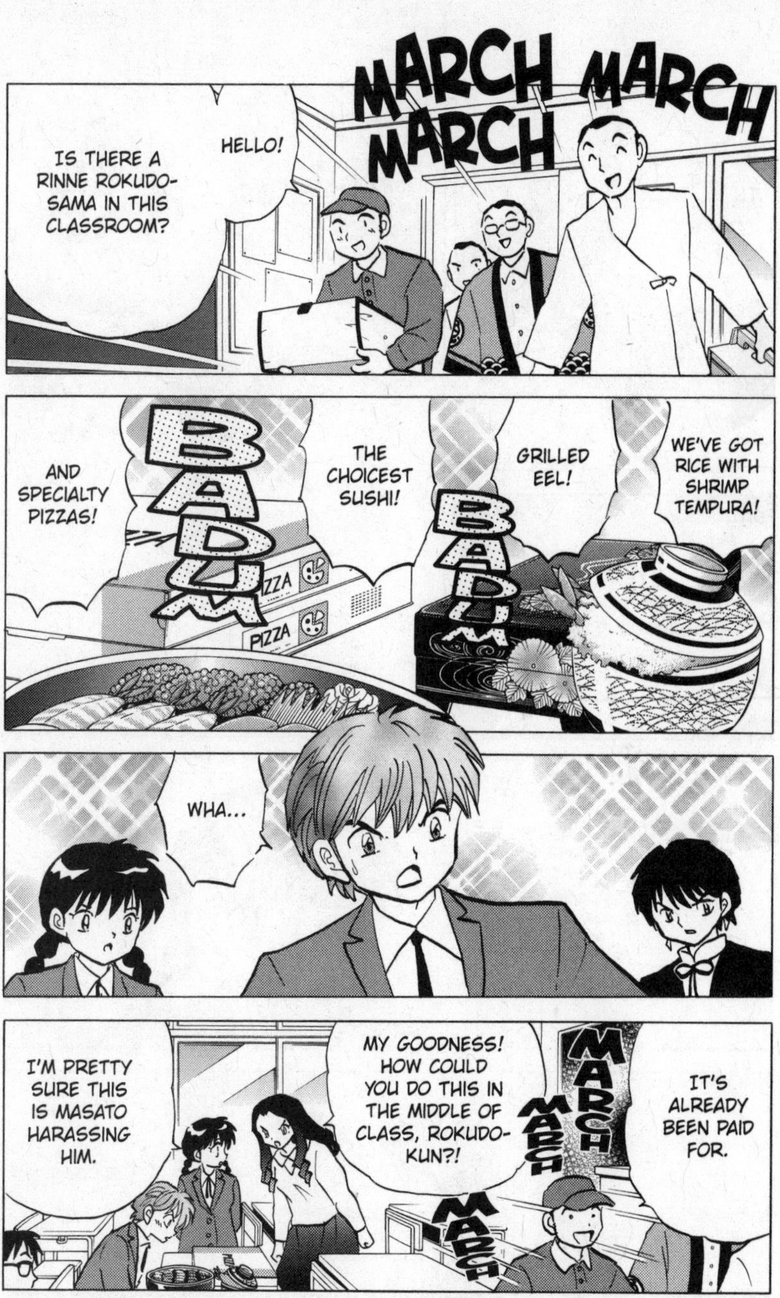
MARCH MARCH
MARCH
HELLO!
IS THERE A RINNE ROKUDO-SAMA IN THIS CLASSROOM?
WE'VE GOT RICE WITH SHRIMP TEMPURA!
GRILLED EEL!
BADUM
THE CHOICEST SUSHI!
BADUM
PIZZA
PIZZA
AND SPECIALTY PIZZAS!
WHA...
IT'S ALREADY BEEN PAID FOR.
MARCH
MARCH
MARCH
MY GOODNESS! HOW COULD YOU DO THIS IN THE MIDDLE OF CLASS, ROKUDO-KUN?!
I'M PRETTY SURE THIS IS MASATO HARASSING HIM.

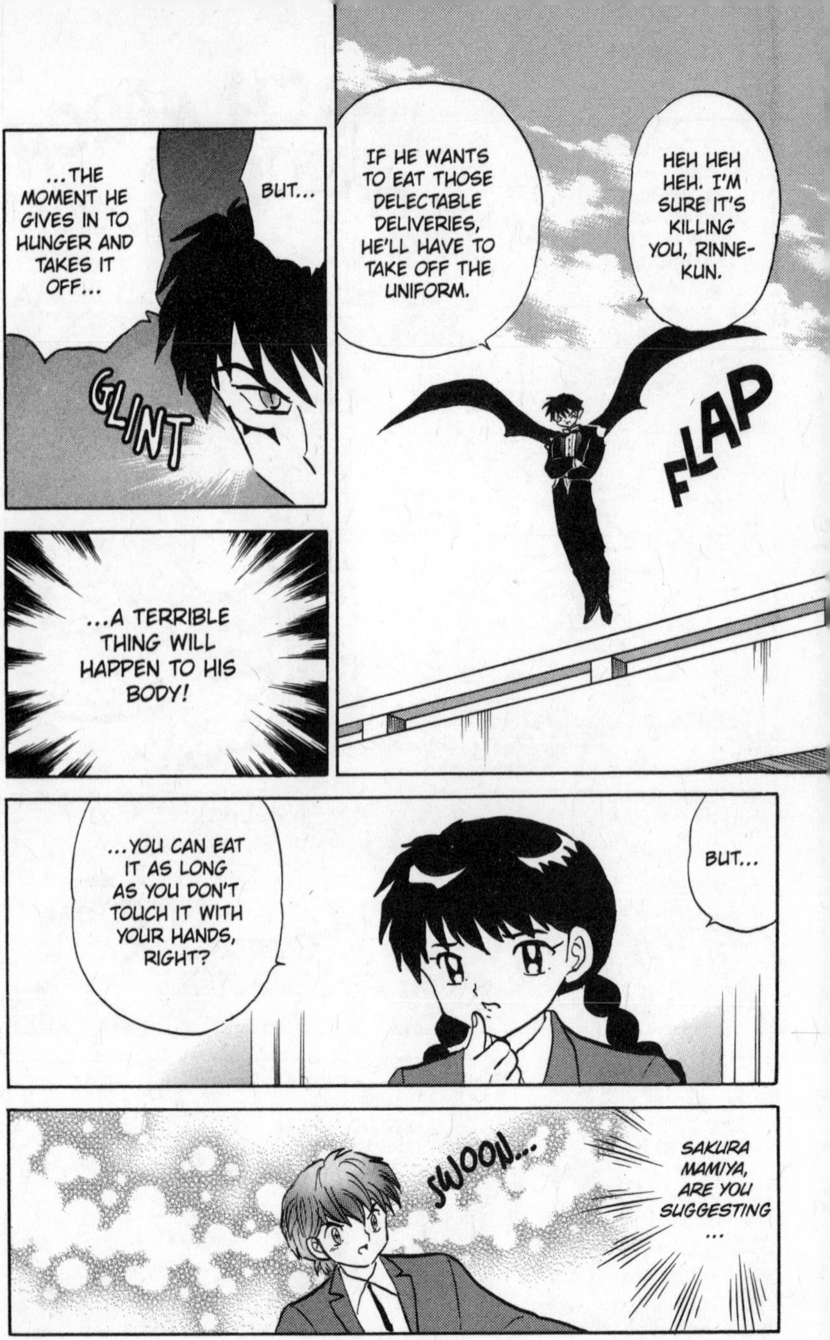
HEH HEH HEH. I'M SURE IT'S KILLING YOU, RINNE-KUN.
IF HE WANTS TO EAT THOSE DELECTABLE DELIVERIES, HE'LL HAVE TO TAKE OFF THE UNIFORM.
FLAP
BUT...
...THE MOMENT HE GIVES IN TO HUNGER AND TAKES IT OFF...
GLINT
...A TERRIBLE THING WILL HAPPEN TO HIS BODY!
BUT...
...YOU CAN EAT IT AS LONG AS YOU DON'T TOUCH IT WITH YOUR HANDS, RIGHT?
SAKURA MAMIYA, ARE YOU SUGGESTING...
SWOON...

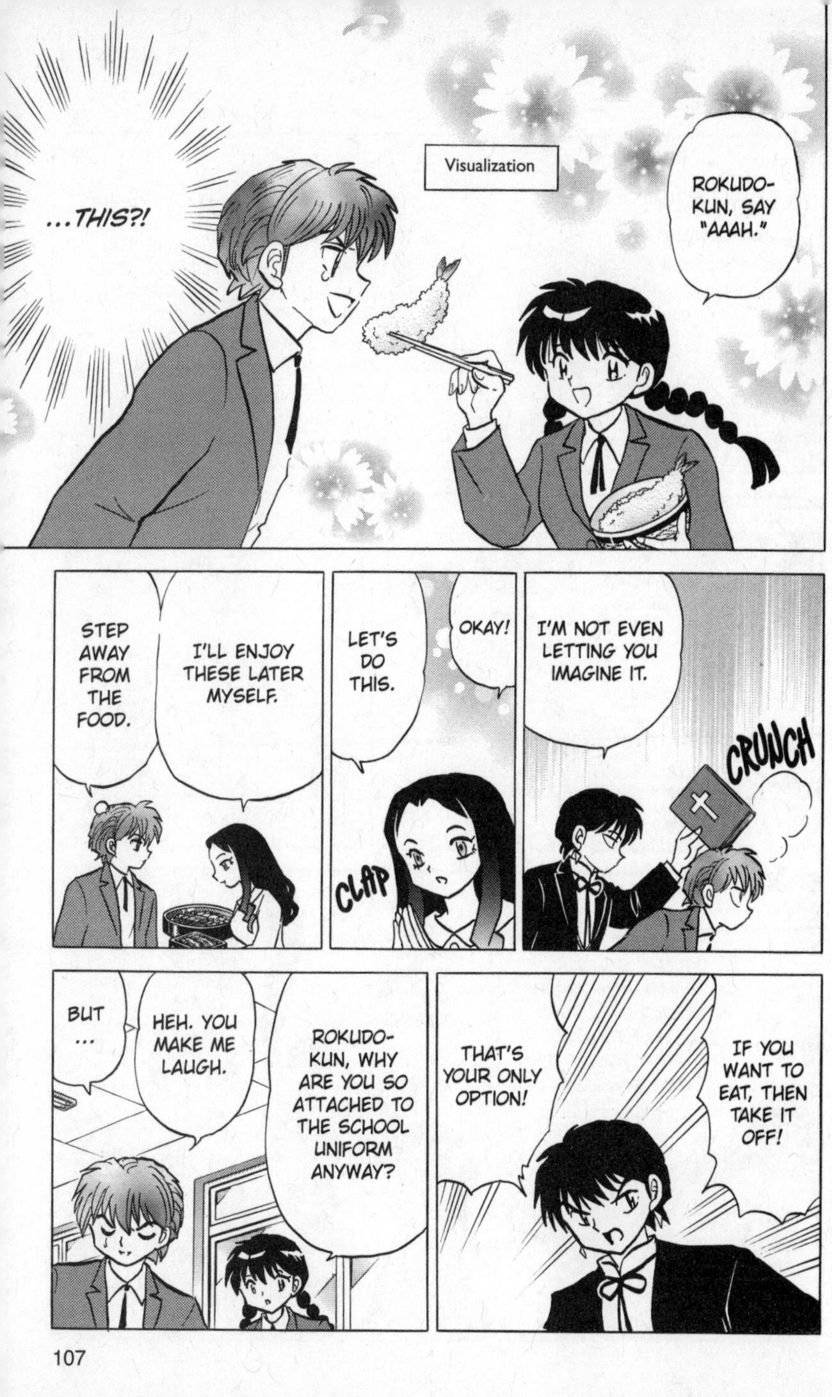
ROKUDO-KUN, SAY "AAAH."
Visualization
...THIS?!
I'M NOT EVEN LETTING YOU IMAGINE IT.
CRUNCH
OKAY!
LET'S DO THIS.
CLAP
I'LL ENJOY THESE LATER MYSELF.
STEP AWAY FROM THE FOOD.
IF YOU WANT TO EAT, THEN TAKE IT OFF!
THAT'S YOUR ONLY OPTION!
ROKUDO-KUN, WHY ARE YOU SO ATTACHED TO THE SCHOOL UNIFORM ANYWAY?
HEH. YOU MAKE ME LAUGH.
BUT ...

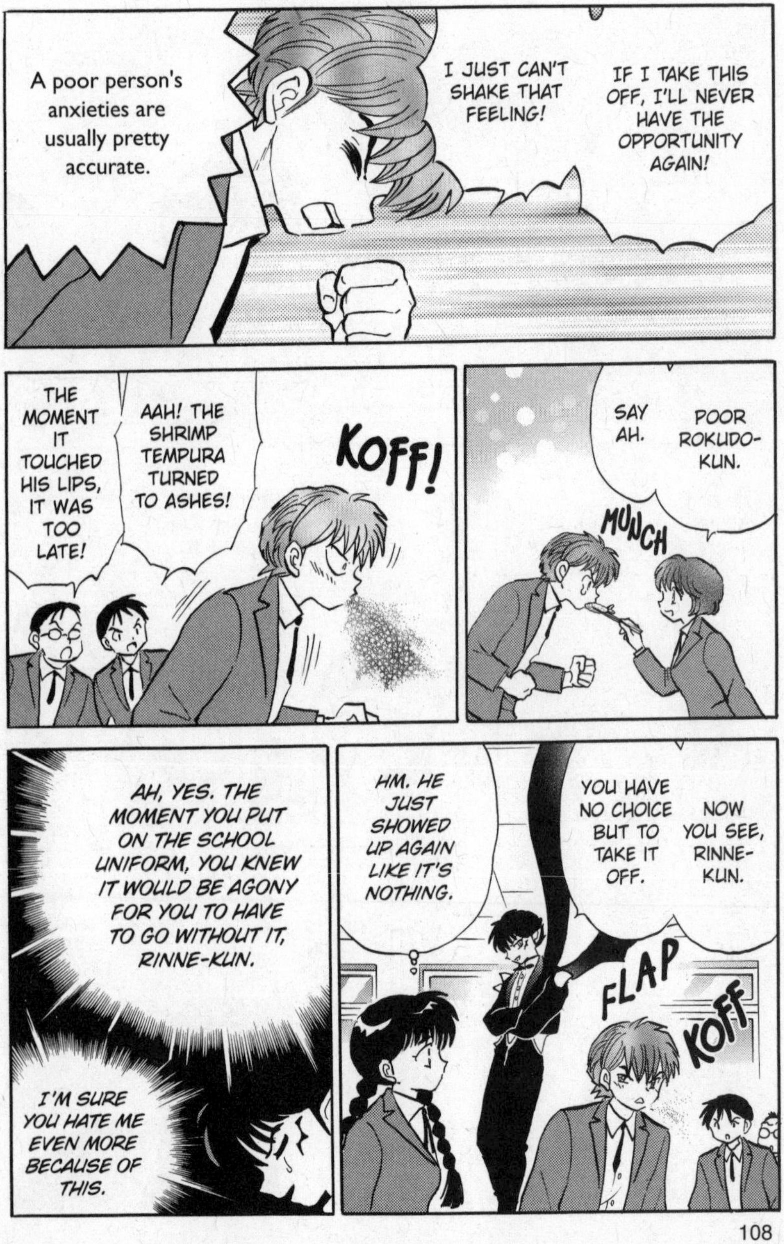
IF I TAKE THIS OFF, I'LL NEVER HAVE THE OPPORTUNITY AGAIN!
I JUST CAN'T SHAKE THAT FEELING!
A poor person's anxieties are usually pretty accurate.
POOR ROKUDO-KUN.
SAY AH.
MUNCH
KOFF!
AAH! THE SHRIMP TEMPURA TURNED TO ASHES!
THE MOMENT IT TOUCHED HIS LIPS, IT WAS TOO LATE!
NOW YOU SEE, RINNE-KUN.
YOU HAVE NO CHOICE BUT TO TAKE IT OFF.
HM. HE JUST SHOWED UP AGAIN LIKE IT'S NOTHING.
FLAP
KOFF
AH, YES. THE MOMENT YOU PUT ON THE SCHOOL UNIFORM, YOU KNEW IT WOULD BE AGONY FOR YOU TO HAVE TO GO WITHOUT IT, RINNE-KUN.
I'M SURE YOU HATE ME EVEN MORE BECAUSE OF THIS.

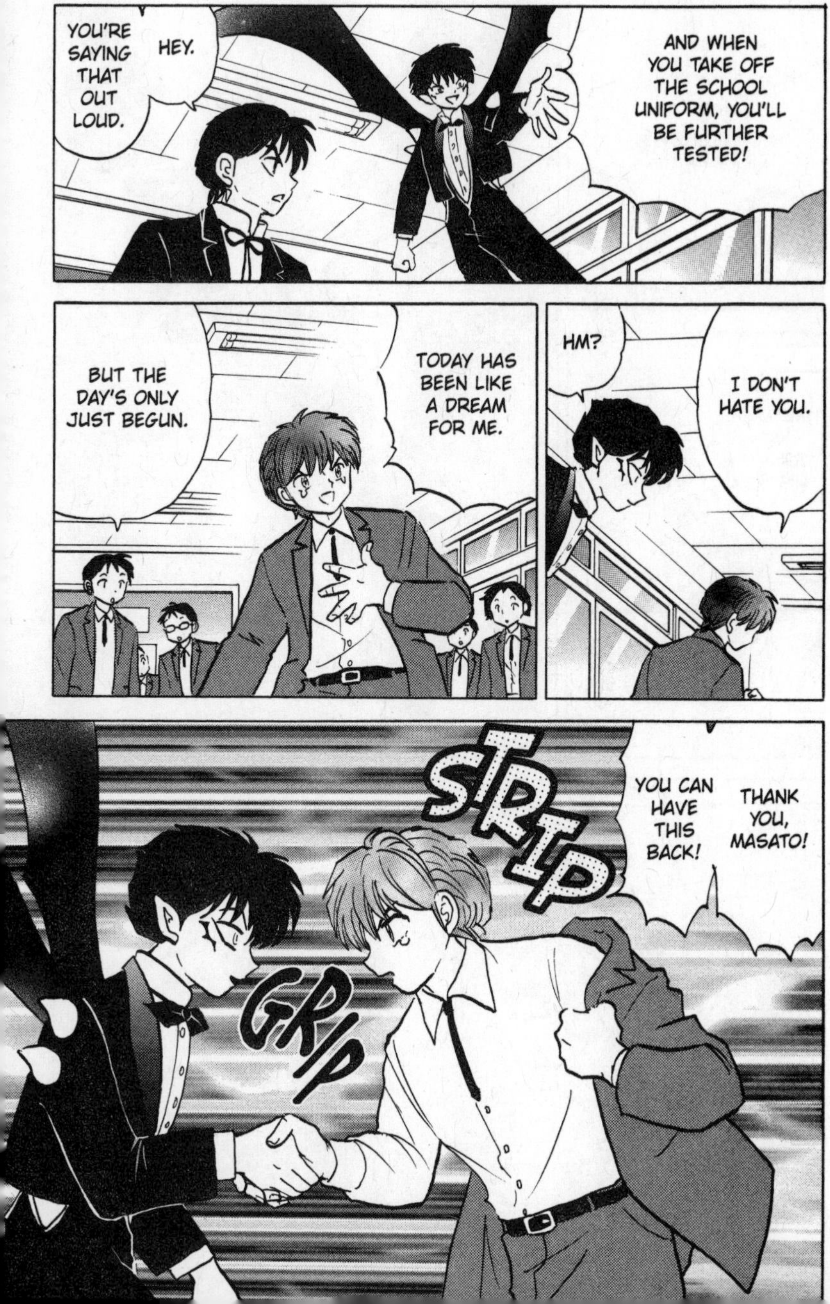
AND WHEN YOU TAKE OFF THE SCHOOL UNIFORM, YOU'LL BE FURTHER TESTED!
HEY.
YOU'RE SAYING THAT OUT LOUD.
I DON'T HATE YOU.
HM?
TODAY HAS BEEN LIKE A DREAM FOR ME.
BUT THE DAY'S ONLY JUST BEGUN.
THANK YOU, MASATO!
YOU CAN HAVE THIS BACK!
STRIP
GRIP

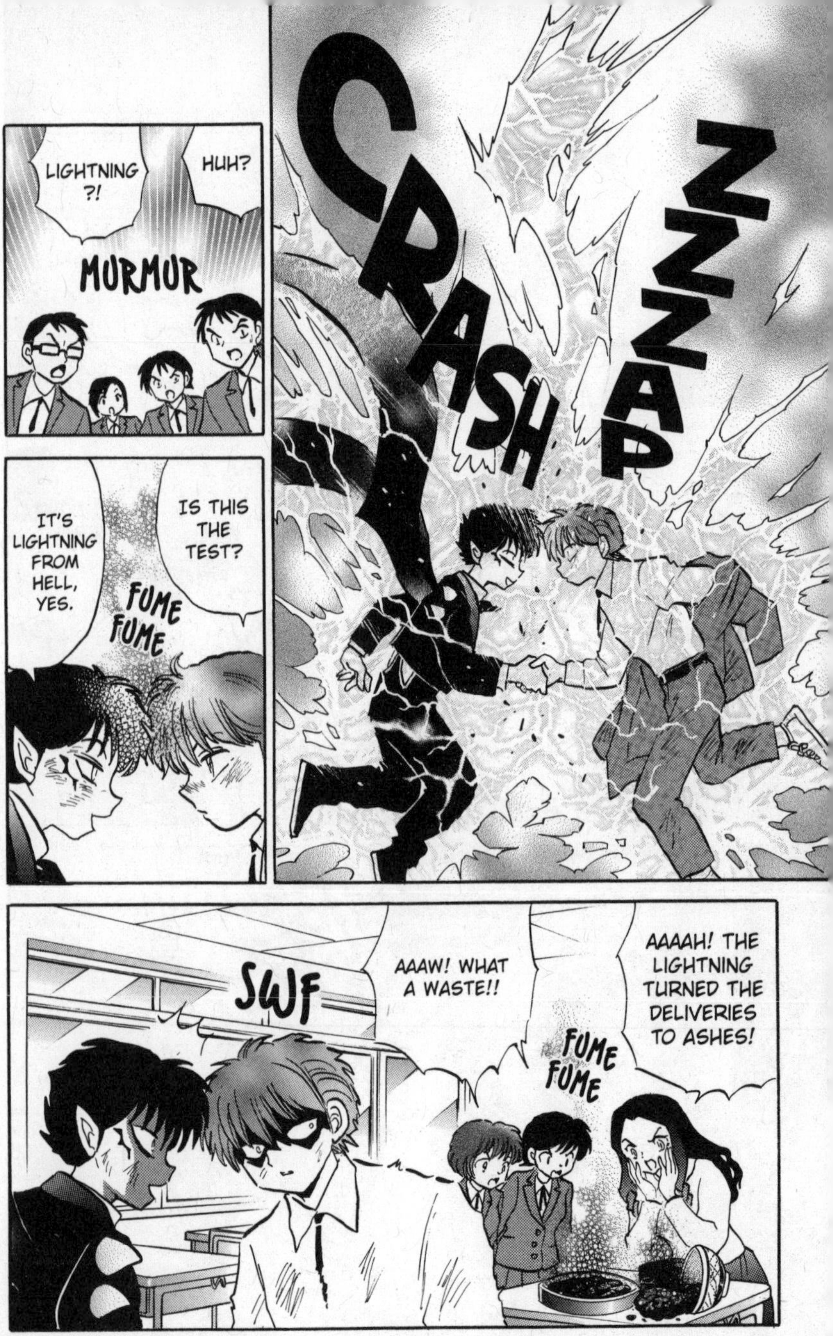
ZZZAP
CRASH
HUH?
LIGHTNING ?!
MURMUR
IS THIS THE TEST?
IT'S LIGHTNING FROM HELL, YES.
FUME FUME
AAAAH! THE LIGHTNING TURNED THE DELIVERIES TO ASHES!
AAAW! WHAT A WASTE!!
FUME FUME
SWF

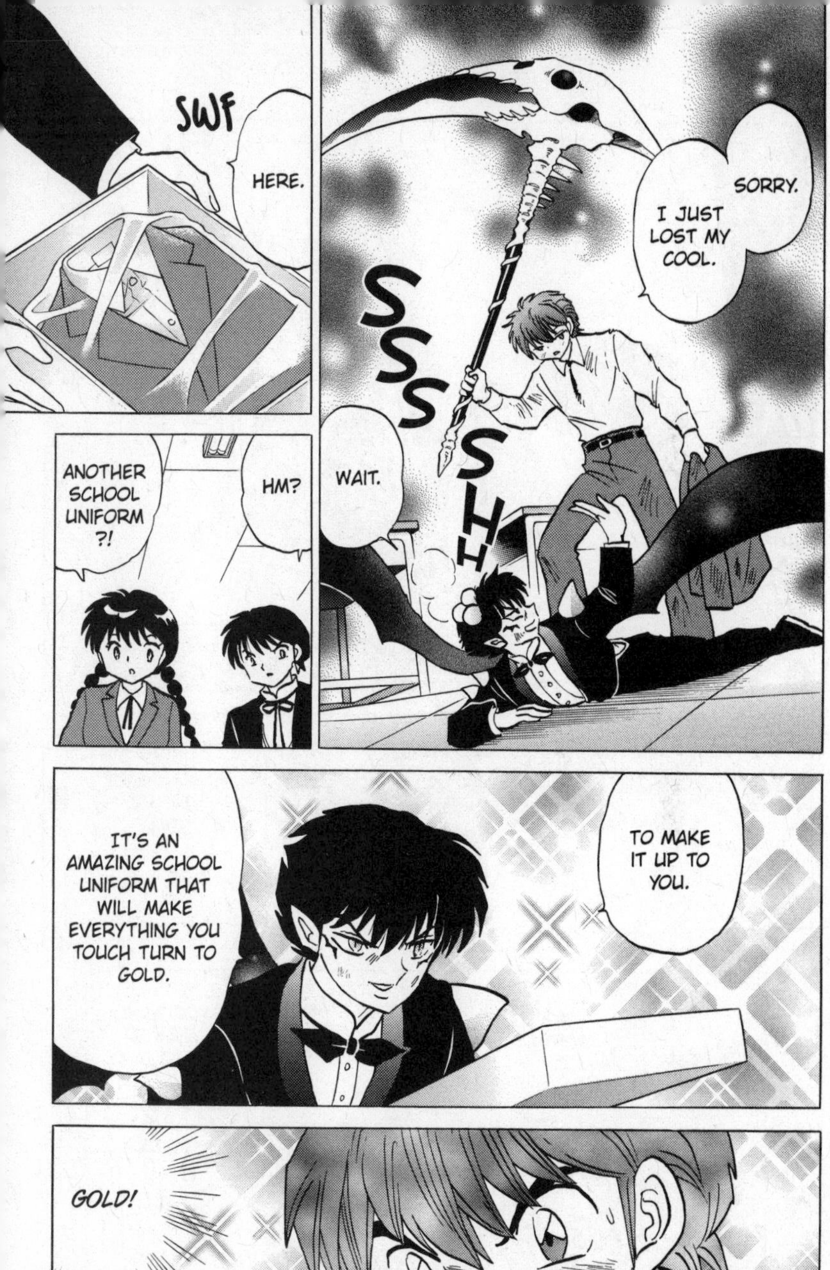
SORRY.
I JUST LOST MY COOL.
SSSSHH
WAIT.
SWF
HERE.
HM?
ANOTHER SCHOOL UNIFORM ?!
TO MAKE IT UP TO YOU.
IT'S AN AMAZING SCHOOL UNIFORM THAT WILL MAKE EVERYTHING YOU TOUCH TURN TO GOLD.
GOLD!

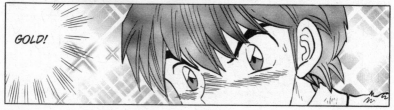

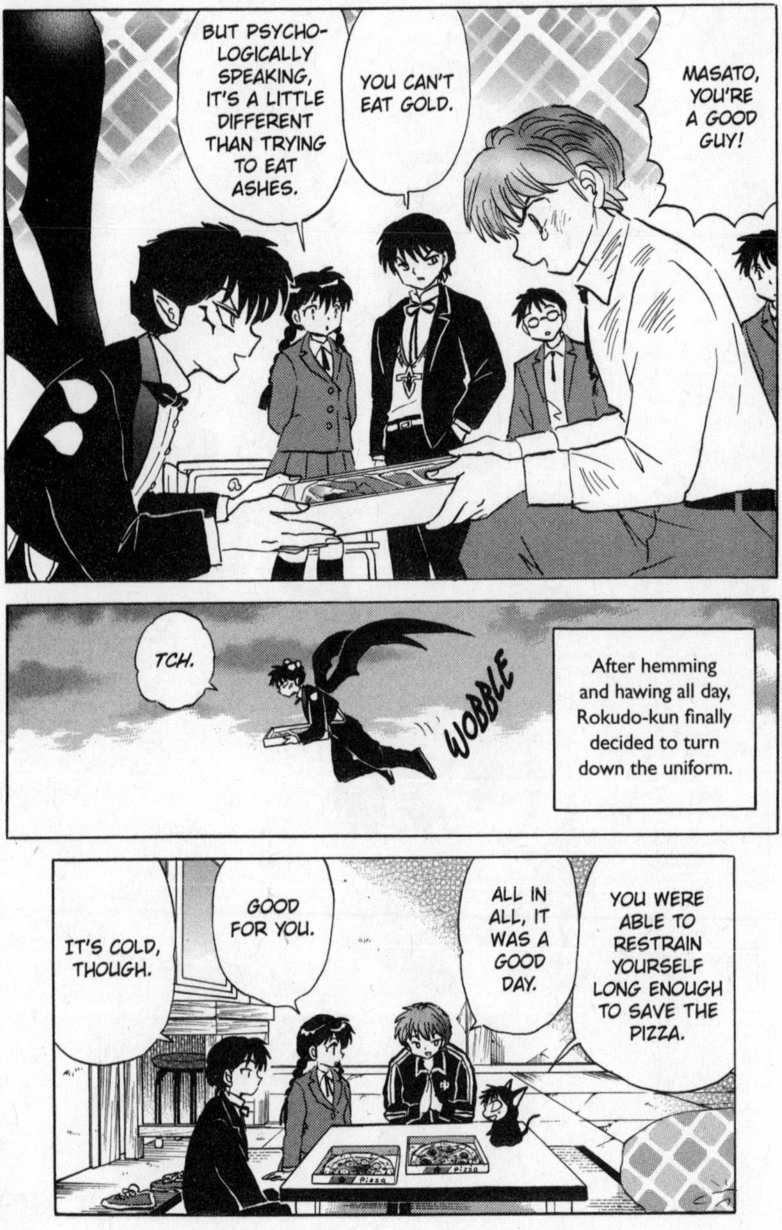
MASATO, YOU'RE A GOOD GUY!
YOU CAN'T EAT GOLD.
BUT PSYCHO-LOGICALLY SPEAKING, IT'S A LITTLE DIFFERENT THAN TRYING TO EAT ASHES.
After hemming and hawing all day, Rokudo-kun finally decided to turn down the uniform.
WOBBLE
TCH.
YOU WERE ABLE TO RESTRAIN YOURSELF LONG ENOUGH TO SAVE THE PIZZA.
ALL IN ALL, IT WAS A GOOD DAY.
GOOD FOR YOU.
IT'S COLD, THOUGH.

CHAPTER 275: CINDERELLA DATE

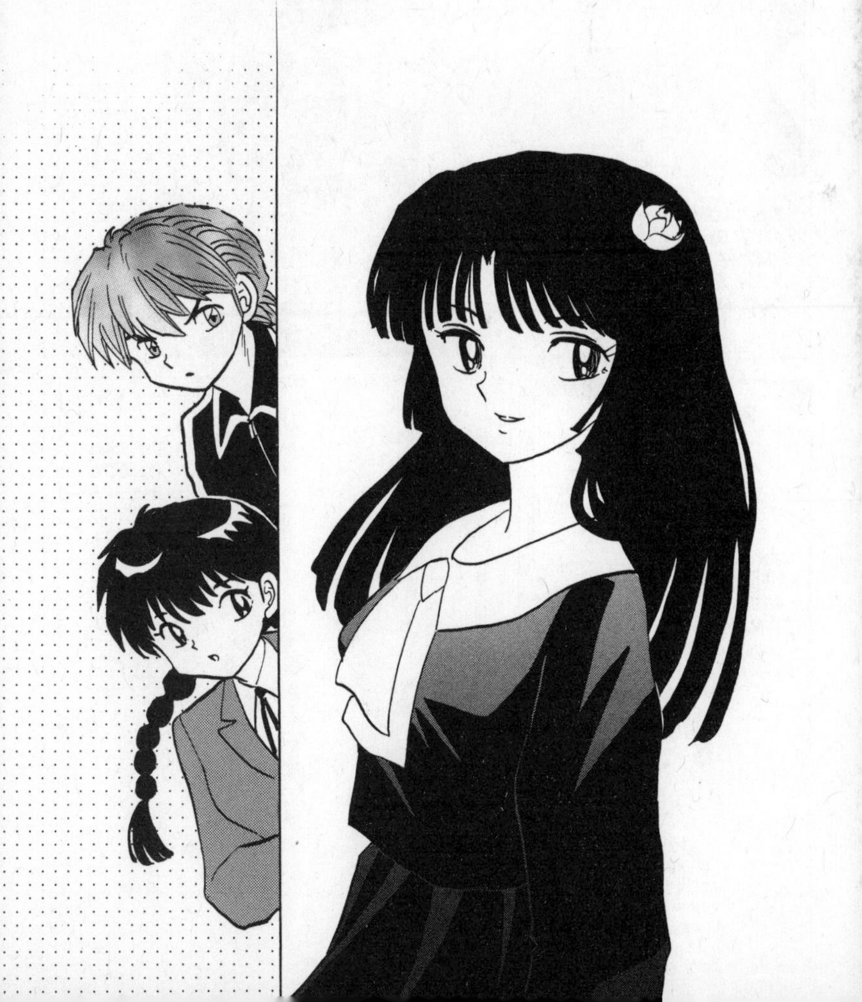

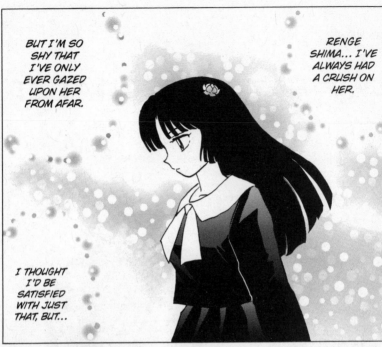

RENGE SHIMA... I'VE ALWAYS HAD A CRUSH ON HER.
BUT I'M SO SHY THAT I'VE ONLY EVER GAZED UPON HER FROM AFAR.
I THOUGHT I'D BE SATISFIED WITH JUST THAT, BUT...
THE CALL WE GOT WASN'T FOR ANY SUPER-NATURAL ACTIVITY.
WE'LL BE MOVING DUE TO MY PARENTS' WORK, SO I'LL BE GOING TO A NEW SCHOOL.
Junya Uchiki
Second-year, Class 3
ROKUDO-KUN. MAMIYA-SAN.
YOU'RE FRIENDS WITH SHIMA-SAN, RIGHT?

In Japanese, Uchiki is pronounced the same as the word "shy."

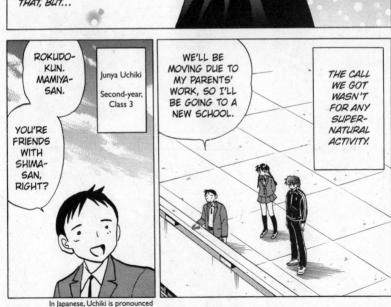

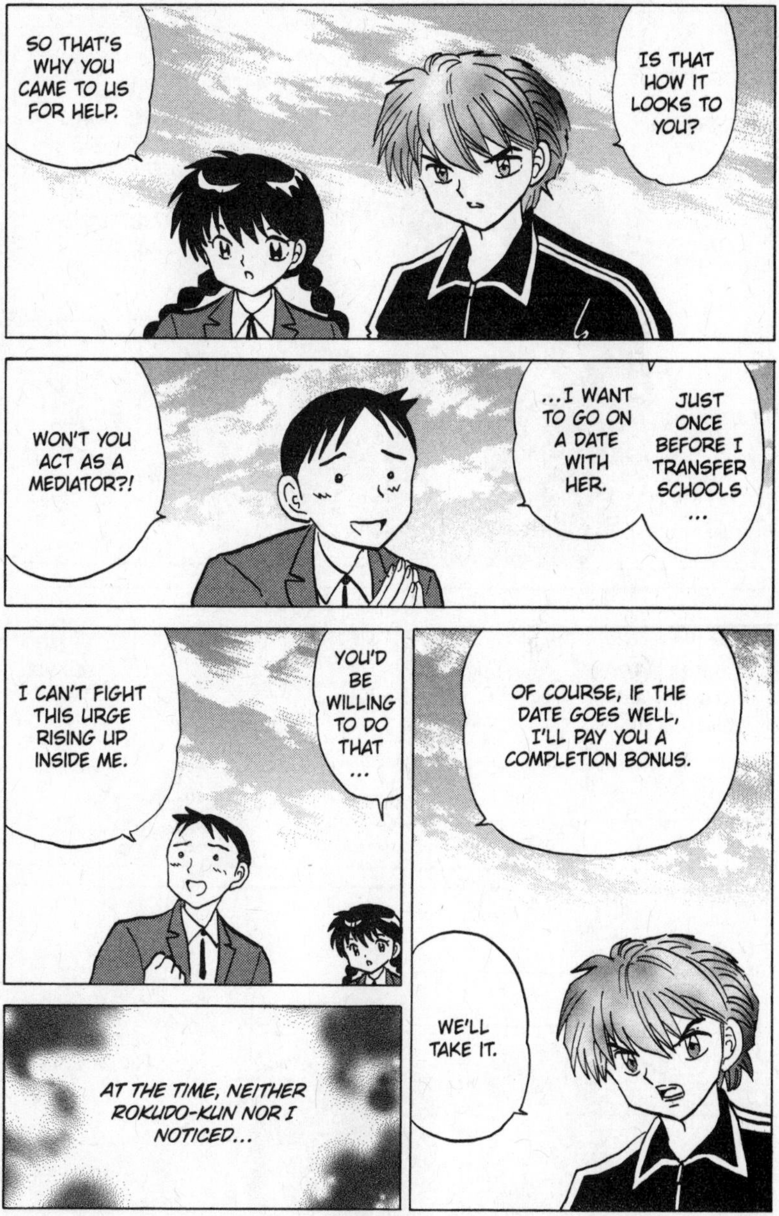
IS THAT HOW IT LOOKS TO YOU?
SO THAT'S WHY YOU CAME TO US FOR HELP.
JUST ONCE BEFORE I TRANSFER SCHOOLS ...
...I WANT TO GO ON A DATE WITH HER.
WON'T YOU ACT AS A MEDIATOR?!
OF COURSE, IF THE DATE GOES WELL, I'LL PAY YOU A COMPLETION BONUS.
WE'LL TAKE IT.
YOU'D BE WILLING TO DO THAT ...
I CAN'T FIGHT THIS URGE RISING UP INSIDE ME.
AT THE TIME, NEITHER ROKUDO-KUN NOR I NOTICED...

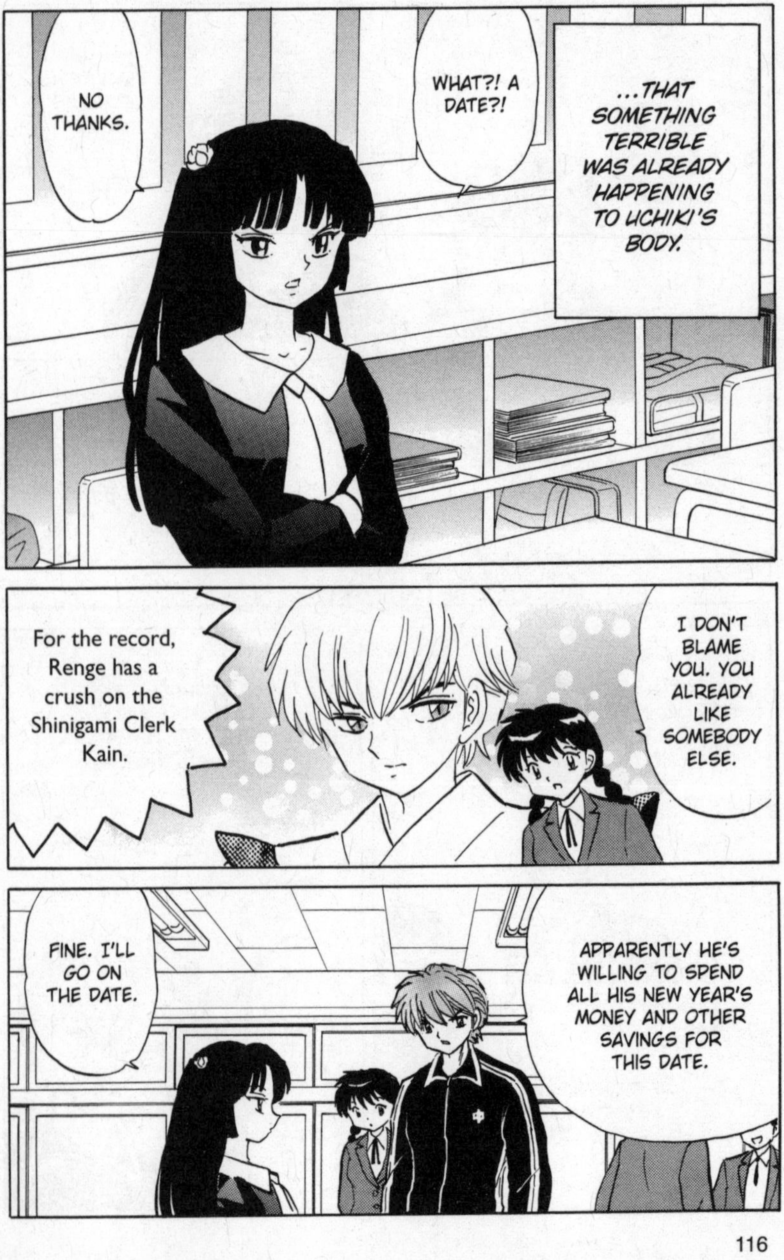
...THAT SOMETHING TERRIBLE WAS ALREADY HAPPENING TO UCHIKI'S BODY.
WHAT?! A DATE?!
NO THANKS.
I DON'T BLAME YOU. YOU ALREADY LIKE SOMEBODY ELSE.
For the record, Renge has a crush on the Shinigami Clerk Kain.
APPARENTLY HE'S WILLING TO SPEND ALL HIS NEW YEAR'S MONEY AND OTHER SAVINGS FOR THIS DATE.
FINE. I'LL GO ON THE DATE.

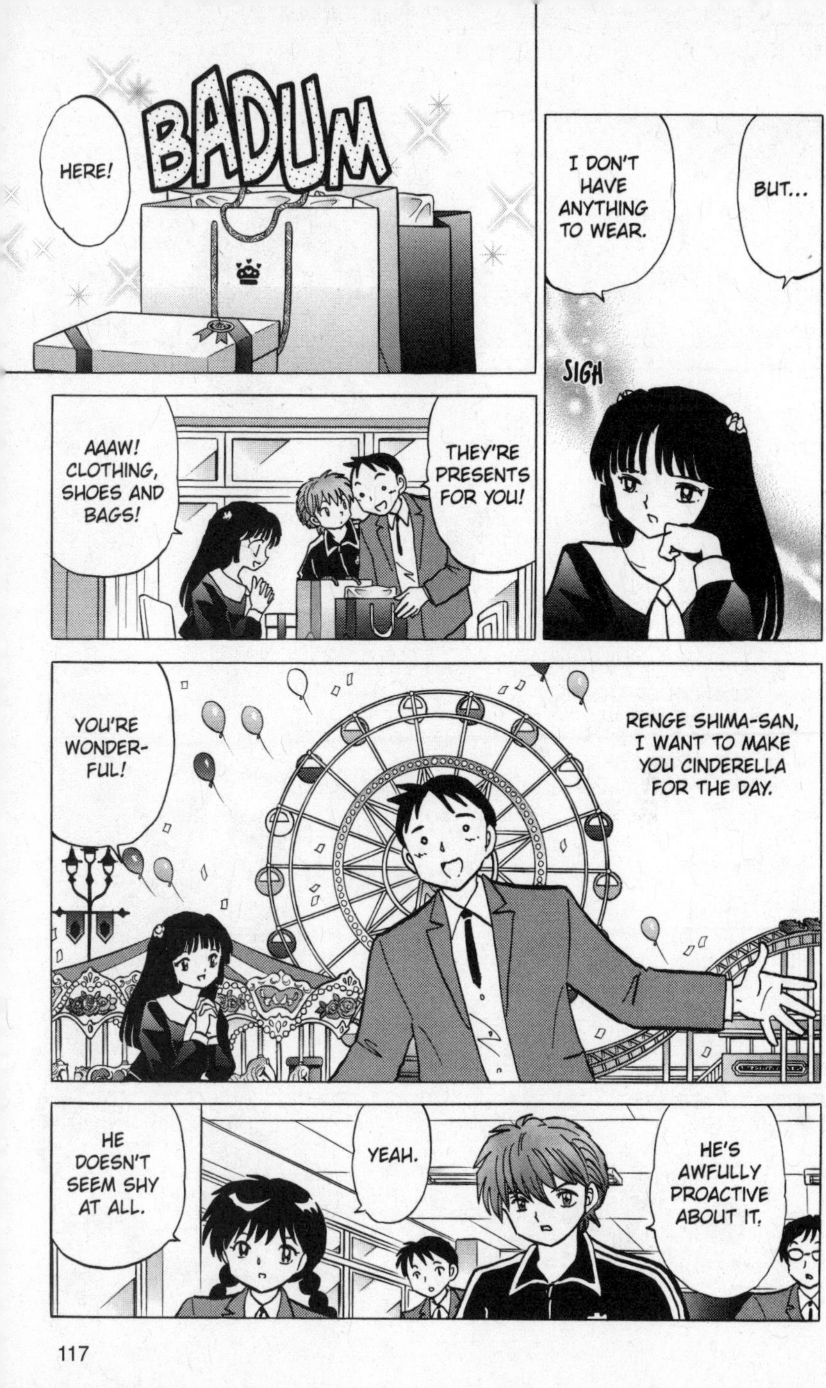
BUT...
I DON'T HAVE ANYTHING TO WEAR.
SIGH
BADUM
HERE!
THEY'RE PRESENTS FOR YOU!
AAAW! CLOTHING, SHOES AND BAGS!
RENGE SHIMA-SAN, I WANT TO MAKE YOU CINDERELLA FOR THE DAY.
YOU'RE WONDER-FUL!
HE'S AWFULLY PROACTIVE ABOUT IT.
YEAH.
HE DOESN'T SEEM SHY AT ALL.

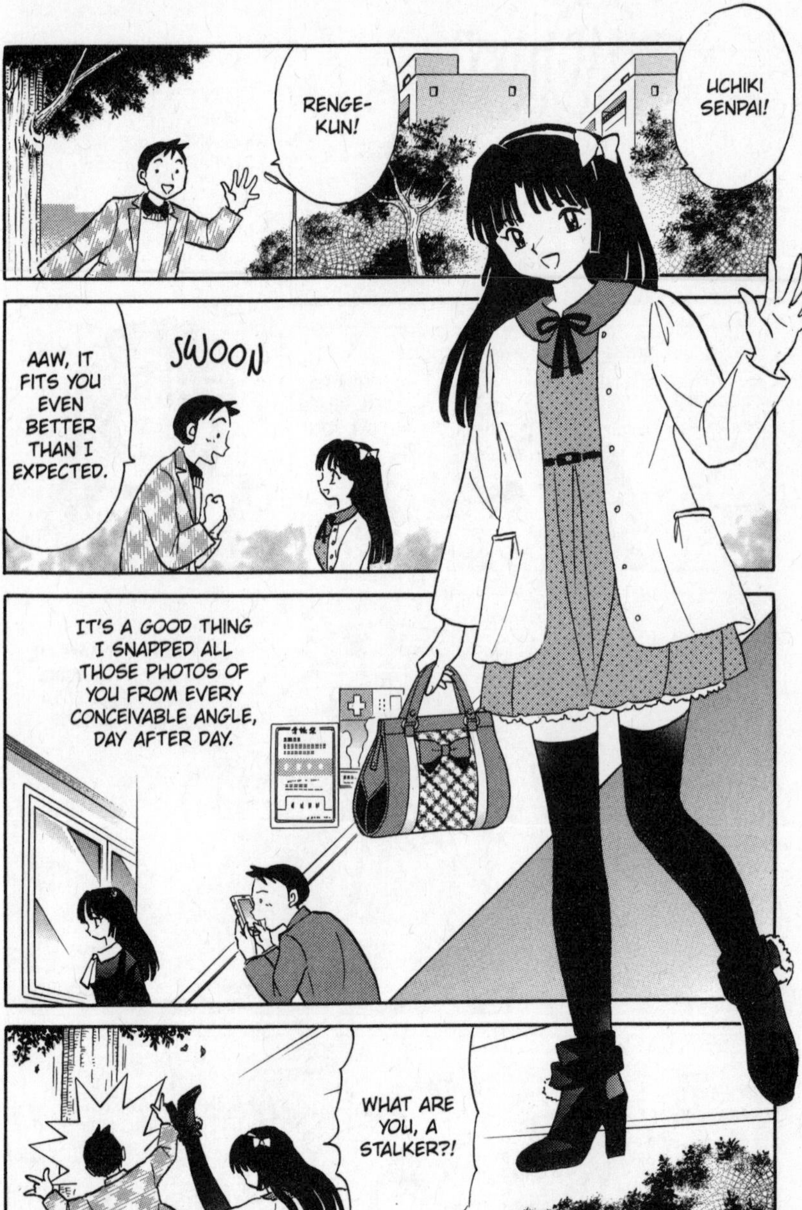
UCHIKI SENPAI!
RENGE-KUN!
SWOON
AAW, IT FITS YOU EVEN BETTER THAN I EXPECTED.
IT'S A GOOD THING I SNAPPED ALL THOSE PHOTOS OF YOU FROM EVERY CONCEIVABLE ANGLE, DAY AFTER DAY.
WHAT ARE YOU, A STALKER?!

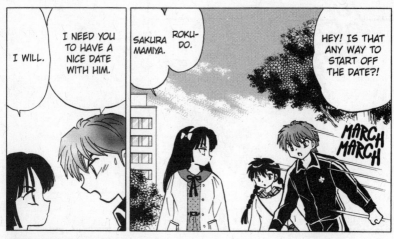

HEY! IS THAT ANY WAY TO START OFF THE DATE?!
MARCH MARCH
ROKU-DO.
SAKURA MAMIYA.
I NEED YOU TO HAVE A NICE DATE WITH HIM.
I WILL.
HUH ...?
ZSH
OKAY, UCHIKI SENPAI. LET'S GO ON OUR DATE.
I CAN'T WAIT!
IS HIS SOUL... COMING OUT?

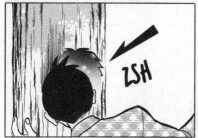

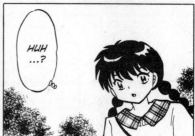

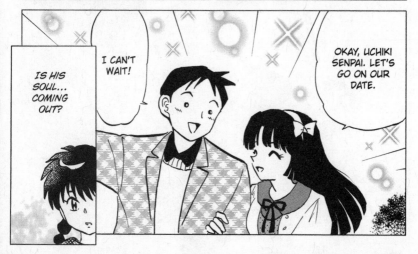

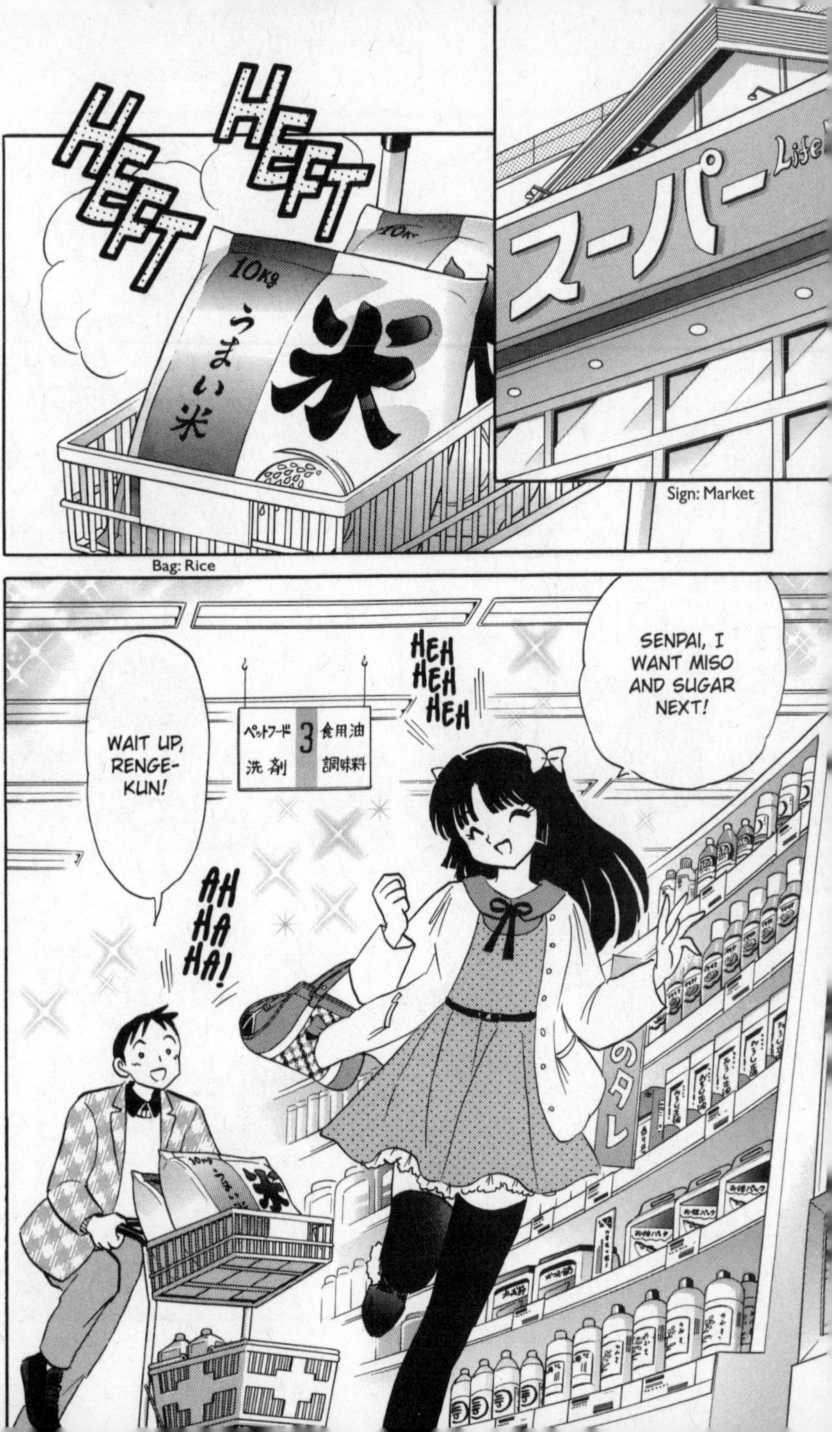

スーパー
Life
Sign: Market
HEFT
HEFT
10kg
うまい米
米
Bag: Rice
SENPAI, I WANT MISO AND SUGAR NEXT!
HEH HEH HEH
ペットフード 3 食用油
洗剤 調味料
WAIT UP, RENGE-KUN!
AH HA HA HA!
のタレ

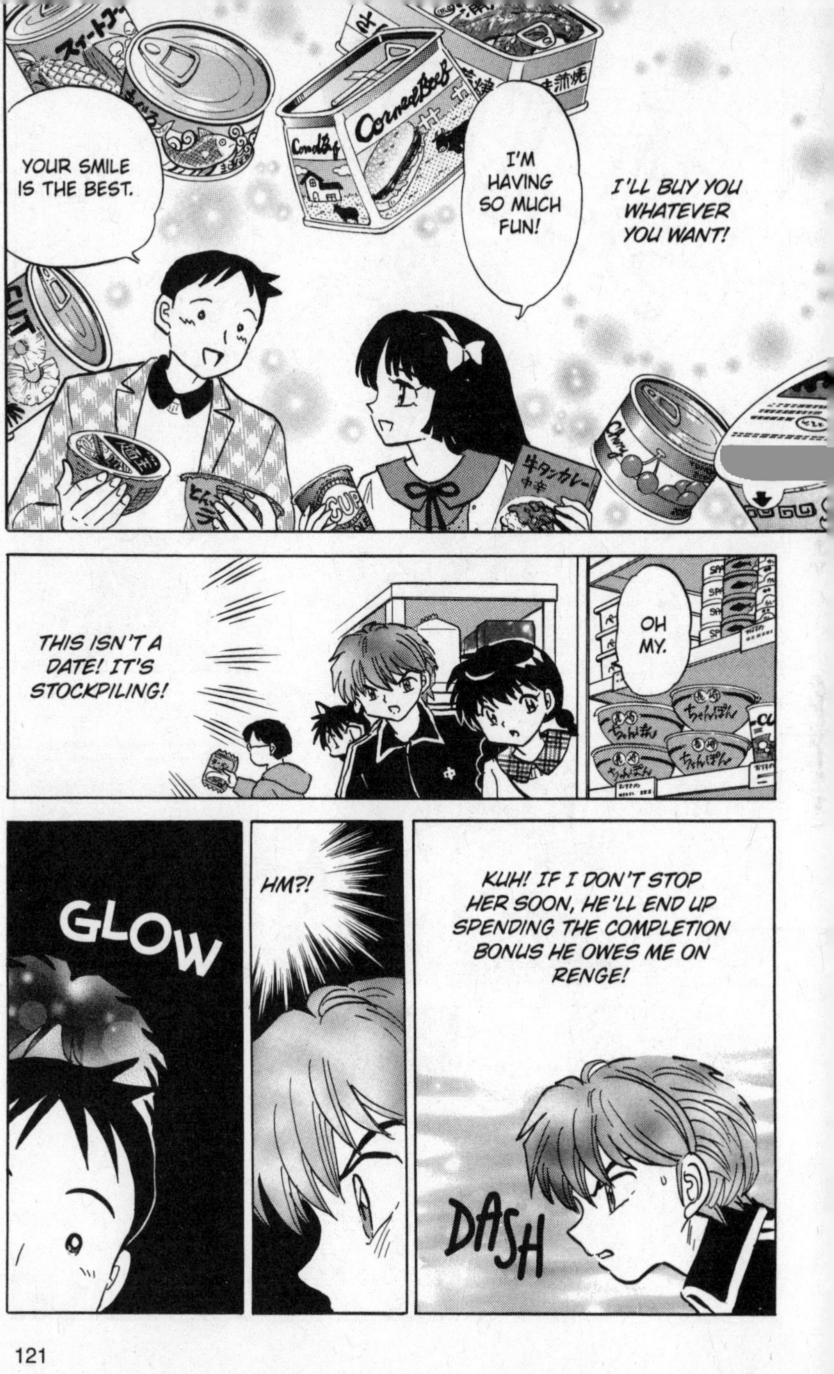
I'LL BUY YOU WHATEVER YOU WANT!
I'M HAVING SO MUCH FUN!
YOUR SMILE IS THE BEST.
OH MY.
THIS ISN'T A DATE! IT'S STOCKPILING!
KUH! IF I DON'T STOP HER SOON, HE'LL END UP SPENDING THE COMPLETION BONUS HE OWES ME ON RENGE!
DASH
HM?!
GLOW

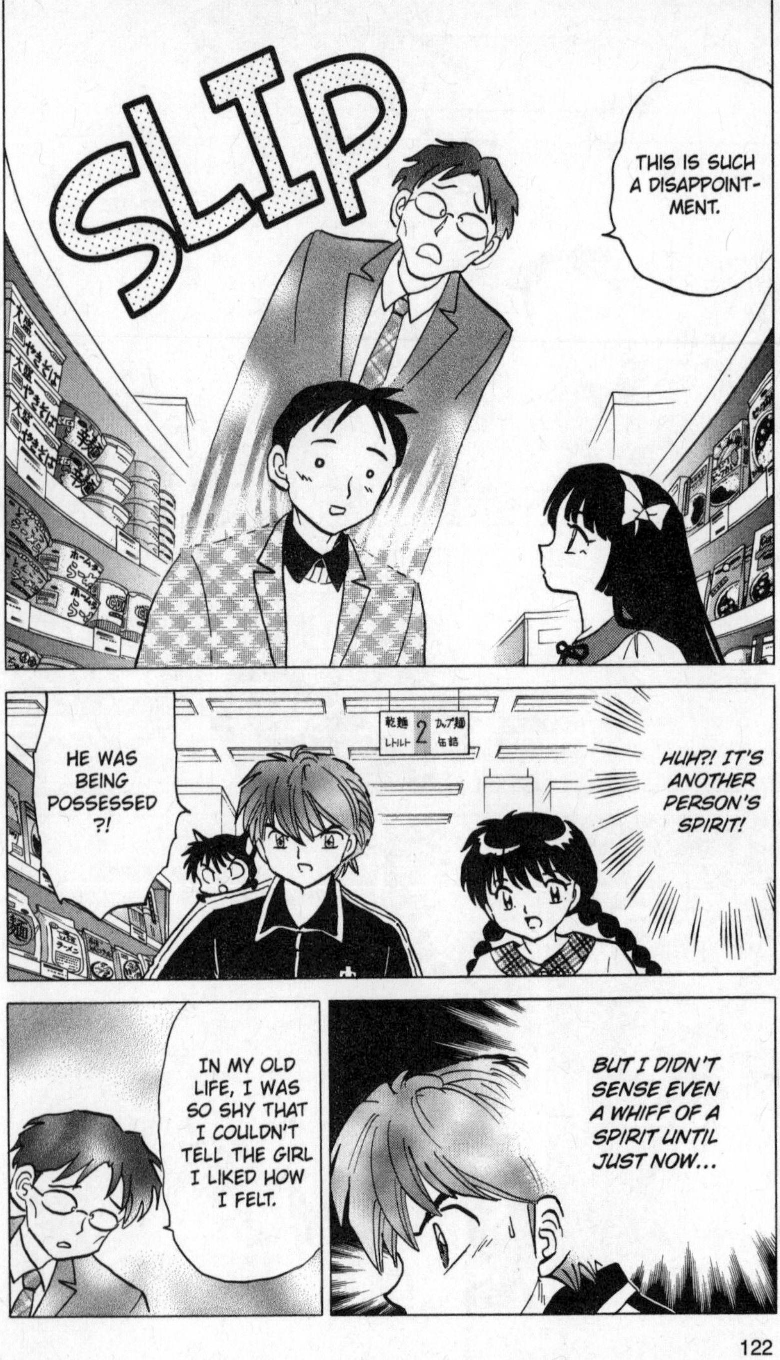
THIS IS SUCH A DISAPPOINT-MENT.
SLIP
HUH?! IT'S ANOTHER PERSON'S SPIRIT!
HE WAS BEING POSSESSED?!
BUT I DIDN'T SENSE EVEN A WHIFF OF A SPIRIT UNTIL JUST NOW...
IN MY OLD LIFE, I WAS SO SHY THAT I COULDN'T TELL THE GIRL I LIKED HOW I FELT.

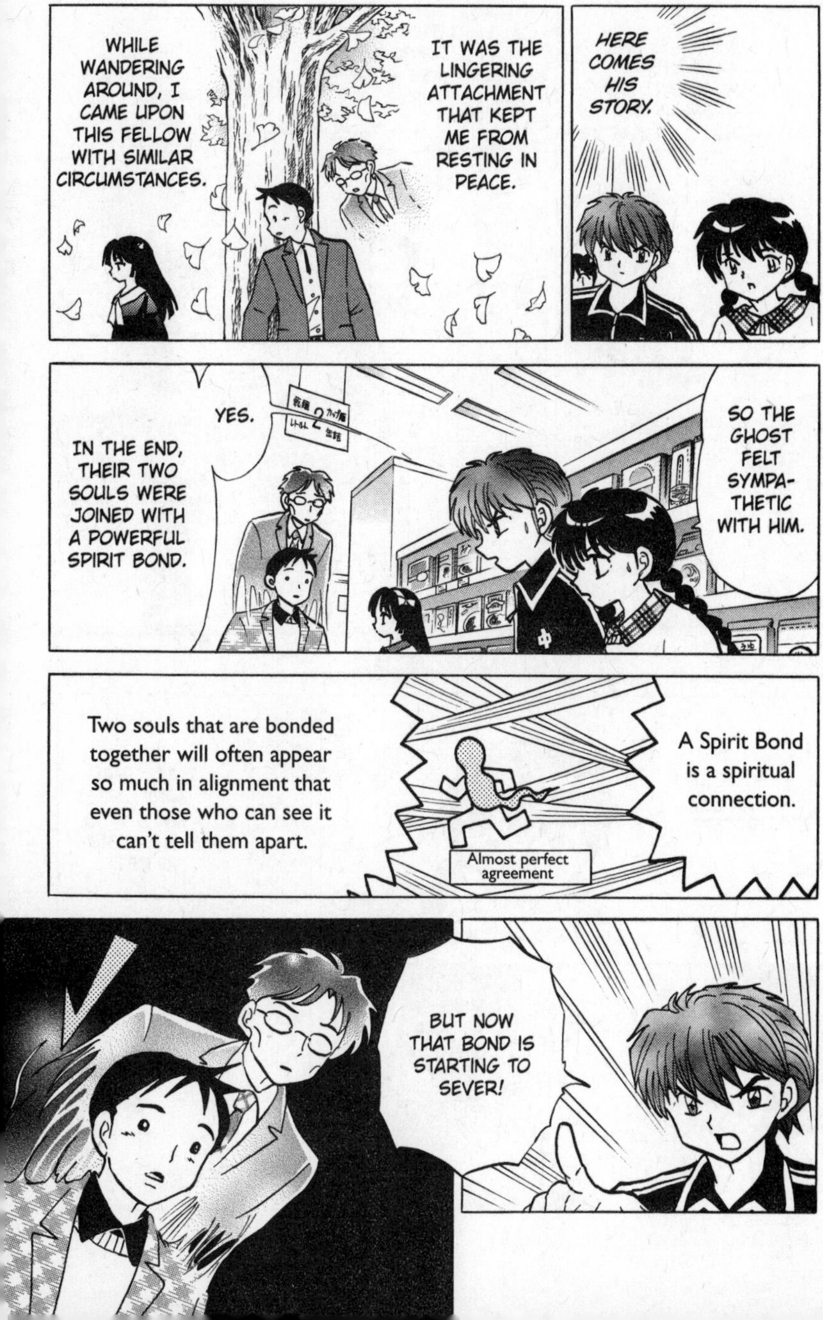
HERE COMES HIS STORY.
IT WAS THE LINGERING ATTACHMENT THAT KEPT ME FROM RESTING IN PEACE.
WHILE WANDERING AROUND, I CAME UPON THIS FELLOW WITH SIMILAR CIRCUMSTANCES.
SO THE GHOST FELT SYMPA-THETIC WITH HIM.
YES.
IN THE END, THEIR TWO SOULS WERE JOINED WITH A POWERFUL SPIRIT BOND.
A Spirit Bond is a spiritual connection.
Two souls that are bonded together will often appear so much in alignment that even those who can see it can't tell them apart.
Almost perfect agreement
BUT NOW THAT BOND IS STARTING TO SEVER!

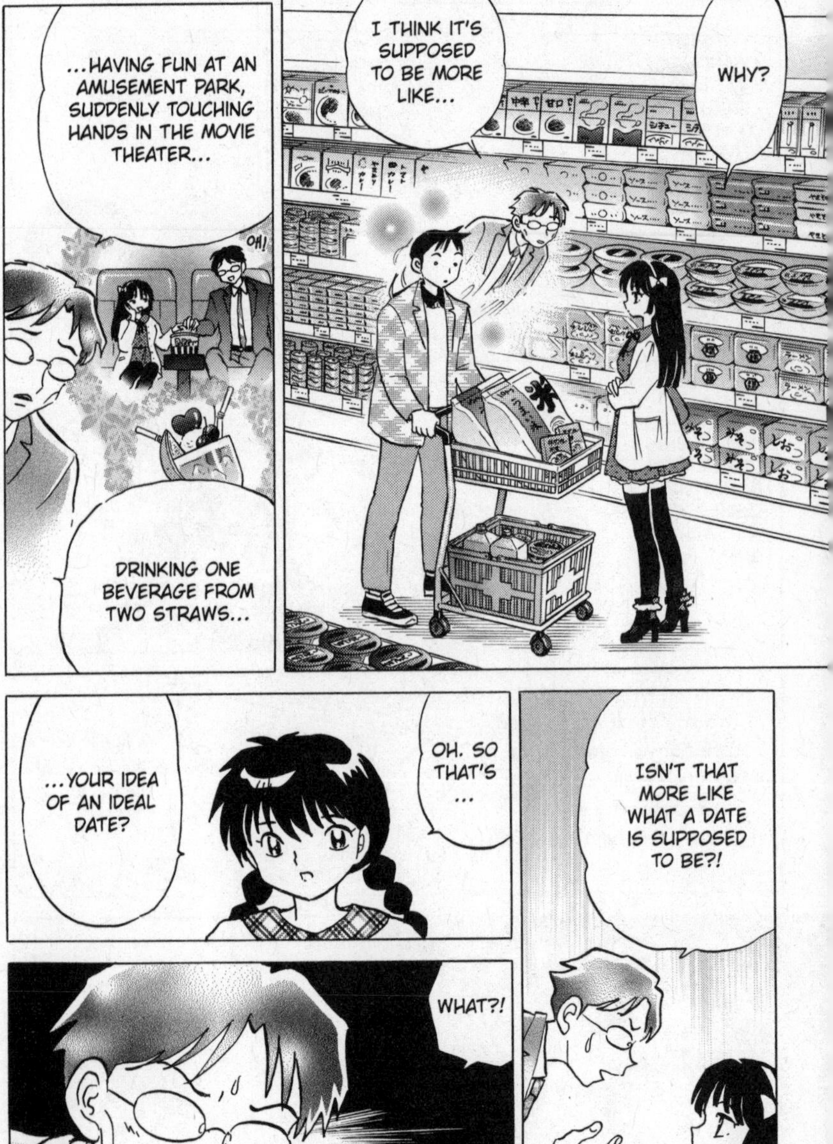
WHY?
I THINK IT'S SUPPOSED TO BE MORE LIKE...
...HAVING FUN AT AN AMUSEMENT PARK, SUDDENLY TOUCHING HANDS IN THE MOVIE THEATER...
OH!
DRINKING ONE BEVERAGE FROM TWO STRAWS...
ISN'T THAT MORE LIKE WHAT A DATE IS SUPPOSED TO BE?!
OH. SO THAT'S...
...YOUR IDEA OF AN IDEAL DATE?
WHAT?!

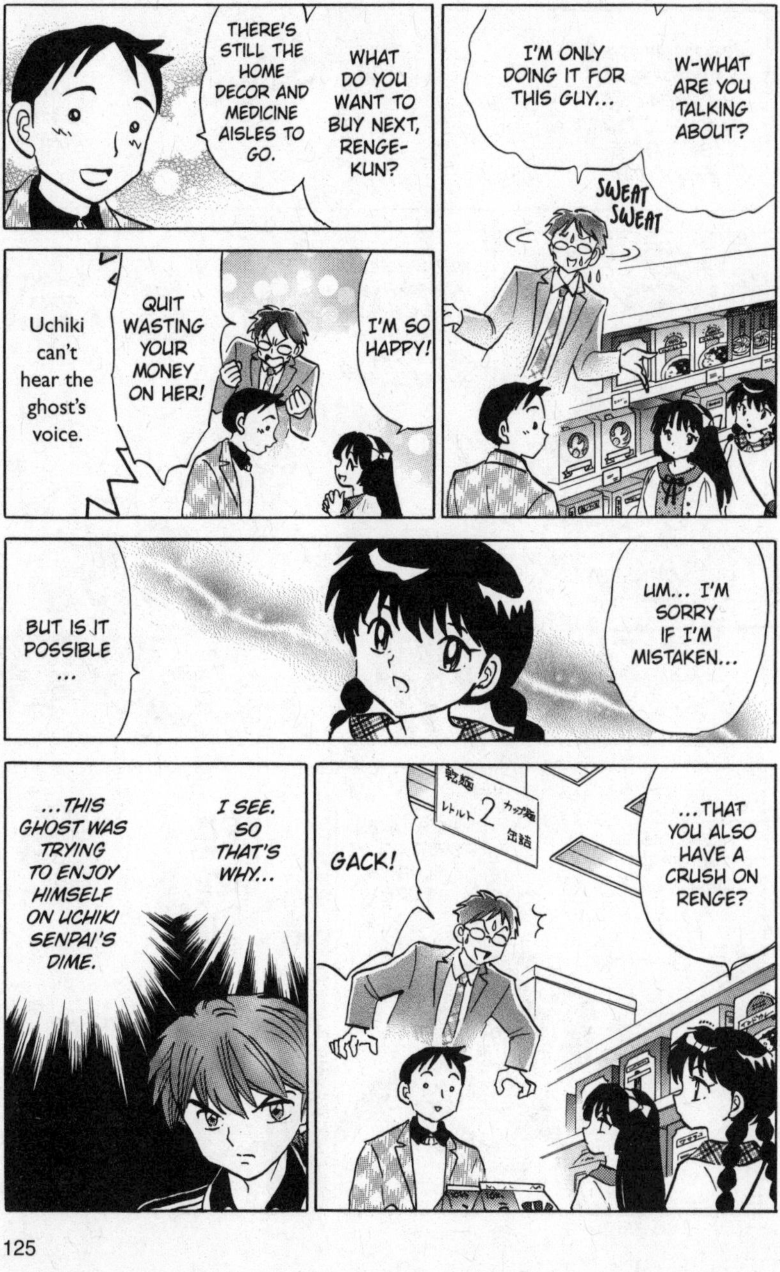
W-WHAT ARE YOU TALKING ABOUT?
I'M ONLY DOING IT FOR THIS GUY...
SWEAT SWEAT
WHAT DO YOU WANT TO BUY NEXT, RENGE-KUN?
THERE'S STILL THE HOME DECOR AND MEDICINE AISLES TO GO.
I'M SO HAPPY!
QUIT WASTING YOUR MONEY ON HER!
Uchiki can't hear the ghost's voice.
UM... I'M SORRY IF I'M MISTAKEN...
BUT IS IT POSSIBLE ...
...THAT YOU ALSO HAVE A CRUSH ON RENGE?
GACK!
I SEE. SO THAT'S WHY...
...THIS GHOST WAS TRYING TO ENJOY HIMSELF ON UCHIKI SENPAI'S DIME.

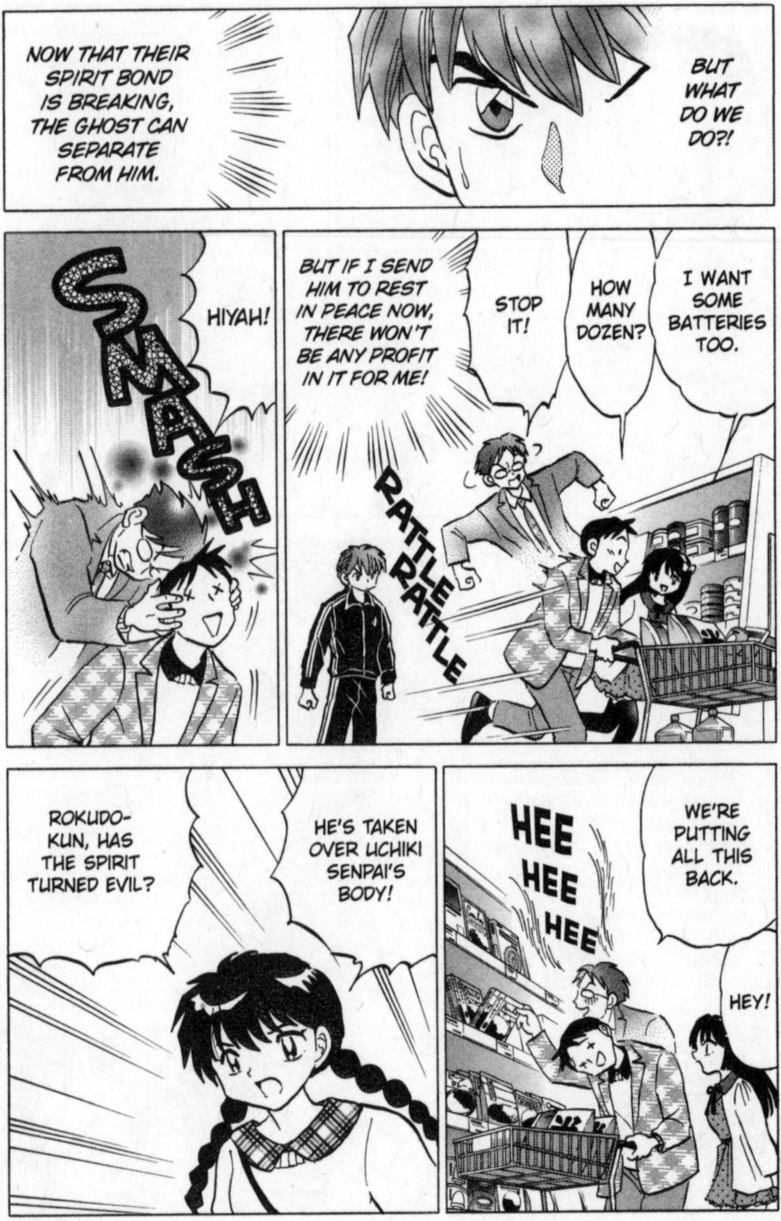
NOW THAT THEIR SPIRIT BOND IS BREAKING, THE GHOST CAN SEPARATE FROM HIM.
BUT WHAT DO WE DO?!
I WANT SOME BATTERIES TOO.
HOW MANY DOZEN?
STOP IT!
BUT IF I SEND HIM TO REST IN PEACE NOW, THERE WON'T BE ANY PROFIT IN IT FOR ME!
RATTLE RATTLE
HIYAH!
SMASH
WE'RE PUTTING ALL THIS BACK.
HEE HEE HEE
HEY!
ROKUDO-KUN, HAS THE SPIRIT TURNED EVIL?
HE'S TAKEN OVER UCHIKI SENPAI'S BODY!

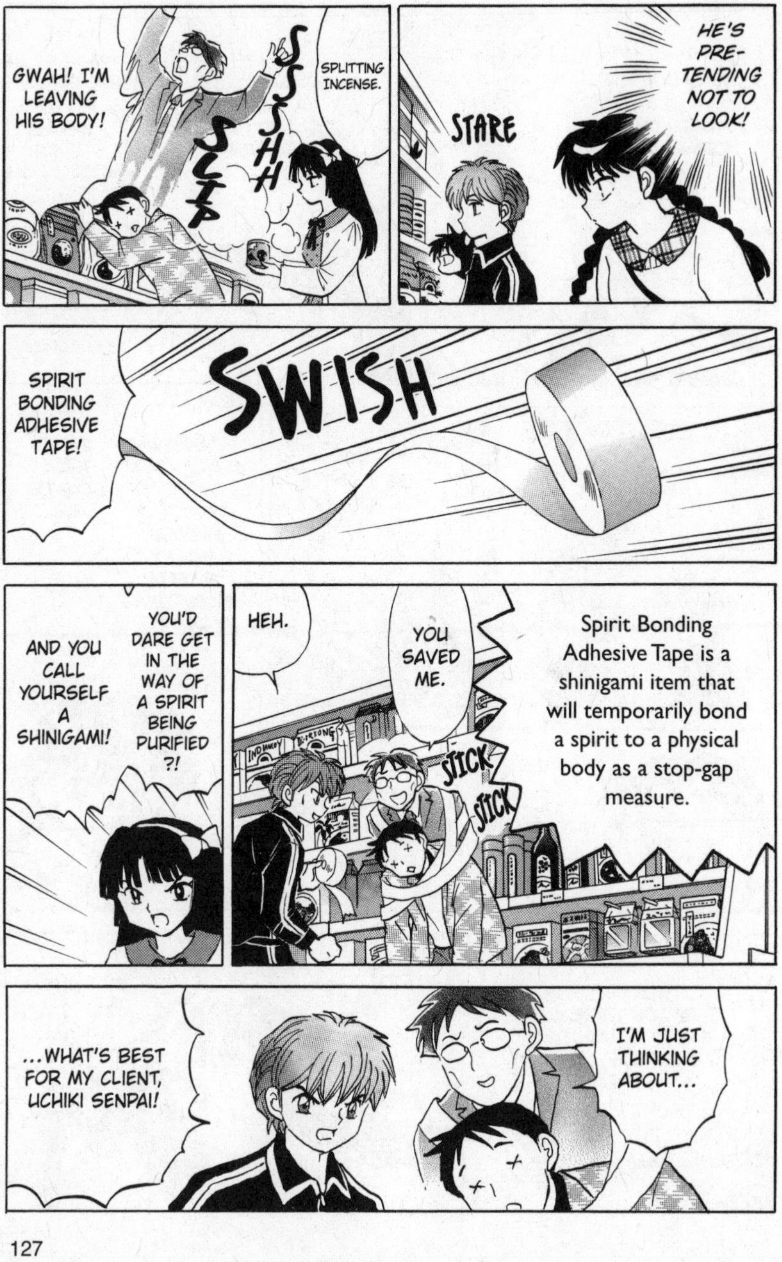
HE'S PRE-TENDING NOT TO LOOK!
STARE
SPLITTING INCENSE.
SSSHH
SLIP
GWAH! I'M LEAVING HIS BODY!
SWISH
SPIRIT BONDING ADHESIVE TAPE!
Spirit Bonding Adhesive Tape is a shinigami item that will temporarily bond a spirit to a physical body as a stop-gap measure.
YOU SAVED ME.
HEH.
STICK
STICK
YOU'D DARE GET IN THE WAY OF A SPIRIT BEING PURIFIED ?!
AND YOU CALL YOURSELF A SHINIGAMI!
I'M JUST THINKING ABOUT...
...WHAT'S BEST FOR MY CLIENT, UCHIKI SENPAI!

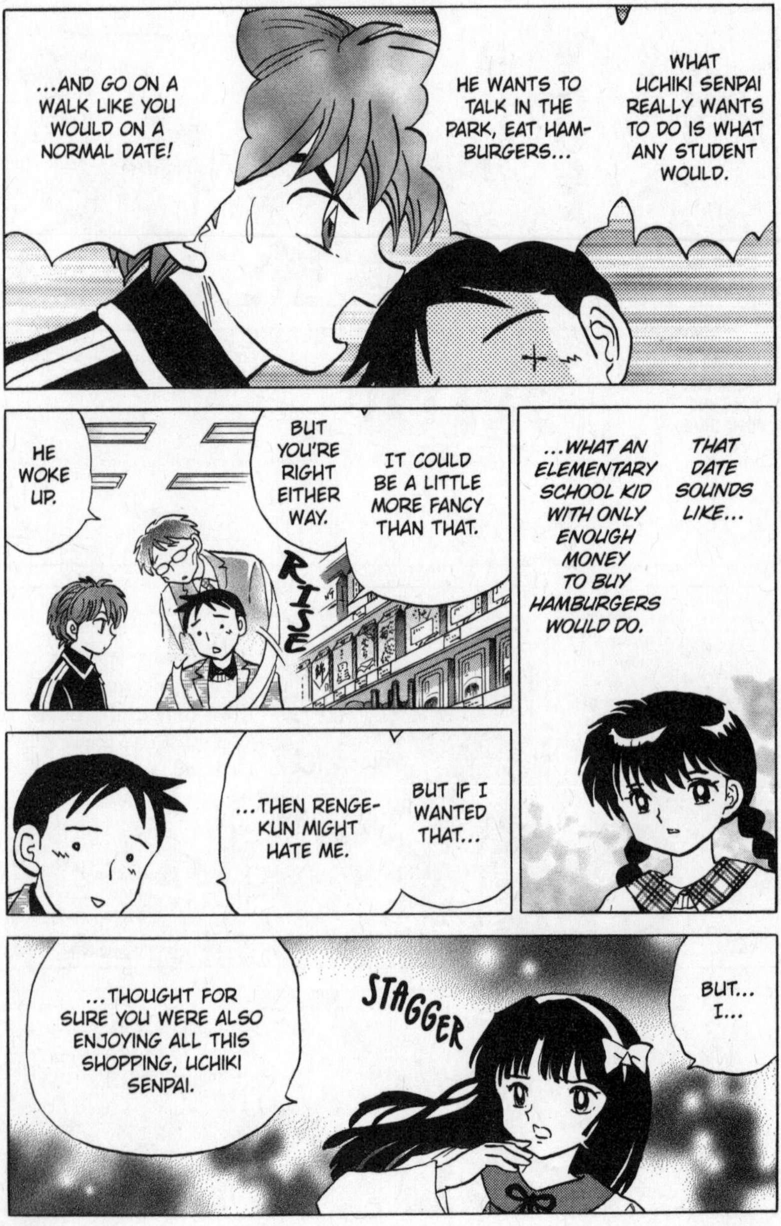
WHAT UCHIKI SENPAI REALLY WANTS TO DO IS WHAT ANY STUDENT WOULD.
HE WANTS TO TALK IN THE PARK, EAT HAMBURGERS...
...AND GO ON A WALK LIKE YOU WOULD ON A NORMAL DATE!
THAT DATE SOUNDS LIKE...
...WHAT AN ELEMENTARY SCHOOL KID WITH ONLY ENOUGH MONEY TO BUY HAMBURGERS WOULD DO.
IT COULD BE A LITTLE MORE FANCY THAN THAT.
BUT YOU'RE RIGHT EITHER WAY.
RISE
HE WOKE UP.
BUT IF I WANTED THAT...
...THEN RENGE-KUN MIGHT HATE ME.
BUT... I...
STAGGER
...THOUGHT FOR SURE YOU WERE ALSO ENJOYING ALL THIS SHOPPING, UCHIKI SENPAI.

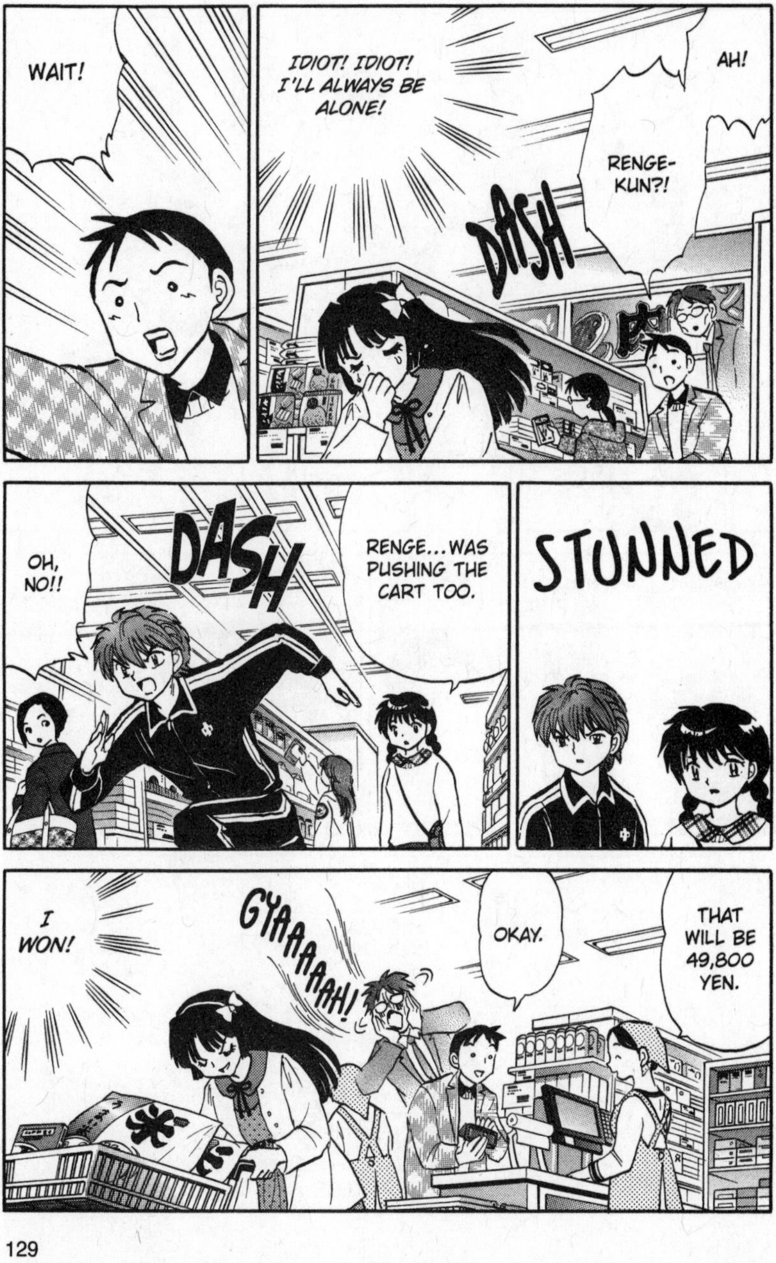

AH!
RENGE-KUN?!
IDIOT! IDIOT! I'LL ALWAYS BE ALONE!
DASH
WAIT!
STUNNED
RENGE...WAS PUSHING THE CART TOO.
DASH
OH, NO!!
THAT WILL BE 49,800 YEN.
OKAY.
GYAAAAAH!
I WON!

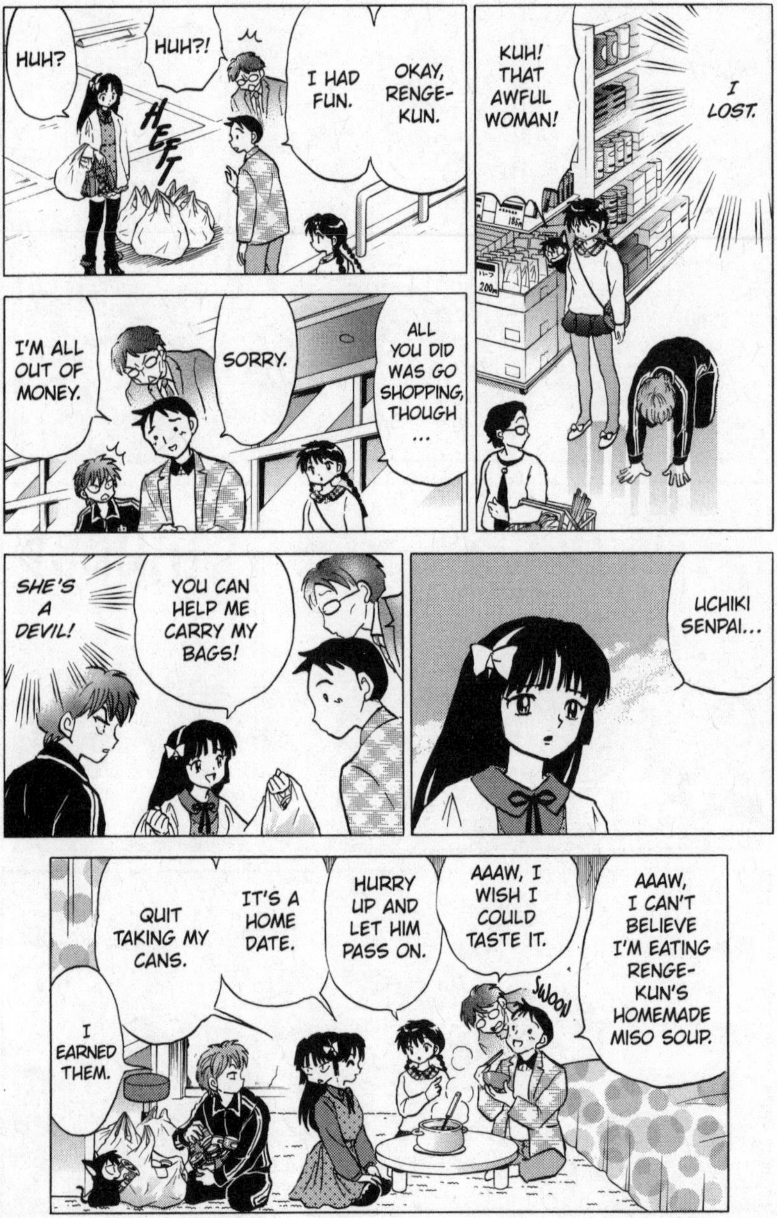
I LOST.
KUH! THAT AWFUL WOMAN!
OKAY, RENGE-KUN.
I HAD FUN.
HUH?!
HEFT
HUH?
ALL YOU DID WAS GO SHOPPING, THOUGH...
SORRY.
I'M ALL OUT OF MONEY.
UCHIKI SENPAI...
YOU CAN HELP ME CARRY MY BAGS!
SHE'S A DEVIL!
AAAW, I CAN'T BELIEVE I'M EATING RENGE-KUN'S HOMEMADE MISO SOUP.
SWOON
AAAW, I WISH I COULD TASTE IT.
HURRY UP AND LET HIM PASS ON.
IT'S A HOME DATE.
QUIT TAKING MY CANS.
I EARNED THEM.

CHAPTER 276: PLEASE CHARGE ME

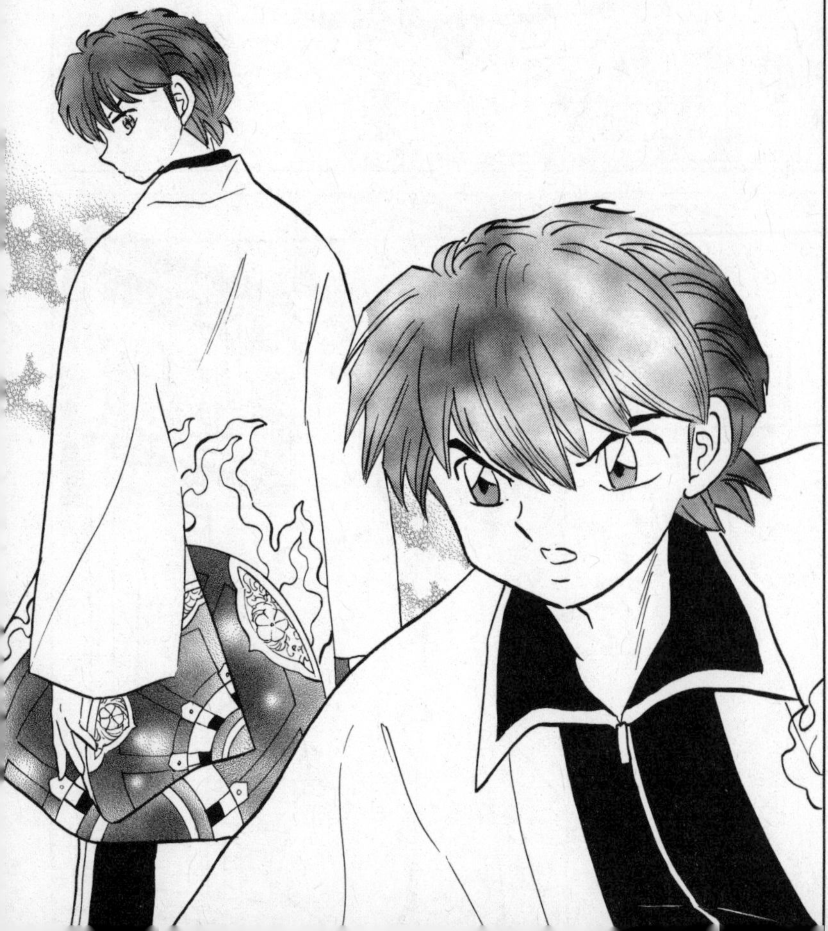

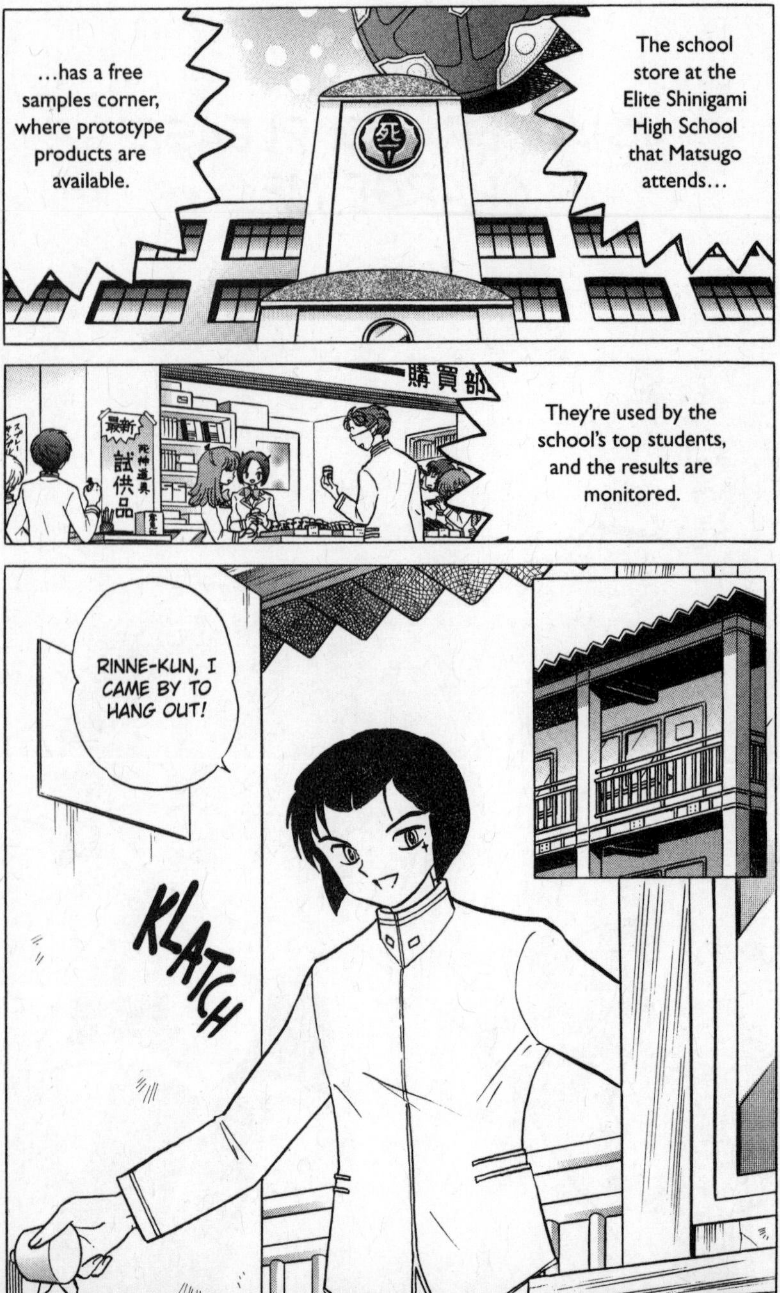
The school store at the Elite Shinigami High School that Matsugo attends…
…has a free samples corner, where prototype products are available.
購買部
最新
死神道具
試供品
They're used by the school's top students, and the results are monitored.
RINNE-KUN, I CAME BY TO HANG OUT!
KLATCH

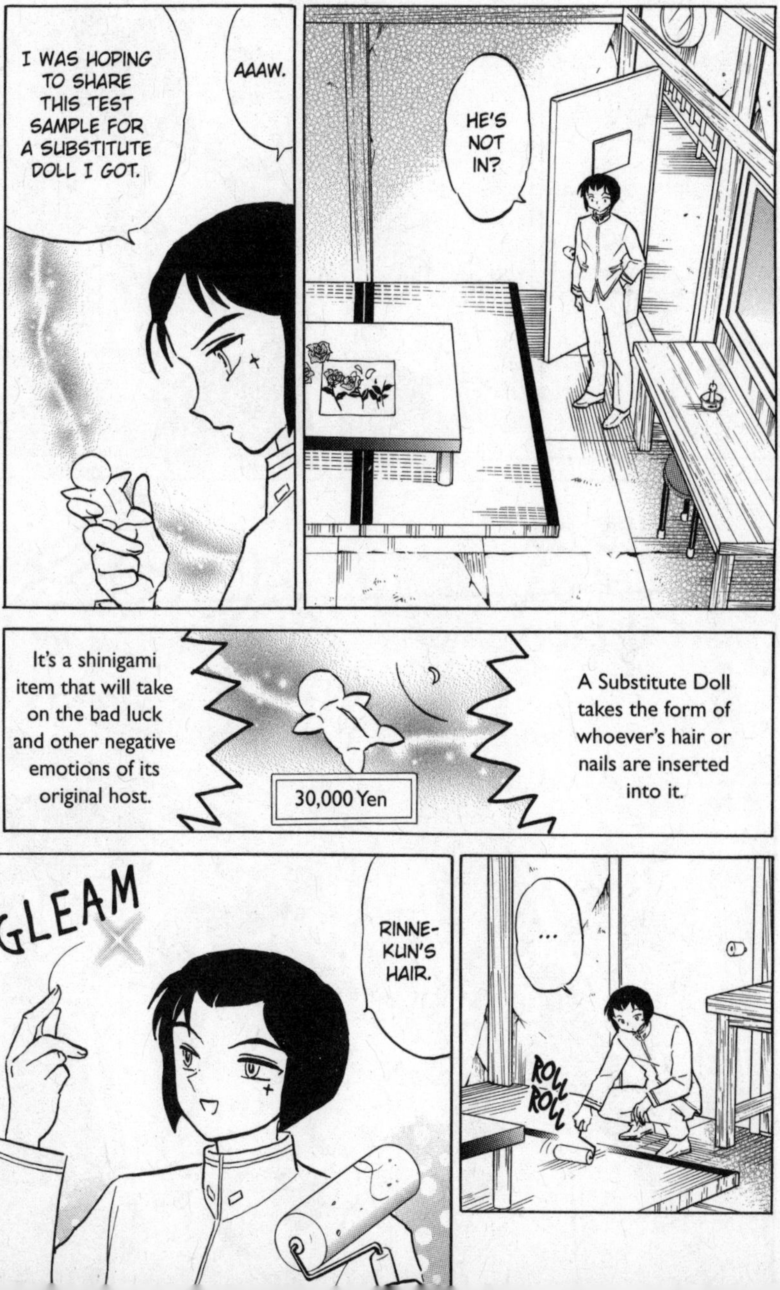
HE'S NOT IN?
AAAW.
I WAS HOPING TO SHARE THIS TEST SAMPLE FOR A SUBSTITUTE DOLL I GOT.
A Substitute Doll takes the form of whoever's hair or nails are inserted into it.
30,000 Yen
It's a shinigami item that will take on the bad luck and other negative emotions of its original host.
...
ROLL ROLL
RINNE-KUN'S HAIR.
GLEAM

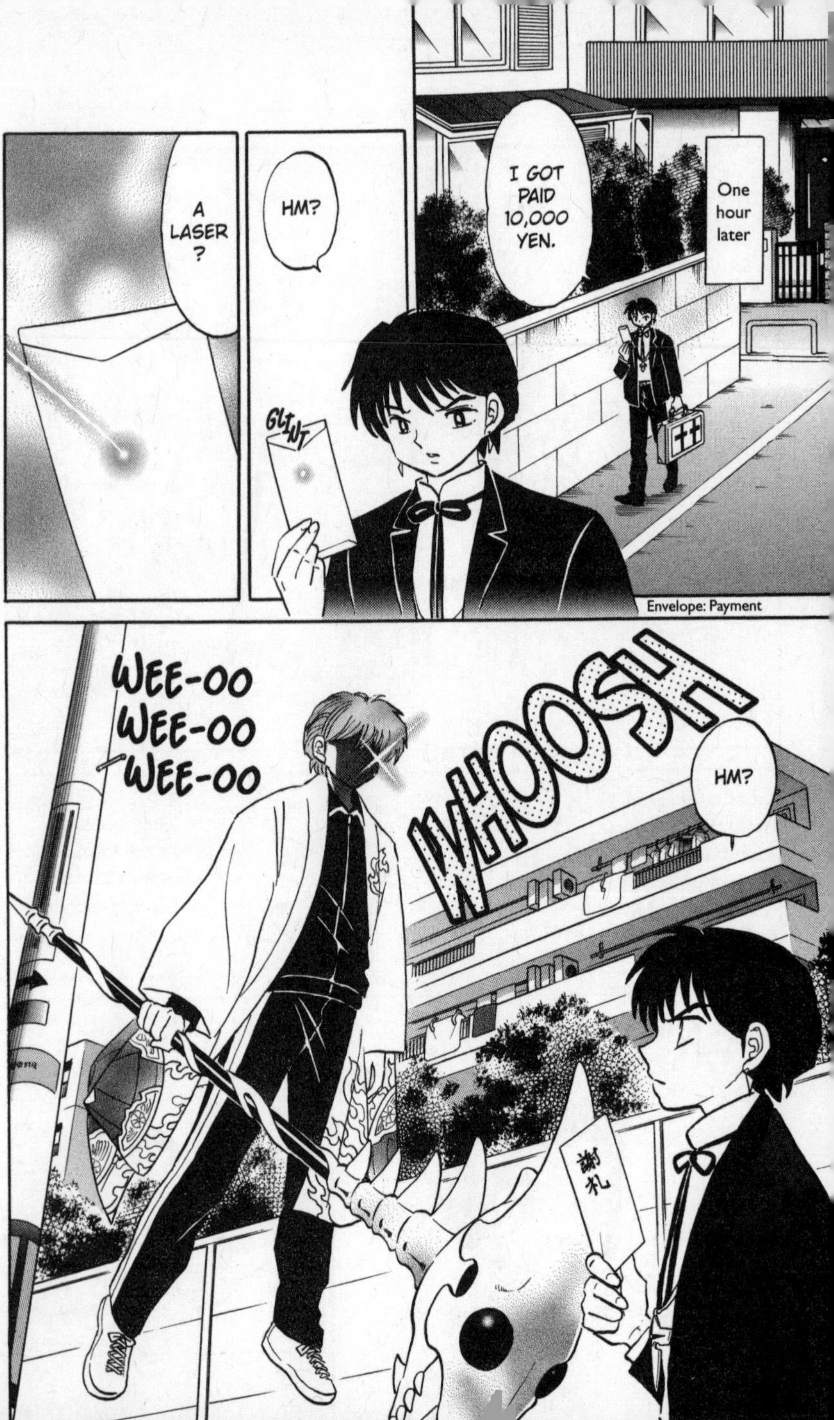
One hour later
I GOT PAID 10,000 YEN.
GLINT
Envelope: Payment
HM?
A LASER ?
HM?
WHOOSH
WEE-OO WEE-OO WEE-OO
謝礼

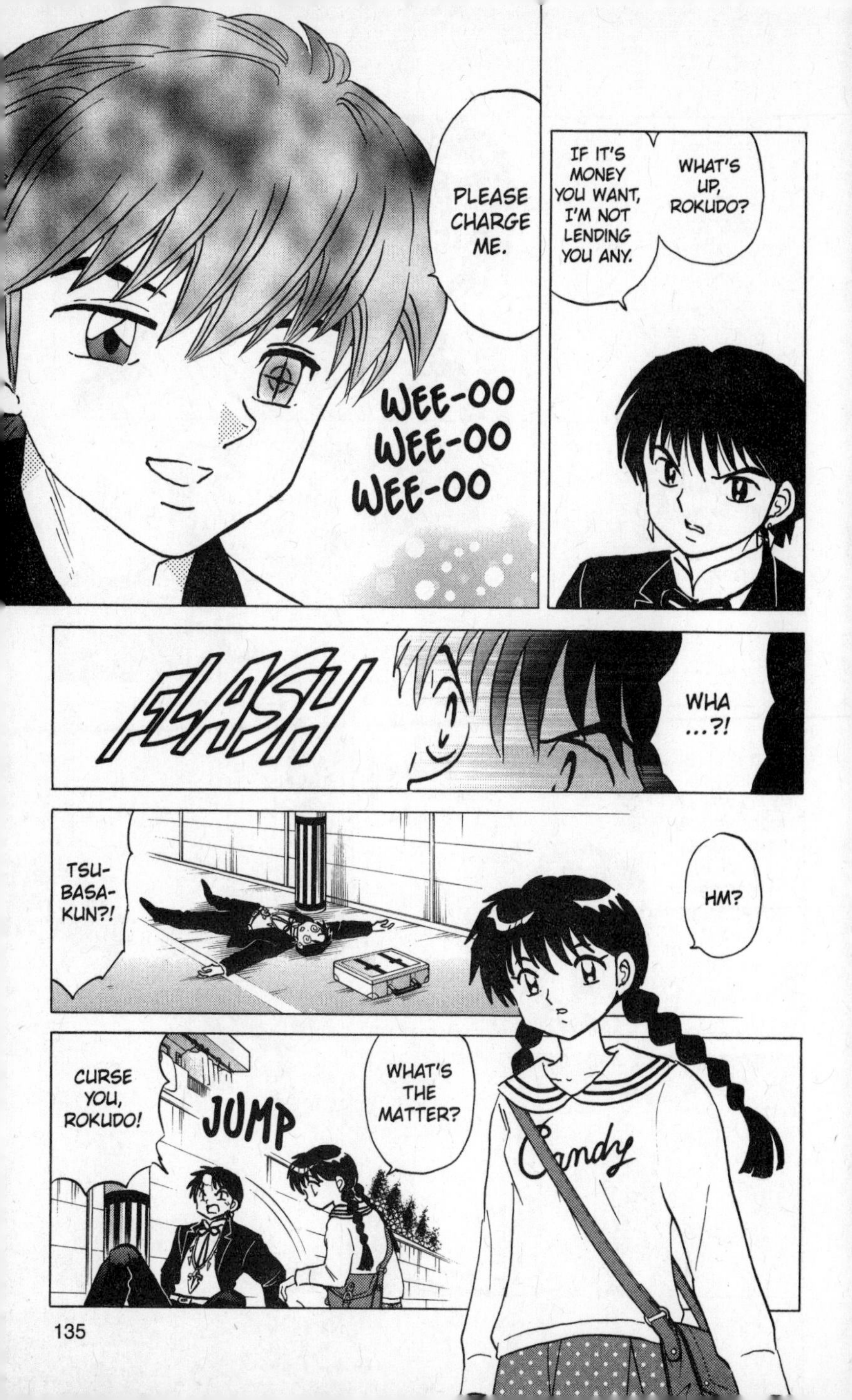
WHAT'S UP, ROKUDO?
IF IT'S MONEY YOU WANT, I'M NOT LENDING YOU ANY.
PLEASE CHARGE ME.
WEE-OO WEE-OO WEE-OO
WHA ...?!
FLASH
HM?
TSU-BASA-KUN?!
WHAT'S THE MATTER?
JUMP
CURSE YOU, ROKUDO!

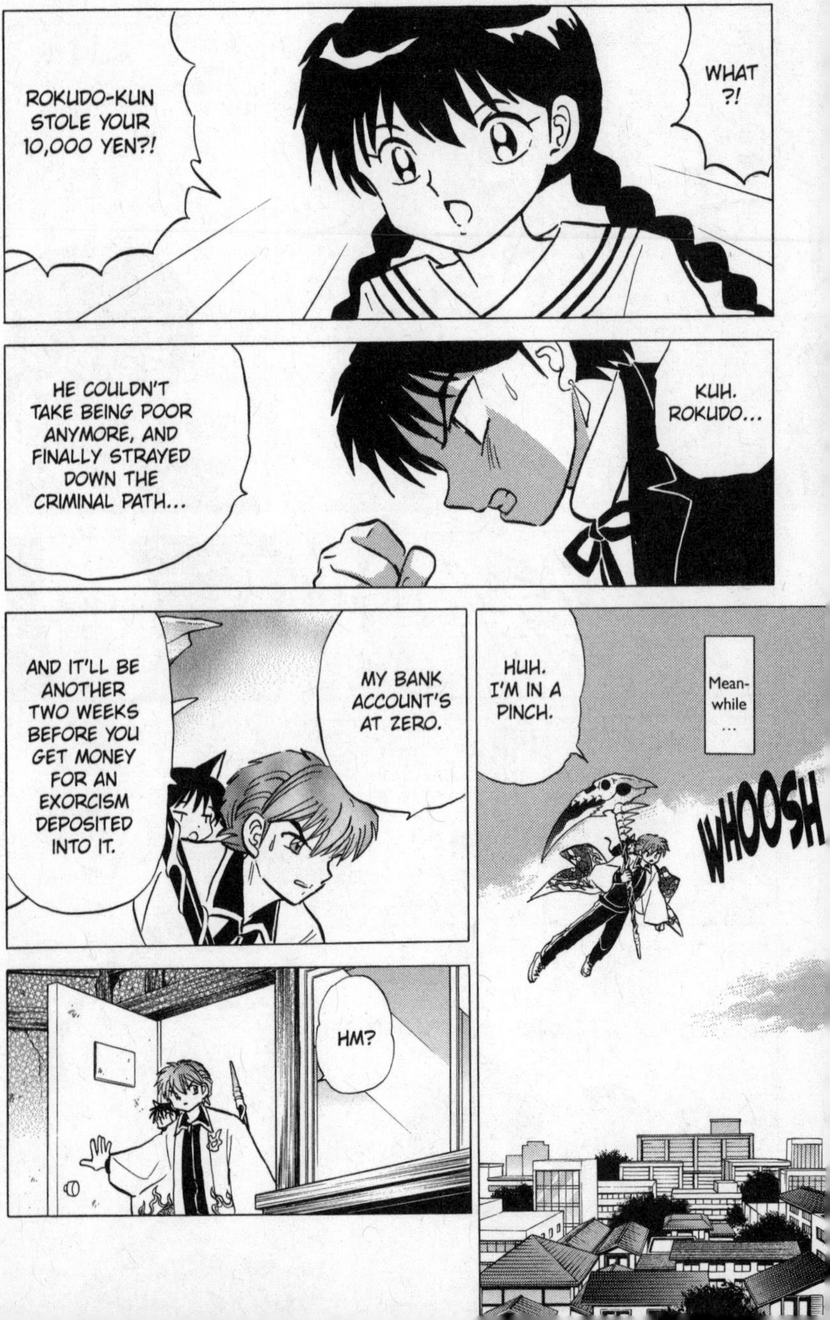
WHAT ?!
ROKUDO-KUN STOLE YOUR 10,000 YEN?!
KUH. ROKUDO...
HE COULDN'T TAKE BEING POOR ANYMORE, AND FINALLY STRAYED DOWN THE CRIMINAL PATH...
Mean-while ...
HUH. I'M IN A PINCH.
WHOOSH
MY BANK ACCOUNT'S AT ZERO.
AND IT'LL BE ANOTHER TWO WEEKS BEFORE YOU GET MONEY FOR AN EXORCISM DEPOSITED INTO IT.
HM?

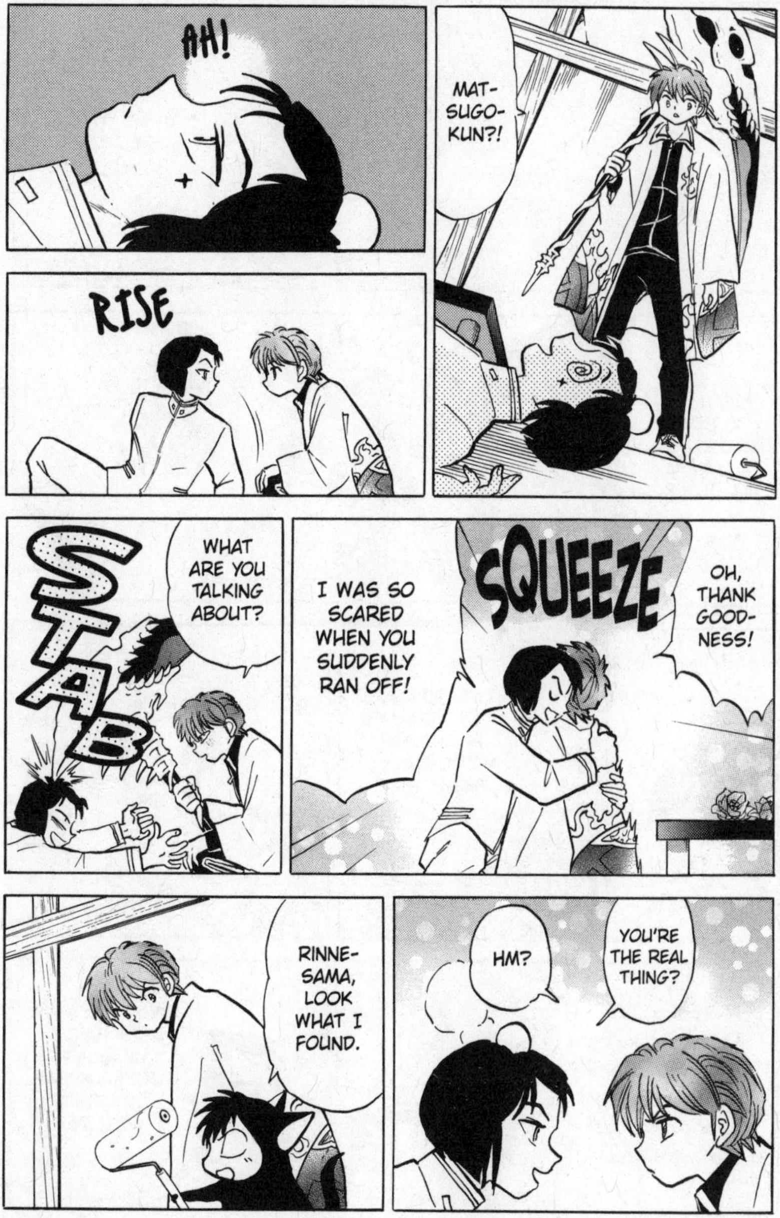
MAT-SUGO-KUN?!
AH!
RISE
SQUEEZE
OH, THANK GOOD-NESS!
I WAS SO SCARED WHEN YOU SUDDENLY RAN OFF!
WHAT ARE YOU TALKING ABOUT?
STAB
YOU'RE THE REAL THING?
HM?
RINNE-SAMA, LOOK WHAT I FOUND.

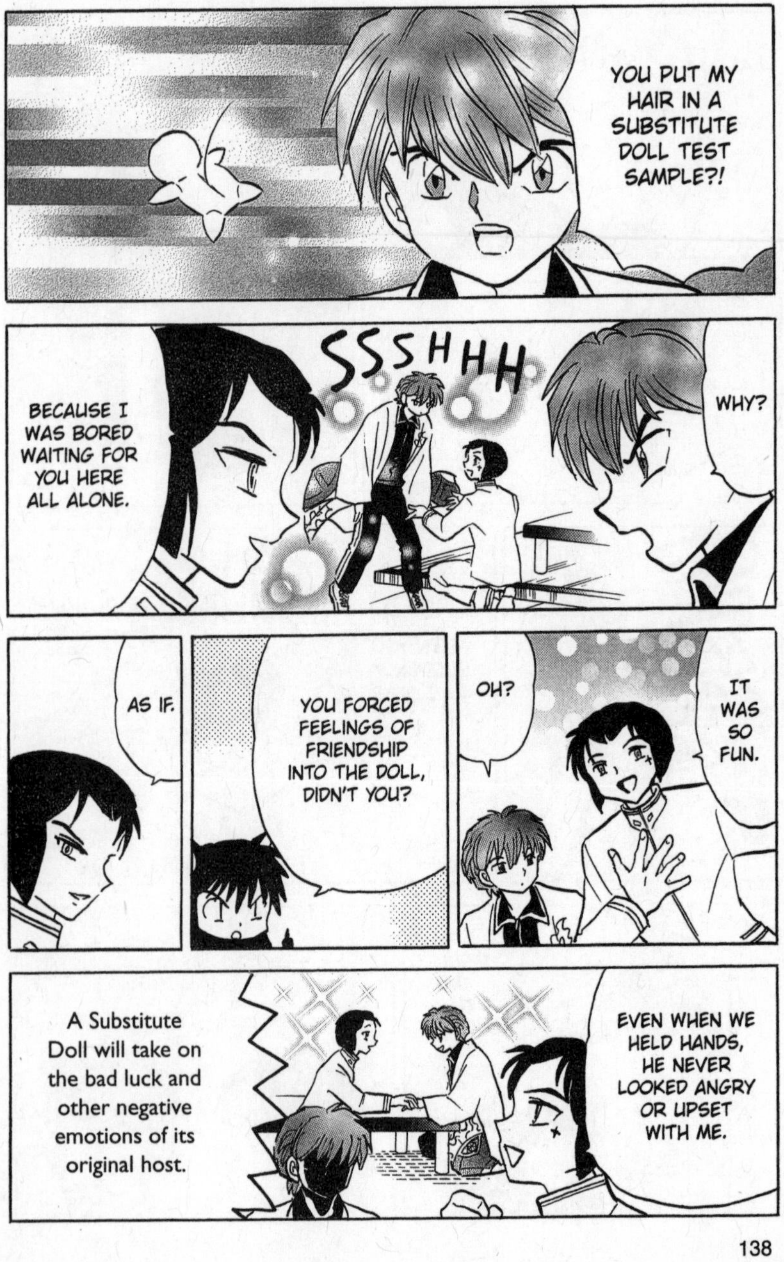
YOU PUT MY HAIR IN A SUBSTITUTE DOLL TEST SAMPLE?!
WHY?
SSSHHH
BECAUSE I WAS BORED WAITING FOR YOU HERE ALL ALONE.
IT WAS SO FUN.
OH?
YOU FORCED FEELINGS OF FRIENDSHIP INTO THE DOLL, DIDN'T YOU?
AS IF.
EVEN WHEN WE HELD HANDS, HE NEVER LOOKED ANGRY OR UPSET WITH ME.
A Substitute Doll will take on the bad luck and other negative emotions of its original host.

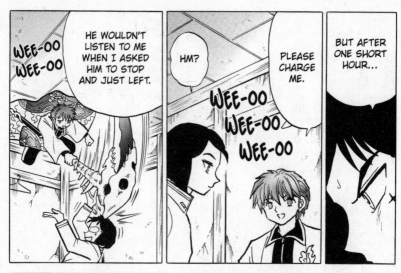

BUT AFTER ONE SHORT HOUR...
PLEASE CHARGE ME.
HM?
WEE-OO WEE-OO WEE-OO
HE WOULDN'T LISTEN TO ME WHEN I ASKED HIM TO STOP AND JUST LEFT.
WEE-OO WEE-OO
IT WAS A SAMPLE, RIGHT?
SO COULD IT BE DEFECTIVE?
NO.
IT'S A NEW FUNCTION.
Normal Substitute Dolls revert back to being a doll after three hours, but...
IT SAYS HERE IT CAN FILL ITSELF UP WITH ENERGY TO KEEP ACTIVE SEMI-PERMANENTLY.
ENERGY?!

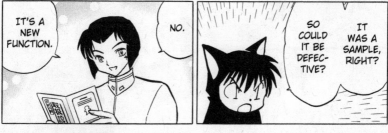

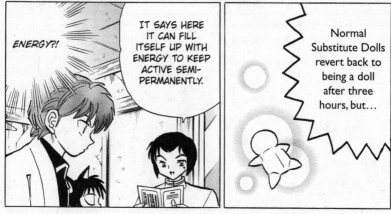

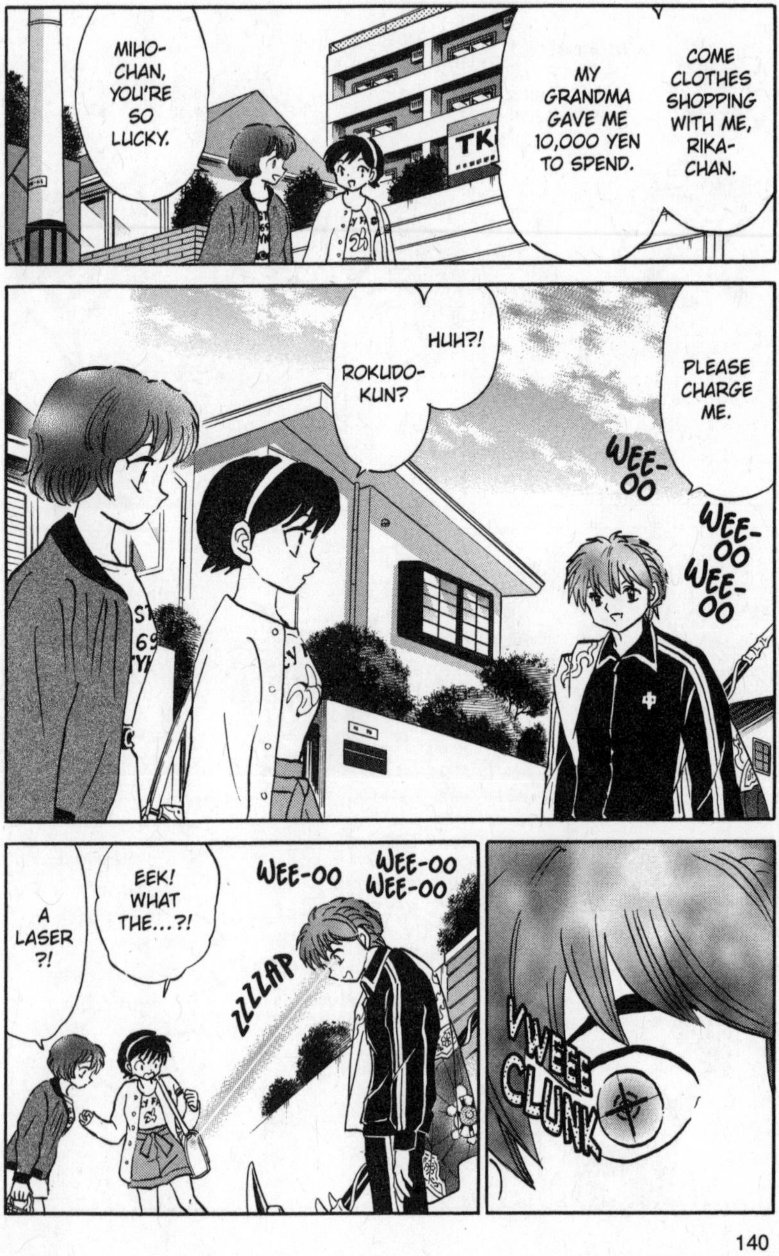
COME CLOTHES SHOPPING WITH ME, RIKA-CHAN.
MY GRANDMA GAVE ME 10,000 YEN TO SPEND.
MIHO-CHAN, YOU'RE SO LUCKY.
PLEASE CHARGE ME.
WEE-OO
WEE-OO WEE-OO
HUH?!
ROKUDO-KUN?
VWEEE CLUNK
WEE-OO WEE-OO
WEE-OO
ZZZZAP
EEK! WHAT THE...?!
A LASER?!

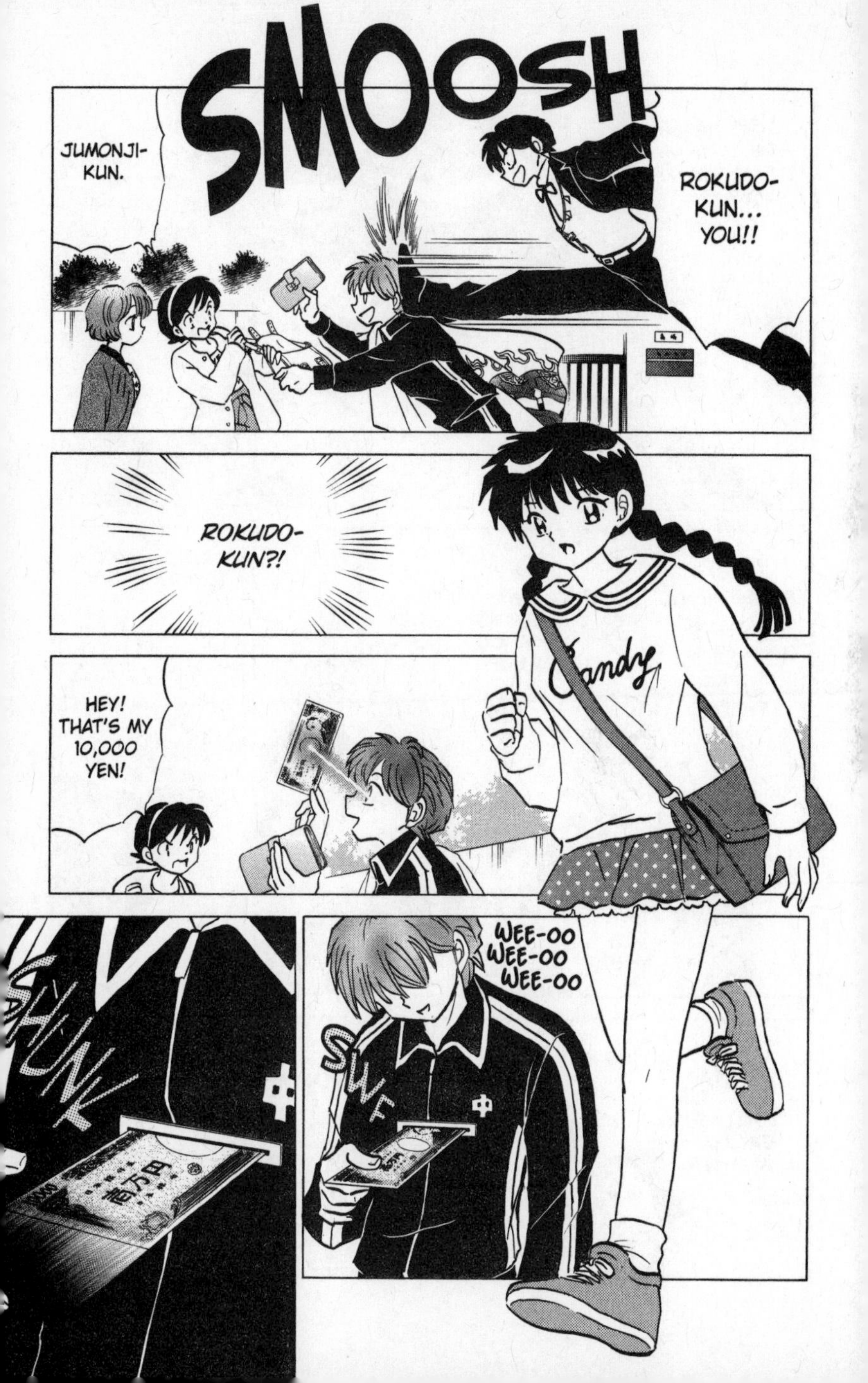
SMOOSH
ROKUDO-KUN... YOU!!
JUMONJI-KUN.
ROKUDO-KUN?!
HEY! THAT'S MY 10,000 YEN!
WEE-OO WEE-OO WEE-OO
SWF
SHUNK

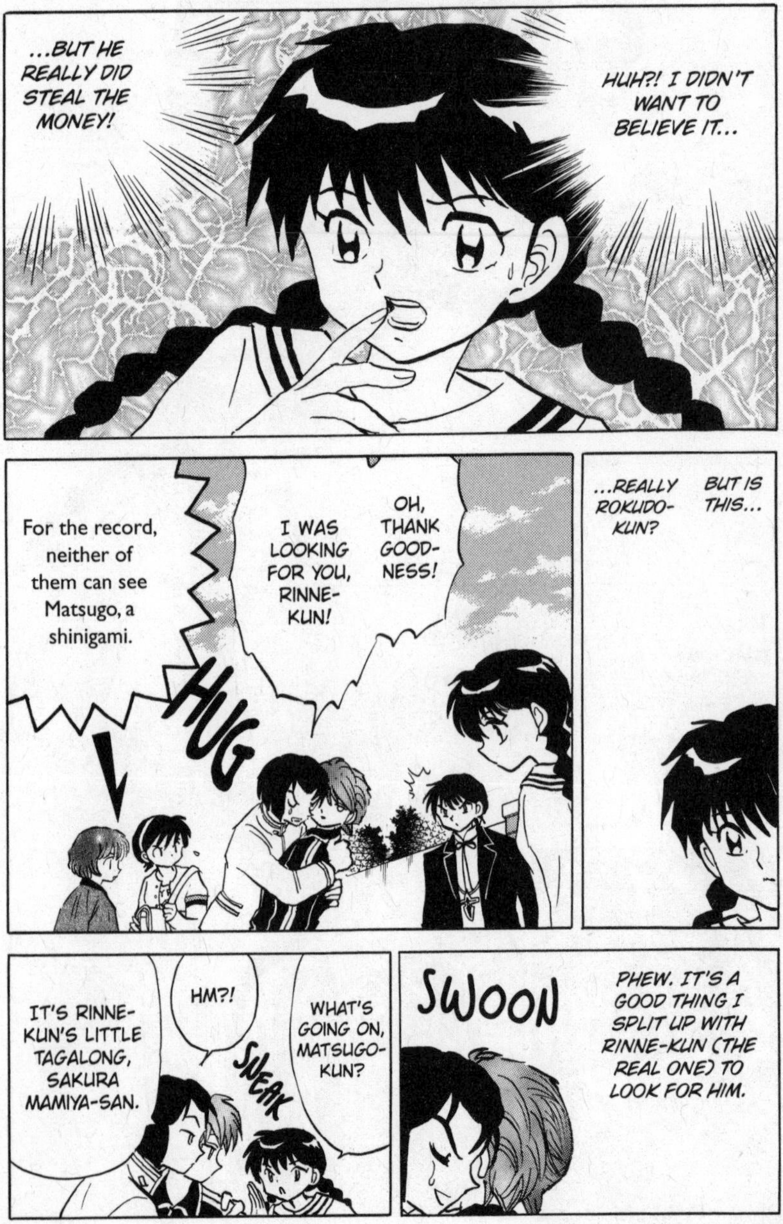
HUH?! I DIDN'T WANT TO BELIEVE IT...
...BUT HE REALLY DID STEAL THE MONEY!
BUT IS THIS...
...REALLY ROKUDO-KUN?
OH, THANK GOOD-NESS!
I WAS LOOKING FOR YOU, RINNE-KUN!
HUG
For the record, neither of them can see Matsugo, a shinigami.
PHEW. IT'S A GOOD THING I SPLIT UP WITH RINNE-KUN (THE REAL ONE) TO LOOK FOR HIM.
SWOON
WHAT'S GOING ON, MATSUGO-KUN?
SNEAK
HM?!
IT'S RINNE-KUN'S LITTLE TAGALONG, SAKURA MAMIYA-SAN.

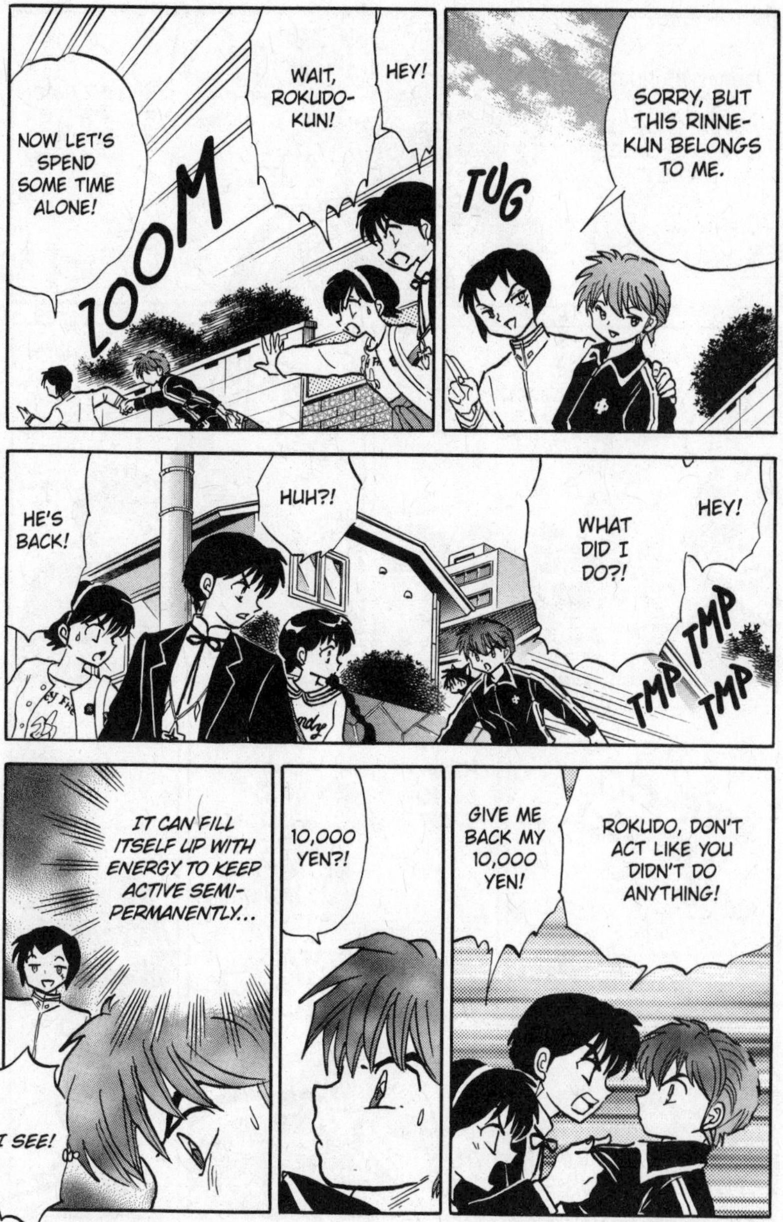
SORRY, BUT THIS RINNE-KUN BELONGS TO ME.
TUG
HEY!
WAIT, ROKUDO-KUN!
NOW LET'S SPEND SOME TIME ALONE!
ZOOM
HEY!
WHAT DID I DO?!
TMP TMP TMP TMP
HUH?!
HE'S BACK!
ROKUDO, DON'T ACT LIKE YOU DIDN'T DO ANYTHING!
GIVE ME BACK MY 10,000 YEN!
10,000 YEN?!
IT CAN FILL ITSELF UP WITH ENERGY TO KEEP ACTIVE SEMI-PERMANENTLY...
I SEE!

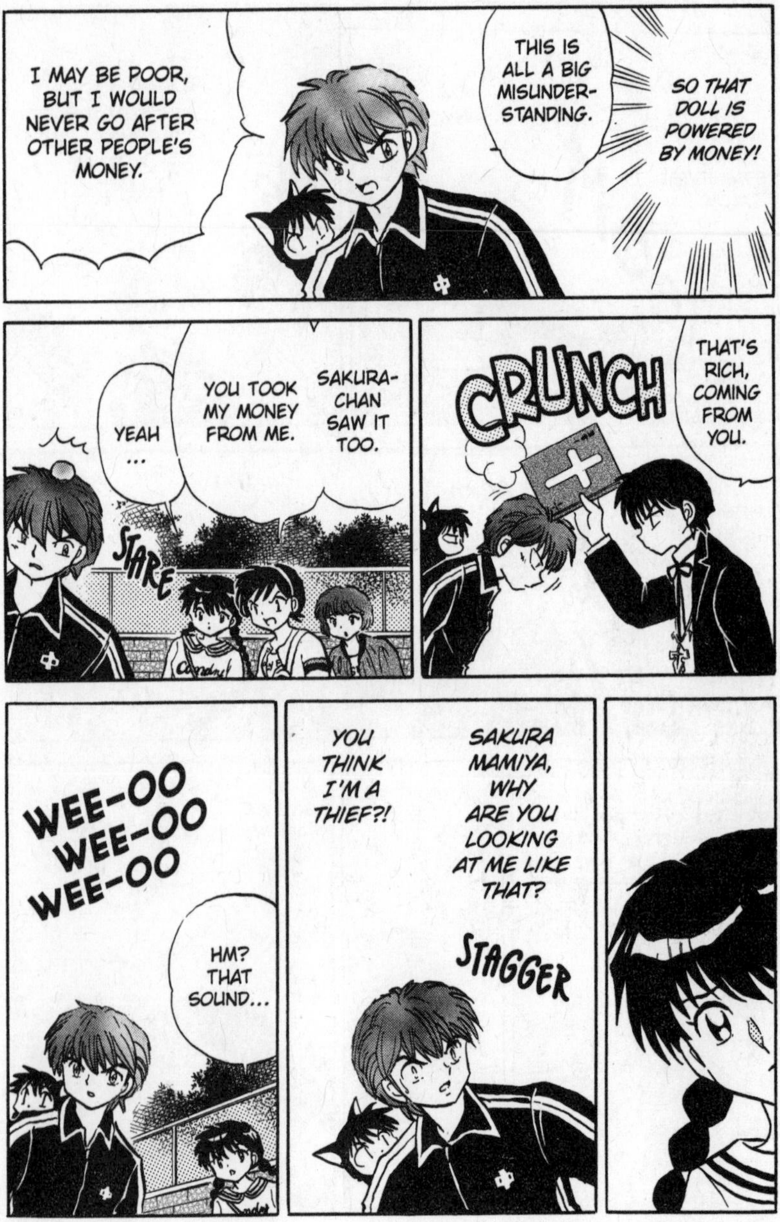
SO THAT DOLL IS POWERED BY MONEY!
THIS IS ALL A BIG MISUNDER-STANDING.
I MAY BE POOR, BUT I WOULD NEVER GO AFTER OTHER PEOPLE'S MONEY.
CRUNCH
THAT'S RICH, COMING FROM YOU.
SAKURA-CHAN SAW IT TOO.
YOU TOOK MY MONEY FROM ME.
YEAH ...
STARE
SAKURA MAMIYA, WHY ARE YOU LOOKING AT ME LIKE THAT?
YOU THINK I'M A THIEF?!
STAGGER
WEE-OO WEE-OO WEE-OO
HM? THAT SOUND...

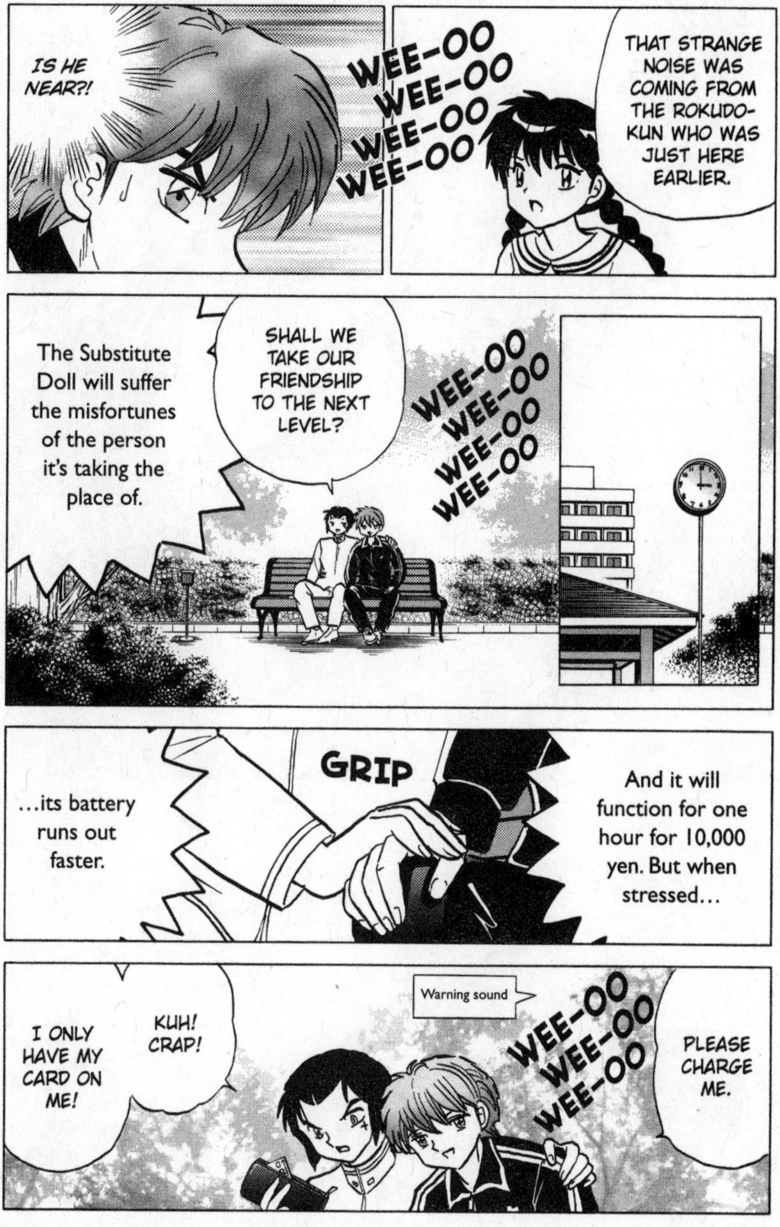
THAT STRANGE NOISE WAS COMING FROM THE ROKUDO-KUN WHO WAS JUST HERE EARLIER.
WEE-OO WEE-OO WEE-OO WEE-OO
IS HE NEAR?!
WEE-OO WEE-OO WEE-OO WEE-OO
SHALL WE TAKE OUR FRIENDSHIP TO THE NEXT LEVEL?
The Substitute Doll will suffer the misfortunes of the person it's taking the place of.
And it will function for one hour for 10,000 yen. But when stressed...
GRIP
...its battery runs out faster.
PLEASE CHARGE ME.
WEE-OO WEE-OO WEE-OO
Warning sound
KUH! CRAP!
I ONLY HAVE MY CARD ON ME!

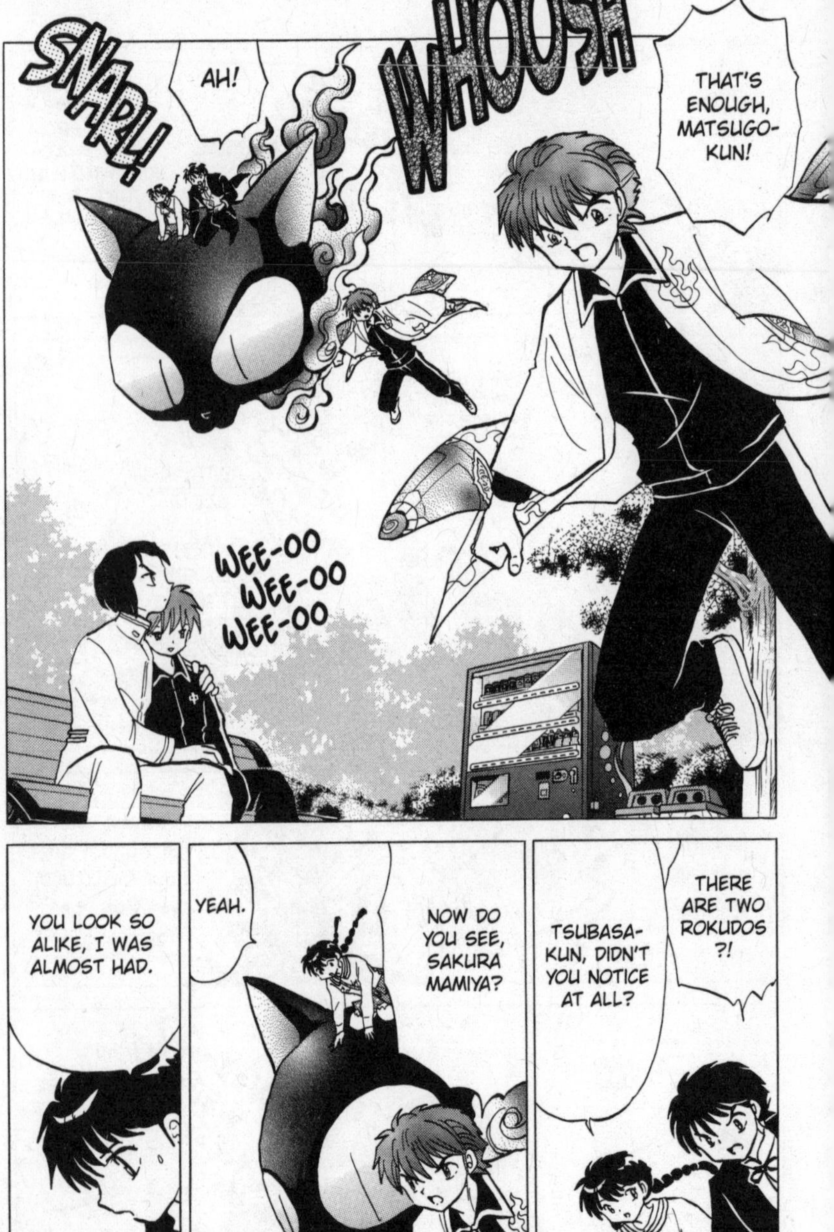
THAT'S ENOUGH, MATSUGO-KUN!
WHOOSH
AH!
SNARL!
WEE-OO WEE-OO WEE-OO
THERE ARE TWO ROKUDOS?!
TSUBASA-KUN, DIDN'T YOU NOTICE AT ALL?
NOW DO YOU SEE, SAKURA MAMIYA?
YEAH.
YOU LOOK SO ALIKE, I WAS ALMOST HAD.

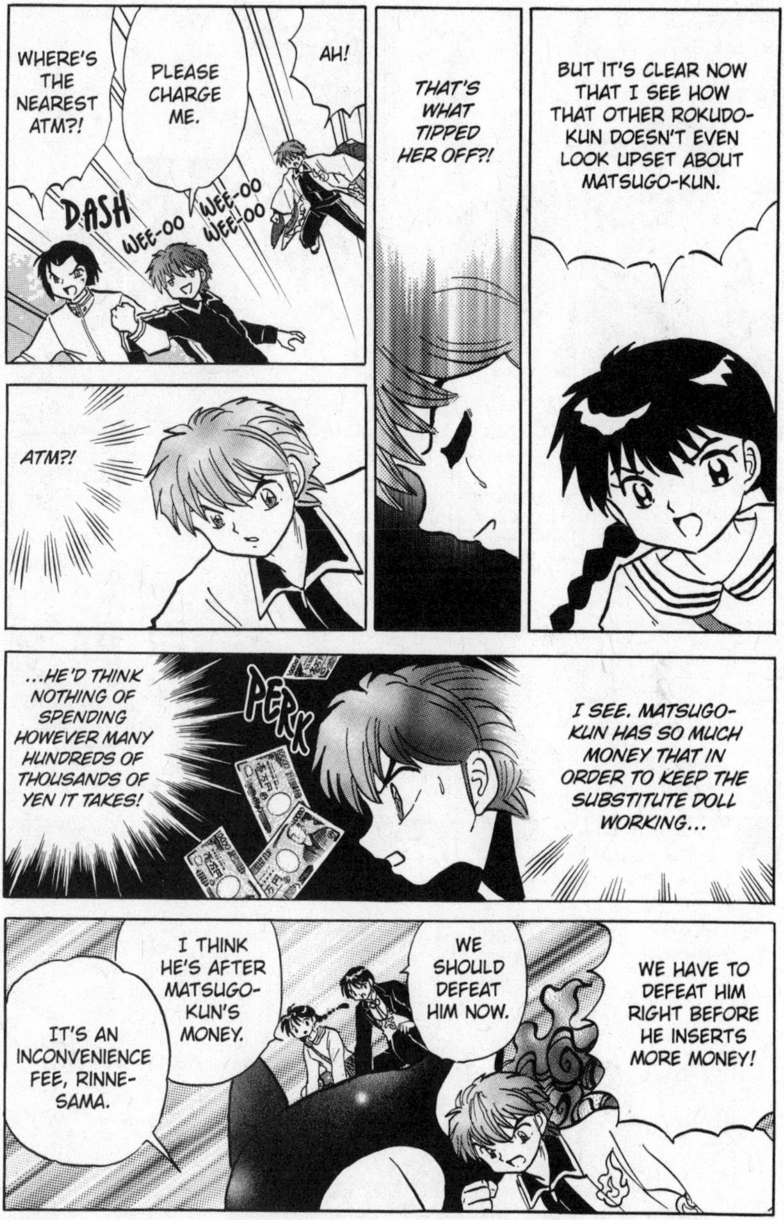
BUT IT'S CLEAR NOW THAT I SEE HOW THAT OTHER ROKUDO-KUN DOESN'T EVEN LOOK UPSET ABOUT MATSUGO-KUN.
THAT'S WHAT TIPPED HER OFF?!
AH!
PLEASE CHARGE ME.
WHERE'S THE NEAREST ATM?!
DASH
WEE-OO WEE-OO
WEE-OO
ATM?!
I SEE. MATSUGO-KUN HAS SO MUCH MONEY THAT IN ORDER TO KEEP THE SUBSTITUTE DOLL WORKING...
PERK
...HE'D THINK NOTHING OF SPENDING HOWEVER MANY HUNDREDS OF THOUSANDS OF YEN IT TAKES!
WE HAVE TO DEFEAT HIM RIGHT BEFORE HE INSERTS MORE MONEY!
WE SHOULD DEFEAT HIM NOW.
I THINK HE'S AFTER MATSUGO-KUN'S MONEY.
IT'S AN INCONVENIENCE FEE, RINNE-SAMA.

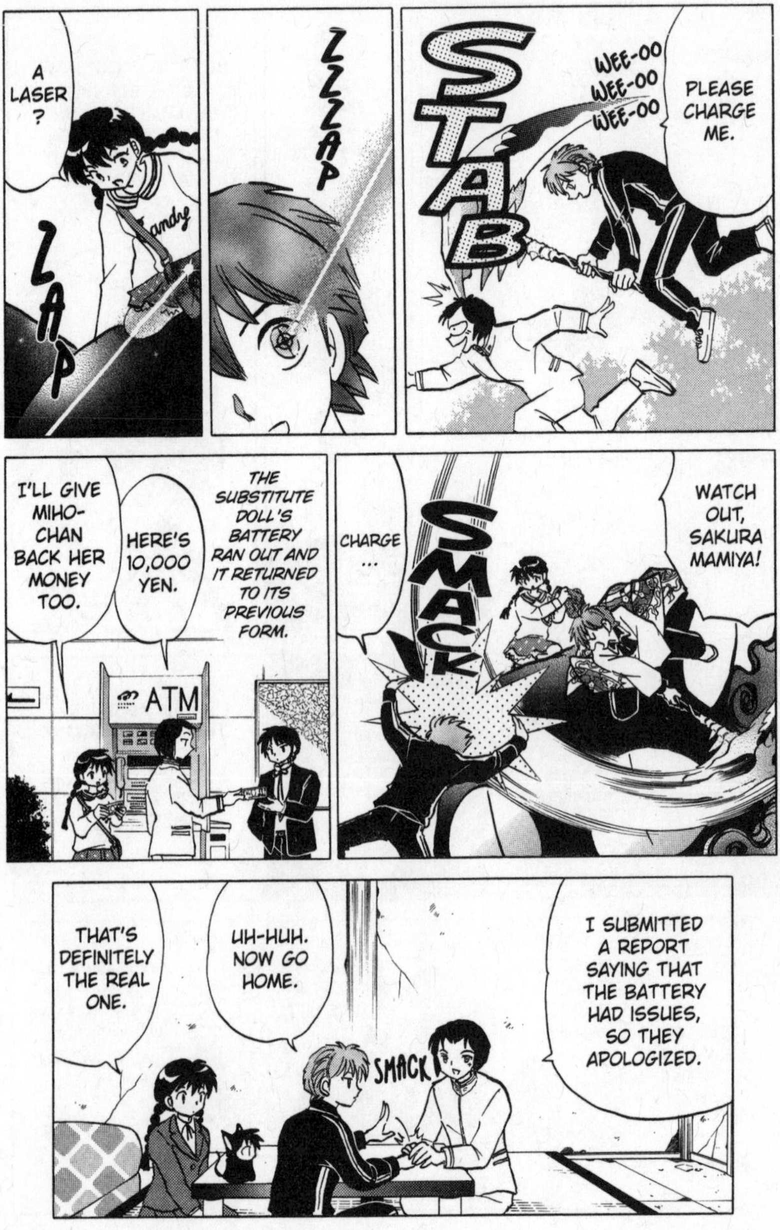
PLEASE CHARGE ME.
WEE-OO WEE-OO WEE-OO
STAB
ZZZZAP
A LASER?
ZAP
WATCH OUT, SAKURA MAMIYA!
SMACK
CHARGE...
THE SUBSTITUTE DOLL'S BATTERY RAN OUT AND IT RETURNED TO ITS PREVIOUS FORM.
HERE'S 10,000 YEN.
I'LL GIVE MIHO-CHAN BACK HER MONEY TOO.
ATM
I SUBMITTED A REPORT SAYING THAT THE BATTERY HAD ISSUES, SO THEY APOLOGIZED.
SMACK
UH-HUH. NOW GO HOME.
THAT'S DEFINITELY THE REAL ONE.

CHAPTER 277: THE FRUITS OF HARD WORK

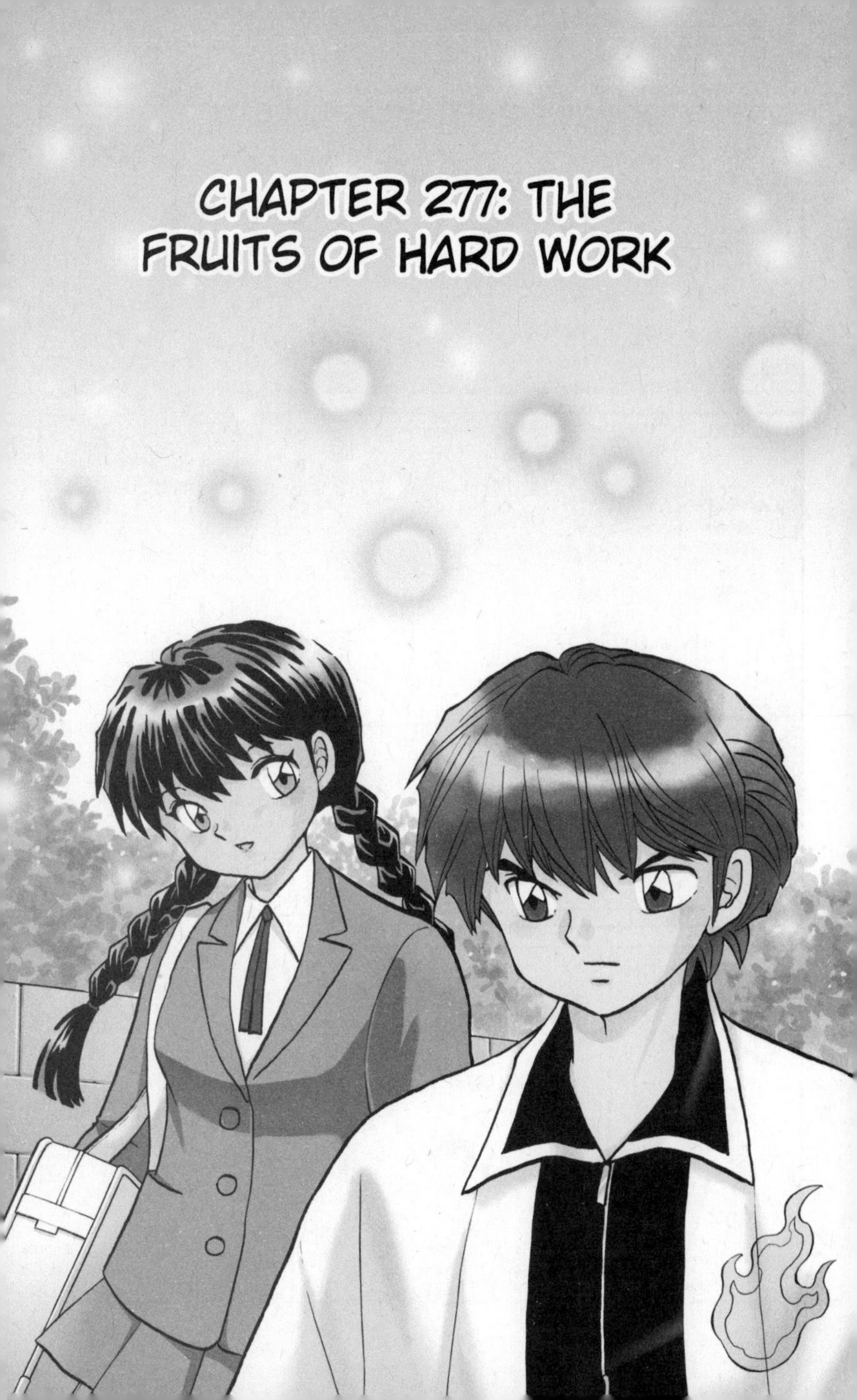

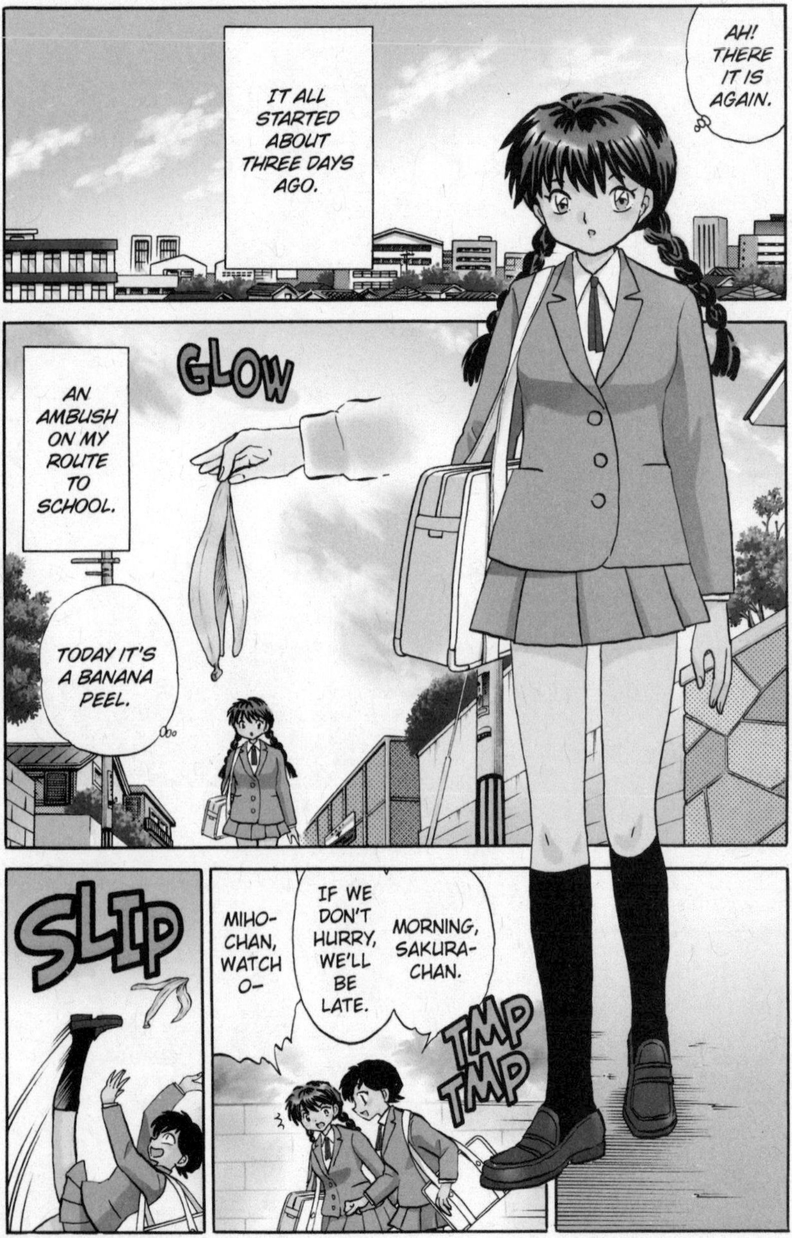

AH! THERE IT IS AGAIN.
IT ALL STARTED ABOUT THREE DAYS AGO.
GLOW
AN AMBUSH ON MY ROUTE TO SCHOOL.
TODAY IT'S A BANANA PEEL.
MORNING, SAKURA-CHAN.
IF WE DON'T HURRY, WE'LL BE LATE.
MIHO-CHAN, WATCH O-
TMP TMP
SLIP

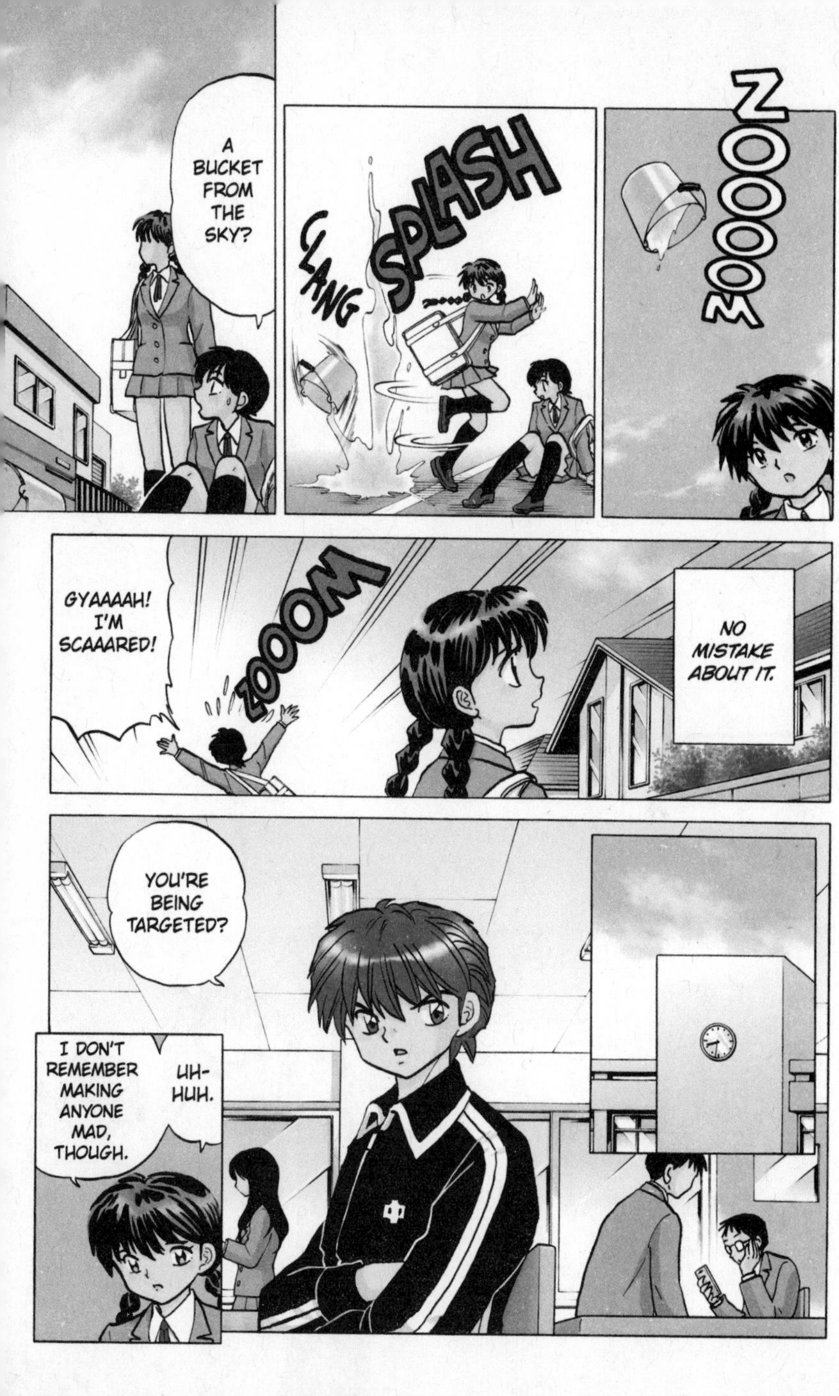
ZOOOOM
SPLASH
CLANG
A BUCKET FROM THE SKY?
NO MISTAKE ABOUT IT.
ZOOOOM
GYAAAAH! I'M SCAAARED!
YOU'RE BEING TARGETED?
UH-HUH.
I DON'T REMEMBER MAKING ANYONE MAD, THOUGH.

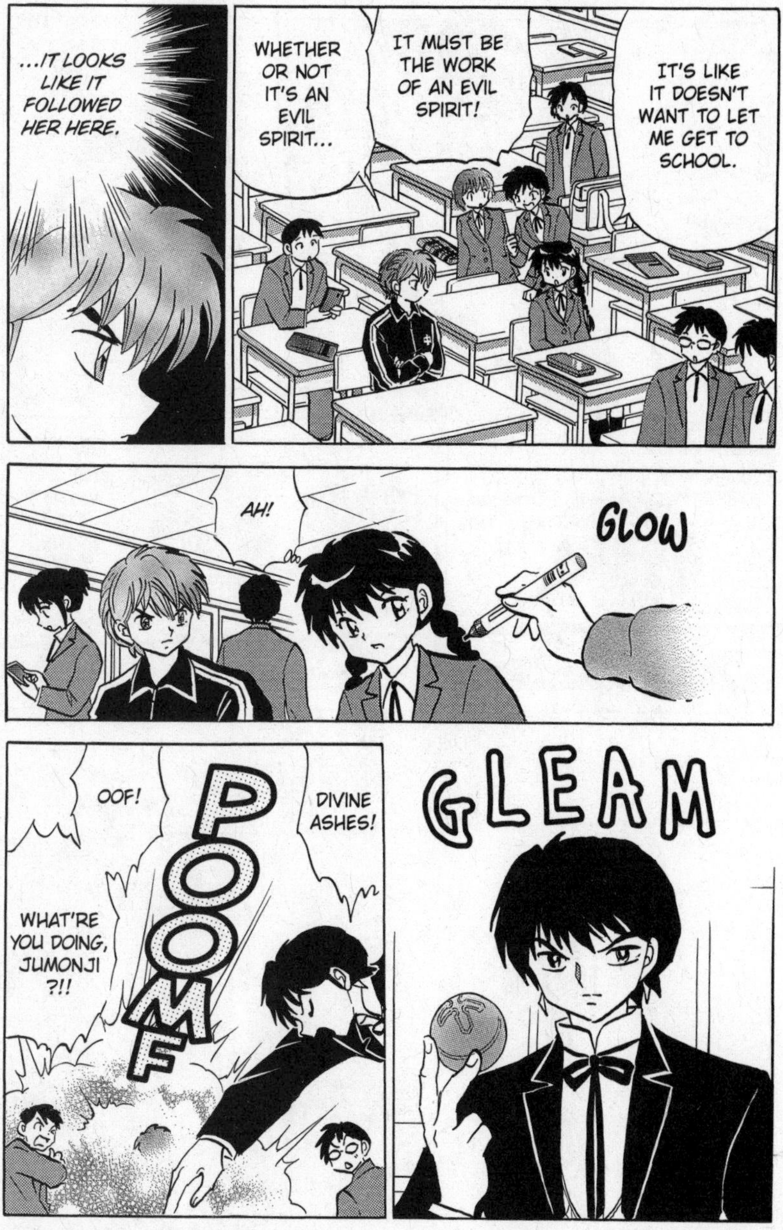
IT'S LIKE IT DOESN'T WANT TO LET ME GET TO SCHOOL.
IT MUST BE THE WORK OF AN EVIL SPIRIT!
WHETHER OR NOT IT'S AN EVIL SPIRIT...
...IT LOOKS LIKE IT FOLLOWED HER HERE.
GLOW
AH!
GLEAM
DIVINE ASHES!
POOOMF
OOF!
WHAT'RE YOU DOING, JUMONJI?!!

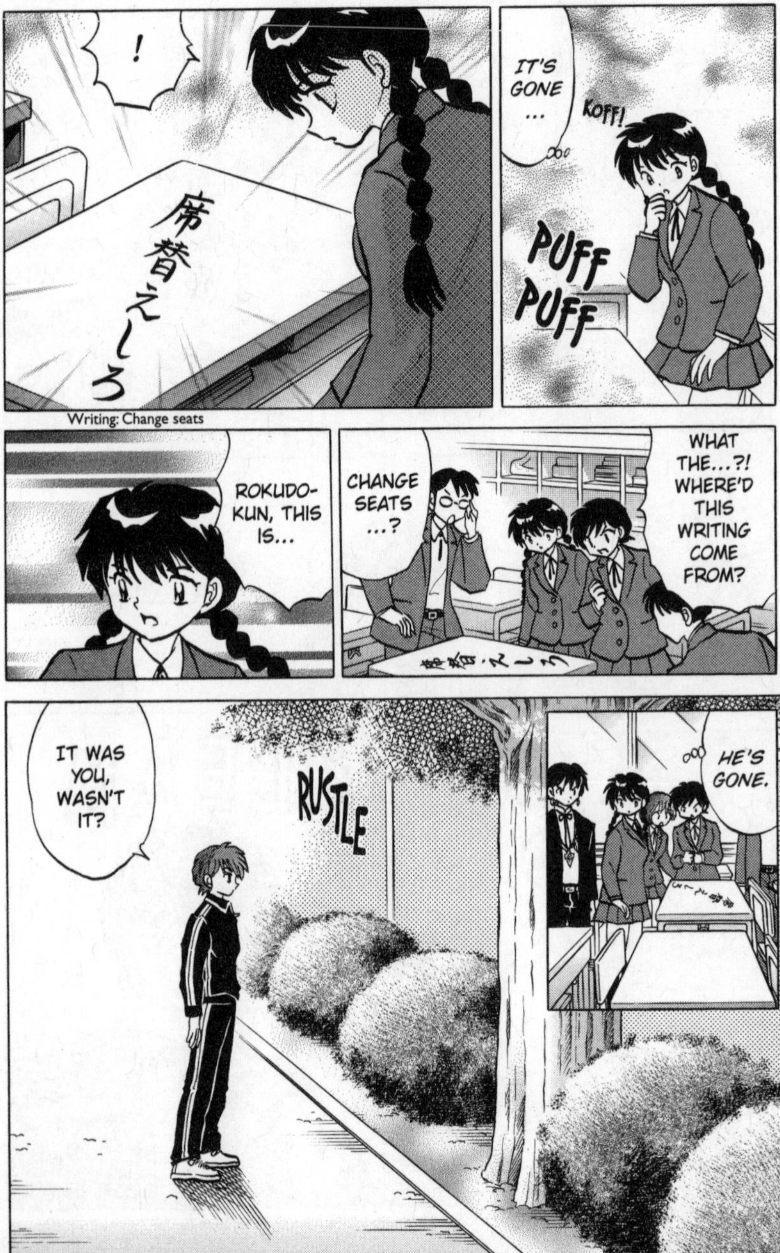
IT'S GONE ...
KOFF!
PUFF PUFF
!
席替えしろ
Writing: Change seats
WHAT THE...?! WHERE'D THIS WRITING COME FROM?
CHANGE SEATS ...?
ROKUDO-KUN, THIS IS...
HE'S GONE.
RUSTLE
IT WAS YOU, WASN'T IT?

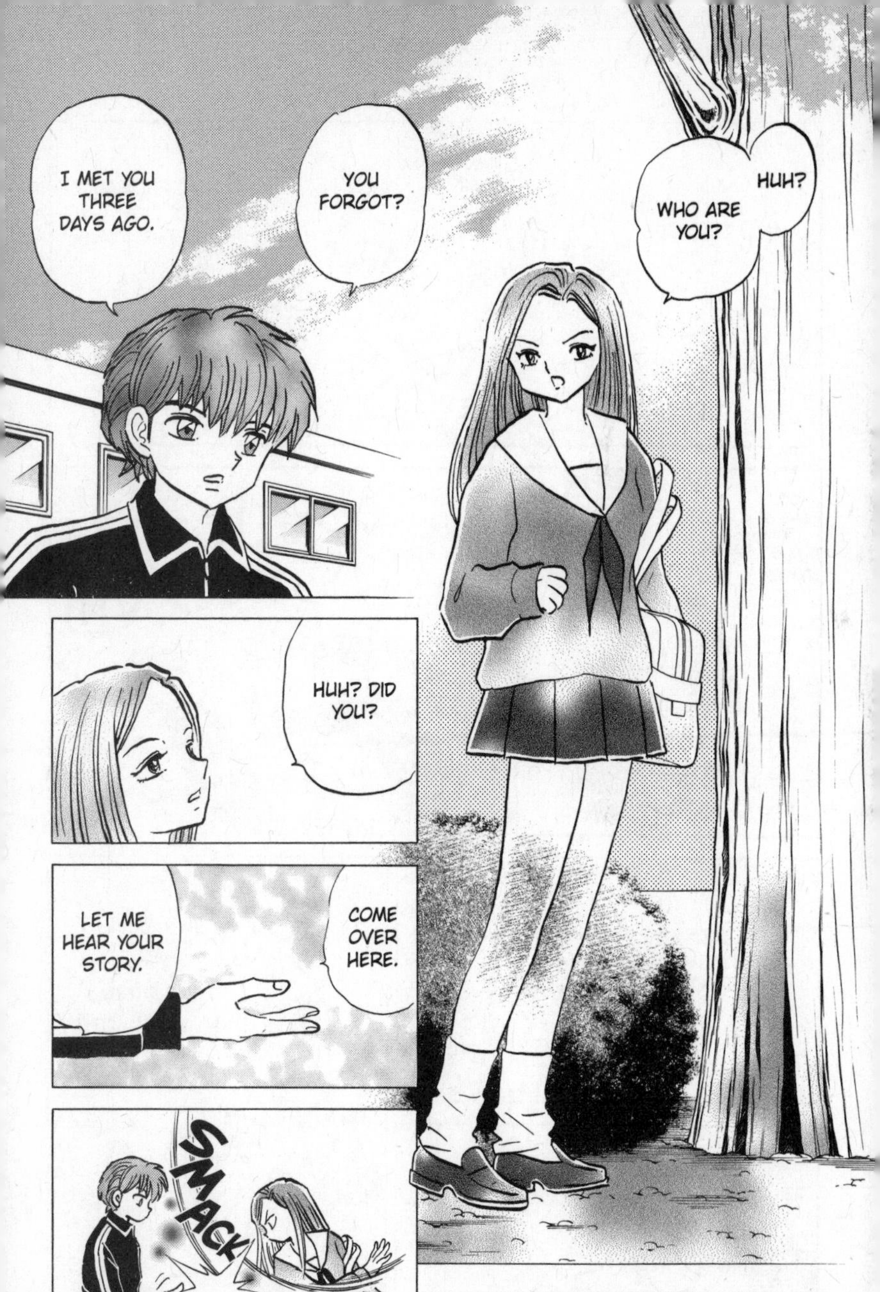
HUH?
WHO ARE YOU?
YOU FORGOT?
I MET YOU THREE DAYS AGO.
HUH? DID YOU?
COME OVER HERE.
LET ME HEAR YOUR STORY.
SMACK

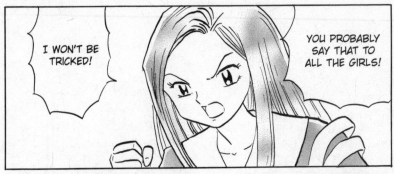

YOU PROBABLY SAY THAT TO ALL THE GIRLS!
I WON'T BE TRICKED!
SHOVE
ROKUDO, DO YOU KNOW HER?
MARCH MARCH
LOOSE SOCKS.
SO SHE'S AN OLD GHOST ?!
Loose socks were a fashion trend among high school girls in the 90's.
THREE DAYS AGO...
I TOOK MY FIRST STEP AS A HIGH SCHOOL STUDENT.
HERE IT COMES.

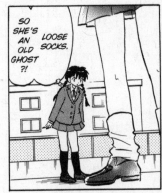

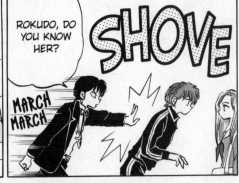

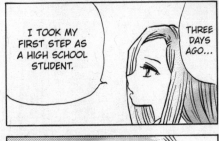

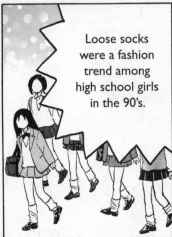

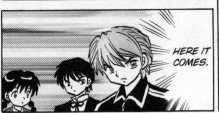

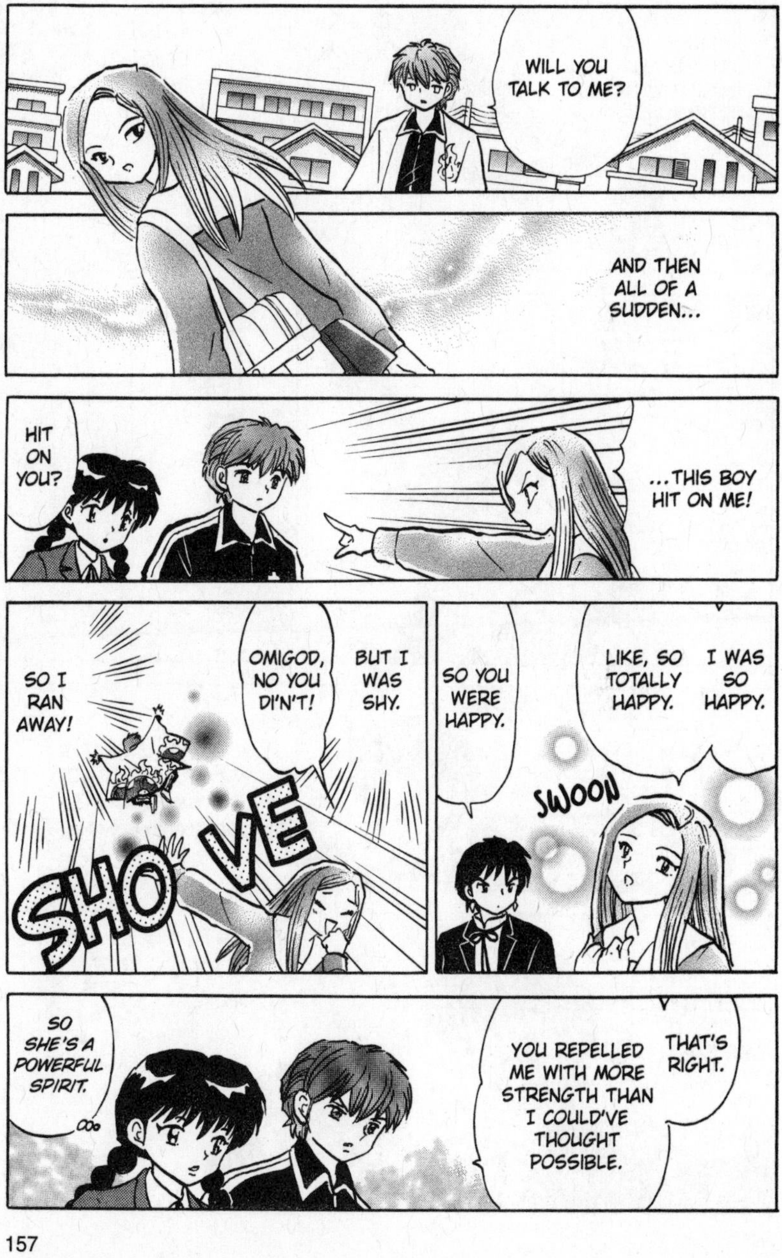
WILL YOU TALK TO ME?
AND THEN ALL OF A SUDDEN...
...THIS BOY HIT ON ME!
HIT ON YOU?
I WAS SO HAPPY.
LIKE, SO TOTALLY HAPPY.
SO YOU WERE HAPPY.
SWOON
BUT I WAS SHY.
OMIGOD, NO YOU DI'N'T!
SO I RAN AWAY!
SHOVE
THAT'S RIGHT.
YOU REPELLED ME WITH MORE STRENGTH THAN I COULD'VE THOUGHT POSSIBLE.
SO SHE'S A POWERFUL SPIRIT.

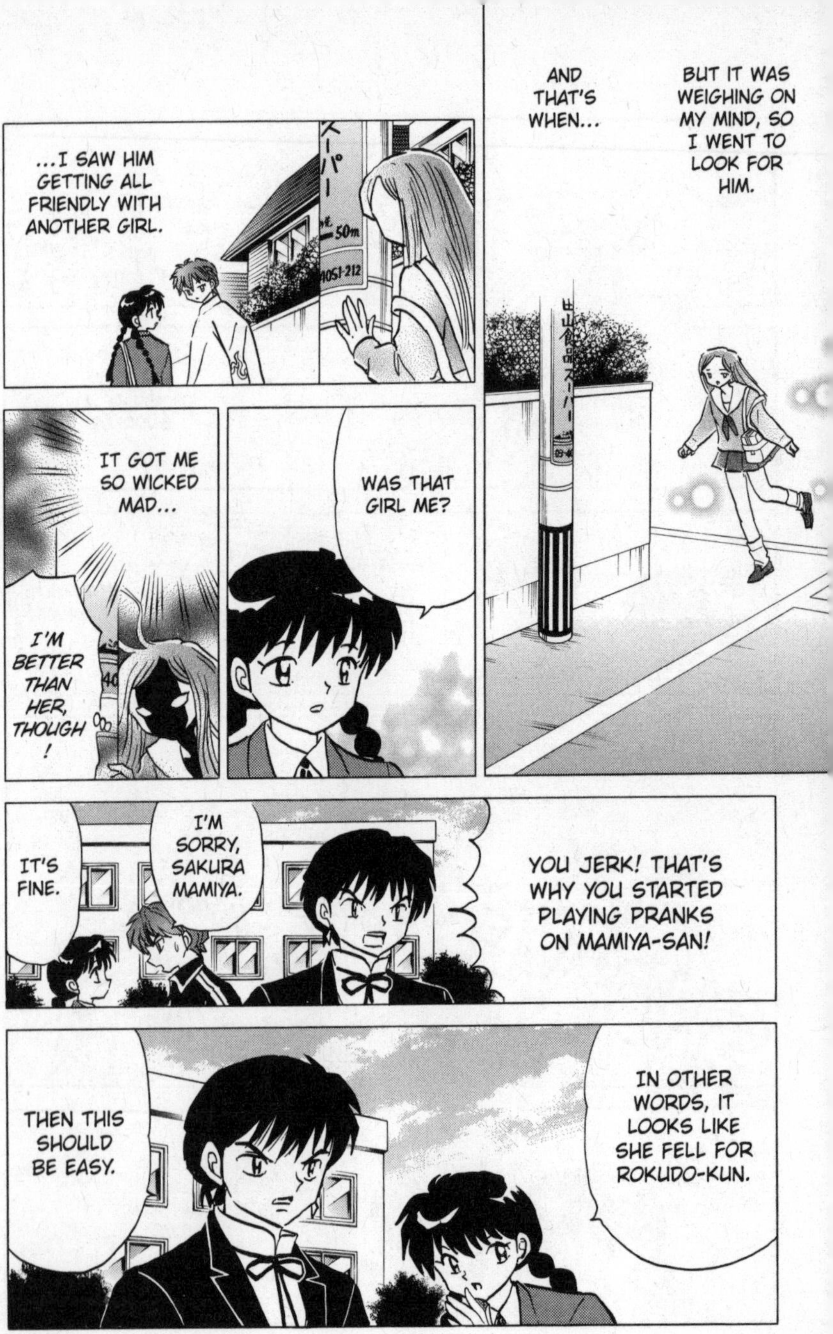
BUT IT WAS WEIGHING ON MY MIND, SO I WENT TO LOOK FOR HIM.
AND THAT'S WHEN...
...I SAW HIM GETTING ALL FRIENDLY WITH ANOTHER GIRL.
WAS THAT GIRL ME?
IT GOT ME SO WICKED MAD...
I'M BETTER THAN HER, THOUGH!
YOU JERK! THAT'S WHY YOU STARTED PLAYING PRANKS ON MAMIYA-SAN!
I'M SORRY, SAKURA MAMIYA.
IT'S FINE.
IN OTHER WORDS, IT LOOKS LIKE SHE FELL FOR ROKUDO-KUN.
THEN THIS SHOULD BE EASY.

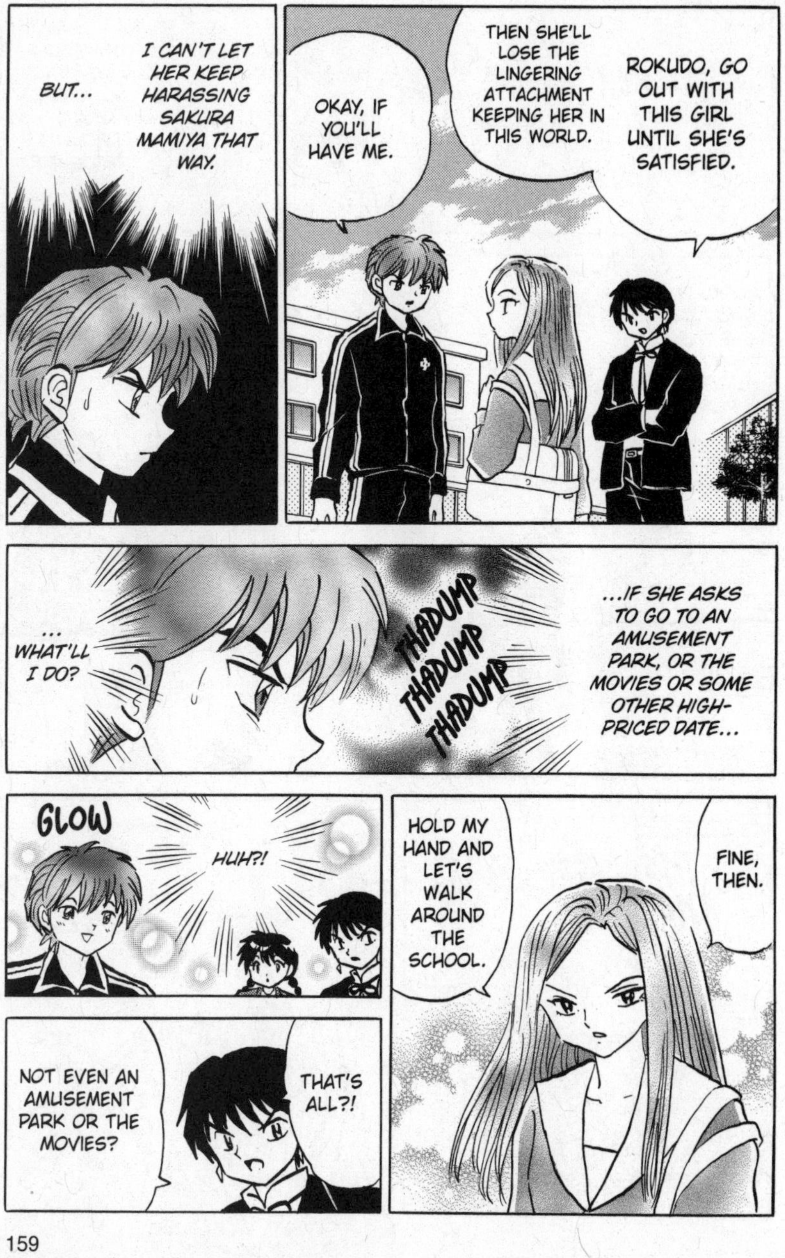
ROKUDO, GO OUT WITH THIS GIRL UNTIL SHE'S SATISFIED.
THEN SHE'LL LOSE THE LINGERING ATTACHMENT KEEPING HER IN THIS WORLD.
OKAY, IF YOU'LL HAVE ME.
I CAN'T LET HER KEEP HARASSING SAKURA MAMIYA THAT WAY.
BUT...
...IF SHE ASKS TO GO TO AN AMUSEMENT PARK, OR THE MOVIES OR SOME OTHER HIGH-PRICED DATE...
THADUMP
THADUMP
THADUMP
...WHAT'LL I DO?
FINE, THEN.
HOLD MY HAND AND LET'S WALK AROUND THE SCHOOL.
GLOW
HUH?!
THAT'S ALL?!
NOT EVEN AN AMUSEMENT PARK OR THE MOVIES?

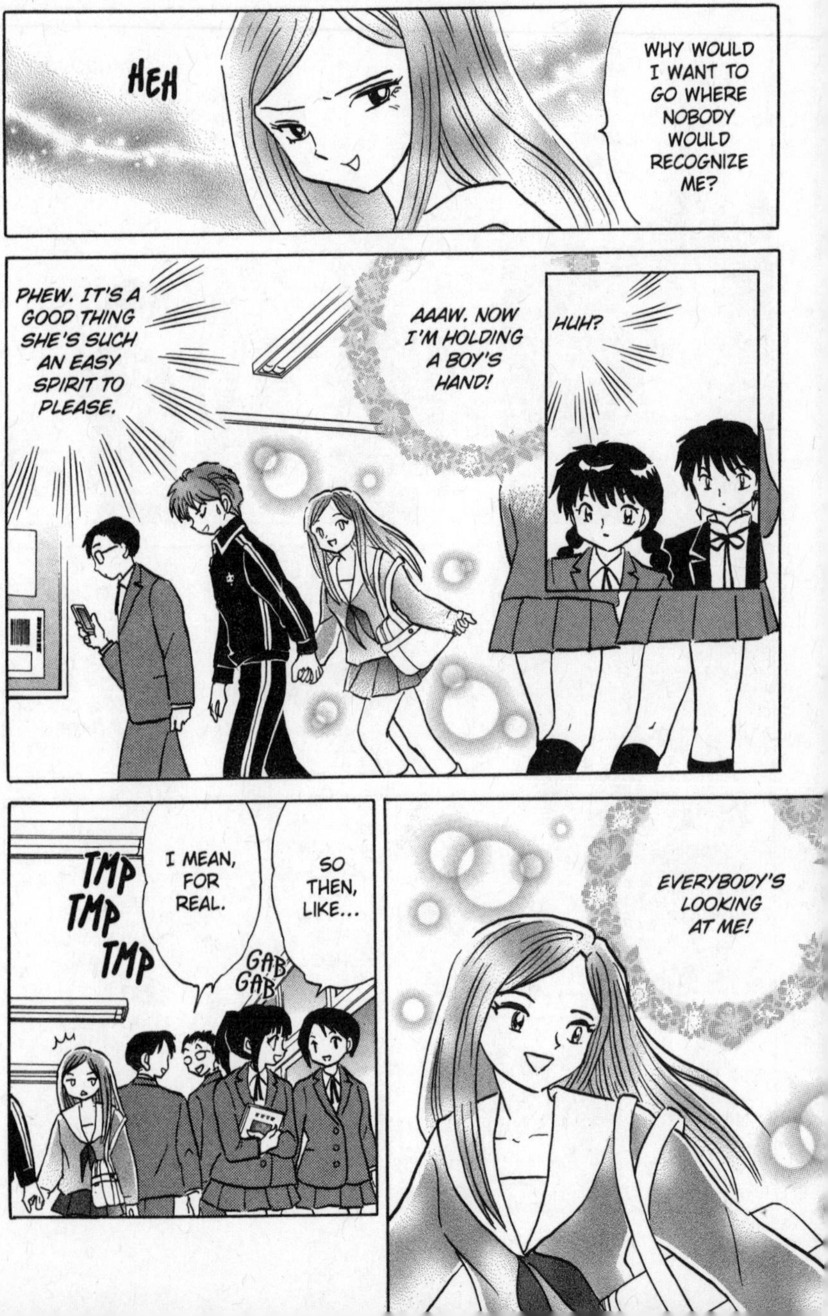
WHY WOULD I WANT TO GO WHERE NOBODY WOULD RECOGNIZE ME?
HEH
HUH?
AAAW. NOW I'M HOLDING A BOY'S HAND!
PHEW. IT'S A GOOD THING SHE'S SUCH AN EASY SPIRIT TO PLEASE.
EVERYBODY'S LOOKING AT ME!
SO THEN, LIKE...
I MEAN, FOR REAL.
GAB GAB
TMP TMP TMP

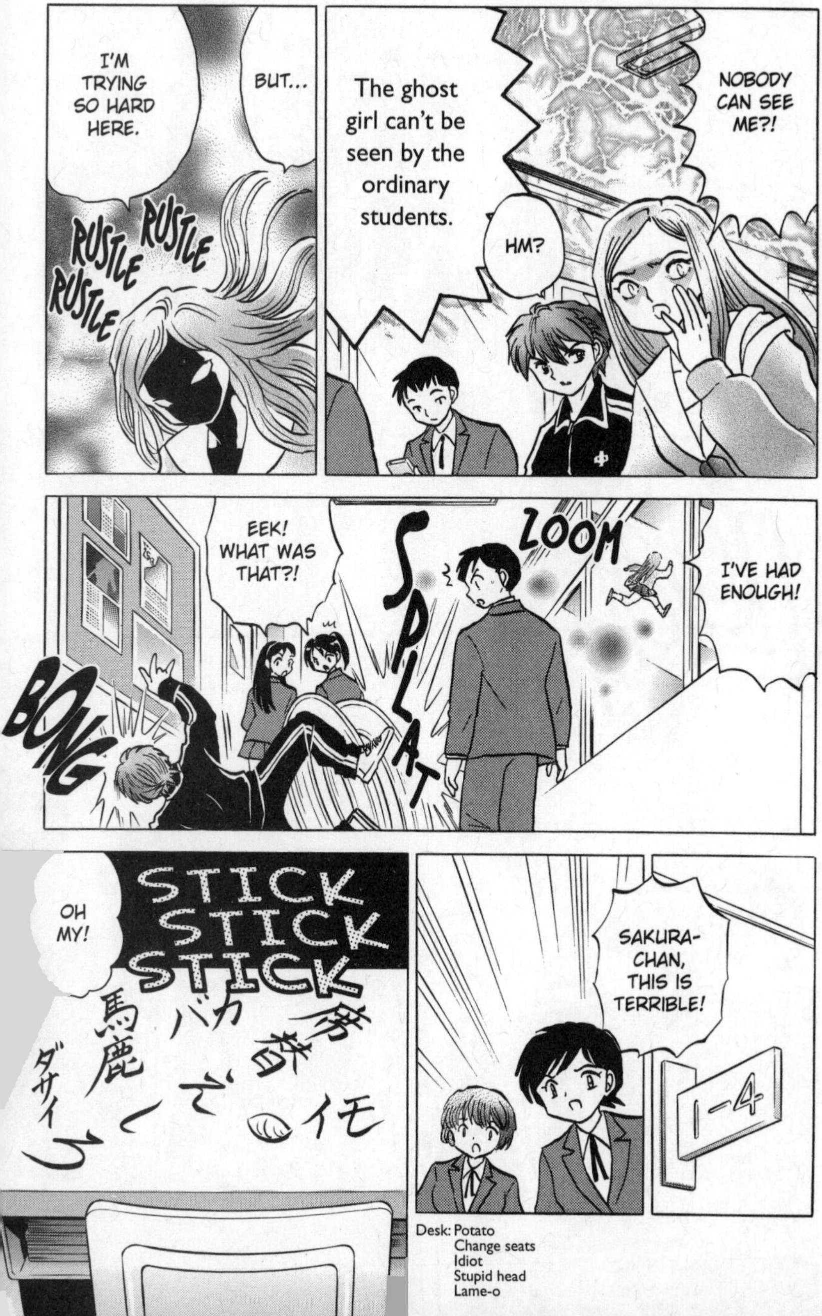
NOBODY CAN SEE ME?!
The ghost girl can't be seen by the ordinary students.
HM?
BUT...
I'M TRYING SO HARD HERE.
RUSTLE
RUSTLE
RUSTLE
I'VE HAD ENOUGH!
ZOOM
SPLAT
EEK! WHAT WAS THAT?!
BONG
SAKURA-CHAN, THIS IS TERRIBLE!
STICK STICK STICK
OH MY!

Desk: Potato
Change seats
Idiot
Stupid head
Lame-o

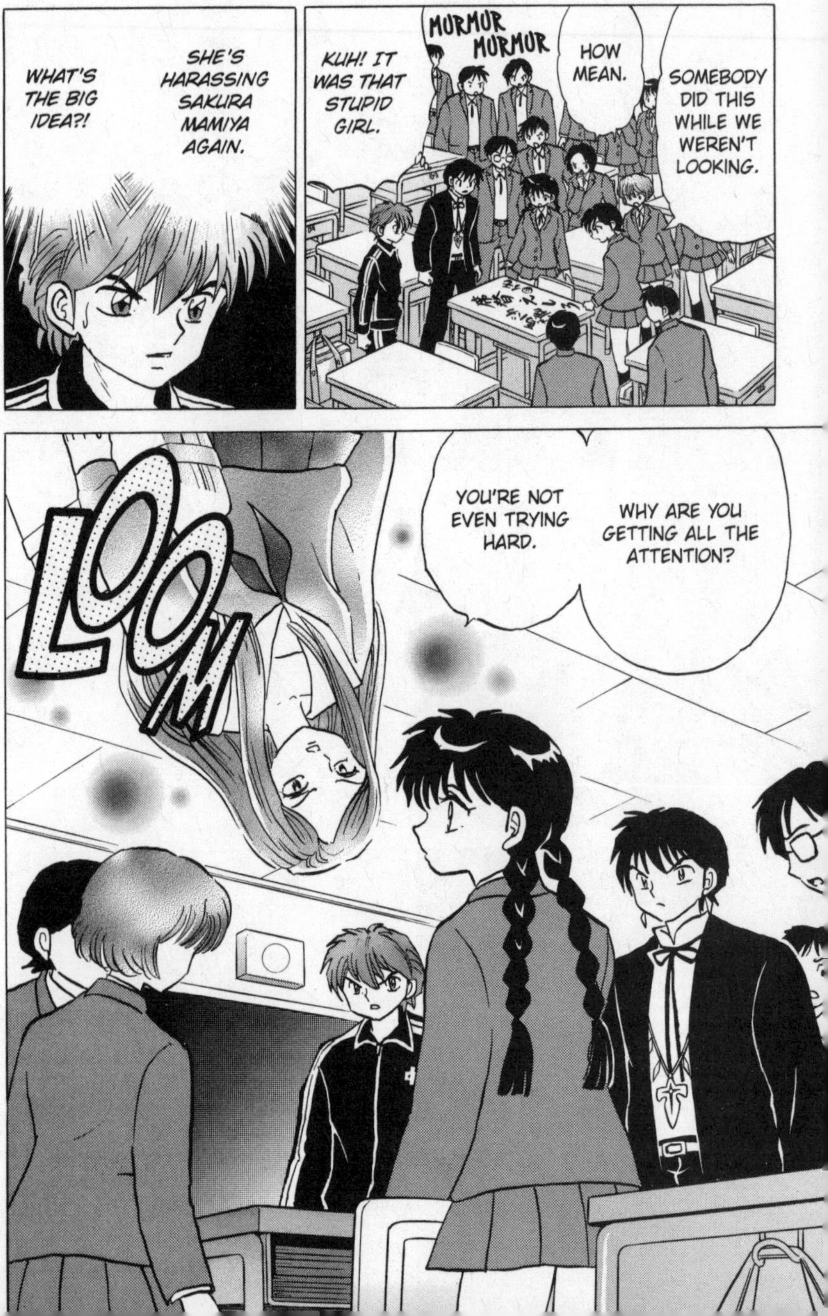
SOMEBODY DID THIS WHILE WE WEREN'T LOOKING.
HOW MEAN.
MURMUR MURMUR
KUH! IT WAS THAT STUPID GIRL.
SHE'S HARASSING SAKURA MAMIYA AGAIN.
WHAT'S THE BIG IDEA?!
WHY ARE YOU GETTING ALL THE ATTENTION?
YOU'RE NOT EVEN TRYING HARD.
LOOM

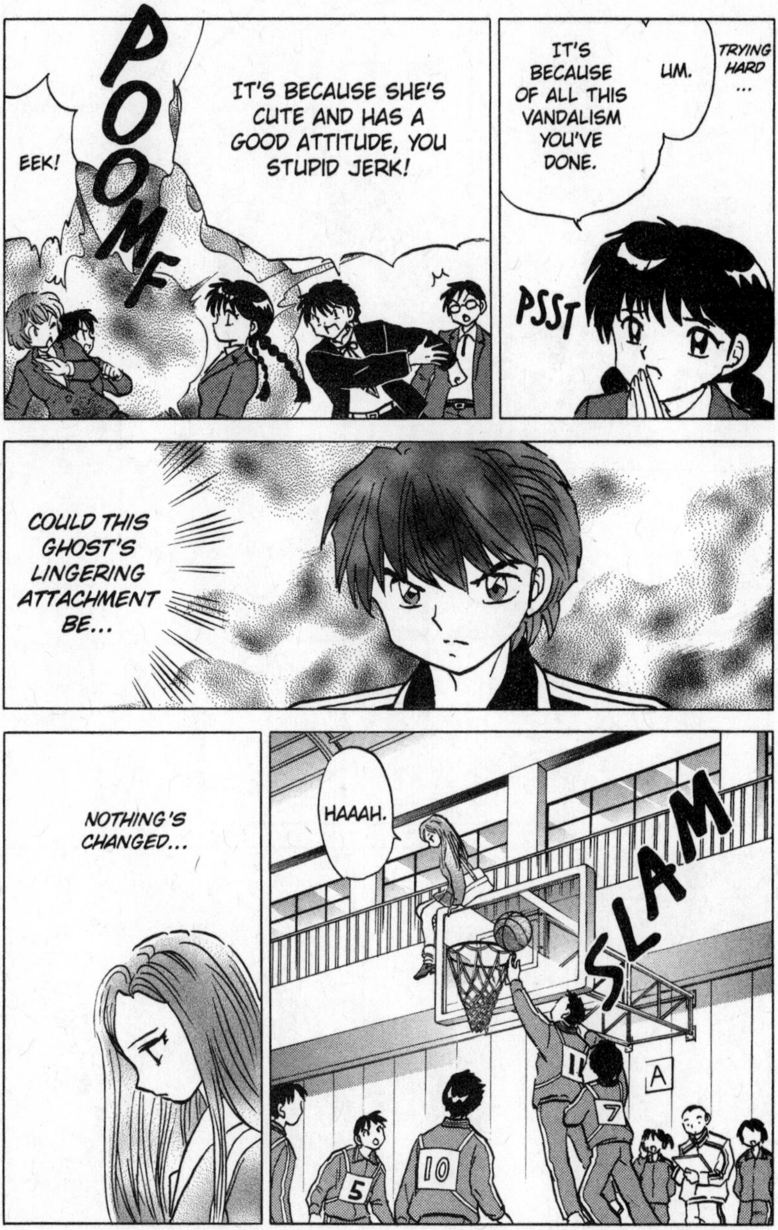
TRYING HARD ...
UM.
IT'S BECAUSE OF ALL THIS VANDALISM YOU'VE DONE.
PSST
IT'S BECAUSE SHE'S CUTE AND HAS A GOOD ATTITUDE, YOU STUPID JERK!
POOMF
EEK!
COULD THIS GHOST'S LINGERING ATTACHMENT BE...
SLAM
HAAAH.
NOTHING'S CHANGED...

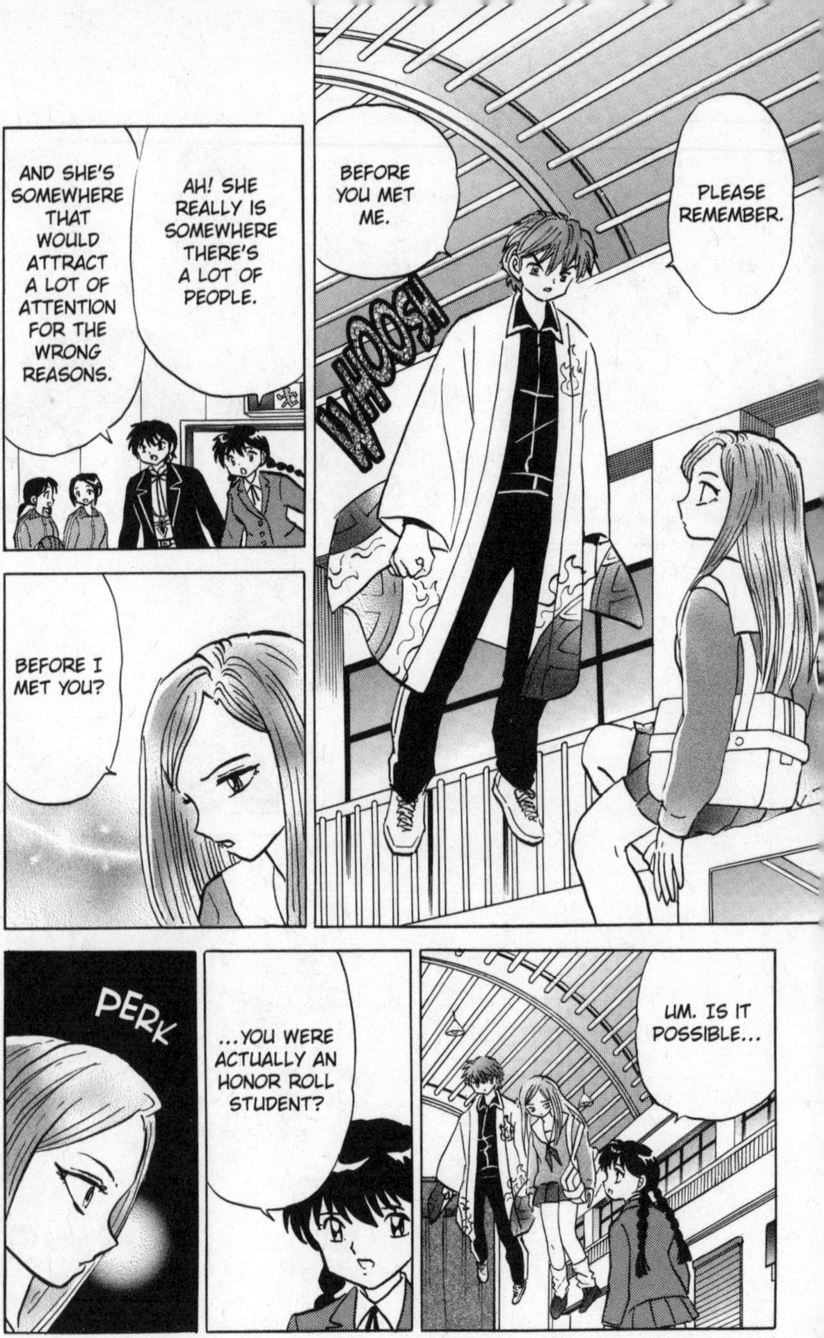
PLEASE REMEMBER.
BEFORE YOU MET ME.
WHOOSH!
AH! SHE REALLY IS SOMEWHERE THERE'S A LOT OF PEOPLE.
AND SHE'S SOMEWHERE THAT WOULD ATTRACT A LOT OF ATTENTION FOR THE WRONG REASONS.
BEFORE I MET YOU?
UM. IS IT POSSIBLE...
...YOU WERE ACTUALLY AN HONOR ROLL STUDENT?
PERK

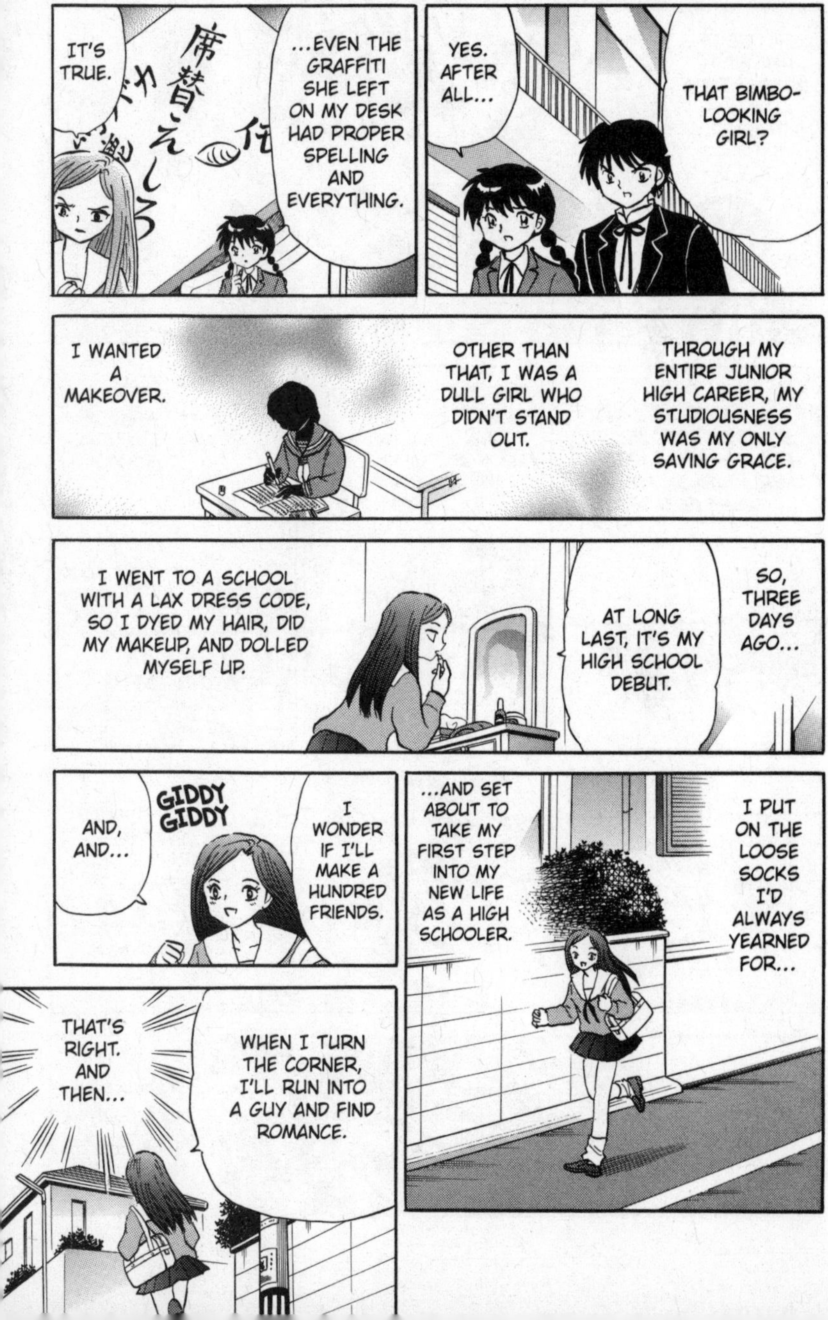
THAT BIMBO-LOOKING GIRL?
YES. AFTER ALL...
...EVEN THE GRAFFITI SHE LEFT ON MY DESK HAD PROPER SPELLING AND EVERYTHING.
席替えしろ
IT'S TRUE.
THROUGH MY ENTIRE JUNIOR HIGH CAREER, MY STUDIOUSNESS WAS MY ONLY SAVING GRACE.
OTHER THAN THAT, I WAS A DULL GIRL WHO DIDN'T STAND OUT.
I WANTED A MAKEOVER.
SO, THREE DAYS AGO...
AT LONG LAST, IT'S MY HIGH SCHOOL DEBUT.
I WENT TO A SCHOOL WITH A LAX DRESS CODE, SO I DYED MY HAIR, DID MY MAKEUP, AND DOLLED MYSELF UP.
I PUT ON THE LOOSE SOCKS I'D ALWAYS YEARNED FOR...
...AND SET ABOUT TO TAKE MY FIRST STEP INTO MY NEW LIFE AS A HIGH SCHOOLER.
I WONDER IF I'LL MAKE A HUNDRED FRIENDS.
GIDDY GIDDY
AND, AND...
WHEN I TURN THE CORNER, I'LL RUN INTO A GUY AND FIND ROMANCE.
THAT'S RIGHT. AND THEN...

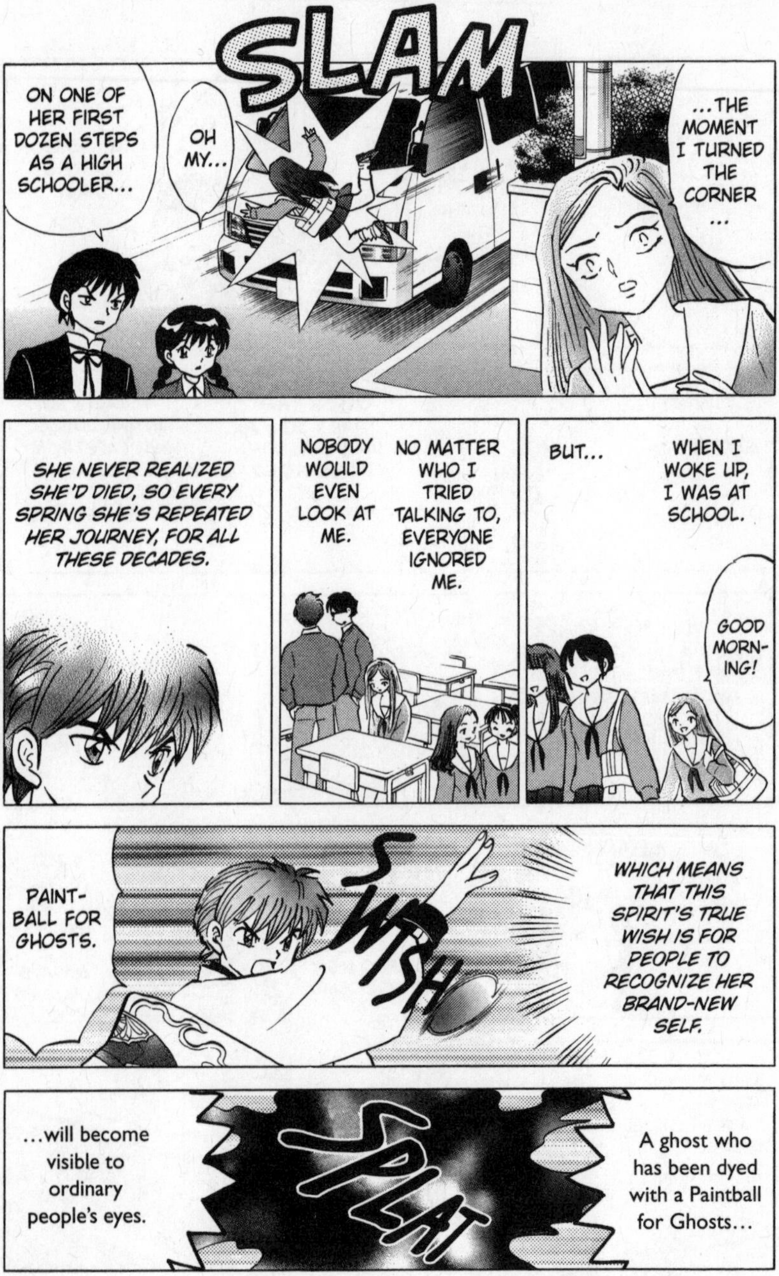
SLAM
...THE MOMENT I TURNED THE CORNER ...
OH MY...
ON ONE OF HER FIRST DOZEN STEPS AS A HIGH SCHOOLER...
WHEN I WOKE UP, I WAS AT SCHOOL.
BUT...
GOOD MORNING!
NO MATTER WHO I TRIED TALKING TO, EVERYONE IGNORED ME.
NOBODY WOULD EVEN LOOK AT ME.
SHE NEVER REALIZED SHE'D DIED, SO EVERY SPRING SHE'S REPEATED HER JOURNEY, FOR ALL THESE DECADES.
WHICH MEANS THAT THIS SPIRIT'S TRUE WISH IS FOR PEOPLE TO RECOGNIZE HER BRAND-NEW SELF.
SWISH
PAINT-BALL FOR GHOSTS.
A ghost who has been dyed with a Paintball for Ghosts...
SPLAT
...will become visible to ordinary people's eyes.

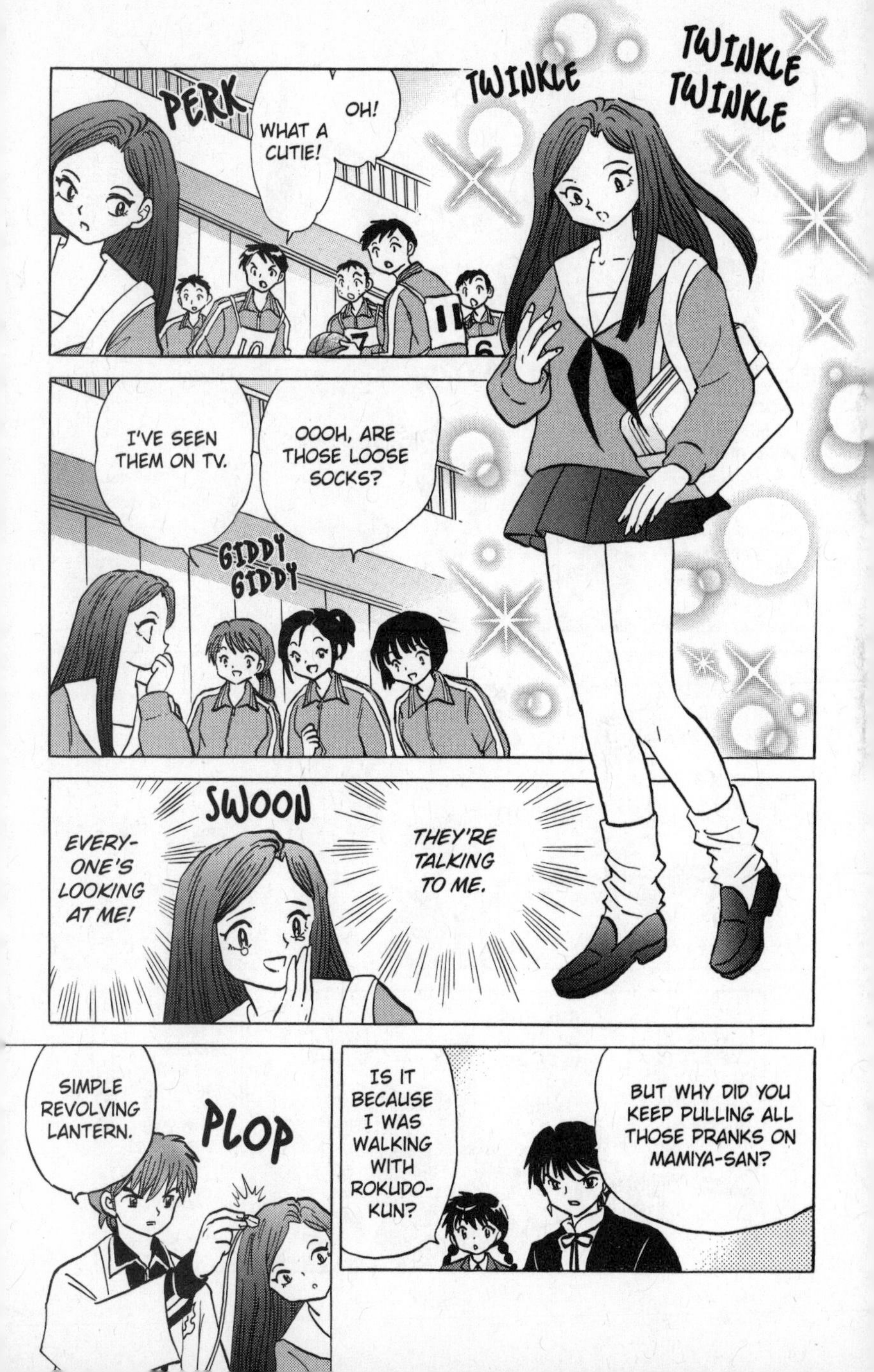
TWINKLE TWINKLE
TWINKLE
OH!
WHAT A CUTIE!
PERK
OOOH, ARE THOSE LOOSE SOCKS?
I'VE SEEN THEM ON TV.
GIDDY GIDDY
SWOON
THEY'RE TALKING TO ME.
EVERY-ONE'S LOOKING AT ME!
BUT WHY DID YOU KEEP PULLING ALL THOSE PRANKS ON MAMIYA-SAN?
IS IT BECAUSE I WAS WALKING WITH ROKUDO-KUN?
SIMPLE REVOLVING LANTERN.
PLOP

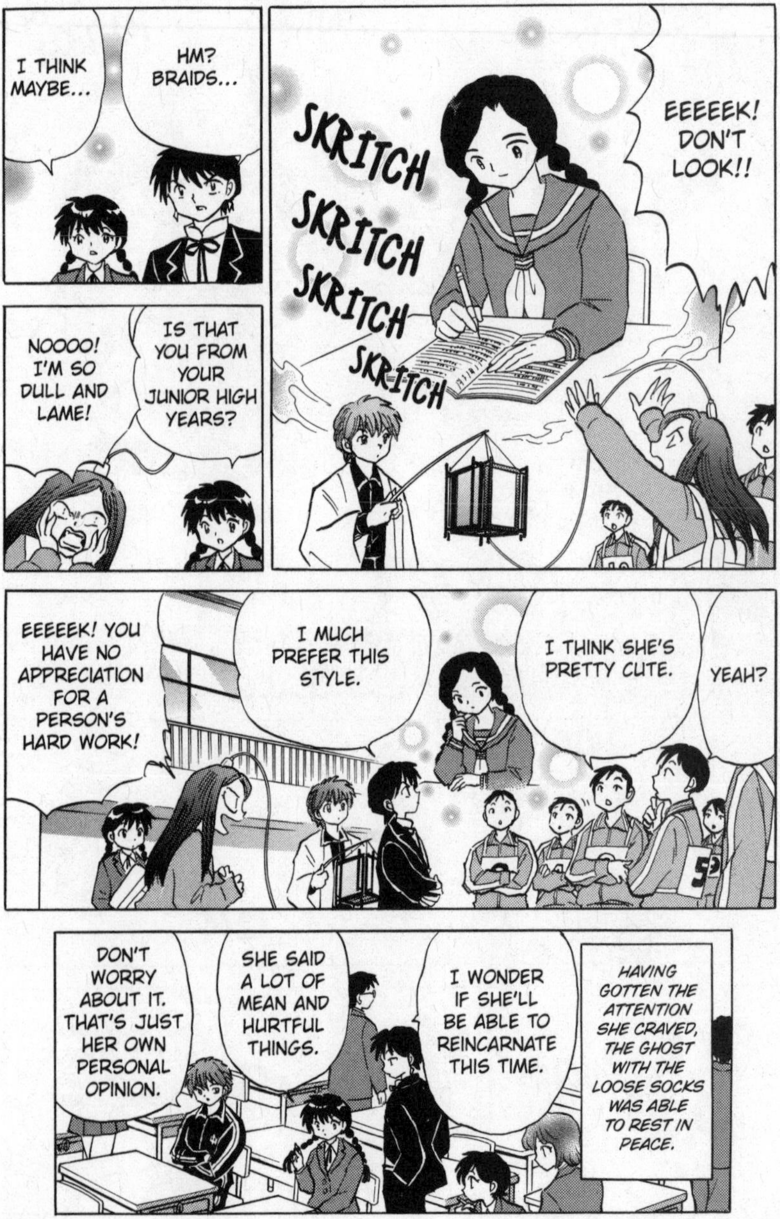
EEEEEK! DON'T LOOK!!
SKRITCH
SKRITCH
SKRITCH
SKRITCH
HM? BRAIDS...
I THINK MAYBE...
IS THAT YOU FROM YOUR JUNIOR HIGH YEARS?
NOOOO! I'M SO DULL AND LAME!
YEAH?
I THINK SHE'S PRETTY CUTE.
I MUCH PREFER THIS STYLE.
EEEEEK! YOU HAVE NO APPRECIATION FOR A PERSON'S HARD WORK!
HAVING GOTTEN THE ATTENTION SHE CRAVED, THE GHOST WITH THE LOOSE SOCKS WAS ABLE TO REST IN PEACE.
I WONDER IF SHE'LL BE ABLE TO REINCARNATE THIS TIME.
SHE SAID A LOT OF MEAN AND HURTFUL THINGS.
DON'T WORRY ABOUT IT. THAT'S JUST HER OWN PERSONAL OPINION.

CHAPTER 278: SPRINGTIME MATCH

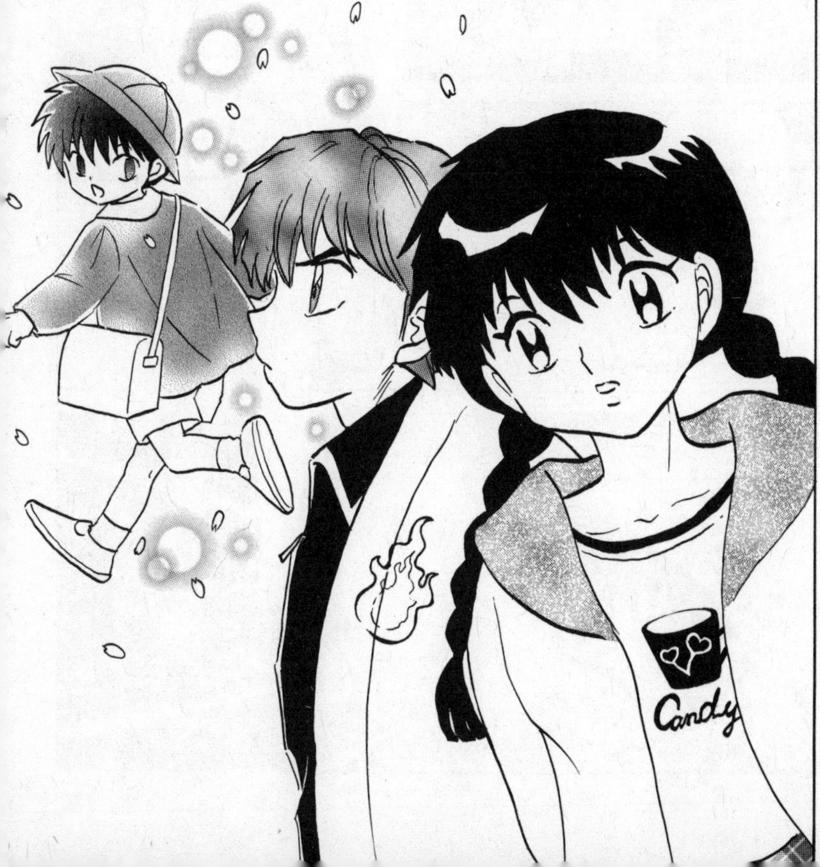
Candy

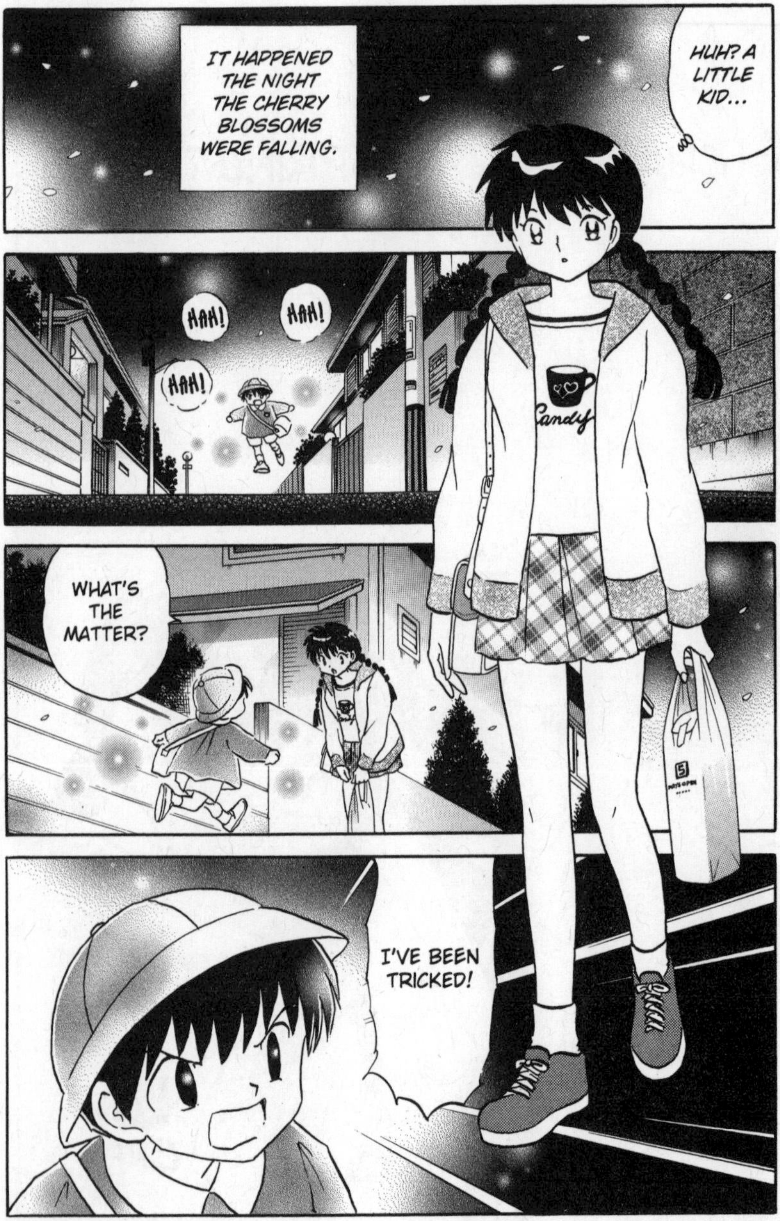
HUH? A LITTLE KID...
IT HAPPENED THE NIGHT THE CHERRY BLOSSOMS WERE FALLING.
HAH!
HAH!
HAH!
WHAT'S THE MATTER?
I'VE BEEN TRICKED!

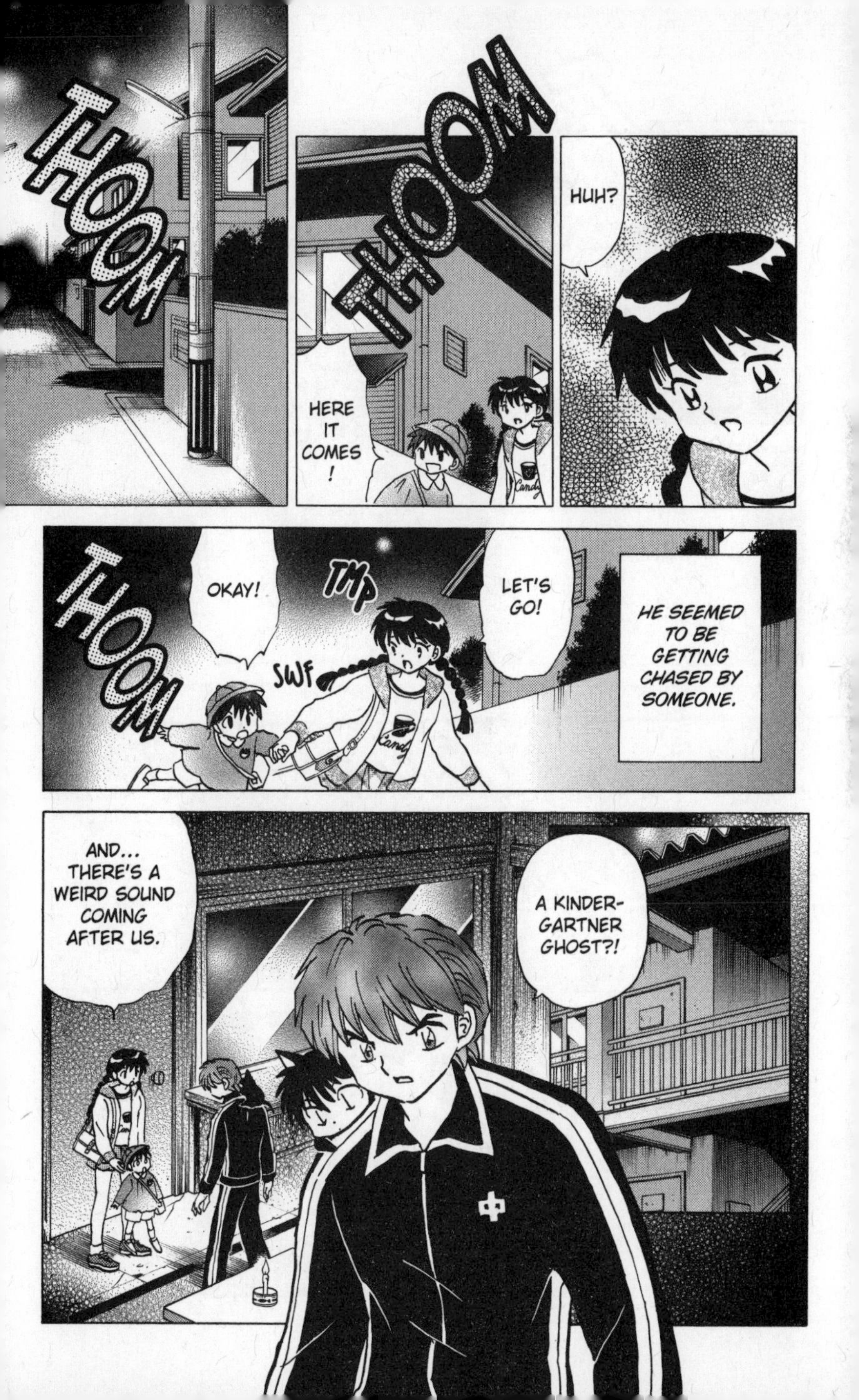
HUH?
THOOM
HERE IT COMES!
THOOM
HE SEEMED TO BE GETTING CHASED BY SOMEONE.
LET'S GO!
TMP
SWF
OKAY!
THOOM
A KINDER-GARTNER GHOST?!
AND... THERE'S A WEIRD SOUND COMING AFTER US.

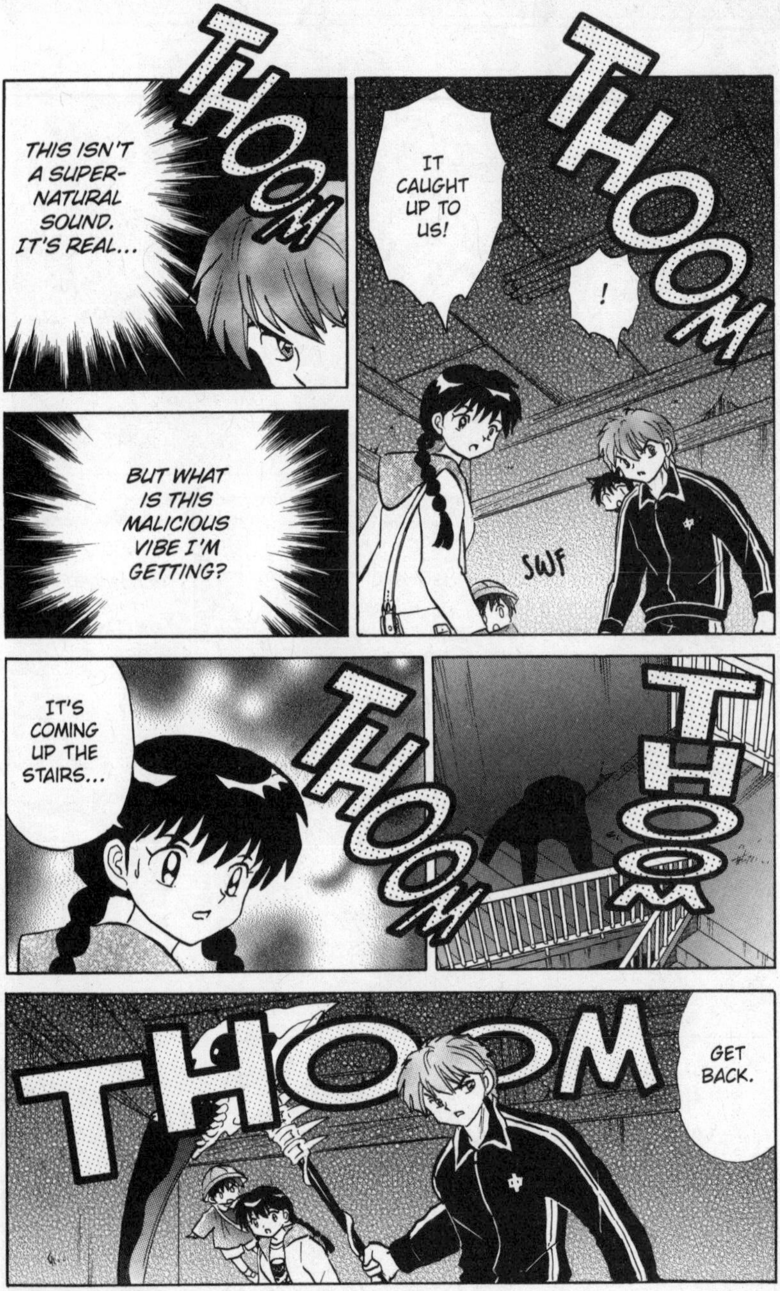
THOOM
IT CAUGHT UP TO US!
!
SWF
THOOM
THIS ISN'T A SUPER-NATURAL SOUND. IT'S REAL...
BUT WHAT IS THIS MALICIOUS VIBE I'M GETTING?
THOOM
IT'S COMING UP THE STAIRS...
THOOM
GET BACK.
THOOM

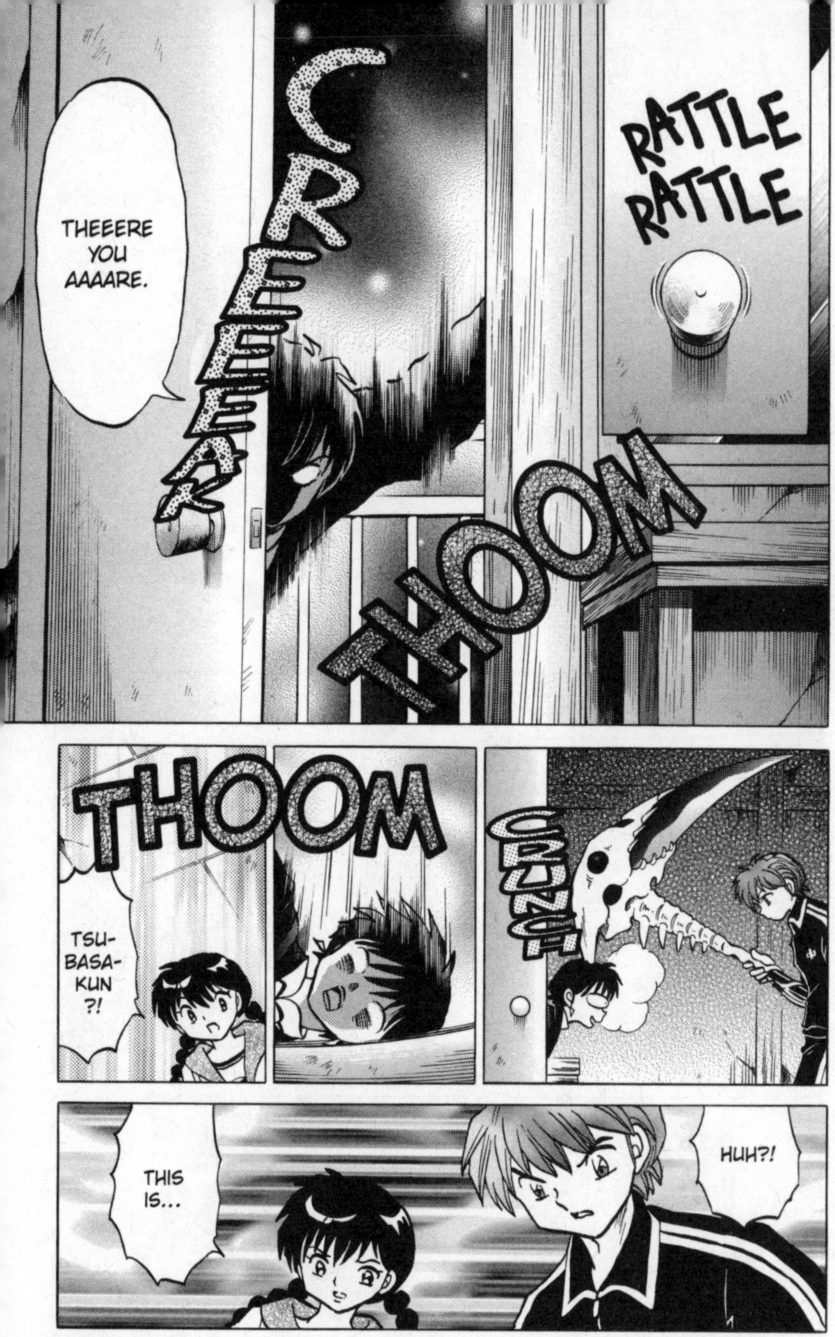
RATTLE RATTLE
CREEEEAK
THEEERE YOU AAAARE.
THOOM
CRUNCH
THOOM
TSU-BASA-KUN ?!
HUH?!
THIS IS...

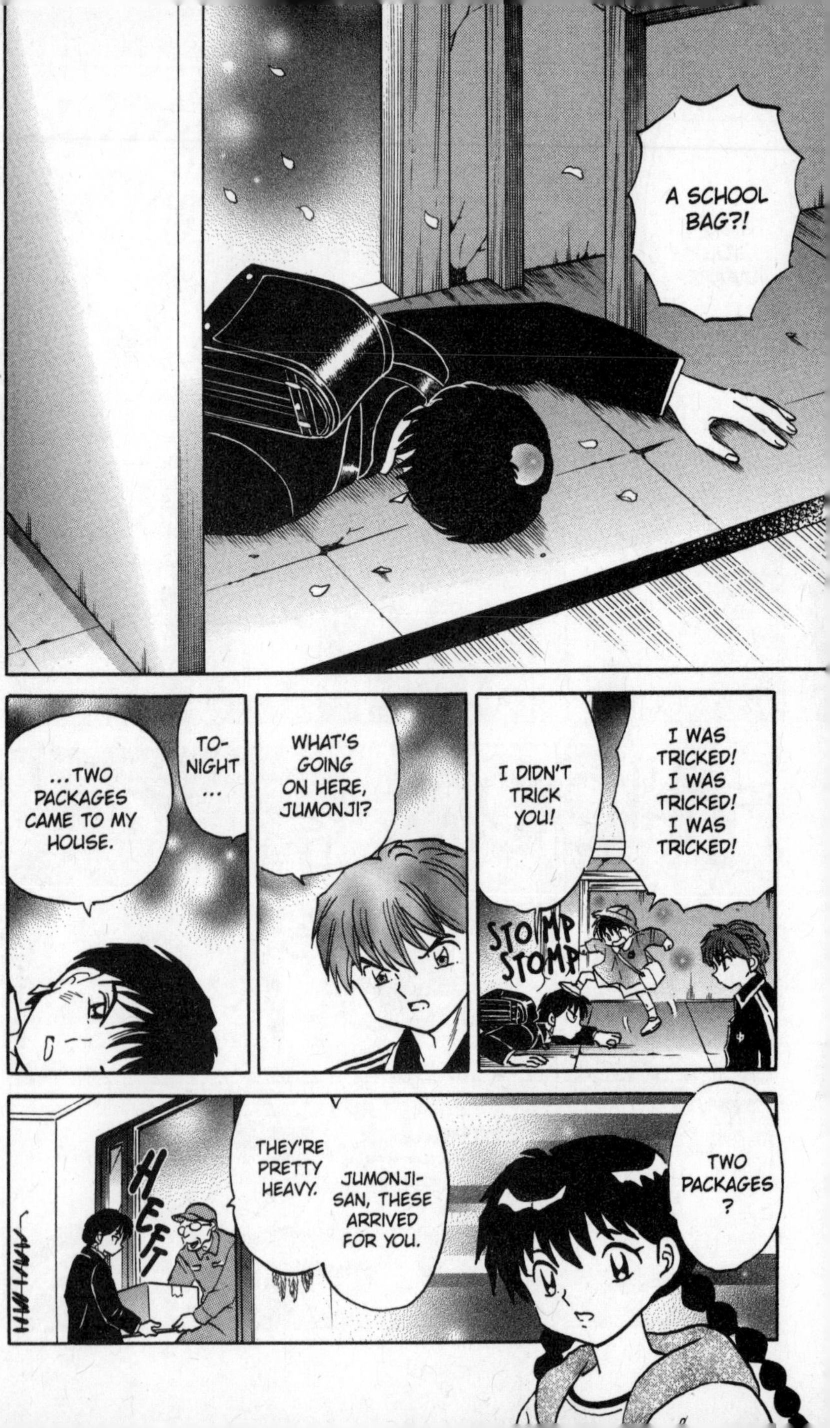
A SCHOOL BAG?!
I WAS TRICKED! I WAS TRICKED! I WAS TRICKED!
I DIDN'T TRICK YOU!
STOMP STOMP
WHAT'S GOING ON HERE, JUMONJI?
TO-NIGHT ...
...TWO PACKAGES CAME TO MY HOUSE.
TWO PACKAGES?
JUMONJI-SAN, THESE ARRIVED FOR YOU.
THEY'RE PRETTY HEAVY.
HEFT

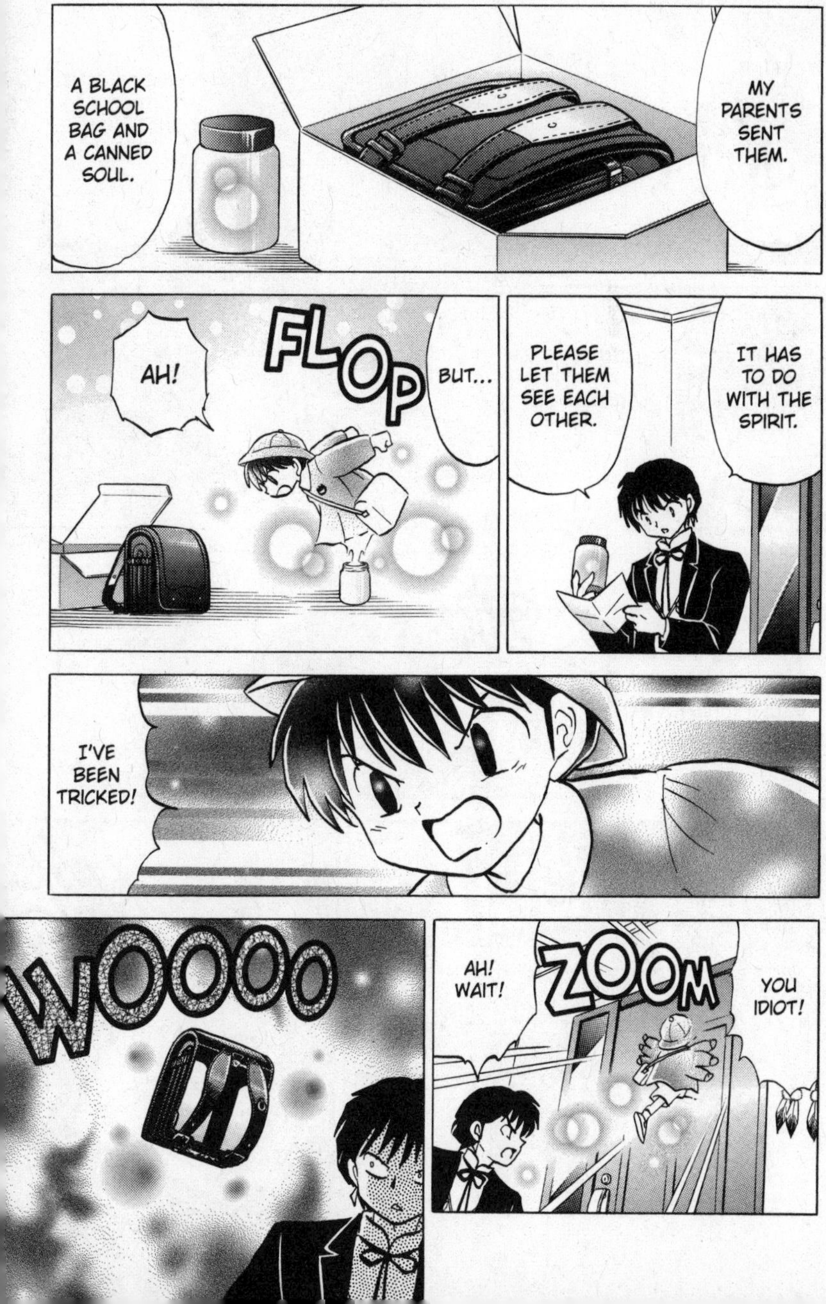
MY PARENTS SENT THEM.
A BLACK SCHOOL BAG AND A CANNED SOUL.
IT HAS TO DO WITH THE SPIRIT.
PLEASE LET THEM SEE EACH OTHER.
BUT...
FLOP
AH!
I'VE BEEN TRICKED!
YOU IDIOT!
ZOOM
AH! WAIT!
WOOOO

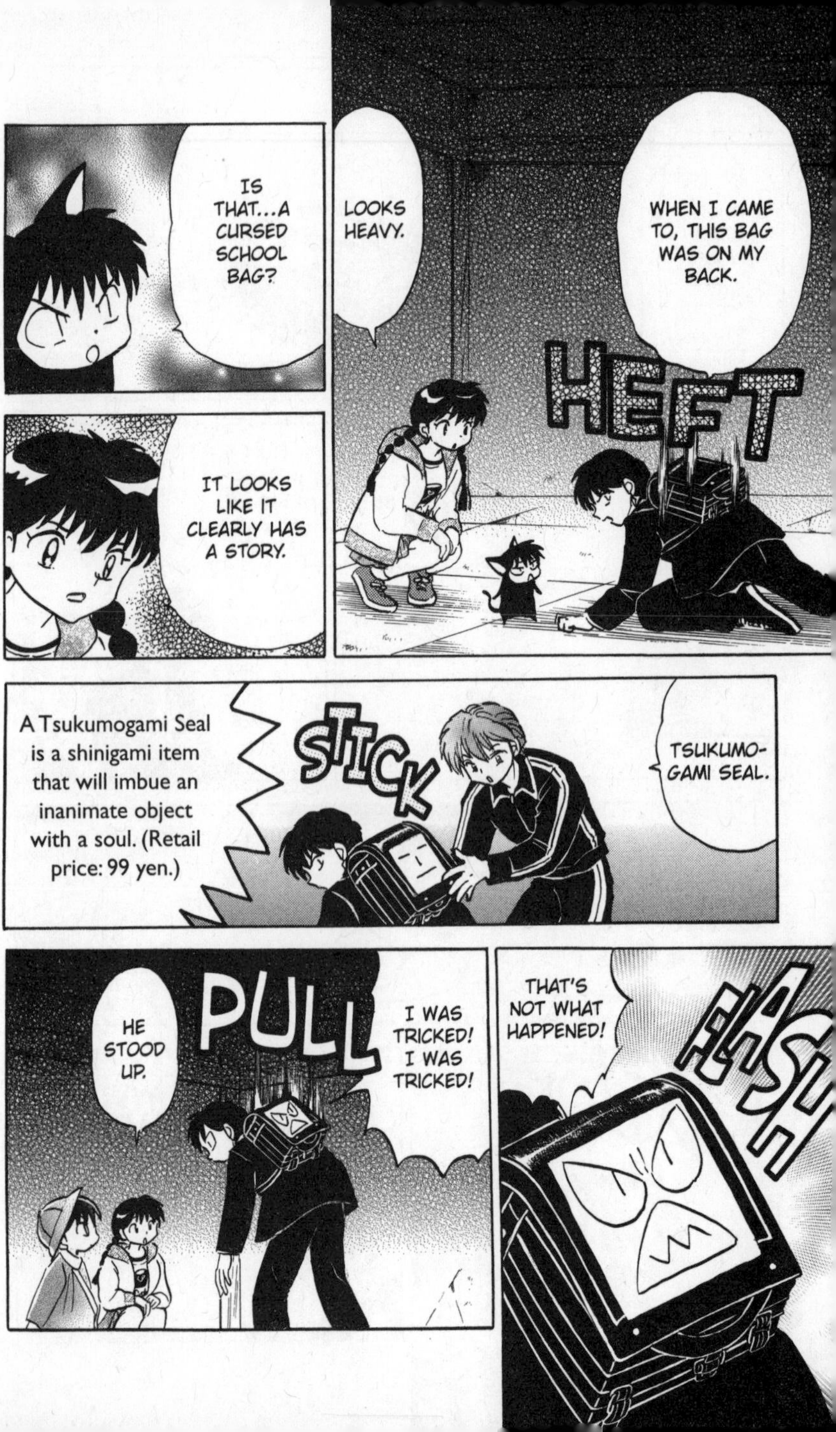
WHEN I CAME TO, THIS BAG WAS ON MY BACK.
HEFT
LOOKS HEAVY.
IS THAT...A CURSED SCHOOL BAG?
IT LOOKS LIKE IT CLEARLY HAS A STORY.
TSUKUMO-GAMI SEAL.
STICK
A Tsukumogami Seal is a shinigami item that will imbue an inanimate object with a soul. (Retail price: 99 yen.)
THAT'S NOT WHAT HAPPENED!
FLASH
I WAS TRICKED! I WAS TRICKED!
PULL
HE STOOD UP.

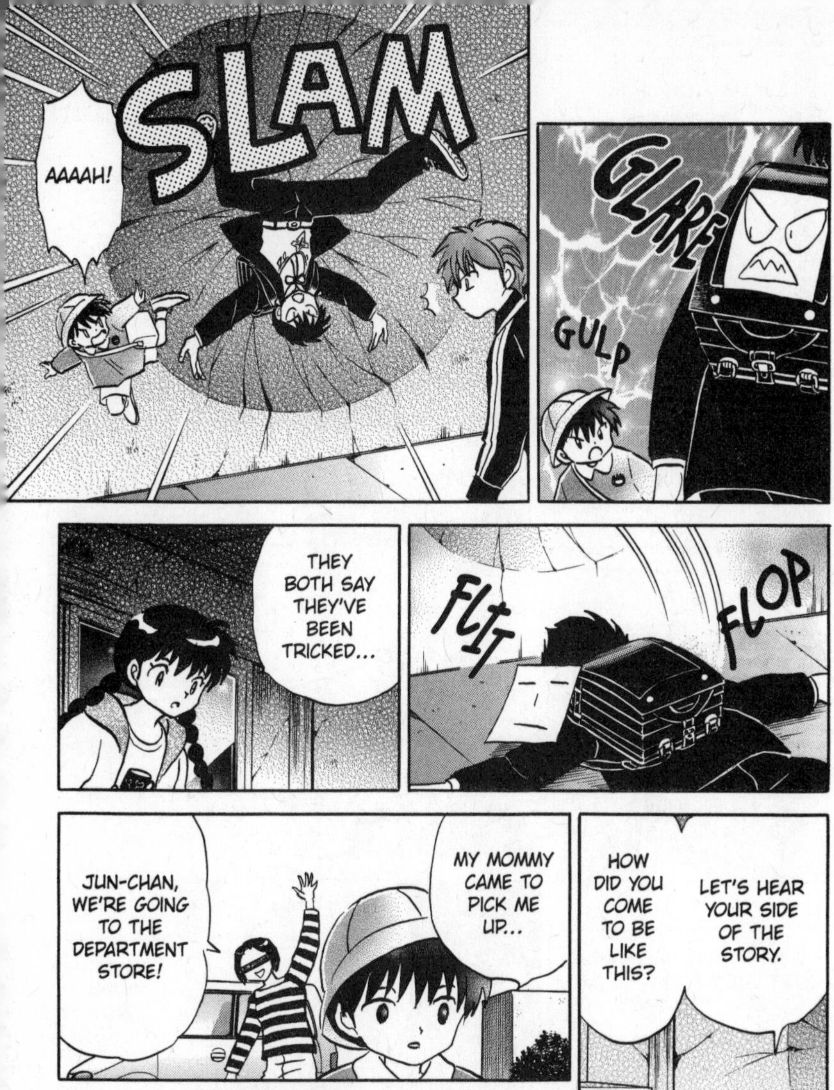
GLARE
GULP
SLAM
AAAAH!
FLIT
FLOP
THEY BOTH SAY THEY'VE BEEN TRICKED...
LET'S HEAR YOUR SIDE OF THE STORY.
HOW DID YOU COME TO BE LIKE THIS?
MY MOMMY CAME TO PICK ME UP...
JUN-CHAN, WE'RE GOING TO THE DEPARTMENT STORE!
WHAT?! A SCHOOL BAG?!
YOU'LL BE A FIRST-GRADER IN THE SPRING.

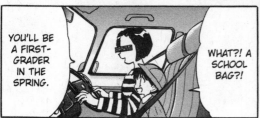

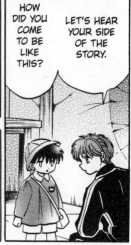

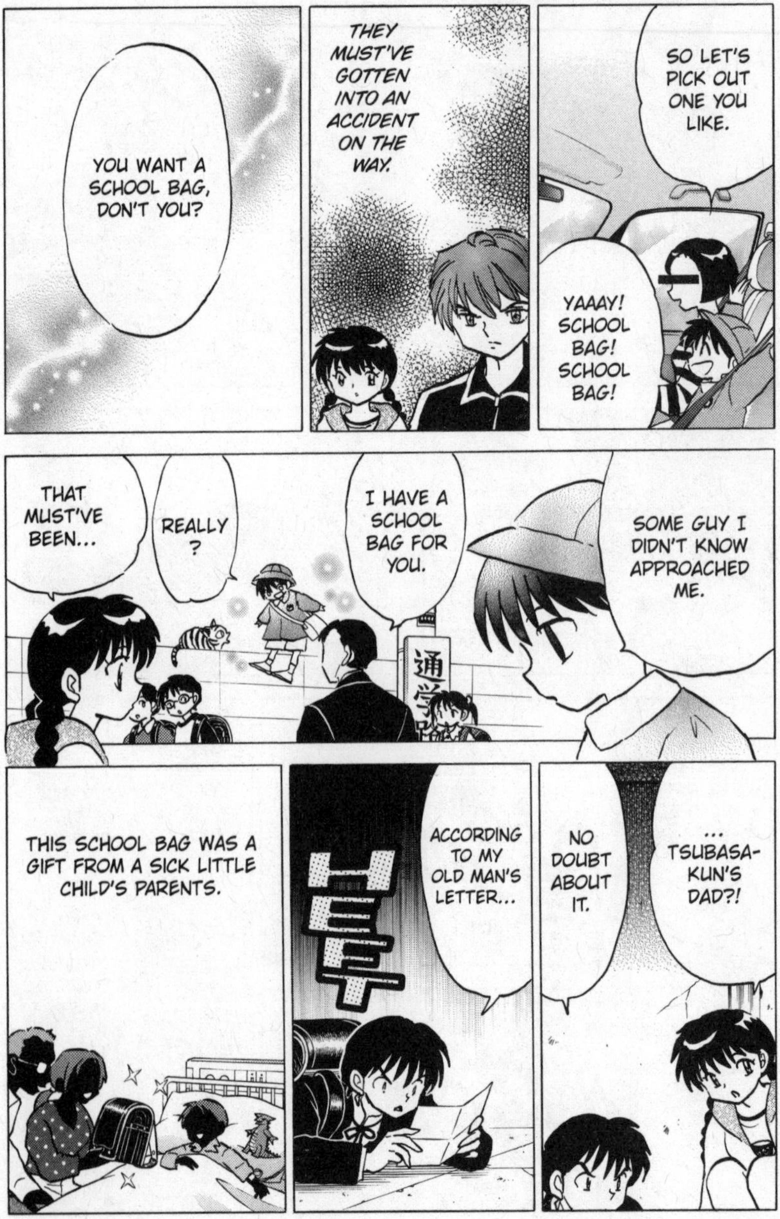
SO LET'S PICK OUT ONE YOU LIKE.
YAAAY! SCHOOL BAG! SCHOOL BAG!
THEY MUST'VE GOTTEN INTO AN ACCIDENT ON THE WAY.
YOU WANT A SCHOOL BAG, DON'T YOU?
SOME GUY I DIDN'T KNOW APPROACHED ME.
I HAVE A SCHOOL BAG FOR YOU.
REALLY?
THAT MUST'VE BEEN...
... TSUBASA-KUN'S DAD?!
NO DOUBT ABOUT IT.
ACCORDING TO MY OLD MAN'S LETTER...
HEFT
THIS SCHOOL BAG WAS A GIFT FROM A SICK LITTLE CHILD'S PARENTS.

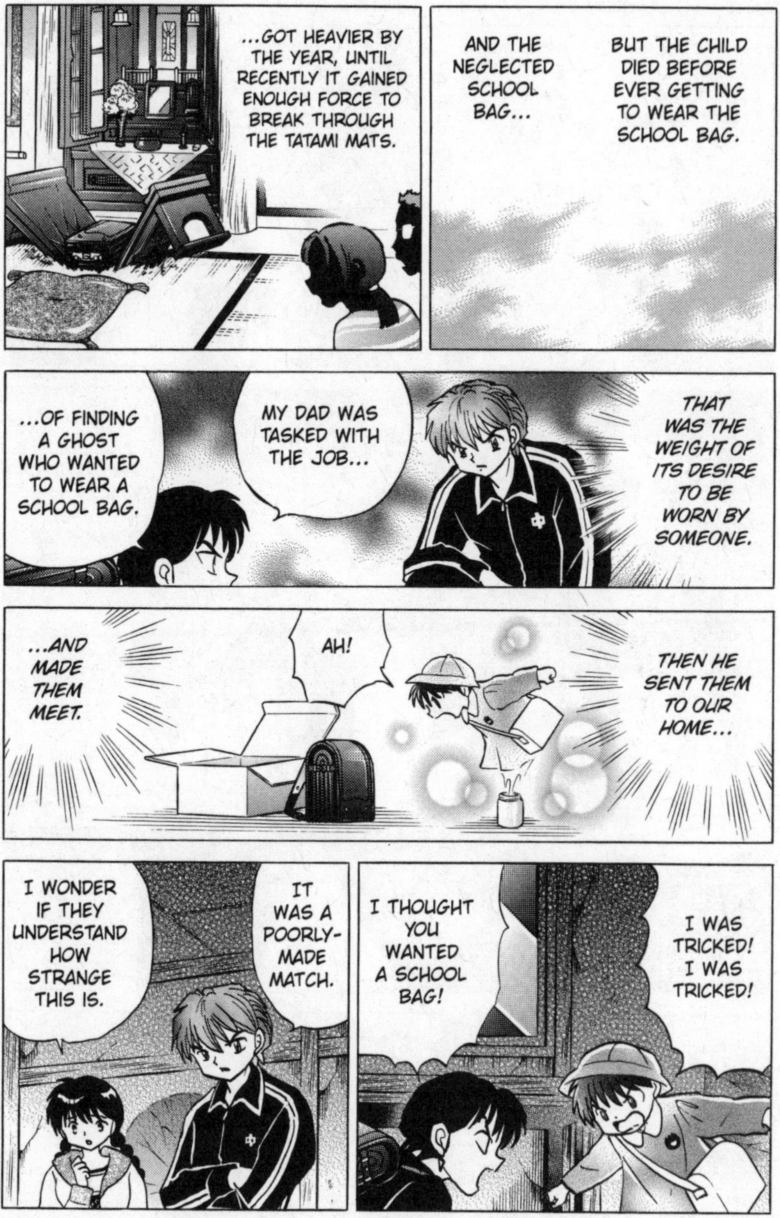
BUT THE CHILD DIED BEFORE EVER GETTING TO WEAR THE SCHOOL BAG.
AND THE NEGLECTED SCHOOL BAG...
...GOT HEAVIER BY THE YEAR, UNTIL RECENTLY IT GAINED ENOUGH FORCE TO BREAK THROUGH THE TATAMI MATS.
THAT WAS THE WEIGHT OF ITS DESIRE TO BE WORN BY SOMEONE.
MY DAD WAS TASKED WITH THE JOB...
...OF FINDING A GHOST WHO WANTED TO WEAR A SCHOOL BAG.
THEN HE SENT THEM TO OUR HOME...
AH!
...AND MADE THEM MEET.
I WAS TRICKED! I WAS TRICKED!
I THOUGHT YOU WANTED A SCHOOL BAG!
IT WAS A POORLY-MADE MATCH.
I WONDER IF THEY UNDERSTAND HOW STRANGE THIS IS.

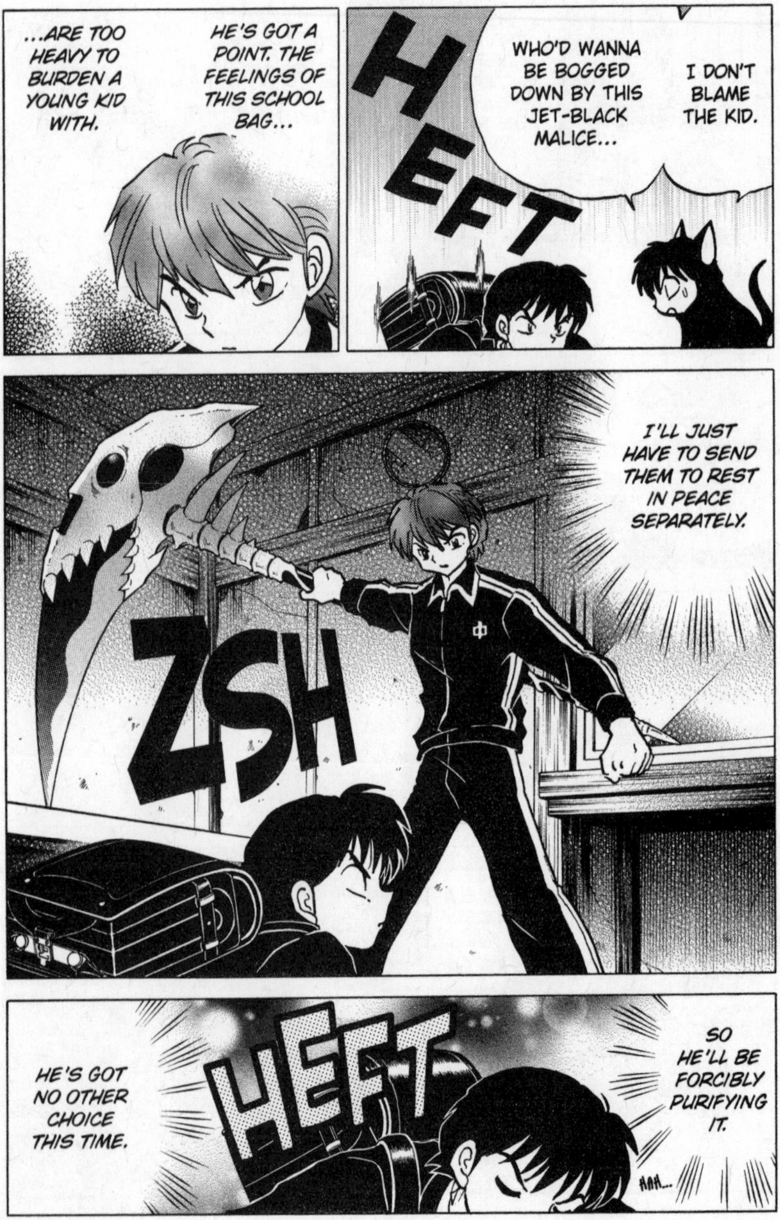
I DON'T BLAME THE KID.
WHO'D WANNA BE BOGGED DOWN BY THIS JET-BLACK MALICE...
HEFT
HE'S GOT A POINT. THE FEELINGS OF THIS SCHOOL BAG...
...ARE TOO HEAVY TO BURDEN A YOUNG KID WITH.
I'LL JUST HAVE TO SEND THEM TO REST IN PEACE SEPARATELY.
ZSH
SO HE'LL BE FORCIBLY PURIFYING IT.
HAH...
HEFT
HE'S GOT NO OTHER CHOICE THIS TIME.

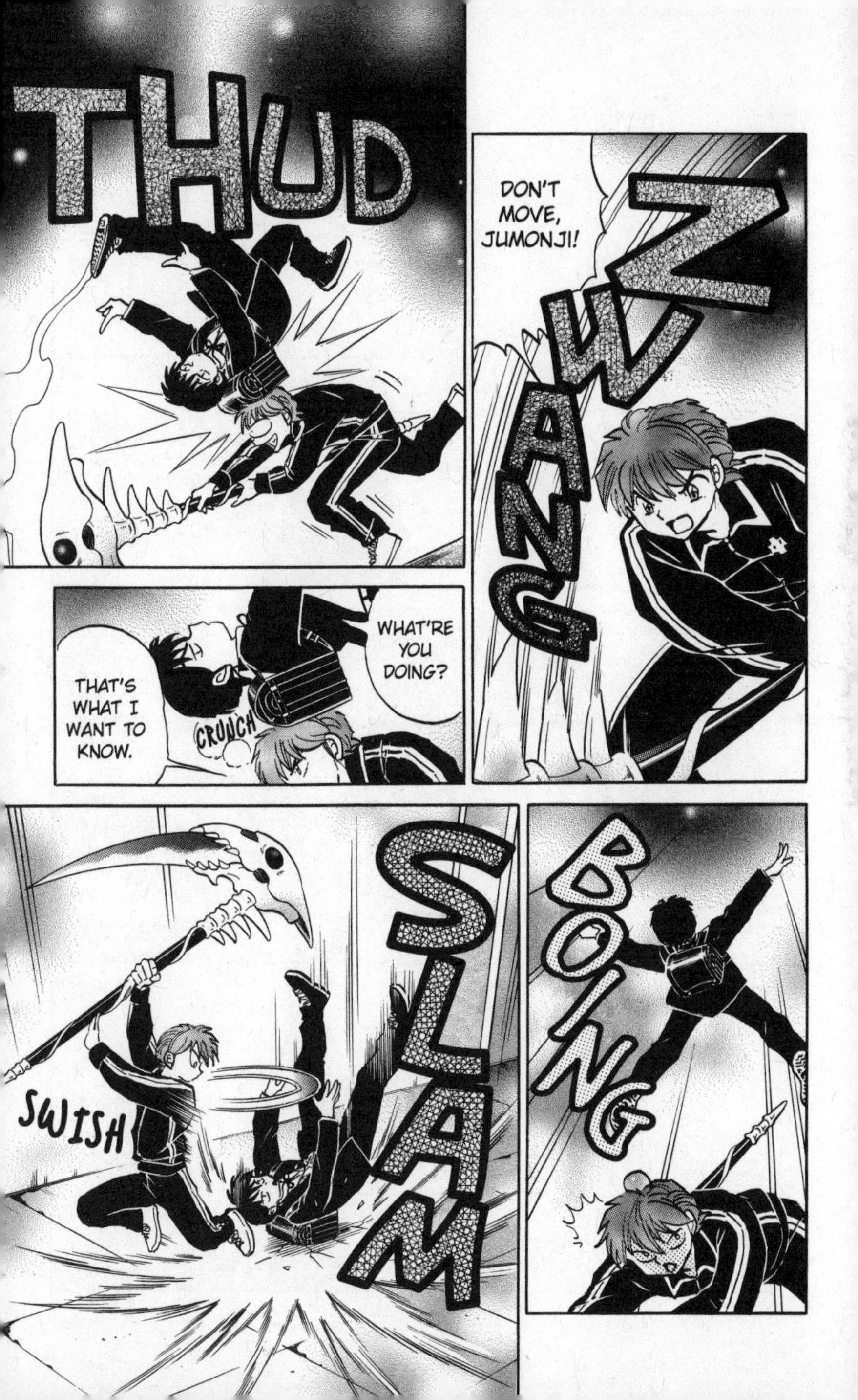
DON'T MOVE, JUMONJI!
ZWANG
THUD
WHAT'RE YOU DOING?
CRUNCH
THAT'S WHAT I WANT TO KNOW.
BOING
SLAM
SWISH

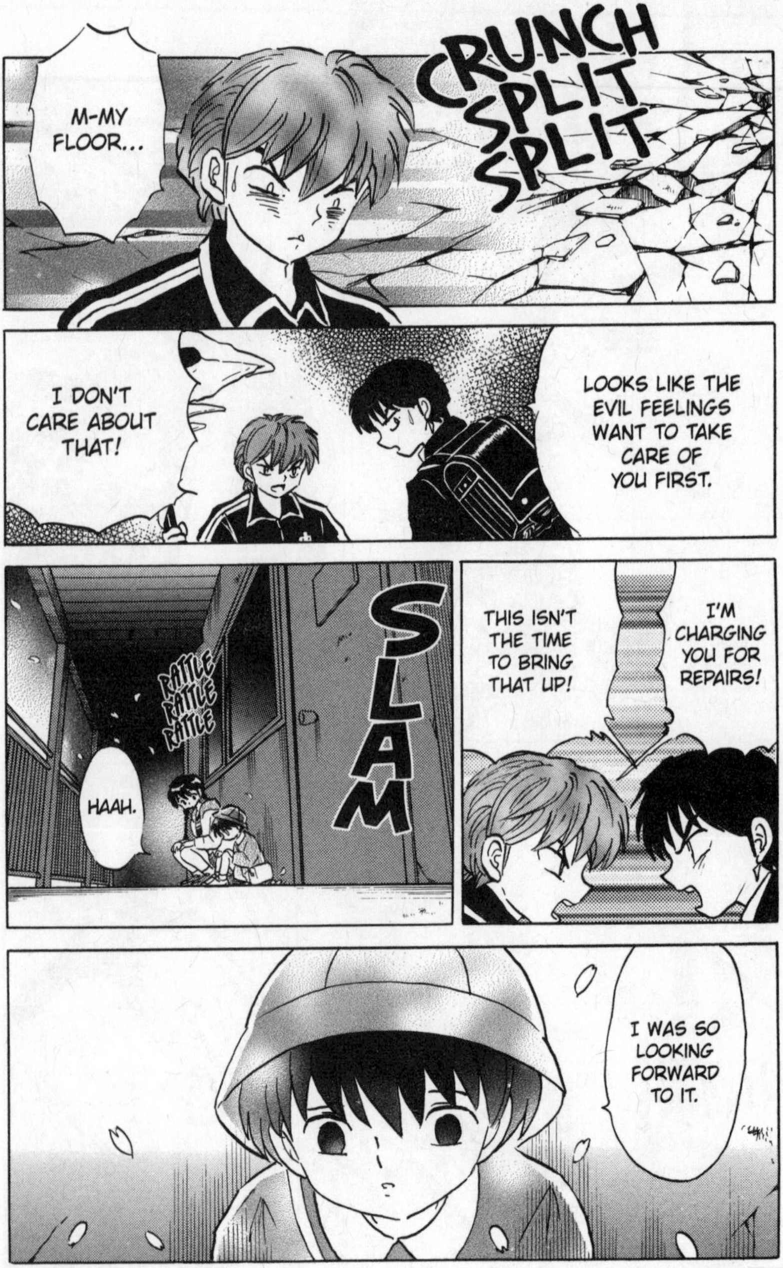
CRUNCH SPLIT SPLIT
M-MY FLOOR...
LOOKS LIKE THE EVIL FEELINGS WANT TO TAKE CARE OF YOU FIRST.
I DON'T CARE ABOUT THAT!
I'M CHARGING YOU FOR REPAIRS!
THIS ISN'T THE TIME TO BRING THAT UP!
SLAM
RATTLE RATTLE RATTLE
HAAH.
I WAS SO LOOKING FORWARD TO IT.

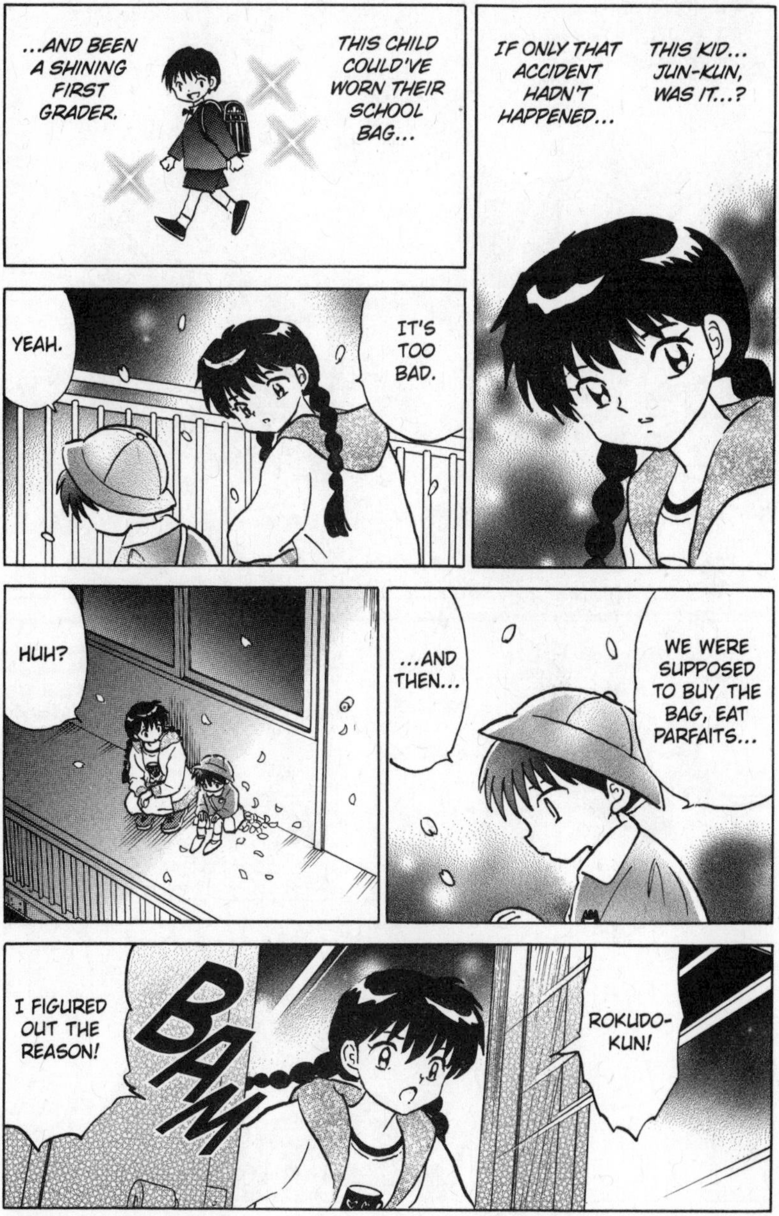
THIS KID... JUN-KUN, WAS IT...?
IF ONLY THAT ACCIDENT HADN'T HAPPENED...
THIS CHILD COULD'VE WORN THEIR SCHOOL BAG...
...AND BEEN A SHINING FIRST GRADER.
IT'S TOO BAD.
YEAH.
WE WERE SUPPOSED TO BUY THE BAG, EAT PARFAITS...
...AND THEN...
HUH?
ROKUDO-KUN!
BAM
I FIGURED OUT THE REASON!

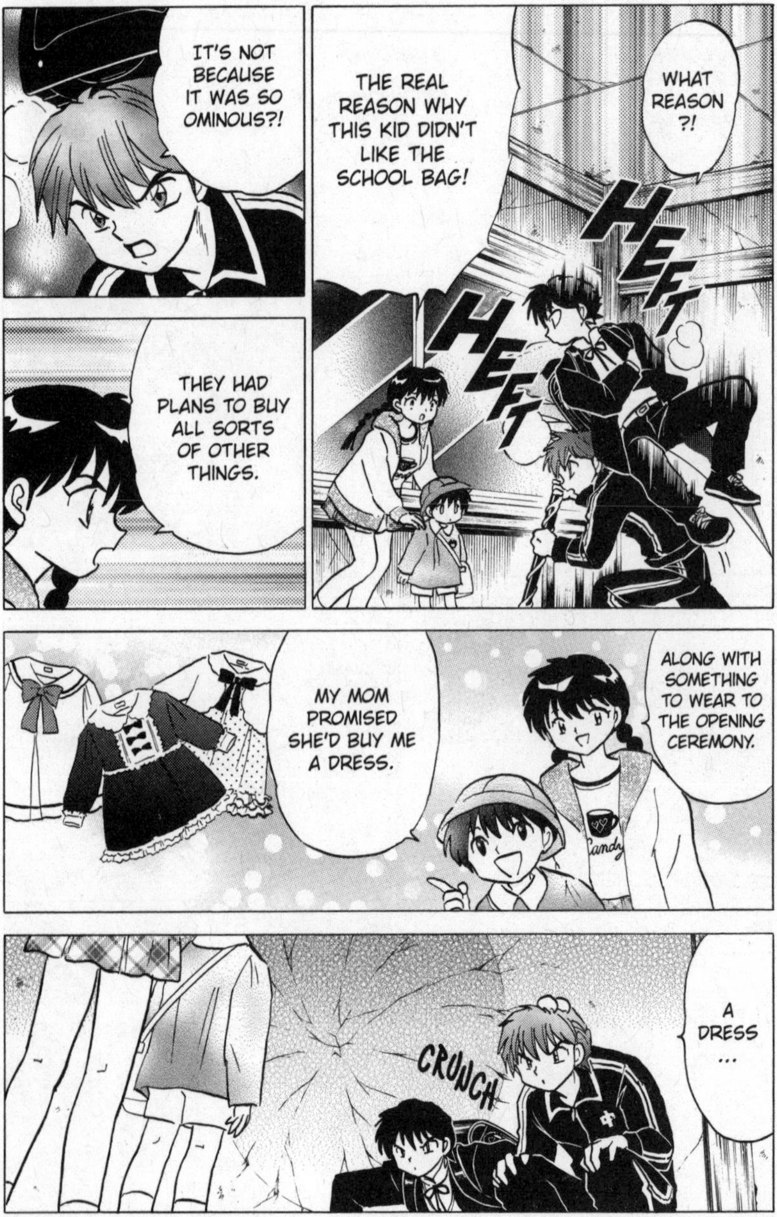
WHAT REASON ?!
THE REAL REASON WHY THIS KID DIDN'T LIKE THE SCHOOL BAG!
HEFT
HEFT
IT'S NOT BECAUSE IT WAS SO OMINOUS?!
THEY HAD PLANS TO BUY ALL SORTS OF OTHER THINGS.
ALONG WITH SOMETHING TO WEAR TO THE OPENING CEREMONY.
MY MOM PROMISED SHE'D BUY ME A DRESS.
A DRESS ...
CRUNCH

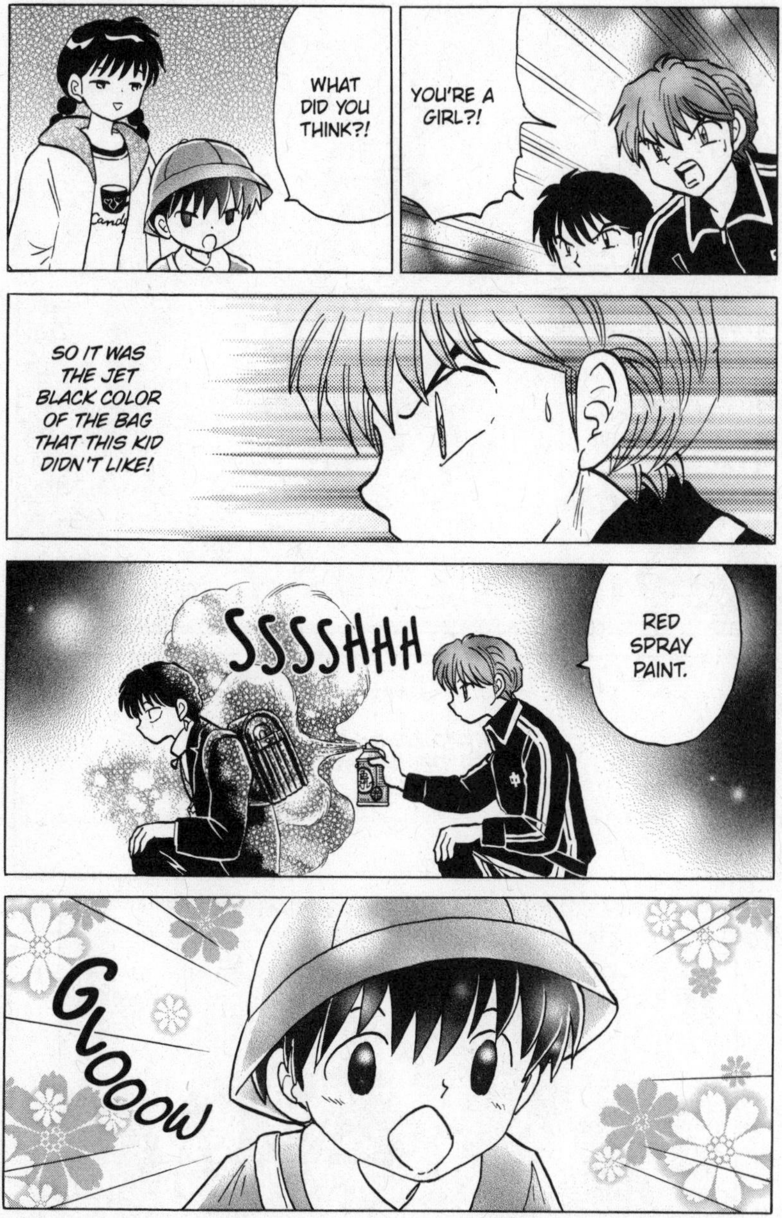
YOU'RE A GIRL?!
WHAT DID YOU THINK?!
SO IT WAS THE JET BLACK COLOR OF THE BAG THAT THIS KID DIDN'T LIKE!
RED SPRAY PAINT.
SSSSHHH
GLOOOW

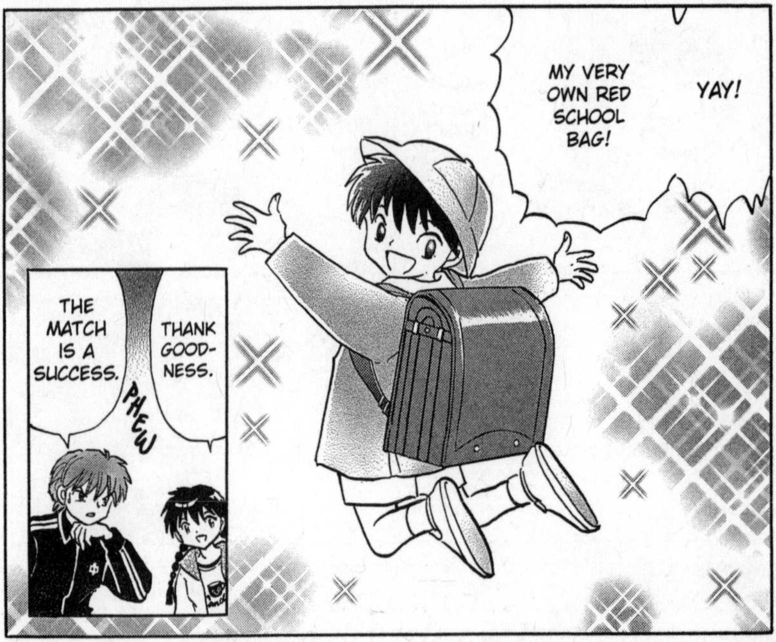
YAY!
MY VERY OWN RED SCHOOL BAG!
THANK GOOD-NESS.
PHEW
THE MATCH IS A SUCCESS.

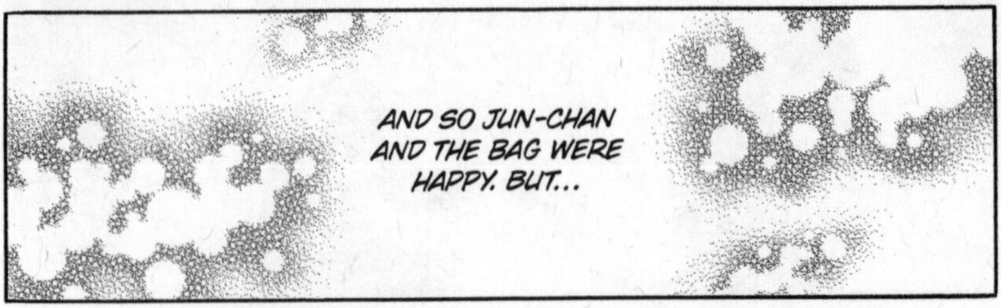
AND SO JUN-CHAN AND THE BAG WERE HAPPY. BUT...

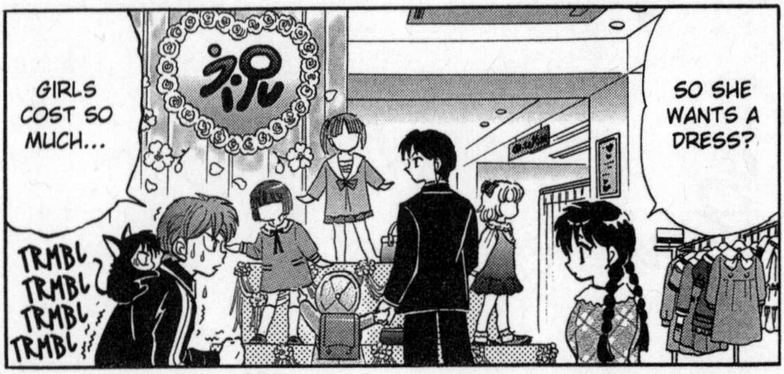
SO SHE WANTS A DRESS?
GIRLS COST SO MUCH...
TRMBL TRMBL TRMBL TRMBL

Heart: Celebrate

RIN-NE VOLUME 28 - END -

Rumiko Takahashi

The spotlight on Rumiko Takahashi's career began in 1978 when she won an honorable mention in Shogakukan's annual New Comic Artist Contest for *Those Selfish Aliens*. Later that same year, her boy-meets-alien comedy series, *Urusei Yatsura*, was serialized in *Weekly Shonen Sunday*. This phenomenally successful manga series was adapted into anime format and spawned a TV series and half a dozen theatrical-release movies, all incredibly popular in their own right. Takahashi followed up the success of her debut series with one blockbuster hit after another—*Maison Ikkoku* ran from 1980 to 1987, *Ranma ½* from 1987 to 1996, and *Inuyasha* from 1996 to 2008. Other notable works include *Mermaid Saga*, *Rumic Theater*, and *One-Pound Gospel*.

Takahashi won the prestigious Shogakukan Manga Award twice in her career, once for *Urusei Yatsura* in 1981 and the second time for *Inuyasha* in 2002. A majority of the Takahashi canon has been adapted into other media such as anime, live-action TV series, and film. Takahashi's manga, as well as the other formats her work has been adapted into, have continued to delight generations of fans around the world. Distinguished by her wonderfully endearing characters, Takahashi's work adeptly incorporates a wide variety of elements such as comedy, romance, fantasy, and martial arts. While her series are difficult to pin down into one simple genre, the signature style she has created has come to be known as the "Rumic World." Rumiko Takahashi is an artist who truly represents the very best from the world of manga.

RIN-NE
VOLUME 28
Shonen Sunday Edition

STORY AND ART BY
RUMIKO TAKAHASHI

KYOKAI NO RINNE Vol. 28
by Rumiko TAKAHASHI
© 2009 Rumiko TAKAHASHI
All rights reserved.
Original Japanese edition published by SHOGAKUKAN.
English translation rights in the United States of America,
Canada, the United Kingdom, Ireland, Australia and New
Zealand arranged with SHOGAKUKAN.

Translation/Christine Dashiell
Touch-up Art & Lettering/Evan Waldinger
Design/Yukiko Whitley
Editor/Megan Bates

Printed in the U.S.A.

Published by VIZ Media, LLC
P.O. Box 77010
San Francisco, CA 94107

10 9 8 7 6 5 4 3 2 1
First printing, November 2018

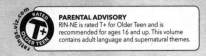

viz.com

shonensunday.com

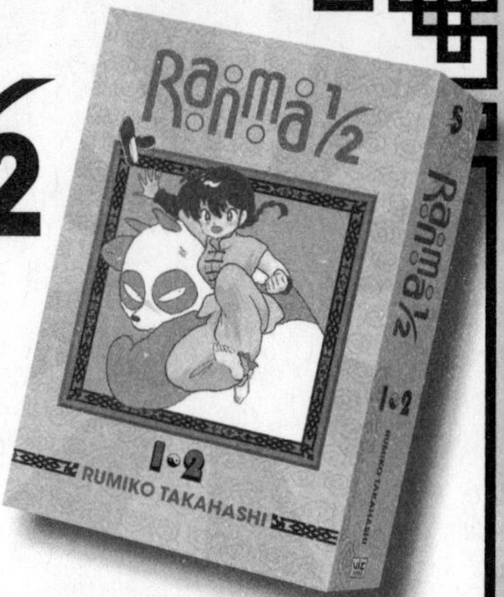

Ranma 1/2
1•2
RUMIKO TAKAHASHI

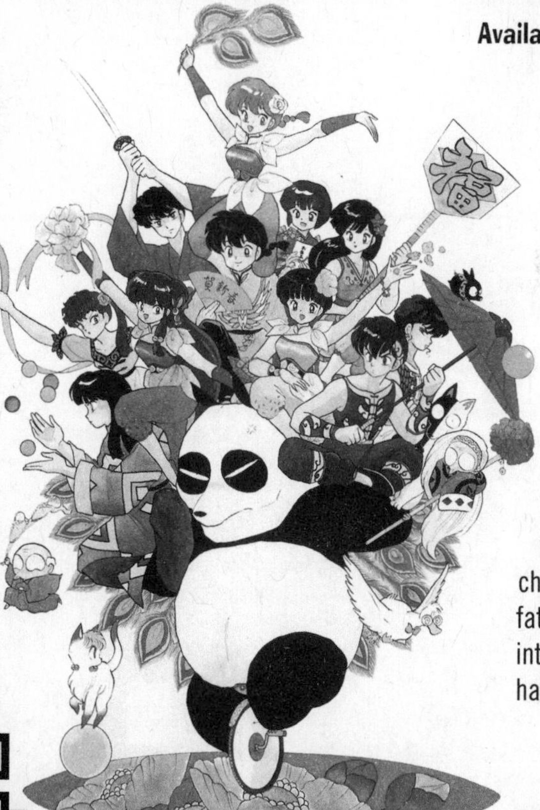

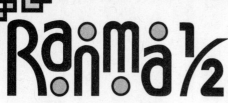

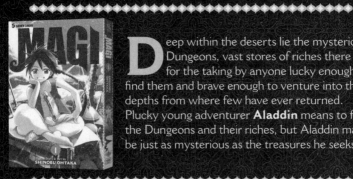

Hey! You're Reading in the Wrong Direction!

This is the end of this graphic novel!

To properly enjoy this VIZ graphic novel, please turn it around and begin reading from right to left. Unlike English, Japanese is read right to left, so Japanese comics are read in reverse order from the way English comics are typically read.

This book has been printed in the original Japanese format in order to preserve the orientation of the original artwork. Have fun with it!

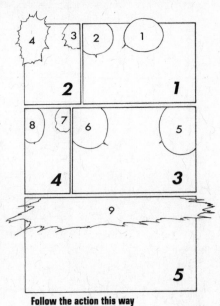

Follow the action this way